ENGLISH RECUSANT LITERATURE
1558–1640

Selected and Edited by
D. M. ROGERS

Volume 229

THOMAS HARDING
An Answere to Maister
Iuelles Chalenge
1565

THOMAS HARDING

An Answere to Maister
Iuelles Chalenge
1565

The Scolar Press
1975

ISBN 0 85967 214 x

Published and printed in Great Britain by
The Scolar Press Limited, 59-61 East Parade,
Ilkley, Yorkshire and
39 Great Russell Street,
London WC1

NOTE

Reproduced (original size) from a copy in the library of the Brompton Oratory, by permission of the Provost and Fathers.

References: Allison and Rogers 373; STC 12759.

AN ANSVVERE
TO MAISTER IVELLES
CHALENGE, BY DOCTOR
HARDING.

augmented vvith certaine quotations and additions.

I. COR. 14.

An à vobis ve. bum Dei proceſſit? aut in vos ſolos
peruenit ?

Hath the word of God proceded from you?
Or hath it come among you only?

SCRVTA  MINI.

Imprinted in Antwerpe,
At the golden Angel by *William* Syl-
vius the Kinges Maiesties printer.

M. D. LXV.
VVith priuilege.

PRIVILEGIVM.

Regiæ Maiestatis Priuilegio, permissum est D. Thomæ Harding sacræ Theologiæ professori, vti per aliquem Typographum admissorum in his hereditarijs Ditionis Regiæ terris, imprimat, aut alibi impressam distrahat, *Responsionem ad articulos Ioannis Iuelli* eodem authore in Catholicæ fidei defensionem Anglica lingua conscriptam, & omnibus alijs inhibitû ne præter eiusdem Priuilegij authoritatem librum hunc imprimant aut imprimi faciant, sub pœna in priuilegio contenta.

Datum Bruxellæ.15.Ianuarij.Anno. 1563. Subsig.

Facuvvez.

The table of the Articles here treated, and of the chiefe pointes in the same touched, is put in the ende, after the Exhortation to M Iuell.

THE CORRECTOVR

TO THE READER.

F thou wilt knowe gentill Reader for what causes and by whom this booke is now set forth in print againe, here mayst thou see both the same declared, and his name subscribed. First the booke being good, and conteyning true, holsome, and Catholike doctrine, the more it is made common, the more good thereby is done. Againe whereas many be desyrous of the same, as well in Scotland, Ireland, as in England: in so easy and so profitable à thing not to answer their desires, it were byside all humanitie. Thirdly for asmuch as it is often and constantly reported, that an answere to this booke hath this long time ben and

A 2   is

is yet in hande, that, when the same
shall come forth men may the better see
by conferēce of bookes, where true dea=
ling is, and where falsehed is vsed: it
may to any man appeare reasonable,
that for so honest and so good a purpose
the copies by meane of a newe print be
multiplied. That thou findest here sun=
dry quotations, and also certaine briefe
additions, which the copies of the first
print had not: to the intent I make thee
priuey to all, thus it hath ben done.
About halfe a yere past coming into
M. D. Hardinges chambre, (which
to his frēdes is neuer shutte) and there
finding a booke newly quoted, and
with some annotations augmēted with
his owne hande: vppon affiance of his
frendship, I was so bolde in his absen=
ce, as for a time to take it with me, and
according to the same to note myne owne boo-

ne booke, not mynding as then euer to
set it in print, but to vse it to my priuate instruction. And the same now
hath serued the printer for his copie.
VVhereas J haue aduentered thus to
do without the authours knowledge, whereto him selfe by sundry persons
moued could neuer yet be induced : as
J knowe not why I should be blamed
of any other, so I trust the greatnes of
the profit that hereof is like to folowe,
shall procure me easy pardon of him,
whose slackenes I haue supplied. If faultes be founde in the print, they are myne and the printers: the authour therewith is not touched. VVho doubtles had he taken the ouersight of it
him selfe, would haue done better: as
the mothers eye tendereth the childe
more then an other bodies. Yet I promise the best of myne endeuour. How so

euer it be, I wishe oure louing countrie
men to consider how harde it is for a-
liantes to print English truly, who neither vnderstand, nor can pronounce
the tongs rightly. As for the corectour,
where the faultes of the printers be infinite for the vnskill of the language,
were he as full of eyes as Argus, or as
sharpsighted as Lynx, yet shoudle he
passe ouer no small number vnespied.
VVere there here an English mã vvho
had skill in settig a print, and knevve
the right Orthographie of ouer speach,
then mightest thou reader looke for
bookes more correctly set forth : for
lacke vvhereof vve do as vve maye.
I praye the in this distresse beare vvith
my litle ouersigth, and accept my greate good vvil: Fare vvel, at Antvver-
pe. 12. Januarij 1565.

John Martiall.
TO

TO THE READER.

VHERE as Horace ſayeth, they that rŭne ouer the ſea, chaunge the ayer, not the mynde, yet is it ſo reader, that I paſſingouer the ſea out of England into Brabant, haue in ſome parte chaunged alſo my mynde. For vvhere as being there, I mynded to ſend this treatiſe but to one frend, vvho required it for his priuate inſtruction, and neuer to ſet any thing abroade: novv being arriued here in Louaine, I haue thought good, by putting it in printe, to make it common to many. Yet to ſaye the trovvth, hereto I haue bē prickte more by zelouſe perſuaſions of others, then induced by myne ovvne lyking. For though dutie require, be it vvith ſhame, or be it vvith fame, to employe 2. Cor. 6. all endeuour to the defence of the Catholike faith, in theſe moſt perilouſe times much impugned: yet partely by a

A 4   certaine

certaine covvardly iudgement, and
specially by naturall inclination, I haue
euer lyked more that olde counsell vt-

Λαθὶ βιώ-
ϲαϲ.

tered by the Grekes in tvvo vvordes,
vvich aduiseth a man so to lyue secretly, as it be not knovven, he hath lyued.
VVherefore as this labour in that respecte deserueth lesse thanke, so for my
parte it ought lesse to be blamed. if
ought be fovvnde amysse, the blame
thereof rightly diuided betvven my
frendes and me, the greater portion
shall redovvnde to thē, the lesser to me
on vvhom the spotte of vnskille only
shall cleaue, but the note of vndiscreti-
tion shall remaine to them. For as the
defectes be myne and none others, so
ouersight of setting forth that, vvhich
vvas of lesse sufficiencie, is to be imputed to them, not to me. Hovv so
euer it be, the meaning of vs bothe is
only this Christen reader, hereby to
minister vnto thee, matter of comforte
in these sorovvful, of staye in these vva-
uering, of vnderstanding the truth, in
these erroneouse times: vvithall, to call
him

him backe, vvho in denying thefe articles, hath ouerrunne him felfe. VVherein I am not al together voyde of hope. Oure lord graunt, the fpirite of herefie, pride, ftoutenes of hart in gaine-
faying, eftimation of him felfe, and regarde of this vvorld, ftoppe not from
him the holy ghoftes vvorking.

VVould god he maye vveigh this my
dooing fo indifferétly, as my meaning
tovvardes him is right, holefom, and
frendly. But in cafe that deepe vvoon-
de may not be cured vvith fuch falue,
yet my truft is, it fhall doo thee good,
reader, vvho art either yet hole, or not
fo defperatly vvoonded : vvich if it
doo, I fhall thinke my labour vvel re-
quitted, and my felfe to haue acheued
that revvard, vvhich I fought.

Novv this much I haue thought
good here to vvarne the of, that
vvhere as at the firft, I appointed this
to my priuate frend only, and not to
all in common, (though in fundry
places I folovv the maner of fuch as
mynde to publifh their vvritinges): I
A 5   haue

haue so both ordered the matter and
tempered the style, as I iudge it might
haue ben liked of my frend at home,
and doubte vvhether it may beare the
light abroade. I see mennes stomakes
of oure time to be very delicate and
diuerse. Some require svvete iunket-
tes, some sovver and sharpe savvces,
some esteme the curiositie of cooke-
rye, more then the holesomnes of vi-
andes, some can like no dishe, be it ne-
uerso vvell dighte. In this diuersitie no
man can please all. VVho so euer see-
keth it, shal fynde him selfe decciued. I
vvene the best vvaye is, if a man herein mynde to doo ought, to make his
prouision of the thinges only, vvhich
be holesome. So shal he displease many, hurte none, and please al the good.
VVho so euer in doing this directeth
his vvhole purpose and endeuour to
this ende, that he may profite and helpe all: in my iudgement, he doth the
dutie of an honest and a good man.
Verely in this treatise this hath ben
myne onely purpose, and the meane
to bring the same to effecte, hath ben
                                    such,

such, as vvhereby I studied to profite holesomely, not to please delicately. Hovv much good I haue performed, I knovv not, my conscience (vvhich is ynough) beareth me vvitnes of good vvill. VVhat the Apostles haue plãted, in this great barraynesse and drovvth of faith, I haue desyred againe to vva- ter. God geue encreace.

If the multitude of allegations brought for confirmation of some the- se Articles, shal seme tediouse, no mer- ueile. I shuld mislike the same in an other my selfe. I graunt herein I haue not alvvayes kepte due comlynes. For symply to saye, vvhat I thinke (hauing leaue to retourne to my former meta- phore) soothly in some courses, I haue ouer charged the borde vvith dishes. Merueile not, I haue done that, I discõ- méd my selfe, to a uoyde a more reprou fe in greater respecte, I haue vvittingly done a thing, in some degree reproueã- ble. Neither thinke I greatly to offen- de, if in this time of spirituall famine, I folow the woont of some feastemakers, vvho of their neighbours tvvited vvith
nyggardnes

gardnes, to shevve their largesse and
bountie, feafte them vvith lauishe. The
aduerfaire, as here thou mayft fee, hath
not fpared to irke vs vvith reproche of
penurie, of fcarcitie, of lacke: I meane
of proufes for maintenance of fome
good parte of oure religiō. In this cafe
to me it femed a parte of iuft deféce to
vtter fome good ftore. And the nyggar-
des feafte by olde prouerbe is vvell cō-
méded, thou knovveft pardie. Neither
yet haue vve empted all our fpence, as
hereafter it fhal apeare, if nede require.

If fome doo not alovve this confideration, vvho fo euer the fame fhall
blame, him here concluding, fhortly
I anfvvere vvith *Alexander* king of Ma-
cedons. vvho to *Leonidas* one of his
Mynnions fynding faute vvith fpéding
much frankencenfe in facrifices, vvrote
thus in fevve. Franckencenfe and myr-
re to the vve haue fent plentie, that
novv to the Goddes thou be no
more a nyggard. Fare vvell,
at Louaine: 14. of Iune:
1563.

Thom. Harding.

A COLLECTION OF
CERTAINE PLACES OVT OF
MAISTER IVELLES BOOKE CON-
teining his sermon, his answeres and Replyes
to Doctor Cole: in which he maketh his Chalenge, avaunteth him selfe, boasteth of the
assuráce of his doctrine, pretendeth and low-
dely affirmeth, the Catholikes to haue nothing for their parte, ouer peartly, as to sober wittes it semeth, egging and pro-
uòking them, to bring somewhat
in their defence.

Mercifull God, who would thinke the- Iuell.
re coulde be so muche wilfulnes in the In the ser-
heart of man? O Gregorie, O Augu- mon. fo-
stine, O Hierome, O Chrysostome, lio. 43.
O Leo, O Dionise, O Anacletus, O Sistus, O Pau-
le, O Christ. If we be deceiued herein, ye are they
that haue deceiued vs. Ye haue taught vs these
schismes and diuisions, ye haue taught vs these he-
resies. Thus ye ordred the holy communion in
your tyme, thesame we receiued at your hand,
and haue faithfully delyuered it vnto the people.
And that ye maye the more meruel at the wilful-
nes of such men, they stand this daye against so
many old fathers, so many Doctoues, so many
examples of the primitiue churche, so manifest
and so plaine wordes of the holy scriptures: and
yet haue they herein, not one father, not one Do-
ctour,

ctour, not one allowed example of the primitiue churche, to make for them. And when ʒ ſaye, not one; ʒ ſpeake not this in vehemēcie of ſpirite, or heate of talke, but euen, as before God, by the waye of ſimplicitie and truth: leaſt any of you ſhould happely be deceiued, and thinke, there is more weight in the other ſyde, then in concluſion there ſhall be foounde. And therefore once againe I ſaye, of all the wordes of the holy ſcriptures, of all the examples of the primitiue churche, of all the old fathers, of all the auncient Doctours in theſe cauſes they haue not one.

Here the matter it ſelf, that I haue now in hand, putteth me in remembraunce of certaine things that I vttered vnto you; to the ſame purpoſe, at my laſt being in this place. I remember I layed out thē here before you, a number of things that are now in controuerſie, where vnto our aduerſaries wil not yelde. And ʒ ſayd perhaps boldly, as it might then ſeeme to ſummie mā, but as I my ſelf and the learned of our aduerſaries them ſelues do wel knowe, ſyncerely: and truly: that none of all them, that this daye ſtand againſt vs, are hable or ſhal euer be hable to proue againſt vs, any one of all thoſe points, eyther by the ſcriptures or by example of the primitiue churche, or by the olde Doctours, or by the auncient generall councelles. Synce that tyme, it hath ben reported in places, that I ſpake then more, then I was hable to iuſtifie and make good. How be it, theſe reportes were onely made in corners, and therfore ought the leſſe to trouble me. But if my ſayinges had ben ſo weake, and might ſo eaſely haue bē reproued, I maruaile that the parties neuer came to the light, to take the aduauntage. For my promiſe was, and that openly, here before you all: that if any man were able to proue the contrarye, I would yelde and ſubſcribe to him, and he ſhuld depart with the victorie. Loth I am to trouble you, with reherſall of ſuch thinges, as I haue ſpoken afore, and yet becauſe the caſe ſo requyreth, I ſhall deſyre you, that haue all ready heard me, to beare the more with me in this behalf. Better it were, to trouble your eares with twiſe hearing of one thing, then to betray the truth of God. The wordes that I then ſpake, as neare as I can call them to mynde, were theſe.

If any learned man of oll our aduerſaries, or if all the learned men that be alyue, be hable to bring any one ſufficient ſentence out of any olde catholike Doctour or father, out of any one olde generall councell, out of the holy ſcriptures of God, or any one example of the primitiue church: wherby it may be clearely and plainely proued,

That there was any priuate Maſſe in the **Article 1.** world at that tyme, for the ſpace of ſyxe hundred yeares after Chriſt:

Or that, there was then any Communion miniſtred vnto the people vnder one kinde: **2.**

Or that, the people had theire common prayers thē in a ſtraūge, tonge that they vnderſtoode not: **3.**

Or that,

4   Or that, the Bisshop of Rome was then called an vniuersall Bisshop, or the head of the vniuersall churche:

5   Or that the people was then taught to beleue, that Christes body is really, substantially, corporally, carnally or naturally, in the Sacrament.

6   Or that, his body is, or may be in a thousand places or mo at one tyme:

7   Or that, the priest dyd then hold vp the Sacrament ouer his head:

8   Or that, the people dyd then fall downe and worship it with godly honour:

9   Or that, the Sacramēt was then, or now ought to be hanged vp vnder a canopie:

10   Or that, in the Sacrament after the wordes of Consecration, there remayneth onely the accidentes and shewes without the substaunce of bread and wine:

11   Or that, the priest then diuyded the Sacrament in three partes, and afterwarde receiued him self all alone:

12   Or that who so euer had sayde, the Sacramēt is a figure, a pledge, a token, or a remembraunce of Christes bodye, had therefore ben iudged for an heretike:

13   Or that, it was lawfull then, to haue xxx. xx. xv. x. or v. Masses sayd in one churche in one daye:

14   Or that, Images were then set vp in the churches, to the entēt the people might worship them

Or

Or that, the laye people vvas then forbydden to reade the vvorde of God in their ovvne tonge.

If any mã a lyue were hable to proue any of these Articles, by any one cleare or plaine clause or sentence, eyther of the scriptures, or of the old doctours, or of any old generall councell, or by any exãple of the primitiue churche: I promysed thẽ, that I vvould geue ouer and subscribe vnto him.

These vvordes or the very like I remember I spake here openly before you all. And these be the thinges, that summe men sayde, I haue spoken, and can not iustifie.

But I for my part, wil not onely not call in any thing, that I then sayde (being well assured of the truth there in) but also will laye more matter to the same. That if they that seeke occasiõ haue any thing to the contrary, they may haue the larger scope to replye against me.

VVherefor besyde all that I haue sayde allready, I will saye farther, and yet nothing so much as might be sayde.

If any one of all our aduersaries be hable clearely and plainely to proue by such authoritie of the scriptures, the olde Doctoures and councelles, as I sayde before,

That it was then lavvfull for the priest to pronounce the vvordes of cõsecration closely, and in silence to him self:

Or that the priest had auctoritie to offer vp Christ vnto his father:

Or, to communicat and receiue the Sacramẽt

B   for

15

16

17

18

for an other, as they doo:

19   Or, to applye the vertue of Christes death and passion to any man by the meane of the Masse.

20   Or that it was then thought a sownde doctrine, to teache the people, that the masse ex opere operato, that is, euen for that it is sayde and done, is hable to remoue any part of oure synne:

21   Or that then any Christian man called the Sacrament his lorde and God:

22   Or that the people was then taught to beleue that the body of Christ remaineth in the Sacrament, as long as the accidentes of the bread remayne there with out corruption:

23   Or that a Mouse, or any other worme, or beaste maye eate the body of Christ: (for so some of oure aduersaries haue sayd and taught)

24   Or that when Christ sayde, Hoc est corpus meum. This word Hoc, pointeth not the bread, but indiuiduū vagum, as summe of them saye:

25   Or that the accidentes or formes or shewes of bread and wyne, be the Sacramentes of Christes body and bloud and not rather the very bread and wyne it selfe:

26   Or that the Sacrament is a signe or token of the body of Christ, that lyeth hydden vnderneathe it.

27   Or that Ignoraunce is the mother and cause of true deuotion and obedience.

These be the highest mysteries and greatest keyes of theire Religion, and with out them, their doctrine can neuer be mainteined and stand vpright. If any one of all oure aduersaries be hable to

ble to auouch any one of all these articles , by any
such sufficient authoritie of scriptures , doctours
or councelles , as I haue required : as I sayde before , so saye I now agayne , I am content to yelde
vnto him and to subscribe.

But I am well assured, they shall neuer be hable truly to alleage one sentence . And because
I know it , therefor I speake it , lest ye happely
shuld be deceiued.

They that haue auaunted them selues of do- Fol. 5.
ctours and councelles and continuance of tyme
in any of these pointes , when they shall be called
to tryall , to shew their proufes : they shall open
their handes, and fynde nothing. I speake not this
of arrogancie (thou lord knowest it best , that
kuowest all thinges) But for as muche as
it is godes cause , and the truth of
God: I shuld doo God great
iniurie, if I shuld con-
cele it.

B 2   THE

THE SAME CHALEN-
GE AND OFFER AND IM-
puting to the catholikes of vnhablenes to
defend their doctrine, vttered by
M. Iuell in other places of his
booke, as folo-
weth.

In the
first an-
svver to
D. Coles
letter. fol.
4.

Y offer was this (he meaneth in the sermon wich he made in the courte) that if any of all those thinges that I the rehearsed, could be proued of your syde by any sufficient authoritie other of the scriptures, or of the auncient Councelles, or by any one allowed exāple of the primitiue churche, that the I woulde be cōtēt to yelde vnto you. I saye you haue none of all those helps, nor scriptures, nor councelles, nor doctours, nother any other antiquitie, and this is the negatiue. Now it standeth you vpon, to proue but one affirmatiue to the contrary, and so to requyre my promise. The Articles that I sayde could not be proued of your parte, were these. That it can not appeare by any authoritie other of the olde doctours, or of the auncient Councelles, that there was any priuate Masse in the whole churche of Christ at that tyme: Or that there was then any communion ministred, &c. the articles rekened, there it foloweth.

Fol. 5.

And if any one of all these articles can be sufficiently proued by such authoritie as I haue sayde,

sayde, and as ye haue borne the people in hand ye can proue them by: I am wel content to stand to my promise.

I thought it best to make my entree with such thinges, as where in $ was well assured, ye shuld be able to finde not so much as any colour at all.

After in the first ansvver to D.C. fol.6.

But to couclude, as $ begane, I answer, that in these Articles $ hold only the negatiue, and therefore $ looke how you wil be able to affirme the contrarie, and that, as $ sayde afore, by sufficient authoritie, which if ye doo not, you shall cause me the more to be resolued, and others to stand the more in doubt of the rest of your learning.

In the ende there. fol.7.

In my Sermon at Poules and els where, I required you to bring forth on your part eyther sum scripture, or sum old doctour, or sum auncient councell, or els some allowed example of the primitiue churche. For these are good growndes to buyld vpō. And I would haue marueiled that you brought nothing all this while, sauing that I knew ye had nothing to bring.

In the second ansvver to D.C. fo.13

As truly as god is god, if ye wold haue vouchesaued to folow either the scriptures, or the auncient doctours, and councelles, ye wold neuer haue restored agayne the Supremacie of Rome, after it was once abolished, or the priuate Masse, or the communion vnder one kinde etc. Now if ye thinke ye haue wrong, shew your euidence out of the doctours, the councels or scriptures, that you may haue your right and reentre. I require

In the 2. ansvver. fol.15.

There fol. 17.

B 3   you to

you to no great paine, one good sentence shall be sufficient.

Fol. 18.

You wold haue your priuate Masse, the bisshop of Romes supremacie, the common prayer in an vnknowē tonge: and for defence of the same ye haue made no small a doo.

Me thinketh it reasonable ye bring sum one authoritie besyde your owne, to auouche the same with all. Ye haue made the vnlearned people beleue, ye had all the doctours, all the councelles, and fiften hundred yeres on your syde. For your credites sake, let not all these great vauntes comme to naught.

Fol. 18.

Ye desyre ye may not be put of, but that your suite maye be consydered. And yet this half yeare long, I haue desyred of you, and of your brethren but one sentence, and still I know not how, I am cast of, and can get nothing at your handes.

21

You call for the special proufes of our doctrine, which would require a whole booke, where as if you of your part could vouchesafe to bring but two lines, the whole matter where concluded. We only tell the people, as our dewtie is, that you withstand the manifest truth, and yet haue neither doctour, nor councell, nor scripture for you, and that ye haue shewed such extremitie, as the like hath not ben seene, and now can giue no rekening why. Or if ye can, let it appeare.

Fol. 23.

You are bownde ye saye, and maye not dispute, etc. But I would wish the quenes Maiestie world not only set you at libertie in that behalfe, but also com-

commaunde you to shewe your growndes. Where as you saye, you would haue the sainges of bothe parties weighed by the balãce of the olde doctours, ye see, that is oure only requeſt, and that in the matters ye write of, I deſire euen ſo to be tried. But why throw you awaye theſe balance, and being ſo earneſtly requyred, why be ye ſo loth to ſhew forth but one olde doctour of your ſyde? ye make me beleue ye would not haue the matter cõme to tryal, etc.

What thinke ye is there now iudged of you, that being ſo long tyme requyred yet can not be wonne to bring one ſentence in your own defence?

I proteſt before God, bring me but one ſuf-Fol. 26. ficient authoritie in the matters I haue requyred, and afterward I wil gentilly and quietly conferre with you farther at your pleaſure. Wherefore for as much it is goddes cauſe, if ye meane ſimply, deale ſimply, betraie not your right, if ye maye ſaue it by the ſpeaking of one worde.

The people muſt nedes muſe ſome what at your ſilence, and miſtruſt your doctrine, if it ſhall appeare to haue no grownde, neither of the olde coũcelles, nor of the doctours, nor of the ſcripture, nor any alowed example of the primitiue churche, to ſtand vpon: and ſo fiften hundred yeres, and the conſent of antiquitie and generalitie, that ye haue ſo long and ſo much talkte of, ſhall comme to nothing. For thinke not that any wiſe man will be ſo much your frend, that in ſo weighty matters will be ſatisfied with your ſilence.

Here I leaue, putting you eftſones gently in

B 4   remem-

In the ende of the 2. anſwer to D.C. fol.27.

remembraunce, that being ſo often and ſo openly deſyred to ſhew forth one doctour, or Councell &c. in the matters a fore mencioned, yet hither to ye haue brought nothing: and that if ye ſtand ſo ſtill, it muſt needes be thought, ye doo it conſcientia imbecillitatis, for that there was nothing to be brought.

In the reply to D. Coles laſt letter. fol. 43.

You ſaye we lacke ſtuffe to proue our purpoſe. O would to God your ſtuffe and oures might be layed together, then ſhuld it ſone appeare, how true it is that ye ſaye, and how faithfully ye haue vſed the people of God.

Fol.44.

Me thinketh bothe reaſon and humanitie would, ye ſhuld haue anſwered me ſumwhat, ſpecially being ſo often and ſo openly required, at the leaſt you ſhuld haue alleaged Auguſtine, Ambroſe, Chryſoſtome, Hierome &c. VVhereas a mã hath nothing to ſaye, it is good reaſon, he kepe ſilence, as you doo.

Fol.53.

You know that the matters that lie in queſtion betwen vs, haue ben taught, as we now teache them, bothe by Chriſt him ſelf, and by his Apoſtles, and by the olde doctours, and by the auncient generall Councelles: and that you hauing none of theſe or like authorities, haue ſet vp a religion of your owne, and built it only vpon your ſelfe. Therefor I may iuſtly and truly conclude, that you now teache and of lõg tyme haue taught the people, touching the Maſſe, the Supremacie, the common prayers, &c. is naught: For neither Chriſt, nor his Apoſtles, nor the olde Doctours,

*Doctours, Tertulliane, Cypriane, S. Hierome,
Augustine, S. Ambrose, S. Chrisostom &c.
euer taught the people, so as you haue taught thē.
Not withstanding your great vawntes that ye* Fol. 62.
*haue made, ye see now ye are discomfyted, ye see
the field is almost lost, where ar now your crakes
of doctours, and councelles? Why stampe ye
not your bookes? why comme ye not forth with
your euidence? Now ye stand in nede of it, now we
it will serue and take place, if ye haue any.*

As I haue offred you oftentymes, bring ye but Fol. 65.
two lines of your syde, and the field is yours.

Hilarius sayeth vnto the Arians, cedo aliud Fol. 110.
Euangelium, *shew me some other gospel, for
this that ye bring, helpeth you not. Euen so will I
aye to you,* Cedo alios doctores, *shew me some
other doctours, for these that ye bring, are not
worthy the hearing. I hoped ye would haue cō-
me in with some fressher bande. It must nedes
be some miserable cause, that can fynde no better
patrones to cleaue vnto. I know it was not for
lacke of good will of your part, ye would haue
brought other doctours, if ye could haue fownd
them.* Fol. 112.

*O Master Doctour, deale simply in Gods
causes, and saye ye haue doctours, when ye haue
them in dede: and when ye haue them not, neuer laye the fault (of not alleaging them to the
defence of your doctrine) in your recognisa-
unce.*

Fol. 114.

*But alas small rhetorike would suffise, to shew
how litle ye haue of your syde to alleage for your
selfe.*

In the cō-
clusion of
the replyes
to D. Cole
fol 129.

*Here once againe I conclude as before, putting
you in remembrance, that this long I haue desyred you to bring forth some sufficient authoritie,
for prouf of your partie, and yet hitherto cā obteine nothing. VVich thing I must nedes now pronounce simply and plainely, because it is true,
with out if, or and, ye doo* conscientia imbecillitatis, *because as ye know,
there is nothing to be
brought.*

THE

THE PREFACE TO
Maister Iuell.

HIS heape of Arti-
cles which you haue
layde to gether Mai-
ster Iuell, the greater
it ryseth, the lesse is
your aduantage. For
whereas you require
but one sentence for
the auouching of any one of them all : the
more groweth your number, the more en-
larged is the libertie of the answerer. It semeth you haue conceiued a great confiden-
ce in the cause, and that your aduersaries (so
it liketh you to terme vs whom God hath
so stayde with his grace as we can not beare
you companie in departing from his catholike churche) haue litle or nothing to saye
in their defence. Els what shuld moue you
both in your printed Sermon, and also in
your answeres and Replyes to Doctour Cole, to shew such courage, to vse such amplifi-
cation of wordes, so often and with such vehemencie, to prouoke vs to encounter, and
as it were at the blast of a trumpet, to make
your chalenge ? What, feared you reproche
of dastardnes, if you had called forth no more but

re but one learned man of all your aduersaries, and therefore to shew your hardinesse,
added more weight of wordes to your pro-
clamatiō, and chalenged all the learned men
that be a lyue? Amōg cowardes perhappes it
serueth the tourne some tymes, to looke fier
cely, to speake terribly, to shake the weapon
furiously, to threatē bloudily, no lesse thē cut
ting, hewing and killing: but among such we
see many tymes sore frayes foughtē, and neuer a blowe geuen . With such bragges of
him self, and reproche of all others, Homer
the wisest of all poetes setteth forth *Thersi-
tes* , for the fondest man of all the Grecians,
that came to Troye . Goliath the giaunt so
stoute as he was, made offer to fight but with
one Israelite . Choose out a man amongst
you (quoth he) and let him come and fight
with me man for man. But you Maister Iuell
in this quarell , aske not the combate of one
catholike man only , but as one suer of the
victory before proufe of fight, cast your glo-
ue as it were , and with straunge defyaunce,
prouoke all learned men that be a lyue to
campe with you.

Now if this matter shall so fall out, as the-
ouerthrowe appeare euidētly on our syde, ād
the victory on youres, that is to witte , if we
cā not bring one sentence for proufe of any
one of all these articles, out of the scriptures
auncient councelles, doctours , or exāple of
the

In the ser-
mō fol. 46.

1.Reg.17.
Eligite ex
vobis vi-
rū, & des-
cendat ad
singulare
certamen.

the primitiue churche : yet wise and graue
mē, I suppose, would haue lyked you better,
if you had meekely and soberly reported the
truth. For truth as it is playne and simple, so
it needeth not to be set forth with bragge of
high wordes. You remember that old saying **Euripides**
of the wise, *Simplex veritatis oratio*, the vtte- **in Phœniss.**
raunce of truth ought to be simple.

But if the victory (loth I am to vse this in-
solent word were it not to folow the metaphore which your chalenge hath dryuen me
vnto) fal to our syde , that is to saye , if we
shall be able to alleage some one sufficiēt sentence for proufe of some one of all these articles : yea if we shal be able to alleage diuerse
and sundry sentences places and authorities
for confirmation of sundry these articles : In
this case I wene, you shall hardly escape amōg
sober men , the reproche of rashnes, among
humble men, of presumption, among godly
men, of wickednes. Of rashnes, for what can
be more rashe, then in so weighty matters, as
some of these articles import, so boldly to af
firme that , the contrary where of may sufficiently be proued? of presumption, for what
can be more presumptuouse, then in matters
by you not thoroughly sene and weighed, to
impute ignoraunce and vnablenes to auouche thinges approued and receiued by the
churche , to all learned men a lyue? Of wickednes , for what is more wicked, then (the
                                     former

former cafe ftanding) fo to remoue the hartes of the people from deuotion, fo to bring
the churche in to contempte , fo to fet at
nought the ordinances of the holy ghoft?

As you folow the new and ftraunge doctrine of *Theodorus Beza*, and Peter Martyr, the
plocutours of the Caluiniã churches in Fraunce, whofe fcolar a lõg tyme you haue bé: fo
you diuerte farre frõ that prudécie, fobrietie,
which in their owtward demeanor, they fhewed in that foléne and honorable affemble at
Poyffi in Septéber 1561. as it appeareth by the
oration which Beza pronoũced there in the
name of all the Caluiniftes. In which oration
with hũble and often proteftation, they fub-
mitte thé felues, if caufe fhall fo appeare, to
better aduife and iudgemét , as though they
might be deceiued, vttering thefe and the like wordes in fundry places. *If we be deceiued,
we would be gladde to know it.*] Ité, [*For the fmal
meafure of knowledge that it hath pleafed God to
impart vnto vs, it femeth that this trãfubftantia-
tion, etc.*] Ité, [*if we be not decieued,*] Ité, [*In cafe
we be decieued, we would be gladde to vnderftãd
it, etc.* } But you Maifter Iuell, as though you
had readde al that euer hath bé writté in thefe pointes, and had borne a waye all that euer
hath bé taught, and were ignorãt of nothing
touchíg the fame: and none other befyde you
had fene ought and were able to faye ought:
faye merueloufe confidently, and that in the
moft

moſt honorable and frequēt audience of this
Realme, that you are well aſſured, that none
of your learned aduerſaries, no nor all the learned, mē alyue, ſhall euer be able to alleage
one ſentéce for any one of theſe Articles, and In the ſer-
that becauſe you knovv it, therefor you ſpea- mō fol. 49.
ke it, leaſt happely your hearers ſhuld be deceiued. Likewiſe in your anſwere to Doctour
Coles firſt letter, you ſaye, ſpeaking of theſe
Articles, you thought it beſt to make your Fol. 62.
entre in your preaching vvith ſuch thinges,
wherein you vvere vvell aſſured, vve ſhuld
be hable to fynde not ſo much as any colour
or ſhadovv of Doctours at all. Wherein you
vvithdravv your ſelf from plaineneſſe, ſo
much as you doo in your preſumptuouſe
chalenge, from modeſtie. For being demaunded of D. Cole, why you treate not rather
of matters of more importance, then theſe
Articles be of, which yet lye in queſtion bet-
wixt the churche of Rome and the proteſtā-
tes, as of the preſence of Chriſtes body and
bloud in the Sacrament, of Iuſtification, of
the valew of good workes, of the ſacrifice
of the Maſſe, and of ſuch other: not vn-
vvitting how much and hovv ſufficient authoritie maye be brought againſt your ſyde for proufe of the catholike doctrine rhe-
rein, leaſt all the world ſhuld eſpye your
weakenes in theſe pointes, you anſwer,
that you thought it beter to begynne with
ſmaller

smaller matters, as these Articles be, because you assure your self, we haue nothing for confirmation of them. Thus craftely you shifte your handes of those greater pointes, wherin you know scriptures, councelles, doctours, and examples of the primitiue churche to be of our syde, and cast vnto vs, as a bone to gnaw vpon, this number of Articles of lesse weight, a fewe excepted, to occupie vs withall. Which be partly concerning order, rather then doctrine, and partly sequeles of former and confessed truthes, rather then principal pointes of faith, in th'exact treatie of which, the auncient doctours of the churche haue not imployed their studie and trauaile of writing. For many of them being sequeles depending of a cófessed truth, they thought it needelesse to treate of them. For as much as a principall point of truth graunted, the graunting of all the necessarie sequeles is implyed. As in a chayne, (which cómparison S. Basile maketh in the like case) he that draweth the first lynk after him, draweth also the last lynke. And for this cause in dede the lesse number and weight of such auncient auctorities may be brought for th'auouching of them. And yet the thinges in them expssed be not iustly improued by any clause or sentence, you haue sayde or vttered hytherto.

Epist. ad
Gregoriū
fratrem.

    Verely M.Iuell if you had not ben more
desyrouse

desyrouse to deface the catholike churche,
then to set forth the truth : you would neuer
haue rehearced such a long rolle of articles,
which for the more part be of lesse importance : whereby you go about to discredite
vs, ād to make the world beleue, we haue nothing to shew for vs in a great part of our Religiō, and that you be to be taken for zelouse men, right reformers of the churche, and
vndoubted restorers of the gospell. As touching the other weighty pointes, whereupon
almost only your scoolemaisters of Germanie, Suitzerland and *Geneua*, bothe in their
preachinges and also in their writinges treate, you will not yet aduēture the triall of thē
with making your matche with learned mē,
and in the meane tyme set them forth by sermons busyly among the vnlearned and simple people, vntill such tyme, as you haue wō-
ne your purpose in these smaller matters.

Thus you seme to folow a sleight, which
king Alexander the great vsed, to further the
course of his conquestes. Who as Plutarche In vita
writeth, where as he thought verely, that he Alexandrī
was begotē of a God, shewed him self toward Magni.
the Barbarians very haute and proude. Yet
among the Grekes he vsed a more modestie,
and spake litle of his godhead. For they
being rude and of small vnderstanding, he
doubted not but by wayes and meanes to
bring them to such beleue. But the Grekes,
                    C   whom

whom he knew to be mē of excellent knowledge and learning, of them he iudged, as it proued in dede, the matter shuld be more subtyly skanned, then symply bleued. Right so you M. Iuell persuading your self to haue singular skille in diuinitie, amōg the simple people you vtter the weighty and high pointes of Christen Religiō that be now in question, in such wise, as the protestantes haue vvritten of thē, and vvith vehemēt affirmations, with misconstrevved and falsefied allegations, and with pitifull exclamations, you leade the seely soules in to dangerouse errours. But in your vvritinges, vvhich you knevv shuld passe the iudgement of learned men, the pointes of greater importaunce you coouer with silence, and vtter a nūber of Articles of lesse vveight for the more part in respect of the chiefe, though for good cause receiued and vsed in the churche, (I speake of thē as they be rightly taken) denying thē all, and requyring the catholikes your aduersaries, to prooue them. Where in you shevv your self not to feare cōtrolmēt of the ignorant, but to mistrust the triall of the learned.

Likevvise in the holy Canon of the Masse you fynde faultes, vvhere none are, as it may easely be proued, thinking for defence thereof, vve had litle to saye. But of the prayer there made to the virgine Mary, the Apostles and martyrs, of the suffrages for the departed

parted in the faith of Chrift: in your whole booke you vtter neuer a worde, though
you miflike it, and otherwheres fpeake a-
gainft it, as all your fecte doth. And why?
Forfooth becaufe you know right well, we
haue ftore of good authorities for pufe thereof. And by your will, you will not yet ftryue
with vs in matters, wherein by the iudgemét
of the people, to whom you lene much, you
fhuld feme ouermatched. And therefore you
ferch out fmall matters in comparifon of the
greateft, fuch as the old doctours haue paffed
ouer with filéce, and for that can not of our
part by anciét authorities be fo amply affirmed, at leaft waye as you thinke your felf
affured. And in this refpecte you laye on lo-
de of blame, cótumelies and fclaunders vpó
the churche, for mainteining of thé. Where
in the marke you fhoote at, euery má percei-
ueth what it is: euen that when you haue
brought the catholike churche in to contép-
te, and borne the people in hand, we are not
able to proue a number of thinges by you
denyed, for lacke of fuch proufes, as your
felf fhall allow, in certaine particular pointes of fmall force, (which falfely you report
to be the greateft keys and higheft myfteries
of our Religió): thé triúphing againft vs and
defpyfing the anciét and catholike Religió
in generall, you may fet vp a new Religió of
your own forging, a new church of your own
C 2   framing,

framing, a new gospell of your own deuise.
Well may I further saye, *cathedram contrà cathedram*, but not I trowe, as S. Augustine termeth such state of religion, *altare contrâ altare*. For what so euer ye set vp, if ye set vp any
thing at all, and pull not downe onlye: all maner of aulters must nedes be throwē downe.

Now being sorye to see the catholike churche by your stoute and bolde bragges thus
attempted to be defaced, the truth in maner
outfaced, and the seely people so dāgerously
seduced: Imbarred of libertie to preache by
Recognisance, and yet not so discharged in
conscience of dutie apperteyning to my calling: I haue now thought good to set forth
this treatise in writing, whereby to my power
to saue the honour of the churche, which is
our common mother, to defend the truth, in
whose quarell none aduenture is to be refused, and to reduce the people from deceite
and errour, which by order of charitie we
are bownde vnto.

For the doing here of if you be offended,
the conscience of good and right meaning
shal sone ease me of that griefe. Verely myne
intēt was not to hurt you, but to profite you,
by declaring vnto you that truth, which you
seme hytherto not to haue knowen. For if
you had, I wene you would not haue preached and written, as you haue: Your yeres, your maner of studie, and the partie
you

you haue ioyned your self vnto confydered, it may well be thought you haue not thoroughly sene, how much may be sayde in defence of the catholike doctrine touching these Articles, which you haue denyed.

For the maner of doing, I am verily persuaded, that neither you, nor any of your felowes, which of al these new sectes by your syde professed so euer he lyketh best, shall haue iust cause to complaine. The whole treatise is written with out choler, with out gaull, with out spite. What I mislike in you, and in the of your syde, I could not allow in my self. Where truthes cause is treated, humaine affections, where by the cleare light is dymmed, ought to be layd a parte. Glykes, nyppes and scoffes, bittes, cuttes and gyrdes, become not that stage. Yet if I shall perhappes sometymes seme to scarre or lawnce a festered bunche, that deserueth to be cut of, you will remembre I doubte not, how the meekest and the holyest of the auncient fathers in reprouing heretikes, oftentymes haue shewed them selues zelouse, earnest, eager, seuere, sharpe and bitter.

Whose taste so euer longeth most after such sawce, i this treatise he shall fynde small lyking. For it is occupyed more about the fortifying of the Articles denyed, then about disprouing of the person, who hath denyed them. Wherein I haue some deale folowed the latter parte of Chilo the wife man his counſaile, which I allow better then the firſt. *Ama, tanquàm oſurus, oderis, tanquàm amaturus.* loue, as to hate, hate, as to loue.

If any man that ſhall reade this, be of that humour, as ſhall miſlike it as being colde, lowe, flatte ād dull, ād requyre rather ſuch verder of writing, as is hote, loſty, ſharp ād quycke, which pleaſeth beſt the taſt of our tyme: vnderſtand he, that before I intended to put this forth in printe, I thus tempered my ſtile for theſe cōſyderatiōs. Firſt, where as a certaine exerciſe of a learned mā of ſiue or ſix ſheetes of paper ſpredde abroade in the Realme in defence of ſome of theſe Articles by M. Iuell denyed, was fathered vpō me, which in dede I neuer made ſentéce of, and therefore a ſtorme imminent was myſtruſted: that by chaūging the hew, which many know me by, that know me familiarly, in caſe it ſhuld come to the handes of many, as it was likely, I myght eſcape the dāger of beīg charged with it, and neuer the leſſe ſatisfye my frendes requeſt, and in ſome parte alſo my conſcience, and doo good. Secōdly, that I thought meeke, ſober and cold demeanour of writing to be moſt ſitting for ſuch kynde of argument. Thirdly and ſpecially that my hart ſerued me not to deale with M. Iuel myne old acquaīted, ſelow ād coūtreymā other wiſe, thē ſwetly, gētilly ād courteouſlye. And in dede here I proteſt,

teſt,that I loue M.Iuell,ãd deteſt his hereſies.

And novv Syr, as I loue you,right ſo I am
deſyrouſe of your ſoule helth, vvhich you ſeme either to forgete, or to procure by a wrõg
vvaye . Bethinke you ſelf I praye you, vvhether the waye you walke in, be not the ſame,
and you the man, that Salomon moued with Prouer.16.
the ſpirite of God , ſpeaketh of . *There is a
waye, that ſemeth to a man right, and the ende of
it leadeth to dãnatiõ.* Certaine it is, you are deceiued, and mainteine vntruth, as it ſhall appeare by this treatiſe . Here in you ſuſteine
the euill of humaine infirmitie. Mary , when
deceite is by plaine truth deteĉted , then to
dwell and cõtinewe in errour, that procedeth
not of humaine weakenes , but of deuiliſh
obſtinacie. But you M.Iuell as many mẽ thinke, ãd I truſt, are not yet ſwallowed vp of that
gulfe. Fayne would I doo you good, if I wiſt
how. I feare me your ſore is putrifyed ſo farre, as oyle and lenitiueſwil not ſerue now, but
rather vinegre and coroſiues.You remember
I doubte not, what Cicero ſayth, that mede-
cine to ͜pſite moſt, which cauſeth the greateſt
ſmarte, And what Salomon alſo, *The woondes* Prouer.27.
of à frend, to be better thẽ the kiſſes of an enemie.

The beſt ſalue any man can miniſter vnto
you , verely I thinke , is , to exhorte you to
humilitie , and to denying of your ſelfe.
For if you could be brought to humble your
ſelfe , and to denye your ſelfe , doubtles you
C 4   ſhuld

shuld see in your selfe, that you see not. If
you were humble, you would not be so
pufte vp, and swell against yonr mother
the churche, you would not contemne her,
whom you ought to honor. You wold not
reioyse like the accursed Cham, to shew her
vnsemelynesse, if by corruption of tymes,
any perhappes be growen. For by auctoritie
and publike consent, saye what ye will, none
is maineteined. If you would denye your
self, to be the man you be not, you shuld better see, who and what you be in dede. Denye
your felf to be so well learned, as you seme
to esteme your selfe, and you vvill be a sha-
med to make such straunge crakes and vauntes of your being vvel assured of that you
haue preached and vvritten touching these
Articles, where in you are deceiued. Denye
your selfe to be a bishop, though you haue
put on the bishop of Salesbury his white
Rochet, and you shall be content and thinke
it meet also, to geue a rekening of the doctrine which you preache openly before the
high estates, and therefore conferre with D.
Cole, and with meaner men also, which more insolently then reasonably, you refused to
doo. And by such conference, you shall be
aduertised of your errour. Denye your priuate iudgement and estimation of your long
studie in diuinitie, which you acknowledge
in your replyes and of your great cunning in
the

Genef. 9.

In the be-
gynning of
the first an-
svver to D.
Cole.

the same, ãd you shal euidently see and remẽber, that your tyme hath ben most bestowed
in the studie of humanitie ãd of the latine tõ
ge, and cõcerning diuinitie, your most labour
hath ben imployed to fynde matter against
the churche, rather thẽ about seriouse ãd exacte discussing of the truth: and that in cõpa-
rison of that holy and learned B. Fissher and
others, whom you geste and scoffe at, and
seeke to discredite by fond argumentes of
your owne framing vpon them by you fathered, you are, touching the sownde and diepe
knowledge of diuinitie, skantly a smatterer.

   Agayne denye your selfe to be so great a
man, but that you may take aduertisement
of a man of meaner calling, denye your selfe
to be so honorable, but that it may stand
with your honestie, to abyde by your promise in a most honest matter by your owne pre
pensed offer made : you maye easely learne
how to redresse, that hath ben done amisse,
you maye see your owne infirmities, defectes, ouersightes and ignorances plainely, as
it were in a glasse, all selfe loue and blinde
estimation of your self set a parte : you maye
with the fauour of al good mẽ, with the wyn
ning of your owne soule and many others,
whom you haue pereloufly deceiued, and to
the glory of God, be induced to yelde to the
truth, to subscribe to the same, and to recant
your errours. Where in you shuld doo no

In the ser-
mõ fol. 31.

       C 5   other

other thing, then (thefe Articles which you denye by vs with fufficient proufes and te-ftimonies auouched)you haue already freely and largely offred. Which thing that it maye be done, God geue you the grace of his holy fpirite , to humble your hart , to denye your felfe , and to make a greater accompte of your euerlafting faluation then of your worldly intereft.

Thomas Harding.

BE-

BECAVSE M. IVELL

OFFERETH TO BE TRYED

NOT ONLY BY THE SCRIPTVRES
*and examples of the primitiue Churche, but also
by the Councelles and fathers that were within syx
hundred yeres after Christ: here is set forth a
true note of the tyme of bothe for the
most part, such, as be in this
treatise alleaged.*

AN

AN ANSVVERE TO MAI-
STER IVELLES CHA-
LENGE BY D. HAR-
DING.

IF any learned man of our aduersaries, or if all the learned mē that be alyue, be hable to bring any one sufficient sentence out of any olde catholike doctour or father, or out of any olde generall councell, or out of the holy scriptures of God, or any one example of the primitiue Churche, whereby it may clearely and playnely be proued, that there was any priuate Masse in the whole world at that tyme, for the space of syx hundred yeres after Christ: etc. The conclusion is this: as I sayde before, so saye I now agayne, I am content to yelde and to subscribe.

Of Masse vvithout a number of others receiuing the
Cōmunion vvith the priest at the same tyme
and place, vvhich the gospellers call
priuate Masse.

ARTICLE I.

EVERY Masse is publike, concerning both the oblation, and also the communion, and none priuate. For no mā offereth that dredfull Sacrifice priuately for him selfe alone, but for the whole Churche of Christ in common. The Communion likewi-

likewise of the Sacramét, is a publike feaft by
Chrift through the minifterie of the prieft in
the same prepared for euery faithfull person:
from partaking whereof none is excluded,
that with due examinatió hauing before made him selfe ready, demaúdeth the same. And
so being common by order of the firft Inftitution, and by will of the minifters, it ought
to be reputed for common, not priuate.

That others doo so commonly forebeare
to cómunicate with the prieft, it is through
their owne defaulte ád negligence, not regar-
ding their owne saluatió. Whereof the godly
and carefull rulers of faithfull people, haue
sithens the tyme of the primitiue Churche,
alwayes much complayned. Therefore in
this respecte we doo not acknowledge any
priuate Maffe, but leaue that terme to Luthers schoole, where it was firft deuysed, and
so termed by Sathan him selfe seeking
how to vvithdravv his nouice Luther from
the loue and eftimation of that moft bleffed
Sacrifice, by reasoning vvith him againft the
same in a night vifion, as him selfe recordeth in a litle booke, vvhich he made, *De
Miffa angulari & vnctione sacerdotali*. Yet
vve denye not but that the [a] fathers of some
auncient Councelles, and fithens likewise
[b] S. Thomas, and certaine other schoole doctours, haue called it fometymes a priuate
Maffe, but not after the sense of Luther and
his

a Cócil. Va-
senc cap. 4.
Cócil. Tri-
burien. De-
cretal. li. 5.
tit. 41. ca. 2.
De confe-
crat. dift. 1.
ex Auguft.
quod qui-
dá Grego-

his scholers: but onely as it is contrary to publike and solemne, in consideration of place,
tyme, audience, purpose, rites, and other cir-
cumstances, and for distinction they haue often tymes called it publike, as we may see in
the second councell of Carthage cap. 3. The
varietie and chaunge of which being thinges
accidentarie, can not varie or chaunge the
substance or essentiall nature of the Masse.
M. Iuell an earnest professour of the new do
ctrine of Luther ád of the Sacramétaries, cal
leth, as they doo, that a priuate Masse, whereat the priest hauing no cópanie to cómunicate with him, receiueth the Sacramét alone.

Against this priuate Masse, as he termeth
it, he inueigheth sore in his printed Sermon,
vvhich he preached at Poules Crosse the second Sundaye before Easter in the yere of
our lord, 1560 as he entituleth it, shun-
ning the accustomed name of Passion Sundaye, least (as it semeth) by vsing the terme of the catholike churche, he shuld seme
to fauer any thing that is catholike. In
vvhich Sermó he hath gathered together as
it vvere in to one heape, all that euer he
could fynde writté in derogatió of it in their
bookes, by vvhom it hath ben impugned.
And though he pretende enemitie against
priuate Masse in vvord, yet in dede who so e-
uer readeth his Sermó, ád discerneth his spri-
te, shall easely perceiue, that he extédeth his
whole

whole witte and cunning, vtterly to abolishe the vnbloudy and daily Sacrifice of the Churche, commonly called the Masse. Which, as the Apostles them selues affirme in *Clemét their scoler and felow, being vnbloudy, hath succeded in place of the bloudy sacrifices of the olde lawe, and is by Christes commaundement frequented and offered in remembraunce of his passion and death, and to be vsed all tymes vntill his cōming. But what so euer he, or all other the forerunners of Antichrist speake or worke against it, all that ought not to ouerthrowe the faith of good and true Christé men, hauing for proufe thereof besyde many other places of holy scripture, the figure of Melchisedech, that was before the law, the prophecie of Malachie in the law, and lastly and most plainely, the Institutiō of Christ in the new testamét. Which he lefte to the Apostles, the Apostles to the Churche, and the Churche hath continually kepte and vsed through the whole world vntill this daye.

Touching doctours, they haue with one consent in all ages, in all partes of the world, from the Apostles tyme foreward, bothe with their example, and also testimonie of writing, confirmed the same faith. They that haue ben brought vp in learning, and yet through corruption of the tyme stand doubtfull in this point let them take paines to trauaile

trauaile in studie, and they shall synde by
good aunciét witnes of the priestes and dea-
cós of *Achaia*, that Saint Androw the Apostle touching the substance of the Masse,
worshipped God euery daye with the same
seruice, as priestes now doo in celebrating
the externall Sacrifice of the Churche. They Abdiæ li.7.
shall synd by witnes of *Abdias* first bishop of historiæ A-
Babylő, who was the Apostles scoler and saw postol.
our Sauiour in fleshe, and was present at the
passion and martyrdom of S. Androw, that
S. Matthew the Apostle celebrated Masse in
Æthiopia, a litle before his Martyrdő. They
shall synde by reporte of an auncient Coun-Concilium
cell generall, that S. Iames wrote à liturgie or Constanti-
a forme of the Masse. They shall synde that nopol. in
Martialis one of the lxxij. disciples of Christ, 32.
and Bishop of Bourdeaulx in Fraunce, sent Epistol. ad
thyther by S. Peter, serued God in like sor-Burdega.
te. They shall synde in Clement, the who-Lib. consti-
le order and forme of the Masse, set forth licarum 8.
by the Apostles them selues, aud the same cap. vlt.
celebrated by them after our lord was assumpted, before they went to the ordering
of bishops, priestes, and the vij. deacons,
according to his Institution, and the same
right so declared by Cyrillus bishop of Ierusalem *In mystagogicis orationibus*. They shall
fynde the same most plainely treated of, and
a forme of the Masse much agreable to that
is vsed in these dayes in wryting set forth by
D   S.Dio-

In ecclef.
hierarch.
cap. 3.
Act.17.

S. Dionyse, vvhom S. Paul conuerted to the faith, of vvhom it is mencioned in the actes of the Apostles, vvho had conference vvith Peter, Paul, and Ihon th'euāgelist, and much acquaintance vvith Timothe.

Thus doo I geue thee good Christen reader but a taste as it vvere of proufes, vvithout allegation of the vvordes, for cōfirmation of thy faith, concerning the blessed Masse out of the Scriptures, Apostles, and Apostolike men. I doo further referre the to *Iastinus* the martyr and philosopher, to *Ireneus* the martyr and bishop of Lions, who lyued vvith the Apostles scholers. To the olde bishop and Martyr *Hippolytus*, that Lyued in Origens tyme, vvho in his oration, *De Consummatione mundi* extant in Greke, maketh Christ thus to saye at the generall iudgement vnto bishops. *Venite Pontifices, qui puré mihi Sacrificium dei noctéq, obtulistis ac pretiosum corpus et sanguinem meum immolastis quotidie.* Come ye Bishops, that haue purely offered sacrifice to me daye ād nyght, ād haue sacrificed my pretious body and bloud daily: Finally I referre them in stede of many, to the two worthy fathers Basile and Chrysostome, whose Masses be lefte to the posteritie at this tyme extant: Amongest all *Cyrillus Hierosolymitanus* is not to be passed ouer lightly, vvho at large expoundeth the vvhole Masse vsed in Ierusalem in his tyme, the same, vvhich novv vve fynde

Lib.4.con-
tra hæref.
cap.32.

In mysta-
gogicis ora
tionibus.

fynde in Clemét, much like to that of Bafile and Chryfoſtome, and for the Canon and other principall partes, to that is now alſo vſed in the Latine Churche.

As for the other doctours of the churche, that folowed the Apoſtles and thoſe Apoſtolike mé, many in nûber, excellét in learning, holy of lyfe, to ſhew vvhat may be brought out of their workes for proufe of this mater, that th'oblation of the body and bloude of Chriſt in the Maſſe is the ſacrifice of the Church, and proper to the new teſtamér, it would require a whole volume: and therefore not being moued by M. Iuelles Chalenge to ſpeake ſpecially therof, but as it is priuate after their meaning, and many good treatiſes in defence of this ſacrifice being ſet forth already in printe: at this preſent, I will ſaye nothing, thinking hereof, as Saluſt dyd of Carthago that great citie, that it were better to kepe ſilence, then to ſpeake fewe.

Now this preſuppoſed, that the Maſſe ſtandeth vpon good and ſufficient groundes for the ſtay of all true Chriſten mennes beleefe: let vs come to our ſpeciall pourpoſe, and ſaye ſomewhat of priuate Maſſe, as our aduerſaries call it.

The chiefe cauſe why they ſtorme ſo much againſt priuate Maſſe, is, for that the prieſt receiueth the ſacramét alone: which thing they expreſſe with great vilanie of wordes. Now

D 2   in caſe

in cafe the people might by ftyrred to fuch
deuotion, as to difpofe them felues worthely
to receiue their houfell euery daye with the
prieft, as they dyd in the primitiue church,
when they looked hourely to be caught and
done to death in the perfecution of Paynimes, that they departed not hence, *Sine Via-
tico*, without their viage prouifiō: what fhuld
thefe men haue to faye? In this cafe perhappes they would fynde other defaultes ih the
Maffe, but againft it in this refpect onely that
it is priuate, they fhuld haue nothing to faye
at all. So the right of their caufe dependeth
of the mifdooing of the people which if they
would amende, thefe folke fhuld be dryuen
either to recant, or to holde their peace. To
other defaultes of the Maffe by them vntruly furmyfed, anfwere fhal be made hereafter. Now touching this.

Where no defaulte is committed, there no
blame is to be imputed. That oftentymes
the prieft at Maffe hath no comparteners to
receiue the facrament with him, it procedeth of lacke of deuotion of the peoples parte, not of enuye or malice of his parte.
The feafte is common, all be inuited, they
may come that lyft, they fhall be receiued
that be difpofed and proued: None is thruft
awaye, that thus commeth: it may be obtru-
ded to none violently, ne offred to none ra-
fhely. Well, none cōmeth. This is not a fufficient

eiét cause, why the faithfull and godly priest
enflamed with the loue of God, feeling him
selfe hungry and thirsty after that heauenly
foode and dryncke, shuld be kepte from it,
and imbarred from celebrating the memorie
of our lordes death according to his commaundement, from his dutie of geuing thankes
for that great benefite, from taking the
cuppe of saluation, and calling vpon the na-
me of God: for these thinges be done in the Masse.   Psal.115.

But the enemies of this holy sacrifice saye,
that this is against the Institution of Christ.
God forbydde, the Institution of Christ
shuld not be kepte. But it is a world to see,
how they crye out for the Institution of
Christ, by whom it is most wickedly broken.
For vvhere as in Christes Institutió cócerning
this Sacrament, three thinges are conteined,
which he him selfe dyd, and by his commaundement gaue auctoritie to the Church to
doo the same, the Consecration, the obla-   the Masse.
tion, and the participation, wherein consi-   sentials of
steth the substance of the Masse: they hauing   Three es-
quite aborogated the other two, and not so
much as once naming them in their bookes
of seruice, now haue lefte to the people nothing but a bare Communion, and that after
their ovvn sorte: with what face can they busely crye for Christes Institution, by vvhom
in the chiefe pointes the same is violated?

Of Confecration and Oblation although much might be fayde here againft thē, I wil at this tyme faye nothing. Concerning participation the number of communicantes together in one place that they iangle fo much of, as a thing fo neceffary, that without it, the Maffe is to be reputed vnlaufull : is no parte of Chriftes Inftitution. For Chrift ordeined the Sacrament, after confecration and oblation done, to be receiued and eatē.

Nūber of communicāts, place, tyme, vvith other rites, bee not of Chriftes inftitution.

And for that ende he fayd : *Accipite, manducate, bibite:* take, eate, drinke. Here in confifteth his Inftitution.

Now as for the number of the communicantes, how many fhuld receiue together in one place, and in what place, what tyme, fitting at table (as fome would haue it) ftanding or kneeling, fafting, or after other meates : and whether they fhuld receiue it in their hādes, or with their mowthes, ād other the like orders, maners and circumftances: all thefe thinges perteine to the ceremonie of eating. the obferuation where of dependeth of the churches ordinance, and not of Chriftes Inftitution. And therefore S. Augu-

Epift.118.

ftine writing to *Ianuarius* fayth : *Saluator non pracepit, quo deinceps ordine fumeretur, vt Apoftolis, per quos difpofiturus erat Ecclefiam, ferua- ret hunc locū.* Our Sauiour gaue not cōmaundement in what order it fhuld be receiued, meaning to referue that matter to the Apoftles,

ſtles, by whom he would directe and diſpoſe
his churche. Wherefore the receiuing of the
Sacrament being the Inſtitution of Chriſt,
and the maner, nũber, and other rites of the
receiuing not fixed nor determined by the ſa
me, but ordered by the Churches diſpoſitiõ;
whether many or fewe, or but one, in one pla
ce receiue : for that reſpecte the min iſtra-
tion of the prieſt is not made vnlaufull.

But if they alleage againſt vs the example
of Chriſt, ſaying that he receiued it not alone
but did communicate with his twelue Apoſ-
ſtles, and that we ought to folow the ſame: I
anſwer, that we are bounde to folow this example, *quo ad ſubſtãtiã, nõ quo ad externã cere-
moniã.* for the ſubſtance, not for the outward
ceremonie , to the which perteineth the nũber and other rites, as is a fore ſayde. Chriſtes
example importeth necesſitie of receiuing
onely, the other rites, as number, place, tyme
etc. be of congruence and order . In which
thinges the churche hath taken order, willing and charging, that all ſhall communicate, that be worthy and diſpoſed . And ſo it
were to be wiſhed , as oftétymes as the prieſt
doth celebrate this high ſacrifice, that there vvere ſome , vvho vvorthely diſpoſed ,
might receiue their rightes vvith him , and
be partakers ſacramentally of the body and
bloude of Chriſt vvith him. But in caſe ſuch
do lacke, as as vve haue ſene that lacke com-
mon-

monly in our tyme : yet therefore the continuall and dayly sacrifice ought not to be intermitted. For sith this is done in remēbraūce of Christes oblatiō once made on the crosse for the Redemption of all mankinde, therefore it ought dayly tobe celebrated thorough out the whole churche of Christ, for the better keping of that great benefite in re membraunce: and that though none receiue with the priest. And it is sufficient in that case if they that be present, be partakers of those holy mysteries spiritually, and communicate vvith him in prayer and thanckes geuing, in faith and deuotion, hauing their mynde and will to communicate with him also sacramētally, when tyme shall serue.

M. Iuell and many other of that syde, thinke to haue an argument against priuate Masse, of the word *Communio*, as though the sacrament were called a communion, in consideration of many receiuers together. So he calleth that a Communion, vvhich is for the vvhole congregation to receiue together.

In his sermō fol. 41.

And therefore in his sermon oftentymes he maketh an opposition betvven priuate Masse and communion, and alleaging diuerse pla ces vvhere mention is of a communion, inferreth of eche of them an argument against priuate Masse. But this argument is weake and vtterly vnlearned, as that which procedeth of ignorāce. For it is not so called, becau

se ma-se many, or as M. Iuell teacheth, the whole congregation, communicateth together in one place: but becaufe of the effecte of the Sacramēt, for that by the fame we are ioyned to God, and many that be diuerfe, be vnited together, and made one myfticall body of Chrift, which is the churche, of which body by vertue and effecte of this holy Sacrament, all the faithfuls be membres one of another, and Chrift is the head. Thus diuerfe auncient doctours doo expounde it, and fpecially *Dionyfius Areopagita*, vvhere fpeaking of this facrament, he fayeth *Dignifsimum hoc Sacramentum fua praftantia reliquis facramentis longè antecellit. atque ea caufa illud meritò fingulariter Ccmmunio appellatur. Nam quamuis vnumquodḡ facramētum id agat, vt noftras vitas in plura diuifas, in vnicum illum ftatum, quo Deo iūgimur, colligat, attamē huic Sacramēto Cō munionis vocabulū præcipuè ac peculiariter congruit.* This moft worthy Sacramēt is of fuch excellécie, that it paffeth farre al other facramétes. And for that caufe it is alonely called the Cōmuniō. For albe it euery Sacramēt be fuch as gathereth our lyues that be diuided a funder many wayes in to that one ftate, whereby we are ioyned to God: yet the name of Cōmuniō is fitte and cōueniēt for this facramēt fpecially and peculiarly, more then for any other. By which wordes and by the whole place of that holy father, vve vnderftand.

that this facramét is specially called the Cō-
munió, for the speciall effecte it vvorketh in
vs, which is to ioyne vs nearely to God, so as
vve be in him, and he in vs, and all vve that
beleue in him, one body in Christ. And
for this in dede vve doo not cōmunicate a-
lone. For in asmuch as the vvhole churche
of God is but one house, as Saint Cypriar
sayeth, *Vna est dom⁹ ecclesiæ, in qua agn⁹ editur:*
There is one house of the church, vvherein
the lambe is eaten: and S. Paul sayeth to Timothe, that this house of God is the churche
of the lyuing God: who so euer doth eate
this lambe worthely, doth cōmunicate with
al christen men, of all places and countries,
that be in this house, and doo the like. And
therefore S. Hierom a priest shewing him
selfe loth to contend in writing with S. Auguftine a bishop, calleth him a bishop of his
communion. His wordes be these. *Non enim
conuenit, vt ab adolescentia vsque ad hanc æta-
tem, in monasteriolo cum sanctis fratribus labore
desudans, aliquid contra Episcopum communio-
ris meæ scribere audeam, & eum Episcopum,
quem ante cœpi amare, quàm nosse.* It is not
meete (sayeth he) that I occupied in labour
from my yowth vntil this age, in a poore monasterie with holy brethren, shuld be so bolde as to write any thing against a bishop of
my communion, yea and that bishop, whom
I begāne to loue, er that I knewe him. Thus
vve

De cœna
domini.

1.Tim.3.

Inter epi-
ftolas Au-
guftini.
Epift.14.

we see, that S. Hierom and S. Augustine were of one communion, and dyd comunicate together, though they were farre a sunder, the one at Bethlehem in *Palestina*, the other at *Hippo* in *Aphrica*.

Thus there may be a Comunió, though the comunicantes be not together in one place. What if foure or fyue of sundry houses in a sicknes tyme being at the pointe of death in a parish, requyre to haue their rightes, er they departe? The priest after that he hath receiued the sacramét in the church, taketh his natural sustenaúce ãd dyneth, ãd thé beíg called vpon, carieth the reste a mile or tvvo to the sicke, in eche house none beíg disposed to receiue vvith the sicke, he doth that he is requi red. Doth he not in this case communicate vvith thé, and doo not they cómunicate one vvith an other, rather hauing a vvill to cómunicate together in one place also, if oportunitie serued? Elles if this might not be accompted as alavvful and good cómunió, and therfore notto be vsed : th'one of these great incóueniences shuld wittingly be committed. That either they shuld be denyed that necessarie vitayle of lyfe at their departing hence, which were a cruel iniurie, ãd a thing cótrary to the examples and godly ordinances of the primitiue churche : Or the priest rather for companies sake then of deuotió, shuld receiue that holy meate, after that he had serued

his

his ſtomake with common meates, which likewiſe is againſt the auncient decrees of the churche. Euē ſo the prieſt that receiueth alone at Maſſe, doth communicate with all them that doo the like, in other places and countries.

Neceſſitie of many cō municants to gether, contrarie to the libertie of the goſ-pell.
Now if either the prieſt, or euery other chriſten man or woman might at no tyme receiue this bleſſed Sacrament, but with mo together in one place: then for the enioying of this great and neceſſary benefite, we were bounde to condition of a place. And ſo the churche delyuered from al bōdage by Chriſt and ſet at libertie, ſhuld yet for all that be in ſeruitute, and ſubiectiō vnder thoſe outward things, which S. Paul calleth, *infirma & egena elementa*, weake and beggarly ceremonies after the Engliſh Bibles tranſlation. Then where S. Paul blamyng the Galathiās ſayeth, *Ye obſerue dayes and monethes and tymes*, For this bōdage he might likewiſe blame vs, and ſaye, ye obſerue places. But S. Paul would not we ſhuld retourne againe to theſe, which he calleth elementes, for that were Iewiſhe. And to the Coloſſians he ſayeth, *we be dead with Chriſt from the elementes of this worlde*. Now, if we excepte thoſe thinges, which be neceſſaryly requyred to this Sacrament by Chriſtes inſtitution, either declared by writ-ten ſcriptures, or taught by the holy ghoſt, as bread and wyne mingled vvith water for the

Galat. 4.

Coloſ. 2.

Similiter & calicé miſ-cés ex vino

the matter, the due vvordes of Consecration
for the forme , and the priest rightely ordered , hauing intention to doo as the churche
doth , for the ministerie: all these elementes
and all outvvard thinges be subiecte to vs,
and serue vs being mēbers of Christes churche. In consideration vvhereof S. Paul sayeth
to the Corinthians , *Omnia enim vestra sunt,*
&c. e *All thinges are yours, vvhether it be Paul,*
either Apollo, either Cephas: vvhether it be the
vvorlde, either lyfe, either death, vvhether they be
present thinges , or thinges to come, all are yours,
and ye Christes , and Christ is Gods.

Againe vvhere as the auncient and great
learned Bishop *Cyrillus* teacheth plainely and
at large , the meruelouse vniting and ioyning together of vs vvith Christ , and of our
selues into one bodie by this sacramēt: seing
that all so vnited and made one body, be not
for all that brought together into one place,
for they be dispersed abroade in all the worlde: thereof we may well conclude , that to
this effecte the being together of communicantes in one place is not of necessitie. His
wordes be these, much agreable to *Dionysius*
Areopagita a fore mentioned . *Vt igitur inter*
nos & Deum singulos vniret , quamuis corpore
simul & anima distemus , modum tamen adin-
uenit, consilio patris & sapientiæ suæ conuenien-
tem. Suo enim corpore credentes per communio-
nem mysticam benedicēs, & secum, & inter nos,
vnum

& aqua, & sanctificās, tradidit eis, dicēs: Bibi-te, &c. Cle-mens in Canone Liturgiæ lib. 8. Apostol. cō stit. cap. 17. 1. Cor. 3.

In Ioā. lib. 11. cap. 26.

*vnum nos corpus efficit. Quis enim eos, qui vnius
sancti corporis vnione in vno Christo vniti sunt,
ab hac naturali vnione alienos putabit? Nam si
omnes vnum panem manducamus, vnum omnes
corpus efficimur: diuidi enim atque seiungi Christus non patitur.*

That Christ might vnite euery one of vs
within our selues, and with God, although
we be distant both in body and also in soule,
yet he hath deuised a meane conuenable
to the counsell of the father, and to his
own wisedom. For in that he blesseth them
that beleue, with his own body through the
mysticall Communion, he maketh vs one
body both with him selfe, and also betwen
our selues. For who will thinke them not to
be of this natural vnion, which with the vnion of that one holy body, be vnited in one
Christ?For if we eate all of one bread, thē are
we made all one body: for Christ may not be
diuided, nor done asunder,

Thus we see after this auncient fathers
learning grounded vpon the scriptures, that
all the faithfulles blessed with the body of
Christ through the mysticall cummunion,
bee made one body with Christ, and one
body betwen them selues. Which good
blessing of Christ is of more vertue, and also
of more necessitie, then that it may be made
frustrate by conditiō of place, specially where
as is no wylfull breache nor contempte of
most

moſt ſemely and conuenable order . And
therefore that one may communicate with
an other , though they be not together in
one place, (which M. Iuell denyeth with as
peeuiſh an argument of the vſe of commu-
nication, as any of all thoſe ys , that he ſcof-
feth at ſome catholike writers for) and that
it was thought lawfull and godly by the fathers of the auncient churche neare to the
Apoſtles tyme , it may be well proued by diuerſe good aucterities.

Many
maye com
municate
together,
not being
in one pla-
ce together
Sermon
fol. 51.

Irenæus writing to *Victor* Biſhop of Rome
cōcerning the keping of Eaſter, *As Euſebius
Cæſarienſis* reciteth , to the intēt *Victor* ſhuld
not refrayne from their communion, which
kepte Eaſter after the cuſtome of the churches in *Aſia* fownded by S. Iohn th'Euan-
geliſte, ſheweth , that when biſhoppes came
from forreine parties to Rome , the biſhoppes of that ſee vſed to ſend to them', if they
had ben of the catholike faith, the Sacramēt
to receiue , whereby mutuall communion
betwen thē was declared. *Irenæus* his wordes
be theſe. *Qui fuerunt ante te preſbyteri , etiam
cum nō ita obſeruarent, preſbyteris ecclſiarum,
(cē Romā accederent.) Euchariſtiam mittebāt.*
The prieſtes (by which name in this place biſhoppes are vnderſtanded) that were afore
thy tyme , though they kepte not Eaſter as
they of *Aſia* dyd, yet whē the biſhoppe of the
churches there came to Rome , dyd ſede thē
the

Eccleſiaſ.
hiſt. lib. 5.
cap. 24.

Græca ſic
habent, ali-
ter quàm
Rufini ver-
ſio vulgata.

the facrament . Thus thofe bifhoppes dyd communicate together , before their meeting in one place.

Iuſtinus the Martyr likewiſe deſcribing the maner and order of chriſten Religion of his tyme touching the vſe of the Sacrament , ſayeth thus . *Finitis ab eo , qui præfeſtus eſt ,gratijs & orationibus,& ab vniuerſo populo facta acclamatione, Diaconi, quos ita vocamus , vnicuiq̃ tum temporis præſenti ,panis & aquæ & vini conſecrati dant participationem, & ad eos,qui non adſunt, deferunt.* When the prieſt hath made an ende of thankes and prayers , and all the people therto haue ſayde amen : They , which we call deacons, geue to euery one then preſent , bread and water and wyne conſecrated,to take parte of it for their houſell, and for thoſe that be not preſent,they beare it home to them. Thus in that tyme they that ſerued God together in the commō place of prayer,and ſome others that were abſent , letted from comming to ther companie by ſickenes,buſines,or other wiſe:communicated together,though not in one place , and no mā cryed out of breaking the Inſtitution of Chriſt.

And becauſe M.Iuell is ſo vehemēt againſt priuate Maſſe , for that the prieſt receiueth the Sacrament alone , and triumpheth ſo much , as though he had wonne the fielde, making him ſelfe mery with theſe wordes,in
dede

Apolog .2.

dede without cause: *Where then was the priua-* In his ser-
te Masse? where then was the single Communion mon.fo.43
all this while? he meaneth for the space of syx
hundred yeres after Christ, as there he ex-
presseth: I wil bring in good euidéce and witnes, that long before S. Gregories tyme that
he speaketh of, yea frō the beginning of the
churche, faithfull persones both men and
women receiued the sacrament alone, and
were neuer therefore reproued, as breakers
of Christes Institution. And er I enter into
the rehearsall of the places wich I am able to
shewe for this purpose, one question I demaunde of M. Iuell. If they which remained
at home, of whom *Iustinus Martyr* writeth, receiued the communion by them selues alone laufully, why may not the priest
doo the same in the churche seruing God in
most deuoute wise in the holy sacrifice of the
Masse, lacking comparteners without any
his defaulte? Haue the Sacramentaries any
Religion to condemne it in the priest, and to
alowe it in laye folke? What is in the priest,
that shuld make it vnlawfull to him, more
then to the people? Or may a laye mā or woman receiue it kepte a long tyme, and may
not a priest receiue it forthwith, so sone as he
hath consecrated and offred? And if case of
necessitie be alleaged for the laye, the same
may no lesse be alleaged for the priestes also
wāting compartners without their defaulte.

E   For

For other. vvise the memorie and recording of our lordes death shuld not according to his commaundement be celebrated and done. Well, novv to these places.

Proufes for priuate cómunion.

Tertullian exhorting his vvife, that if he dyed before her, she marye not againe, specially to an Infidell, shevving that if she dyd, it vvould be hard for her to obserue her Religion vvithout great inconuenience, sayeth

Libr. 2. ad vxorem.

thus. *Non sciet maritus, quid secretò ante omnē cibum gustes? Et si sciuerit, panem, non illum credet esse, qui dicitur.* Will not thy husband knowe what thou eatest secretly before all other meate? And if he doo knowe, he will beleue it to be bread, and not him, who it is called. He hath the like saying in his booke, *De corona militis.* Which place plainely declareth vnto vs the beleefe of the churche then in three great pointes by M. Iuel and the rest of our Gospellers vtterly denyed. The one, that the communion maye be kepte: the second, that it may be receiued of one alone without other companie: the third, that the thing renerently and deuoutly before other meates receiued, is not bread, as the infidels then, and the Sacramentaries now beleue: but he who it is sayde to be of Christen people, or who it is called, that is, our maker and Redemer, or, which is the same, our lordes bodye. And by this place of Tertulliā, as also by diuerse other auncièt doctours, we may gather,

1
2
3

ther, that in the tymes of perfecution the
maner was, that the prieftes delyuered to deuoute and godly men and women the Sacrament confecrated in the churche, to carye
home with them, to receiue a parte of it euery morning fafting, as their deuotion ferued
them, fo fecretly as they might, that the infidels fhuld not efpie thē, nor gette any knowledge of the holy myfteries. And this was done, becaufe they might not affemble them
felues in folemne congregation, for feare
of the infidels amongeft whom they dwelte.
Neither fhuld the cafe of neceffitie haue ex-
cufed them of the breach of Chriftes commaundemēt, if the fole communion had ben
expreffely forbyddē, as we are borne in hande by thofe that vphold the contrarie doctrine. And Origen that auncient doctour Origen.in
and likewife S. Auguftine doth write of the Exod.ho-
great reuerence, feare, and warenes, that the milia.13.
men and women vfed in receiuing the Sa- Aug. hom.
crament in a cleane lynnen cloth to cary it 26.in li.50.
home with them for the fame purpofe. hom. & fer

Saint Cyprian writeth of a womā that dyd de tēpore.
the like, though vnworthely, after this forte. In fermone
Cum quædam arcam fuam in qua domini fanctū de lapfis.
fuit, manibus indignis tentaffet aperire, igne
inde furgente deterrita eft, ne auderet attingere.
When a certaine woman went about to o-
pen her chefte, wherein was the holy thing
of our lorde, with vnworthy handes, fhe was
frayed

frayed with fyer that rose frō thence, that she
durst not touche it. This place of S. Cypriane
reporteth the maner of keping the Sacramēt
at home, to be receiued of a deuout Christen
person alone at conuenient tyme. The example of Serapion, of whom *Dionysius Ale-*
xandrinus writeth, recited by *Eusebius*, confirmeth our purpose of the single communion. This Serapion one of *Alexandria*, had
committed idolatrie, and lying at the pointe
of death, that he might be reconciled to the
churche before he departed, sent to the priest
for the Sacrament. the priest being him selfe
sicke and not able to come, gaue to the ladde that came of that errant, *parum Euchari-*
stiæ, quod infusum iussit seni præberi. a litle of
the Sacrament, which he commaunded to
be powred in to the olde mannes mowth.
And when this solennitie was done, (sayeth
the storye) as though he had broken certaine
chaynes and giues, he gaue vp his ghost che-
refully.

Of keping the sacramēt secretly at home,
and how it might be receiued of deuoute
persons alone with out other companie, I
wene none of the auncient doctours wrote
so playnely, as S. Basile, in an epistle, that
he wrote to a noble woman called *Cæsaria*,
which is extāt in greeke, where he sayeth further that this maner beganne not first in his
tyme, but long before. his wordes be these.
Illud

Ecclesiast.
hist. lib. 6.
cap. 34.

1838412

Illud autem in perfecutionis temporibus necessi-
tate cogi quempiam, non praefente facerdote aut
ministro communionem propria manu sume,e,
nequaquam esse graue, superuacaneum est de-
monstrare, propterea quòd longa consuetudine,
& ipso rerum vsu confirmatum est. Omnes enim
in eremis folitariam vitam agentes, vbi non est
facerdos, communionem domi seruantes, à s.ipsis
communicant. In Alexandria verò & in Æ-
gypto, vnusquisque eorū qui sunt de populo, plu-
rimùm habet communionem in domo sua. Semel
enim facrificium sacerdote consecrante & distri-
buente, merito participare & suscipere, credere
oportet. Etenim & in Ecclesia facerdos dat par-
tem, & accipit eam is qui suscipit, cum omni li-
bertate, & ipsam admouet ori propria manu.
Idem igitur est virtute, siue vnam partem acci-
piat quisquā à facerdote, siue plures partes simul.

As concerning this, that it is no greuouse,
offence, for one to be driuen by necessitie in
the tymes of persecution to receiue the com
munion with his owne hand, no priest nor
deacō being present: it is a thing superfluous
to declare, for that by long custome and
practise it hath ben confirmed and taken
place. For all they which lyue a solytary lyfe
in wildernes, where no priest is to be had,
keping the communion at home, doo communicate with them selues alone. And in
Alexandria and in Egypte, euery one of the
people for the most parte hath the commu-

nion at home in his houfe . For when as the
prieſt doth once cōſecrate and diſtribute the
hoſte, it is reaſō we beleue, that we ought to
be partakers of it, and he that taketh it, recei
ueth it without all ſcruple of cōſcience, and
putteth it to his mowth with his owne hāde.
And ſo it is of one vertue, whether any body
take one parte of the prieſt, or mo partes together. This farre S. Baſile. In this ſaying of

1   Baſile , it is to be noted , firſt, that neceſſitie
here hath reſpecte to the lacke of prieſt and
decon: So as in that caſe the Sacramēt might
be receiued of a faithfull perſon with his

2   owne hande. And that for the ratifying of ſo
doing, he alleageth continuance of cuſtome,
which for vs in this point of the ſole receiuing, maye in more ample wiſe be alleaged.

3   Agayne, that holy Eremites lyuing in wildernes a parte from companie , and alſo the deuout people of *Alexandria* and Egypte , receiued the communion alone in their celles

4   and howſes. Furthermore that the hoſte once conſecrated of the prieſt, is algates to be
receiued, whether of many together , or of
one alone, by him it ſemeth not to force.

5   Finally, that whether a man take at the prieſtes hande the bleſſed Sacramēt in one piece
or mo pieces, and receiue them at cōuenient
tymes, when deuotion beſt ſerueth: the vertue , effecte , and power thereof is one. By
which auctoritie reſeruation is auouched.

Reſeruatiō
of the Sa-
crament.

Doub-

Doubteles where he speaketh so precisely
and particularly of sundry cases touching the
order of receiuing, if he had ben of M. Iuelles opinion, that the Sacrament may not be
receiued of one with out a certaine number
of communicantes together, he would not
so haue passed ouer that matter in silence,
much lesse written so plainely of the contrary. Now that the communion thus kepte in
wildernes and in Egypte, places of extreme
heate, where wyne in small quantitie as is for
that purpose conuenient, can not be long kepte frō sowring and chaūging his nature, was
in the forme of bread only, and not also of
wyne: I differre to note it here, because it perteineth to the treatise of the nexte Article.

It appeareth euidētly by witnes of saint Hie
rome also, that this custome of receiuing the
communion priuately at home contynewed
among Christen men at Rome not only in
tyme of persecution, but also afterward when
the churche was at rest and peace, so as the
case of necessitie can not here serue them for
maintenaunce of their straunge negatiue in
this point. These be his wordes. *Scio Romæ* In Apolo-
hanc esse consuetudinem, vt fideles semper Christi gia aduer-
corpus accipiant, quod nec reprehendo, nec probo, sus Iouinia
Vnusquisque enim in suo sensu abundat. Sed ipso- num.
rum conscientiam conuenio, qui eodem die post Rom.14.
coitum communicant, & iuxta Persium, noctem
flumine purgāt: quare ad Martyres ire nō audēt?

Quare non ingrediuntur Ecclesias? An alius in publico, alius in domo Christus est? Quod in Ecclesia non licet, nec domi licet. Nihil Deo clausum est, & tenebræ quoq; lucet apud Deum. Probet se vnusquisq; ; & sic ad corpus Christi accedat.
I know this custome is at Rome, that Chriften folke receiue the body of Christ dayly, which I doo neither reproue, nor allowe. For euery man hath ynough in his owne sense. But I appose their conscience, which doo communicate that same daye, as they haue done wedlocke worke, and as *Persius* sayeth, doo rynce night filth with runnig water. why dare not they goe to Martyrs Shrynes? Why goe not they in to churches? what, is there one Christ abroade, and an other Christ with in the house? what so euer is not laufull in the churche, neither at home is it laufull. To God nothing is hydden : yea darknes also shyneth before God. Let euery one examine him selfe, and so come to the body of Christ. S. Hierome reproueth this in the Romaines; that where as S. Paul ordeined, that for cause of prayer maried folke shuld at tymes forbeare their carnall imbracinges, they not withstanding that, though they had doing with their wyues, yet receiued their rightes neuerthelesse dayly. And yet what daye they had so done they durst not goe to churches, where martyrs toúbes were, there to receiue our lordes body. For it
is to

is to be vnderstanded for better knowledge
hereof, that such as knewe then selues to haue done any vncleānes, were afrayd in th'old
tyme to comme to the Martyrs Sepulchres.
For there commonly by miracle such thin- Hereof
ges were bewrayed, and many tymes by open speaketh
cōfeſſion of rhe parties, whether they would S. Hierom
or no. *Erasmus* in his Scholies vpon this pla- ad Vigilā-
ce of S. Hierome sayeth thus. Of this place tiū, and S.
we gather, that in th'olde tyme euery one was Aug. epi-
wonte to receiue the body of Christ at home stola.137.
in his house, that would. He sayeth further, and Seue-
Idem videtur innuere Paulus, cum ait: an domos rus Sulpi-
non habetis ad manducandum? S. Paul sayeth tius in vi-
he, semeth to meane the same thing, where ta S. Mar-
he sayeth, *haue you not houses to eate in*? Thus tini.dial.3.
Erasmus gathereth proufe of priuate, or as cap.7.
M. Iuell iesteth, *Single Communion*, out of the 1. Cor.11.
scriptures, and he was as wel learned in thē as
M. iuell is. Yet I herein leaue *Erasmus* to his
owne defence. By this we may vnderstand,
that in the auncient tymes of the Churche,
the receiuing of the Communion of one by
him selfe alone, was well alouved. And
though it vvas done but by one faithfull
person at once in one place, yet vvas it called a communion both of S. Basile, and also of S. Hierom, cleane contrary to M. Iuelles sense. It is to be iudged that they knew
the Institution of Christ, so wel las he, or any
other of these nevve Maisters, and that their

conscience was such, as if Christes ordinance
therein had ben broken, they would not haue winckte at it, ne with their vngodly silence confirmed such an vngodly custome. Verely for excuse of this sole receiuing, necessitie can not iustly be alleaged.

Damasus Bishop of Rome in S. Hieromes
tyme writeth *in libro Pōtificali*, that *Milciades*
Pope and Martyr, ordeined that the Sacramēt
in sundry portions consecrated by a bishop,
shuld be sent a broade amōg the churches for
cause of heretikes that the catholike people
of the churches (which vvord here signifieth
as the greke vvord παροικίαι doth, so as it is
not necessarie to vnderstād that the sacramēt
was directed only to the materiall churches,
but to the people of the parrishes) might receiue the catholike communiō, and not com
municate vvith heretikes. Which doubteles
must be vnderstanded of this priuate and single communiō in eche catholike mans house, and that vvhere heretikes bare the svvea,
and priestes might not be suffred to consecrate after the catholike vsage. Elles if the
priestes might vvith out lette or disturbance
haue so done, then vvhat nede had it ben for
Milciades, to haue made such a prouision for
sending abroade hostes sanctified for that
purpose by the consecration of a Bishop? The
place of *Damasus* hath thus. *Milciades fecit,
vt oblationes cōsecratæ per Ecclesas ex cōsecrata
Episcopi*

Episcopi (propter hæreticos) dirigerentur. Milciades ordeined that cõsecrated hoftes fhuld be sent abroade amongeft the churches, prepared by the cõsecratiõ of a bifhop. The two wordes *propter hæreticos,* for heretikes, added by Ado the writer of Martyrs lyues, openeth the meaning and purporte of that decree.

Here haue I brought much for proufe of priuate and single communion, and that it hath not onely ben suffered in tyme of persecution, but also allowed in quiet and peaceable tymes, euen in the Churche of Rome it selfe, where true Religiõ hath euer ben moft exactly obserued aboue all other places of the worlde, and from whence all the churches of the Weft hath taken their light. As the Bishops of all *Gallia* that now is called Fraunce, doo acknowledge in an epiftle sent to Leo the Pope, with these wordes. *Vnde re-* Epiftola *ligionis noftræ propicio Chrifto, fons & origo ma-* proxima *nauit.* From that Apoftolike see by the mer- poft 51. incie of Chrift, the fontaine and spring of our ter epiftolas Leonis. Religion hath come. Yea on which al the endes of the worlde, that truly haue receiued our lorde, do looke, sayeth *Maximus :* and In epift. ad out of which they take the light of the catho Orientales. like and Apoftolike faith.

More could I yet bryng for confirmation of the same, as th'example of *S. Hilaria* the virgine in the tyme of *Numerian⁹,* of *S. Lucia* in Diocletians tyme done to martyrdõ, of *S. Maria*

Maria Aegyptiaca, and of S. *Ambros:* of
which euery one, as auncient testimonies of
ecclesiasticall histories, and of *Paulinus* doo
declare, at the houre of their departure hence
to God, receiued the holy Sacrament of
th'aulter for their viage prouision, alone: But
I iudge this is ynough, and if any man will
not be persuaded with this, I doubte whether with such a one a more number of authorities shall any thing preuaile.

Now that I haue thus proued the single
communion, I vse their own terme, I desire
M. Iuell to reason with me soberly a word of
two. How saye you Syr? doo you reproue the
Masse, or doo you reproue the priuate Masse? I thinke what so euer your opinion is herein, your answer shall be, you allow not the
priuate Masse. For as touching that the Ob-
blation of the body and bloude of Christ
done in the Masse, is the sacrifice of the churche, and proper to the new testament, commaunded by Christ to be frequented according to his institution: if you denye this, make it so light as you liste: al those authorities,
vvich you denye vs to haue for pufe of your
great nūber of articles, wil be fownde againft
you: I meane doctours, general coūcelles the
most auncient, th'example of the primitiue
churche, the scriptures, I adde further reaso,
consent vniuersall and vncontrolled, and tradition. If you denye this, you must denye all

our

our Religion from the Apostles tyme to this
daye, and now in the ende of the world, whē
iniquitie aboundeth, and charitie waxeth
colde,when the sonne of mā comming shall
scarcely finde faith in the earth, begynne a
new. And therefore you M. Iuell knowing
this well ynough, what so euer you doo in
dede, in worde, as it appeareth by the litle
booke you haue set foorth in printe: you
pretende to disallow, yea most vehemently
to improue the priuate Masse.

Vpon this resolution, that the Masse, as
it is taken in generall, is to be allowed: I enter further in reason with you,and make you
this argument. If priuate Masse in respecte
only of that it is priuate after your meaning,
be reproueable, it is for the single communion, that is to saye, for that the priest receiueth the Sacrament alone. But the single
communiō is laufull,yea good and godly: *Er*
go the priuate Masse in this respecte that it
is priuate, is not reproueable,but to be allo-
vved, holden for good and holy, and to be
frequented. If you denye the first proposition,or *maior*,then must you shevv for vvhat
elles you doo reproue priuate Masse in respecte only that it is priuate, then for single
communion. If you shevv any thing elles,
then doo you digresse from our purpose,and
declare,that you reptoue the Masse.The *mi-*
nor you cā not denye,seing that you see hovv
                                    ufficiently

sufficiently I haue proued it . And so the priuate Masse in that respecte only it is priuate,
is to be allowed for good , as the Masse is.
Mary I denye not but that it were more cō-
mendable , and more godly on the churches
parte , if many wel disposed and examined,
would be partakers of the blessed Sacramēt
with the priest . But though the Clergie be
vvorthely blamed for negligence herein,
through vvhich the people may be thought
to haue grovven to this slaknes and indeuo-
tion:yet that notvvithstanding , this parte of
the catholike Religion remaineth sovvnde
and faultles . For as touching the substance
of the Masse it selfe, by the single communion of the priest,in case of the peoples colde-
nes and negligence , it is nothing impaired.
Elles if the publike sacrifice of the churche might not be offered vvith out a number of communicantes receiuing vvith the
priest in one place:then vvould the auncient
fathers in all their vvritinges some vvhere
haue cōplained of the ceasing of that , vvich
euery vvhere they call *quotidianū & inge sacrificium*, the dayly and cōtinuall sacrifice: of
which their opinion is,that it ought dayly to
be sacrificed , that the death of our lord and
the worke of our Redemptiō;might alwayes
be celebrated and had in memorie , and vve
thereby shevve our selues according to our
boundē dutie myndeful and thākeful.But ve
rely

rely the fathers no vvhere complaine of intermitting the daily sacrifice, but very much of the slaknes of the people, for that they came not more often vnto this holy and holesome banket : and yet they neuer compelled thē thereto, but exhorting them to frequent it vvorthely, lefte them to their ovvne conscience

S. Ambros vvitnesseth that the people of the East, had a custome in his tyme to be houseled but once in the yere. And he rebuketh sharply such as folovve them, after this sorte. *Si quotidianus est cibus, cur post annum illum sumis, quemadmodum Græci in Oriente facere consueuerunt?* If it be our daily meate (sayeth he) why takest it but once in the yere, as the Grekes are wōte to doo in the East? S. *Augustine* vttereth the same thinge almost with the same wordes. And in the second booke, *De sermone Domini in monte* the twelfth chapter, expownding the fourth petition of our lordes prayer. *Geue vs this daye our dayly bread*, shewing that this may be taken either for materiall bread either for the sacrament of our lordes body, or for spirituall meate, which he alloweth best : would that concerning the sacrament of our lordes body, they of the Easte shuld not moue question, how it might be vnderstanded to be their dayly bread, which were not dayly partakers of our lordes supper, where

as

Lib. 6. de sacra. ca. 4.

De verbis domini secundū Lucā. ho. 18.

as for all that, this bread is called dayly bread: There he sayeth thus: *Vt ergo illi taceant,
neque de hac re sententiam suam defendant, vel
ipsa auctoritate Ecclesiæ sint contenti, quòd sine
scandalo ista faciunt, neque ab eis qui ecclesijs
præsunt, facere prohibentur, neque non obtempe-
rātes condēnantur.*Wherefore that they holde
their peace, and stand not in defence of their
opinion, let them be content àt leaſt waye
with the auctoritie of the churche, that they
doo these thinges without offence thereof
taken, neither be forbidden of those that be
ouer the churches, neither be condemned,
when they diſobeye. Here we see by S. Auguſtine, that they of the Orient, who so seldom receiued the sacrament, were holden
for all that, for Chriſté people by the authoritie of the churche, none offence thereof
was taken, neither were they inhibited of
their cuſtome, and though they obeyed not
their ſpirituall gouernours mouing them to
receiue more often, yet were they not condemned, nor excommunicated.

In 10.ea.ad
Heb.ho.17 S.*Chryſoſtome* many tymes exhorting his
people to prepare them ſelues to receiue
their rightes at Eaſter, in one place sayeth
thus. What meaneth this? The moſt parte of
you be partakers of this ſacrifice but once in
the yere, ſome twyſe, ſome oftener. Therefore this that I ſpeake, is to all, not to thé onely that be here preſent, but to thoſe alſo that
lyue

lyue in wildernes. For they receiue the sacrament but once in the yere, peraduenture
but once in two yeres. Well what then?
whom shall we receiue? those that come but
once, or that come often, or that come
seldom? Soothly we receiue them that come with a pure and a cleane conscience, with
a cleane harte, and to be shorte, with a bla-
melesse lyfe. They that be such, let them
come allwayes, and they that be not such,
let not them come not so much as once.
Why so? because they receiue to them selues iudgement, damnation, and punishe-
ment. The auncient doctours, specially Chrysostome and Augustine, be full of
such sentences.

Now to this ende I dryue these allegations, leauing out a great number of the same sense. Although many tymes the people
forbare to come to the communion, so as
many tymes none at all were founde dispo-
sed to receiue, yet the holy fathers, bishops ^The peo-
and priestes thought not that a cause why ples fore-
they shuld not dayly offer the blessed sacrifi- bearing the
ce, and celebrate Masse. Which thing may cōmunion,
sufficiently be proued, whether M. Iuell, is no cause
that maketh him selfe so sure of the con- vvhy the
trary, will yelde and subscribe according not saye
to his promise, or no. Of the dayly sacri- masse.
fice these wordes of Chrysostome be plaine. In 10
Quid ergo nos? Nōne per singulos dies, offerimus? ca.ad Heb.
                   offerimus homil. 17.

F

offerimus quidem , ſed ad recordationem facien-
tes mortis eius , & vna eſt hoſtia , non multæ. etc.
Then what doo we ? doo we not offer euery
daye?yeas verely we doo ſo.But we doo it for
recording of his death , And it is one hoſie,
not many.Here I heare M.Iuell ſaye,though
against his will , I grawnt the dayly ſacrifice,
but I ſtand ſtill in my negatiue,that it can not
be ſhewed , there was euer any ſuch ſacrifice celebrated , without a communion , that
is , as they will haue it with out ſome conuenient number to receiue the ſacrament in
the ſame place with the prieſt.For proufe of
this , theſe be ſuch places as I am perſuaded
with all . The better learned men that be
of more reading then I am , haue other I
doubte not .

> By order of the laſte communiõ booke, no communiõ may be ſiyd or had vvithout three doo communicate vvith the miniſter at leaſte,of hovv ſmall num ber ſo euer the parriſhe bee. De conſec. diſt.1.can. hoc quoq; ſtatutum.

Soter Byſhop of Rome about the yere of
our lord. 170. who ſuffred martyrdom vnder *Antoninus Verus* te Emperour,for order
of celebrating the Maſſe , made this ſtatute
or decree . *Vt nullus presbyterorum Miſſarum*
ſolennia celebrare præſumat,niſi duobus præſenti-
bus,ſibiᶀ, reſpõdẽtibus & ipſe tertius habeatur,
quia cũ pluraliter ab eo dicitur, Dominus vobiſ-
cũ,& illud in ſecretis , Orate pro me: apertiſſimè
*conuenit, vt ipſius reſpondeatur ſalutationi.*This
hath ben ordeined,that no prieſt preſume to
celebrate the ſolennitie of the Maſſe,excepte
there be two preſent , and anſwer him , ſo as
he be the third.For whereas he ſayeth (as by
waye

waye of speaking to many) *our lorde be with you :* and lykewise in the Secretes, *Praye ye for me :* it semeth euidently conuenient, that answer be made to his salutatiō accordingly. Which auncient decree requireth not, that all people of necessitie be present, much lesse that all so oftentymes shuld communicate sacramentally, which thing it requireth neither of those two, that ought to be present. If of the bare wordes of this decree a sufficient argument maye not be made for our purpose, inducing of th'affirmation of that one thing there specified, the denyall of that other thing we speake of, which maner of argument is commonly vsed of our aduersaries : then more weight may be put vnto it in this case : for that where as the receiuing of Christes body is a farre greatter matter, then to answer the priest at Masse, if that holy bishop and Martyr had thought it so necessary, as that the Masse might not be done with out it : doubteles of very reason and conuenience, he would and shuld haue specially spoken of that, rather then of the other. But for that he thought otherwise, he required onely of necessitie, the presence of two, for the purpose aboue mentioned.

In a councell holden at Agatha a citie of Fraunce thē called *Gallia*, about the tyme of *Chrisostome*, an olde decree of *Fabianus Bishop* of Ro-

a Ex concilio Agathē. can. 31. Missas die dominico secularibus totas audire, speciali ordine precipimus

F 2

ita vt ante
benedictio
nem sacer-
dotis egre-
di populus
non presu-
mat : quod
si fecerit, ab
Episcopo
publicè cõ
fundantur.

b De conse
dist. 1. cum
ad celebrã-
das Missas.

of Rome and Martyr, and also the coũcel *Eli-bertine* in the tyme of Saint *Syluester, anno Domini* 314. was renewed, that all secular christen folke shuld be houseled thrce tymes euery yere, at Easter, Witsontide, and Christmasse. It was there also decreed, that they shuld heare the whole Masse euery Sunnedaye, and not departe, before the priest had geuen blessing. So they were bownde to heare Masse euery Sunnedaye, and to receiue the communion but thrise in the yere. The selfe same order was decreed in the b Councell of Orleance. Then of like, specialy in small townes and villages, they had masse without the cõmunion of many together, some tymes.

Cap. 21.

In that Councell of Agatha we fynde a decree, made by the fathers assembled there, whereof it appeareth, that priestes oftétymes sayd Masse with out others receiuing with them. And this much it is in English. If any man will haue and oratorie or chappell abroade in the countrie, beside the parrish churches, in which laufull and ordinarie assemble is : for the rest of the holydayes, that he haue Masses there, in consideration of weerynesse of the household, with iust ordinance we permitte. But at Easter, Christes Birth, Epiphanie, the Ascenscion of our lord Witsunnedaye, and Natiuitie of Saint Iohn Baptist, and if there be any other speciall feastes : let them not kepe their Masses, but in
the

the cities and parishes . And as for the cler-
kes , if any will doo or haue their Masses at
the afore sayde feastes in chappelles , onlesse
the bishop so cōmaunde or permit , telet thé
be thrust out from communion . By this decree we learne , that then Masses were commonly say'd in priuat chappelles at home , at
such tymes , as the people were not accustomed to be howseled. For when by commaundement and common order they receiued
their rightes , as in the afore named feastes:
thé were the priestes ₚhibited to saye Masses
in priuate oratories or chappelles with out
the parish churches. And here of we may plai
nely vnderstand , that in such places, priestes
customeably sayde Masses of their owne and
of the householders deuotion, when none of
the household were disposed to receiue with
them. The like decree is to be fownde , *Con-*
cilij Aruernensis.cap.14. Concil.Constantinop.
generalis in Trullo.cap.31.

Now let vs see what examples of the olde fathers we haue for the priuate Masse. *Le-*
ontius a Greke bishop of a Citie in Cypres,
called *Neapolis* , writing the lyfe of Saint
Iohn the holy Patriarke of *Alexandria,*who
for his great charitie was commonly called
eleemosynarius , that is , th'almose geuer ,
telleth this story , whereby it appeareth
that at that tyme priuate Masse was vsed.
Though the translatour through ignorance

vixit tem-
poribus
Mauritij
Imper.vide
Synodi.Ni
cenæ.2.
actioné.4,

of the

of the tyme he lyued in, tourned this lyfe in to latine of meane eloquence, yet for truthes sake, I will not let to recite that, which I take for my purpose, as I fynde it. *Malitiam reseruantem quendam industrium contrà alium principem, audiens hic magnus Ioannes, monuit eum sæpè, & suasit ad concordiam, & non potuit eum conuertere ad pacem. Semel ergo ad eum mittit & adducit eum sanctus, q uasi pro republica, & facit missas in oratorio suo, nullum habens secum nisi ministrum suum. Cum ergo sancta benedixisset Patriarcha, & orationem Dominicam inchoasset, cœperunt dicere tantum tres illi, Pater noster, Et cum peruenissent ad sermonem quo dicitur, Dimitte nobis debita nostra, sicut & nos dimittimus debitoribus nostris: Innuit domestico Patriarcha, vt taceret. Siluit ergo & Patriarcha, & remansit Princeps solus dicens versum, dimitte nobis, sicut & nos dimittimus. Et statim conuersus sanctus, dicit ei mansueta voce. Vide in quàm terribili voce dicas Deo, quoniam sicut ego dimitto, ita & tu dimitte mihi. Et tanquam ab igne statim cruciatum ferens prædictus princeps, cecidit in faciem ad pedes sancti, dicens: Quæcunque iusseris domine, faciet seruus tuus. Et reconciliatus est inimico suo cum omni veritate.* This story soundeth thus in Englifh. This great patriarke Iohn, hearing that a noble man bare malice to an other noble man, warned him oftentymes of it, and treated with him to be accorde, but he could not bring

him

him to be at peace. Wherefore on a daye this
holy father sent for the noble man, and cau-
seth him to come to him, as though it were
about some matter of the common weale.
At that tyme he sayeth Masse in his chappell,
hauing none other body with him but his
seruant. When the Patriarke had consecrated
the sacrament, and had begonne to saye our
lordes prayer, they three onely begonne to
saye *Our father*, and so foorth. When they
were come to those wordes, *Forgeue vs our
trespasses, as we forgeue thē, that trespasse againſt
vs:* the Patriarke made a becke to his seruant,
to holde his peace, then the Patriarke held
his peace also, and the noble man remained
alone, saying foorth the verse, *Forgeue vs, as
we forgeue*: Then the holy father tourning
him selfe toward him, by and by sayeth with
a milde voice. Consider with how terrible
wordes thou sayest to God, that as I forgeue,
so forgeue thou me also. Whereat the sayde
noble man, as though he had felt the tormēt
of fyer, foorth with fell downe on his face at
the holy fathers feete, saying: My lord, what
so euer thou byddest me thy seruant to doo,
I will doo it. And so he was reconciled vnto
his enemie, with out all dissembling.

Here M. Iuell I trowe, will grawnt that
this was a priuate Masse. The place was priuate, the audience not publike nor common,
the purpose touching the noble man, was
priuate

priuate:The cōmunion alſo priuate, I meane
for the patriarkes parte alone,for beſyde that
the ſtory maketh no mētion of any other cō-
municantes , he could not be aſſured of that
noble mā to cōmunicate with him. For whereas he could by no meanesbefore bring him
to forgeue his enemie,he had but a ſmall cō-
iecture he ſhuld bring it to paſſe now. And a-
gayne though he had cōceiued no diſtruſt of
his reconciliation vpon this holy policie , yet
we may doubte,whether the patriarke foorth
with,with out further and more mature pro-
bation and examinatiō,which S. Paul in this
caſe requireth : would haue admitted him to
receiue our lordes body ſo vpō the ſuddeine.
Now for the ſeruāt,it is a ſtreight caſe that ſo
holy and ſo great a Patriake and biſhop of ſo
populouſe a citie,as Alexādria was,vnderſtā-
ding that maſſe cā not be celebrated with out
breach of Chriſtes Inſtitutiō(as M.Iuell holdeth opiniō)excepte he haue a nūber to com
municate with him in the ſame place : ſhuld
haue none of his ſpirituall flocke with him at
ſo weightie a matter of cōſciēce,but one onely,and him his owne houſhold ſeruāt.He was
not ſo ſimple as not to thinke, that the ſeruāt
might be letted frō receiuing by ſome ſuddeine pange cōming vpon him,or with ſome cogitation and conſcience of his owne vnwor-
thines ſuddeinly cōming to his mynde. If either this, or any other let had chaunced, in
what

1. Cor.11.

what case had the patriarke ben then?He had
bē like,by M.Iuelles doctrine,to haue brokē
Christes Institution,and so Gods commaundemēt,through an others defecte,which were straunge.But I iudge,that M.Iuel,who har
peth so many iarring argumentes against pri
uate Masse vpō the very word *Cōmunion,* will
not allowe that for a good and lawfull cōmunion,where there is but one onely to receiue
with the priest.Verely it appeareth by his sermon that all the people ought to receiue, or
to be dryuen out of the church. Now therefore to an other exāple of the priuate Masse.

    Amphilochius byshop of *Iconiū* the head ci-
tie of *Lycaonia,*to whō S. Basile dedicated his
booke *De spiritu sancto,*ād an other booke intituled *Ascetica,* writing the lyfe of S. Basile,
or rather the miracles trough Gods power by
him wrought,which he calleth worthy of record,true,ād great miracles: specially such as
were not by the three most worthy men Gregorie Naziāzene,Gregorie Nyssene,and holy
Ephrem,in their Epitaphicall or funerall treatises before mentioned: among other thinges,reporteth a notable story,wherein we haue a cleare testimonie of a priuate Masse. And
for the thing that the storie sheweth,as much
as for any other,of the same *Amphilochius* he
is called, *Cœlestium virtutum collocutor, & an-
gelicorum ordinum comminister* , a talker together with the heauenly powers , and a felowe

Memora-
bilia,& ve-
ra ac mag-
na miracu-
la,in præfa
tione.

       F 5   seruant

feruant with orders of Angelles. The ftory is
this. This holy bifhop Bafile befoughte God
in his prayers, he would geue him grace, wi-
fedom and vnderftanding, fo as he might offer the facrifice of Chriftes bloude fheding,
propriis fermonibus, with prayers and feruice
of his owne making : and that the better to
atcheue that purpofe, the holy ghoft might
come vpon him . After fyx dayes, he was in a
traunce for caufe of the holy ghoftes comming. When the feuenth daye was come, he
beganne to minifter vnto God, that is to witte, he fayde Maffe, euery daye. After a certaine tyme thus fpent, through faith and prayer
he beganne to write with his owne hande,
myfteria miniftrationis, the Maffe, or the feruice of the Maffe. On a night our lord came
vnto him in a vifion with the Apoftles, and
layde breade to be confecrated on the holy
aulter, and ftirring vp Bafile, fayd vnto him.
*Secūdum poftulationem tuam repleatur os tuum
laude, etc.* According to thy requeft, let thy
mowth be fylled with praife, that with thyne
owne wordes thou mayft offer vp to me facrifice. He not able to abide the vifion with
his eyes, rofe vp with trembling, and goyng
to the holy aulter, beganne to faye, that he
had written in paper, thus. *Repleatur os meum
laude, & hymnū dicat gloria tuæ domine Deus,
qui creafti nos, & adduxifti in vitam hāc, & cæ-
teras orationes fancti minifterij.* Let my mowth
be

be fylled with prayſe , to vtter an hymne to thy glory Lord God , which haſt created vs, and brought vs in to this lyfe , and ſo foorth the other prayers of the Maſſe.It foloweth in the ſtory.*Et poſt finem orationum,exaltauit panem,ſine intermiſſione orans,& dicens: Reſpice domine Ieſu Chriſte etc.* After that he had done the prayers of Conſecration , he lyſted vp the bread,praying cōtinually and ſaying,Looke vpon vs lord *Ieſus* Chriſt out of thy holy tabernacle, and come to ſanctifie vs, that ſitteſt aboue with thy father, and arte here preſent inuiſibly with vs , voucheſafe with thy mighty hand to delyuer to vs,and by vs to all thy people, *Sācta Sanctis*, thy holy thinges to the holy.The people anſwered,one holy,one our lord Ieſus Chriſt,with the holy ghoſt, in glorie of God the father , *Amen* .

Now let vs conſyder , what foloweth perteining moſt to our purpoſe.*Et diuidens panē in tres partes , vnam quidem communicauit timore multo,alteram autem reſeruauit conſepelire ſecum,tertiam verò impoſuit columbæ aureæ, quæ pependit ſuper altare.* He diuided the bread in to three partes , of which he receiued one at his communion with greate feare and reuerence, the other he reſerued, that it might be buried with him , and the third parte he cauſed to be put in a golden pyxe , that was hanged vp ouer the aulter , made in forme and ſhape of a dooue . After this , a litle
before

before the ende of this treatise, it foloweth, how that S. Basile at the houre that he departed out of this lyfe, receiued that parte of the hoste him selfe, which he had purposed to haue enterred with him in his graue, and immediatly as he laye in his bedde, gaue thankes to God, and rendred vp the ghost.

That this was a priuate Masse, no man can denye. Basile receiued the sacrament alone, for there was no earthly creature in that churche with him. The people that answered him, were such, as Christ brought with him. And that all this was no dreame, but a thing by the will of god done in dede, though in a vision as it pleased Christ to exhibite, *Amphilochius* playnely witnesseth, declaring how that one *Eubulus*, and others the chiefe of that clergie, standing before the gates of the churche, whiles this was in dooing, sawe lightes with in the churche, and men clothed in white, and heard a voice of people glorifying god, and behelde Basile standing at the aulter, and for this cause at his comming foorth fell downe prostrate at his feete.

Here M. Iuell and his cosacramentaries doo staggar I doubte not, for graunte to a priuate Masse they will not, what so euer be brought for proufe of it, and therefore some doubte to auoyd this authoritie must be be vsed. But whereof

whereof they fhuld doubte , verely I fee not.
If they doubte any thing of the bringing of
the bread and other neceffaries to ferue for
confecration of the hofte:let thē alfo doubte
of the bread and flefhe , that *Elias* had in the
pōde of Carith . Let thē doubte of the bread
and potte of water,he had vnder the Iuniper
tree in *Berfabée*. Let thē doubte of the potte
of potage brought to *Daniel* for his dyner,
from Iewerie in to the caue of lions at Baby-
lō, by *Abacuck* the prophete. But perhappes
they doubte of the auctoritie of *Amphilochius*,that wrote this ftory . It may well be , that
they would be gladde to difcredite that worthy bifhop. For he was that vigilant paftour
and good gouernour of the churche, who
firft with *Letoius* bifhop of *Melite* , and with
Flauianus bifhop of *Antioche* , ouerthrewe
and vtterly vanquifhed the heretikes called
Meffuliani,otherwife,Euchite,the firft parétes
of the Sacramentarie herefie, Whofe opiniō
was,that the holy Euchariftie,that is the blef
fed Sacramēt oft h'aulter, doth neither good
nor euil neither profiteth ought,nor hurteth
euen as our facramentaries doo afcribe all to
faith onely,and call the moft worthieft facramēt,none other, but tokening bread, which
of it felfe hath no diuine efficacie or operatiō
.Therefore, I wonder the leffe , I faye,if they
would *Amphilochius* his auctoritie to be di-
minifhed . But for this I will matche them
with

3.Reg. 17.
3.Reg. 19.

Daniel. 14.

Theodorit.
in hift. ec-
clef. lib. 4.
cap. 11.
εὐχῖται .i.
precatores.

with greate Basile, who estemed him so much, who loued him so intierly, who honored him so highly with the dedication of so excellent workes. I will ioyne them also with the learned Bishop *Theodoritus*, who semeth to geue him so soueraigne praise, as to any other Bishop, he writeth his stories of, neuer naming him without preface of great honour; now calling him *admirandum*, the wonderful, at an other tyme, *sapientissimum*, the most wise, and most commonly *laudatissimū*, most praise worthy.

Theodor. lib.5. Ecclesiast. hist.cap.16.

If they doubte of Basile him selfe, whether he were a man worthy to obteine byhis prayer of God such a vision, it may please the to peruse what *Gregorius Nyssenus*, what holy *Ephrē* of *Syria*, and specially, what Gregorie Nazianzene wrote of him, which two Gregories be not affrayed to compare him with *Elias*, with *Moses*, with *S.Paul*, and with who so euer was greatest, and for vertue of most renome. Whereby without all enuie he hath obteined of all the posteritie, to be called *Magnus*, Basile the great, much more for deserte of vertue and learning, the those other for merite of chiualrie, the great Charles, the great Pompey, the great *Alexander*.

In monodia.

If they denye the whole treatise, and saye that it was neuer of *Amphilochius* dooing, that were a shifte in dede, but yet the worst of all, and farthest from reason and custome of
the

the beſt learned, and much like the facte of
kyng *Alexander*, who being deſyrouſe to vn-
doo the fa̷all knotte, at *Gordium* a towne in
Phrygia, hearing that the Empier of the
worlde was boded by an olde prophecie to
him, that could vnknitte it, not fynding out
the endes of the ſtrenges, nor perceiuing by
what meanes he could doo it, drewe foorth
his ſworde, and hewed it in pieces, ſupply-
ing want of ſkill with wilfull violence. For
the auctoritie of this treatiſe, this much I can
ſaye. Beſyde, that it is ſet foorth in a booke of
certaine holy mens lyues printed in Colen,
and beſyde very great likelyhode appearing
in the treatiſe it ſelfe: it is to be ſene in the librarie of Saint *Nazarius*, in the citie of *Ve-
rona* in Italie, written in veleme for three
hundred yeres paſt, bearing the name of *Am
philochius* biſhop of *Iconium*.

Now one place more for proufe of priuate Maſſe, at the wyneding vp of this matter,
and then an ende of this article. This place is
twyſe fownd in Chryſoſtó, in an homelie vpõ
the epiſtle to the Epheſians, and more plainely in an homelie *ad populum Antiochenum*.
Where he hath theſe very wordes *Multam*
video rerum inæqualitatem. In alijs quidem tem-
poribus cum puri frequenter ſitis, non acceditis,
In Paſcha vero licet ſit aliquid à vobis patratũ,
acceditis. O conſuetudinem, ô præſumptionem.
Sacrificium fruſtrà quotidianum. In caſſum aſ-
ſiſtimus

Hom.61.
ad popul.
Anthioch.

sistimus altari.nullus qui comuuicetur. I see great inequalitie of thinges among you. At other tymes, when as for the more parte ye are in cleane lyfe, ye come not to receiue your rightes. But at Easter, though ye haue done some thing amysse, yet ye come. O what a custome is this? O what a presumption is this? The dayly sacrifice is offred in vaine. We stand at the aulter, for nought. There is not one, that woll be houseled. Here is to be noted, whereas Chrisostome sayeth, the daily sacrifice was celebrated in vaine, and the priestes stoode at th'aulter in vaine: it is not to be vnderstanded of the sacrifice in it selfe, as though it were in vaine and frustrate : but this is to be referred to the people, it was in vaine for their parte, that shuld haue receiued their communion with the priestes, who waited daily for them, and cryed out as the maner was, *Sancta sanctis,* holy thinges for the holy, and after that they had receiued the breade the selues, shewing the chalice to the people, sayd: *Cu timore Dei, & fide, & dilectio ne accedite*. Come ye vp to receiue with the feare of God, with faith and charitie. But all was in vaine. For none came, so colde was their deuotion in that behalfe.

Now if Chrysostome had cause to complai ne of the peoples slaknes in comming to the comunion, in that great and populouse citie of Antioche, where the scriptures were daily

expown-

A true declaration of Chrysostomes place.

In Missa Chrysost.

expownded and preached, where discipline
and good order was more streightely exacted,where in so great núber some of likelyho
de were of more deuotiõ then others:what is
to be thought of many other litle townes and
villages through the worlde, where litle prea
ching was heard,where discipline slaked,whe
re the núber of the faithful being small , and
they occcupied al together in worldly affaye-
res,fewe gaue good ensample of deuotiõ to
others ? Doubtles in such places was much
lesse resorte of the people at the Masse tyme,
to receiue the Sacrament with their priestes.

And whereas , least this place might seme
plainely to auouche the hauing of Masse
without a number communicating with the
bishop or priest , for auoyding of this auctoritie , the gospellers answere by waye of con-
iecture, that in Chrysostomes tyme the priestes and deacons communicated together
daily with the partie that offred the Sacrifice , though none of the people dyd ? we tell
them , that this poore shifte will not serue
their purpose . For though they saye , some
sufficient number euer communicated with
him that celebrated the dayly sacrifice in that
great and famouse churche of Antioche,whe
re many priestes and deacõs were ,which neither being denyed they shall neuer be able
to proue: what may be sayde or thought of
many thousand otherlesser churchesthrough

G   the

the world, where the prieft that fayd Maffe,
had not always in redynes a fufficient number of other prieftes and deacons to receiue
with him, fo to make vp a communion? Of
fuch churches it muft be fayde, that either
the Sacrifice ceafed, and that was not done
which Chrift commaunded to be done in
his remembrance, which is not to be grawn-
ted: or that the memorie of our lordes death
was oftentymes celebrated by the prieftes in
the daily oblatiõ with out tarying for others
to communicat with them, and fo hadde thefe churches priuate Maffes, as the churches
now a dayes haue.

Now to conclude, of this moft euident
place of Chrifoftome, euery childe is able to
make an inuincible argument againft, M. Iuell for the priuate Maffe, as they call it, in this
forte. By reporte of Chryfoftome, the facrifi-
çe in his tyme was daily offred, that is to faye,
the Maffe was celebrated, but many tymes
no body came to communicare facramental-
ly with the prieftes, as it is before proued:
Ergo there were Maffes done without other
receiuing the Sacrament with the prieftes.
And then further, *Ergo* priuate Maffes in
Chryfoftomes dayes were not ftraunge, and
then yet one fteppe further, there to ftaye:
Ergo M. Iuel according to his owne promife
and offre, muft yelde, fubfcribe and recant.

Or that there was then any communion mi-
nistred vnto the people vnder one kynde .

Of communion vnder one kynde.

ARTICLE II.

His being a Sacrament of vnitie,
euery true christen man ought in
receiuing of it to consyder, how
vnitie may be acheued and kepte,
rather then to shewe a streightnes of conscience aboute the outward formes of bread
and wyne, to be vsed in the administration of
it: and that so much the more, how much the
ende of euery thinge, is to be estemed more
then that, which serueth to the ende. Otherwise herein the breache of vnitie is so litle re-
compésed by the exacte kepinge of th'outward ceremonie, that according to the saying
of S. Augustine, who so euer taketh the myste
rie of vnitie, and kepeth not the bóde of peace, he taketh not a mysterie for him selfe, but
a testimonie against him selfe.

Therefore they haue great cause to weigh
with them selues, what they receiue in this
sacrament, who moued by slender reasons
made for bothe kyndes, do rashely and dan-
geroufly condemne the churche, for geuing
of it vnder one kinde, to all, that doo not in
their owne persons consecrate and offer the,
same in remembraunce of the sacrifice once
G 2   offered

offered on the croſſe. And that they may thin
ke the churche to ſtand vpon good growndes
herein, may it pleaſe them to vnderſtãd, that
the fruite of this ſacramẽt, which they enioye that worthely receiue it, dependeth not
of the outward formes of bread and wine,
but redoundeth of the vertue of the fleſhe
and bloude of Chriſt. And whereas vnder either kynde whole Chriſt is verely preſent,
(for now that he is riſen againe frõ the deade, his fleſhe and bloude can be ſundred no
more, becauſe he dyeth no more) this helthfull ſacrament is of true chriſten people with
no leſſe fruit receiued vnder one kynde, then
vnder bothe. And as this ſpirituall fruite is
not any thinge diminiſhed to him that receiueth one kinde, ſo it is not any whitte increaced to him that receiueth bothe. The Sacra-
mẽtaries that beleue not the truth of Chriſtes
bodye and bloude in this holy Sacramẽt, I re
mitte to ſundry godly treatiſes made in defence of the right faith in that pointe. I thinke it not neceſſarie here to treate thereof, or
of any other matter, which M. Iuell hath not
as yet manifeſtly touched in his ſermon.

Now concerning th'outward formes of
bread and wyne, their vſe is imployed in ſignification onely, and be not of neceſſitie, ſo
as grace may not be obteined by worthy receiuing of the Sacrament, onleſſe bothe kindes be miniſtred. Therefore in cõſecrating of
the

the Sacramét, according to Chriſtes inſtitution, bothe kyndes be neceſſarie, for as much
as it is not prepared for the receiuing onely,
but alſo for renewing and ſtirring vp of the
remébraunce of oure lordes death. So in as
much as the ſacrament ſerueth the ſacrifice,
by which the death and oblation of Chriſt is
repreſented, bothe the kyndes be requeſite:
that by diuerſe and ſundry formes, the blou
de of Chriſt ſhedde for our ſynnes, and ſeparated from his body, may euidently be ſigni-
fied. But in as much as the faithful people do
receiue the ſacramét, thereby to atteine ſpirituall grace and ſaluation of their ſoules, diuer
ſitie of the forme or kyndes, that be vſed for
the ſignification onely, hath no further vſe ne
profite. But by one kynde, becauſe in it whole
Chriſt is exhibited, abundance of all grace is
once geuen: ſo as by the other kynde thereto
ouer added (which geueth the ſame and not
an other Chriſt) no further augmentation of
ſpirituall grace may be atteined.

In côſideration of this, the catholike churche taught by the holy ghoſt all truth, whiles
in the daily ſacrifice the memorie of oure
lordes death and paſſion is celebrated, for
that it is neceſſarie therein to expreſſe moſt
playnely the ſhedding and ſeparating of the
bloude from the bodye, that was crucified:
hath alwayes to that purpoſe, diligently v-
ſed bothe kyndes of breade and wine.

But in diſtributing of the bleſſed ſacrament to Chriſten people, hath vſed her libertie (which Chriſt neuer imbarred by any cōmaundement to the contrary) ſo as it hath euer ben moſt for the behoufe and commoditie of the receiuers: and hath miniſtred ſometymes bothe kyndes, ſometymes one kynde onely, as it hath ben thought moſt expedient, in regard of tyme, place, and perſons.

As touching the wordes of Chriſt, *Bibite ex hoc omnes*, *Drinke ye all of this*: they perteine to the Apoſtles only, and to their ſucceſſours. For to them only he gaue commaundement to doo that, which he dyd in his ſupper, as *Clemēt ſayeth*: To them only ſaying, *doo this in my remembrauce*, he gaue cōmiſſion to conſecrate, offer, and to receiue the ſacrament in remembrance of his death and paſſion, by the ſame wordes ordeining thē prieſtes of the newe teſtament. Wherefore this belongeth not to the laye people, neither can it be iuſtely gathered by this place, that they are bounde of neceſſiitie, and vnder paine of deadly ſynne, to receiue the ſacrament vnder bothe kyndes.

Matth.26.
Chriſtes
vvordes
bynde not
the laitie
to receiue
both kindes.
Ante paſſionem nobis
ſelis præcepit hoc facere, inquiunt
Apoſtoli
apud Clementem.
lib.8.conſtitut. Apoſtolicarum.
cap.vlt.

And this vnderſtoode they, which aboue an hundred yeres paſt, chaunging the olde cuſtome of the churche of receiuing the communion vnder one kynde, by theire priuate auctoritie, would nedes vſurpe the cuppe alſo. For ſeeing them ſelues not to haue

haue sufficient proufe and warrant for their
dooing of these wordes, *drinke ye all of this :*
the better to bolster vp their newe fangled
attempte, they thought it better to alleage
the wordes of Christ in S. Iohn : *Excepte ye* Ioan. 6.
eate the fleshe of the sonne of man, and drinke his
bloude, ye shall not haue lyfe in you: which wordes for all that our new maisters of these xl.
yeres past, will to be vnderstanded of the spirituall and not of the sacramentall eating.
Which place although it be taken for the sacramentall eating, as it may be and is taken
for bothe of the doctours vewed a parte : yet
in all that chapter there is no mention of the
cuppe, nor of wine at all . Wherefore they
that crye so much on the Institution and
commaundement of Christ, can not synde
in all the scriptures neither cōmaundement,
where he gaue charge the sacrament so to be
geuen, neither so much as any example, where Christe gaue it vnder bothe kyndes, to
any other, then to the Apostles . Where as Luc. 24.
contrary wise it may be shewed of our parte, that the sacrament was geuen vnder o- a In Mat-
ne kynde only to the two disciples, that thæum ho-
went to Emaus. For that the bread which mil. 17.
Christ there tooke, blessed, brake, and ga- b De con-
ue to them, was not simple and common bre- sensu Euan
ad, but the Sacrament of the bodye and gelist.lib.3.
bloude of Christ. For so a Chrysostome, b Au- cap. 25.
gustine, c Bede, and d Theophylacte with one Rom. 6.
c In Luc.
d In Lucā.

Act 2. accorde doo witneſſe. It appeareth alſo that the communion vnder one kynde was vſed at Ieruſalem among Chriſtes diſciples, by that S. Luke writeth in the actes of the Apoſtles of the breaking of the bread. If M. Iuell here thinke to auoyde theſe places by their accuſtomed figure *ſynecdoche*, among his owne ſecte happely it may be accepted, but among men of right and learned iudgement, that ſhifte will ſeme ouer weake and vaine. Now to conclude touching the ſixth chapter of S. Ihon, as thereof they can bring no one worde mētioning the cuppe or wyne, for prouſe of their bothe kyndes : ſo it ſheweth and not in very obſcure wiſe, that the forme of breade alone is ſufficient, where as Chriſt ſayeth, *Qui manducat panem hunc, viuet in æternum*, He that eateth this bread, ſhall lyue for euer.

Thus our aduerſaries haue nothing to bring out of the ſcriptures againſt the vſe of the catholike churche in miniſtring the communion vnder one kynde. And yet they ceaſe not crying out vpon the breache of Chriſtes expreſſe commaundement, and M. Iuell for his parte in his firſt anſwere to D. Cole ſayeth, that the councell of Conſtāce pronounced openly againſt Chriſt him ſelfe. But for as much as they are ſo hote in this pointe, I will ſend them to Martin Luther him ſelfe their patriarke that either by his

his fobrietie in this matter they may be fome
what colded, or by his, and his fcolers incon-
ftancie herein, be brought to be a fhamed of
them felues. Though the places be well knowen, as oftentymes cited of the catholike wri
ters of oure tyme againft the gofpellers, yet
here I thinke good to rehearfe them, that
the vnlearned may fee, how them felues make not fo greate a matter of this Article, as fome feme to beare the people in hand it is.

Luther wryteth to them of *Bohemia* thefe very wordes. *Quoniam pulchrum quidem
effet, vtraque ſpecie euchariftiæ vti, & Chriftus
hac in re nihil tanquam neceffarium præcepit:
præftaret pacem & vnitatem quam Chriftus
vbique præcepit, fectari, quã de ſpeciebus Sacramenti cõtendere.* Whereas it were a fayre thinge (fayeth he) to vfe bothe kyndes of the facrament, yet for that Chrift herein hath
commaunded nothing as neceffary, it were
better to kepe peace and vnitie, which Chrift
hath euery where charged vs with all, then to
ftriue for the outward kyndes of the facra-
mẽt. Agayne his wordes be thefe in a declaration that he wrote of the facrament. *Non,
dixi, nequè confului, nequè eft intentio mea,
vt vnus aut aliquot Epiſcopi propria æuthoritate
alicui incipiant vtramque ſpeciem porrigere, nifi
ita conftitueretur & mandaretur in concilio ge-
nerali.* Neither haue I fayde nor counſailed,
nor my minde is, that any one or moe bifhops

Luther and
his ofsprÿg
doth not
necefsitate
Cõmunion
vnder both
kyndes.

G 5   begynne

beginne by their owne auctoritie to geue bothe kyndes (of the sacrament) to any person,
onlesse it were so ordeined and commaunded in a generall councell.

Of his con-
ference
vvith the
deuill, he
vvriteth
libello de
Missa angu-
lari.
Thus he wrote before that he had conceiued perfite hatred against the church. But after that he had ben better acquainted with
the deuill, and of him appearing vnto him
sensibly, had ben instructed with argumentes against the sacrifice of the Masse, that
the memorie of our redemption by Christ
wrought on the crosse, might vtterly be abo-
lyshed: he wrote hereof farre otherwise. *Si
quo casu concilium statueret, minimè ommnium
nos vellemus vtraque specie potiri, imò tunc primum in despectum concily vellemus aut vna, aut
neutra, & nequaquã vtraq́, potiri, & eos planè
anathema habere, quicunq́, talis concily auctoritate potirentur vtraque.* If in any case the councell would so ordeyne, we would in no wise
haue bothe the kyndes, but euen then in
dispite of the councell we would haue one
kynde, or neither of them, and in no wise
bothe, and holde them for accursed, who
so euer by auctoritie of such a coucell would
haue bothe. These wordes declare what spri-
te Luther was of. They shewe him lyke him
selfe. Who so euer readeth his bookes with
indifferent iudgemét, shall fynde, that sythés
the Apostles tyme neuer wrote man so arro-
gãtly ne so dispitefully agaĩst the churche, nor
so con-

contraryly to him selfe. Which markes be so
euident, that who so euer will not see them,
but suffreth him selfe to be caried a waye in
to errour, hatred of the church, and cōtemp-
te of all godlynes, either by him, or by his
scolers: except he repent and retourne, he is
gyltie of his owne damnation, vtterly ouer-
throwen, and synneth inexcusably, as one cō-
demned by his owne iudgement. But for excuse hereof, in his booke of the captiuitie of
Babylon, he confesseth that he wrote thus,
not for that he thought so, nor for that he
iudged the vse of one kynde vnlawfull, but
because he was stirred by hatred and anger
so to doo. His wordes doo sounde so much
plainely. *Prouocatus, imò per vim raptus.* I wrote this (sayeth he) otherwise then I thought
in my hatte, prouoked, and by violence pulled to it, whether I would or no. Here I doub
te not, but wise men will regarde more that
Luther wrote when his minde was quiet
and calme, then when it was enraged with
blustering stormes of naughty affections.

Now to put this matter, that Luther iudged it a thing indifferent, whether one receiue the sacrament vnder one kynde or bothe,
more out of doubte: Philip Melanchthon
his scoler, and neareſt of his coūsell, wryteth,
Sicut edere suillam, aut abstinere a suilla, sic alte-
rutra signi parte vti medium esse. That as it is a
thing indifferent, to eate swines fleshe, or to

> Tit. 3.

> In locis
> communi-
> bus.

forbeare

forbeare swines flesshe , so it is also to vse which parte of the signe , a man lysteth. By the word signe , he meaneth the Sacrament, lyking better that straunge word, then the accustomed word of the churche, leaste he might perhaps be thought of the brethren of his secte , in some what to ioyne with the catholikes.

Bucer also is of the same opinion , who in the conference that was had betwene the catholikes and protestantes for agrement in controuersies of Religion at Ratisbone, confirmed and allowed this article by his full consent, with these wordes. *Ad controuersi- am quæ est de vna aut vtraque specie, tollendam, cum primis conducturum , vt sancta Ecclesia liberam faceret potestatem sacramentum hoc in vna vel in vtraque specie sumēdi . Ea tamen lege, vt nulli per hoc detur occasio , quem vsum tantopere retinuit Ecclesia , temere condemnandi, aut inuicem iudicandi.*

That the controuersie for the one or bothe kindes may be taken awaye, it shall be very well done, that holy churche made it free, to receiue this sacrament in one or bothe kyndes: yet vnder such condition , as hereby no occasion be geuen to any bodye rashely to condemne the vse, which the church hath so long tyme kepte , nor to iudge one an other . Soothly he which would haue it free and at libertie , to receiue the sacrament vnder

der one or bothe kyndes, and holdeth opinion, that the olde custome of the one kynde onely is not to be condemned, semeth plainely ynough to côfesse, that nothing hath ben instituted or cômaunded by Christ touching this matter, as necessarie to saluation.

Thus we may see playnely, that they which haue diuided them selues from the mysticall bodye of Christ, that is his churche, who were of greatest learning and iudgement, make it a matter indifferent (as it is in dede of it selfe lefte to the libertie of the churche) whether the sacrament be ministred vnder one kynde or bothe.

And this much hath ben confessed against M. Iuell and his secte, not onely by the learned aduersaries of the churche in our tyme, but also by a learned man of *Bohemia* aboue six score yeres past. His name is Iohn Przybram, of whose writinges some are set foorth in printe. This learned man whereas he endeuoured to proue the vse of bothe kyndes of the wordes of Christ written by S. Iohn: *Except ye eate the flesh of the sonne man, and drinke his bloude, ye shal not haue lyfe in you:* at length vttereth these wordes according to the eloquence of his tyme. *Veruntamen hic Deum timens, & mores impios aliorum præcauens, fateor quòd quaslibet personas de ecclesia communioni fidelium sub vtraque specie repugnantes, damnare aut hæreticare non intendo.*　In libr. de professione fidei catholicæ cap. 19.

　　　　　　　　　　　　　　But

But here hauing the feare of god before myne eyes, and being well ware, I folowe not
the wicked conditions of otheis, I grawnt,
that what perſones ſo euer of the churche
repine againſt the communiõ of the faithfull
people vnder bothe kyndes, I entend not to
condemne thẽ, nor to holde them for heretikes. But if it be the commaundement of
God, that the Sacrament be receiued of all
vnder bothe kyndes, why ſhuld he be forbydden by the feare of God to condemne
thoſe, that wythſtand that order of communion? Seeing that who ſo euer goeth againſt
Gods commaundement, is worthy to be cõdemned? Therefore by his teſtimonie the v-
ſe of one or bothe kyndes, is indifferent.

Thus we are able to alleage Luther, Melanchthon, Bucer, and that learned Bohe-
mian, for the Indifferencie of the communion to be miniſtred either vnder one kynde, or bothe. Whereby I meane not that the
vſe of the ſacrament is ſo lefte to euery mannes libertie, as he that liſteth, may require
bothe kyndes, and an other may cõtent him
ſelfe with one bynde: not ſo, euery man is bo
wnde to folow the order of the churche, but
the churche is not bownde of neceſſitie by
Gods commaundement, to miniſter it vnder
bothe kyndes to the laitie.

And whereas it was miniſtred in bothe kindes at Corinth, as it appeareth by S.Paul, and
in

In sundry other places, as we finde most euidently in the writinges of diuerse auncient fathers : yet the churche hath ben moued by diuerse and weighty causes to take order, that the people should receiue their communion vnder one kynde, not onely in the councell of Basile, but also in that of Constance, and long before them aboue a thousand yeres, in the first councell of *Ephesus*, as many doo probably gather, and namely *Vrbanus Regius* a doctour of Luthers scoole cōfesseth in his booke, *De locis communibus*. One cause and not the leaste, was, that thereby the heresie of *Nestorius* might the rather be extinguished, who emonge other errours held opinion, that vnder the forme of bread in the Sacramēt is cōteined the body of Christ without his bloude, and vnder the forme of the wine, his bloude onely without his bodye. Many other causes moued those fathers to take that order, for th'auoyding of many inconueniēces, dangers, and offences, which might happen in the vse of the cuppe : as vnreuerence of so high a Sacrament, whereof christen people at the beginning had a meruelouse care and regarde, the lothsomnes of many that can not brooke the taste of wine, the difficultie of getting, and impossibilitie of keping wine from corruption in countries situated neare to the north Pole, in that clime, where is knowen to be great extremi-

Causes mouing the churche to communicate vnder one kinde.

tie of colde, befyde a number of the like. So
that it had ben befide reafon to haue bounde
all to the necefsitie of bothe kyndes.

Now in very dede if we would graunt to
our aduerfaries, which in any wife we do not
graunt, that it hath bē cōmaunded of Chrift,
the laye people fhould communicate vnder
bothe kyndes, by thefe wordes, *Drinke ye all
of this:* yet this notwithftanding, the exacte
ftreightnes of gods ordinance may without
fynne in cafes be omitted , in fuch thinges
which be not necefsaryly to be obferued of
them felues, or of the prefcipte of the lawe
of nature: fo that great and weighty caufes
(the rule of charitie exactely obferued) require the fame. For euident proufe of this, we
haue examples bothe of the olde and alfo of
the newe teftamēt. Dyd not God commaunde that none fhuld eate of the fhewebread,
but the prieftes onely ? Dauid eate thereof,
and yet Chrift cleareth him of all blame. The
lawe of circūcifion fo ftreightly cōmaunded,
was for the fpace of forty yeres by the people
of Ifrael quite omitted, whiles they paffed frō
Egypte to the land of promeffe, and God
fownde no faulte with them for it. God gaue
the law of keping holy the Saboth daye with
out exception. The Machabes notwithftanding ftickte not to arme them felues againft
Antiochus, and to fpende that daye in the fielde in theire defence , hauing no fcruple of
confcien-

Leuit.24.

1.Reg.21.
Mar.1.

Genef.17.
& 34.

Exod 12.
1.Mach.:

confcience for breach of that law. Many the
like examples we fynde in the olde teftamét.
But let vs come to the newe teftament, and
to the Sacraments of the tyme of grace. In
due confideration of which we may fynde,
that Chrift hath fcarcely commaunded any
outward thing, the moderation, qualifying,
and ordering whereof, he hath not lefte to
his churche, as according to the condition of
the tyme it hath ben fene moft expedient for
the common preferment and edifying of the
fame. So that notwithftanding there be no
fwaruing from the fcope, and principal in-
tente, and no creature defrauded of that
good, which by the outward thinges is to be
atteined. Touching the Sacrament of ba-
ptifme, though nothing be fayde of the teaching of them that fhuld be baptized, neyther of the dipping of them in to the water,
which Chriftes charge in this behalfe geuen
femeth plainely to require, go you(fayeth he
to his Apoftles) and teach all nations, ba- Matt.28.
ptizing thé &c. and yet the church hath not
feared to baptife infantes that be without
capacitie of teaching, and for the due adminiftration of this Sacrament, to many, hath
thoughte powring or fprinkling of water vpó
them fufficient: though this be not fpoken of
I faye, it is much to be cófyderęd to this purpofe, that the Apoftles ftickte not for a tyme
to alter and chaúge the very effentiall forme

H   of wor-

wordes, with which Christ would this sacrament to be ministred. For where as he commaunded them to baptise *in the name of the father, and of the sonne, and of the holyghost:* they baptized in the name of Iesus Christ only, intending thereby to make that to be of more fame and celebritie.

So to retourne tō the Sacramēt of the bodye and bloude of Christ, whereof we treate, no man can denye, but many thinges were at th'institution of it done by the example of Christ, and by him cōmaunded, which now be not obserued, and yet in that respecte no faulte is fownde. Christ washed the Apostles feete, and gaue them an expresse commaundement to doo the same with these moste plaine wordes. *If I that am your Maister and lorde, haue washed your feete, you also ought to wash one an others feete. For I haue geuen you an example, that as I haue done, you doo so like wise.* Which commaundement of Christ according to the outward letter verely bindeth no lesse, then these wordes: *Drinke ye all of this:* yet this commaundement is not kepte, but cleane growen out of vse. Though it appeare by Saint Bernard, who calleth it *Magnum Sacramentum*, a great Sacrament, and long before, by reporte of Saint Cyprian, that Christ dyd not onely washe his Apostles feete, but commaūded also by solemne request, ād ordeined that th'apostles afterward should

doo

Act. 8.

Ioan. 6.

In serm. de cœna do.

In serm. de vnctione chrismatis.

doo the same. Whether this ordinance of Christ hath ben abolished, for that it should not be thought a rebaptization, as it may be gathered of S.Augustine, or for any other cau se, it forceth not greatly. But this is much to be merueiled at, that this so earnestly commaunded is so quietly and with such silence suffered vndone, and in the ministration of the Sacrament the vse of the cuppe so factiously and with so much crying out required. Neither in many other rites and ceremonies we do not as Christ dyd. Christ celebrated this sacrament after that he had supped, we do it in the morning, and fasting. Christ sate at the table with his twelue Apostles, neither sytte we at a table, neither thinke we it necessary to obserue such nuber. Christ brake the bread, we thinke it not necessary to breake the hoste that is to be delyuered to the faithfull participates. Here is to be noted, that S.Cyprian rebuking the which thought sprinkling or powring of water not to be sufficient for baptisme, declareth, that the sacraméts be not to be estemed according vnto their extreme and rigotouse obseruation or administration of all the externe eleméte; but rather according to the integritie and soundnes of faith of the geuer and of the receiuer, and that diuine things ges vsed in a compédious sorte, conferre and geue neuerthelesse to the right beleuers their whole vertue. lib. 4. epist. 7.

Ad Iantua-rium.c.118

H 2   Many

Many other commaundementes of God concerning outward thinges might here be rehearsed, which notwithstãding by litle and litle in the churche haue ben omitted, as the forebearing of strangled thinges and bloude:which was cõmaũded by God in the olde testament, and according to the pleasure and aduise of the holy ghost, decreed by the Apostles in the newe testamẽt: yet for as much as concerneth outward thinges, both this, and many other the like, haue in processe of tyme growen out of obseruation, and haue with out any scruple of cõscience ben abrogated.

I truste no man will gather of that I haue sayde here, that it is none offence to doo against Gods commaundement. My meaning is farrre otherwise. Neither saye I, that this saying of Christ in Mathew, *Drinke ye all of this*, or that in Iohn, *Excepte ye eate the flesh of the sonne of man, and drinke his bloude, ye shall not haue lyfe in you* : or other commaundementes of Christ, be not to be kepte: but this is that I saye, and that euery catholike man sayeth: that the vniuersall churche doth better vnderstand, which are the commaundementes of Christ, and how they ought to be kepte, then *Berengarius*, Wiclef, Hus, Luther, *Zuinglius*, Caluine, Crammare, Peter Martyr, or any their scolers and folowers, which now be sundry sectes. As for example: God hath thus commaunded, *thou shalt not sweare*

Matth. 5.

sweare, and, *thow shalt not kylle* , and , *if thine* Matth.5.
eye cause the to offende , *pull him out* , *and cast* Exod.20.
him awaye from the . Whereas certaine sectes
of heretikes , as namely they which be called *VValdenses* , and *Picardi* , by their con-
struction hereof haue mainteined opinion,
that no oth ought to be geuen or made in no
case or respecte : lyke wise that in no case or
respecte a man may doo an other to death,
and also that after the outward letter of the
gospell sometyme a man is bounde to pull
out his eye , and cast it from him : which
thing hath ben done by some of the Picar-
des , as it is reported , as though elles Gods
commaundement were not kepte : this hath
so ben vnderstanded by the catholike churche , confessing neuerthelesse these to be
Gods commaundementes , as in tyme , in
place, and in certaine cases, a man might and
ought without breach of commaundement
bothe sweare , and kylle, and likewise kepe
his eye in his head , and therein offend God
nothing at all . So the catholike churche
vnderstandeth , *Drynke ye all of this* , to be
Christes commaundement, and of necessitie
to be obserued , but of priestes onely, I meane of necessitie, and that, when in the sacrifice of the church , is celebrated the memorie
of Christes death , which in that degree be
the successours of the Apostles , to whom
that commaundement was specially geuen,

when

when they were confecrated prieftes of the new teftamēt, who fo dyd drinke in dede, as S. Marke witnefleth : *Et biberunt ex eo omnes.* And they dranke all of it. To thefe onely, and to none other, the catholike churche hath euer referred the neceſſitie of that commaundemēt. Elles if the neceſſitie of it ſhould perteine to all, and becauſe Chriſt ſayde, *Drinke ye all of this,* if all of euery ſtate and condition of neceſſitie ought to drinke of the cuppe: how is it come to paſſe, that out aduerſaries them ſelues, (who pretende ſo ſtreight a conſciéce herein) kepe frō it infantes and young children, vntill they come to good yeres of diſcretion : ſpecially where as the cuſtome of the primitiue churche was, that they alſo ſhould be partakers of this ſacrament, as it may playnely be ſene, in *S. Dionyſe, Cyprian, Auguſtine, Innocentius, Zoſimus,* an other aunt cient fathers? what better reaſon haue they to kepe the infantes from the cuppe, then the Anabaptiſtes haue to kepe them from theire baptiſme ? If they allege their impotencie of remembring our lordes death. the Anabaptiſtes will likewiſe allege their impotencie of receiuing and vnderſtanding doctrine, that Chriſtes inſtitutiō in this behalfe ſemeth to require.

Thus th' aduerſaries of the the churche them ſelues doo agniſe, that the vſe of the cuppe in the Sacrament perteineth not to all

of ne-

Marc. 14.

of necessitie. So haue they neithet godly charitie to ioyne with the churche, neither sufficient reason to impugne the churche. And although herein we could be content, infantes
not to be spoken of, yet it maye easely be proued, that the communion vnder bothe kyndes hath not euer ben generall. And as we do
not condemne it, but confesse it might be restored agayne by th'auctoritie of the churche lawfully assembled in a general councell,
vppon mature deliberation before had, and a
holesome remedie against the inconuenien-
ces thereof prouided : euen so are we able to
shewe good auctoritre for the defence of the
one kynde , now vsed in the churche . And
because M. Iuell beareth the world in hand
nothing can be brought for it of our syde:so-
me places I will allege here that seme to me
very euidently to proue, that the vse of bothe
kyndes hath not alwaies ben ben thought necessary to all persons, and thath the communion vnder one kynde hathe ben practised
and holden for good within the six hundred
yeres after Christ, that he would so faine
bynde vs vnto .

Here maye be alleaged first the example
of our lord him selfe, out of the 24. chapter of Saint Luke, which is spoken of befo-
re:where it is declared, that he gaue the Sacra
mét to the two disciples at Emaus vnder the
forme of bread only which place ought to

Proufes for communió vnder one kinde.

H 4   haue

haue the more weight of auctoritie in a catho
like mannes iudgemēt, becaufe it is brought
by the councell of Conftance, and alfo by the
councell of Bafile, for proufe of the communion vnder one kynde. That it was the Sacrament, the auncient doctours doo affirme it playnely, and the wordes conferred
with the wordes of our Lordes fupper, doo
agree: and that it is not nedeful of oure owne
head to adde thereto the adminiftration of
the cuppe, as oure aduerfaries doo by their
figure *fynecdoche*: it appeareth by that thofe
two difciples declared to the twelue Apoftles
affembled together in Ierufalem, how they
knew our Lorde *in fractione panis*, in breaking
of the breade to them, which can not be taken for the wine: and as fone as they knewe
him in breaking of the breade, he vanifhed
awaye from theire fyght, er that he tooke
the cuppe in to his handes, and blefted it, and
gaue it vnto them, as it appeareth euidently
ynough to S. Auguftine, to Bede, and to all
other that be not willfully opinatiue.

Agayne what nede is it to vfe violence in
this fcripture, and ioyne vnto it a patche of
oure owne deuife by fo fimple a warrant of a
figure, fith that according to the minde of
the learned fathers Chrift gaue here to the
two difciples not a piece of the facrament,
but the whole Sacrament, as it is proued by
the effecte of the fame: and th'effecte prefuppofeth

poseth the cause. For saint Augustine confesseth by that Sacrament of breade (so he calleth it) *Vnitate corporis participata , remoueri*
impedimentũ inimici, vt Christus posset agnosci.
that thereby they were made partakers of the
vnitie of Christes bodye, that is to saye, made
one bodye with Christ , and that all impedi-
ment or lette of the ennemie the deuil , was
taken awaye, so as Christ might be acknowleged. Wat more should they haue gotten , if
the had receiued the cuppe also?

De cõsensu
Euangeli-
starũ lib. 3.
cap. 25.

Here might be alleaged the place of the
Actes in 2. chapter, where mention is made
of the communion of breaking of the breade, the cuppe not spoken of, which the heretikes called *VValdenses* dyd confesse , that it
must be vnderstanded of the Sacrament , *in*
*confessione ad Vladislaum.*and likewise the place of the twentith chapter, and specially that
of the seuẽ and twẽtith chapter of the Actes.
Where Chrysostome and other fathers vnderstand the breade that saint Paul in perile
of shipwracke tooke , gaue thankes ouer, brake, and eate , to be the holy Sacrament.

It is not to be merueiled at, albe it S. Paul
deliuered to the Corinthians the institution
of oure lordes supper vnder bothe kindes,
that yet vppon occasion geuen , and when
condition of tyme so required, he ministred
the communion vnder one kynde , sith that
with out doubte he tooke that holy mystery

H 5   vnder

vnder one kynde for the whole Sacramēt, as we perceiue by his wordes where he sayeth, *Vnus panis & vnum corpus multi sumus omnes, qui de vno pane participamus.* One breade and one body we being many are, all that doe participate of one breade. Where he speaketh nothing of the cuppe. And likewise by his wordes, where he speaketh desiunctiuely, as the greke and the true latine texte hath, *Quicunque manducauerit panem, vel biberit calicem domini indignè, reus erit corporis & sanguinis domini.* Who so euer eateth the bread, or drynketh of the cuppe of our lord vnworthely, he shall be gylty of the bodye and bloude of our lorde. Whereon dependeth an argument of the contrary, that who so euer either eateth this bread worthely, or drinketh this cuppe worthely, he eateth and drinketh righteousnes and lyfe.

For thys purpose we haue a notable place in the hebrew gospell of S.Matthew, which, S. Hierome saieth, he sawe in the librarie of *Cæsarea*, and translated it. This place is cited by S. Hierome in his booke *de ecclesiasticis scriptoribus, in Iacobo fratre domini.* The wordes touching the cōmunion that S.Hierome rehearseth, agree thoroughly with those of S.Luke 24.chapter. *Matthæus sic refert. Dominus autem etc.* Matthew reporteth thus. When our lorde had geuen his shrowde vnto the bishoppes seruant, he went to Iames, and

2.Cor.10.

1.Cor.11,

and appeared vnto him: for Iames had made an oth, that he would not eate breade, from that howre he dranke of the cuppe of our lorde, vntill he saw him raysed from the dead. It foloweth a litle after. *Afferte ait dominus mensam, & panem, Statimque addit: Tulit panem, & benedixit, ac fregit, & dedit Iacobo iusto, & dixit ei: frater comede panem tuum, quia resurrexit filius hominis à dormientibus.* Bring the table and set on bread quoth our lorde, and by and by it is added: he tooke bread, and blessed it, and brake it, and gaue it to Iames the iust, and sayde vnto him: my brother eate thy breade, for the sonne of man is risen agayne frō the dead. No mā cā doubte but this was the Sacrament. And wine was there none geuen, for any thing that may be gathered. For it is not likely that S. Iames had wyne in his house then, for as much as *Egesippus* who was not long after him witnesseth of him, that he neuer dranke wyne, but at our lordes supper.

But because perhappes oure aduersaries will caste some myste ouer these allegations, to darken the truth with theire clowdy gloses, which be cleare ynough to quiet and sobre wittes, that geue eare to the holy ghost speaking to vs by the mowth of the churche: I will bring forth such witnesses and proufes for this purpose out of auncient fathers, as by no reason or Sophisticall shifte they shall be able be able to auoyde. Many of the places that I alleged in the article before this for priuate communion, may serue to this purpose very well, and therfore I will not lette to recite some of them here also.

Milciades that constant martyr of Christ and bishop of Rome ordeined, that sundry hostes prepared by the consecrating of a bishop shuld be sent abroade among the churches and parishes, that Christen folke, who remayned in the catholike faith, might not through heretikes be defrauded of the holy Sacrament. Which can none other wise be také, then for the forme of breade onlye, because the wine can not conueniently be so caryed abroade from place to place in small quantitie for such vse, much lesse any long tyme be kepte without corruption. The councell of Nice decreed, that in churches, where neither bishop nor priest were present, the deacons them selues bringe forth and eate the holy communion. Which lykewise can not be referred to the forme of wine, for cause of sowring and corruption, if it be long kepte. Where oftentymes we finde it recorded by the fathers, that christen people in tyme of persecution receiued of the priestes at church in fyne linnen clothes the sacrament in sundry portions, to beare with them, and to receiue it secretly in the morninge before other meate, as their deuotion

serued

ferued them:for the fame caufe,and in refpectes of other circumftances,it muft of neceffitie be taken onely for the kynde or forme
of breade.

The places of Tertullian , and fainct Cyprian be knowen. Tertullian writing to his *Libr. 2. ad*
wife,exhorteth her not to marye agayne,fpe- *vxorem.*
cially to an infidell , if he dye before her, for
that if fhe doo, fhe fhall not be able at all tymes for her hufband , to doo as a Chriften
woman ought to doo. Will not thy hufband
know(fayeth he)what thou eateft fecretly before all other meate?and in cafe he doo know
it, he will beleue it to be bread,not him,who
it is called. Saint Cyprian writeth in his fermon *de lapfis,* that when a woman had gonne
aboute with vnworthy handes to open her
cofer , wher the holy thing of our lord was
layde vp , fhe was made affrayde with fyre
that rofe vp from thence , as fhe durft not
touch it.Which doubteles muft be taken for
that one kynde of the Sacrament.

The examples of keping the holy Sacrament vnder the forme of bread onely , to be
in a redines for the ficke, and for others in
tyme of danger ; that they might haue their
neceffarie vitaile of lyfe or viage prouifion
with them at their departure hence , be in
maner infinite.Here one or two may ferue in
ftede of a number. For though M.Iuell maketh his vaunt , that we haue not one fentéce
                                   or claufe

or clauſe ſor proufe of any theſe articles, which he ſo defaceth with his negatiue: yet I wil not accumulat this treatiſe with tediouſe allegation of auctorities. S. Ambroſe at the houre of death receiued the communion vnder one kynde kepte for that purpoſe, as it appeareth by this teſtimonie of *Paulinus*, who wrote his life. And becauſe it may be a good inſtruction to others to dye well, I will here recite his wordes. At the ſame tyme as he departed frō vs to our lorde, from about the eleuenth howre of the day vntill the howre that he gaue vp the ghoſt, ſtretching abroade his handes in maner of a croſſe he prayed. We ſawe his lippes moue, but voice we heard none. *Horatus* a prieſt of the churche of Vercelles being gone vp to bedde, heard a voice three tymes of one calling him and ſaying to him, aryſe, and haſte the, for he will departe hence by and by. Who going downe, gaue to the Sainte our lordes bodye, which taken, and ſwalowed downe he gaue vp the ghoſt, hauing with him a good voiage prouiſion, ſo as the ſoule being the better refreſhed by the vertue of that meate, maye now reioyſe with the companie of Angelles, whoſe life he leade in the earth, and with the felowſhip of *Elias*.

Eccleſiaſ.
hiſt.lib.6.
cap.44. *Dionyſius Alexādrinus* aboute the yere of our lord 200. as *Euſebius Cæſarieſis* reciteth, manifeſtly declareth, how that an olde man called

called *Serapion* was houseled vnder one kinde at his ende . This *Serapion* after that he
had layen speacheles three dayes, sent for
the Sacrament . The priest for sickenes not
able to come him selfe , gaue to the ladde
that came of that errant a litle of the Sacrament, commaunding him to weate it, and so
being moisted to powre it in to the olde manes mowth , this much is expressed by the
wordes there, as the greke is to be côstrewed. ἀπεβρέ-
The ladde being retourned home, moisted ξαι μελεύ-
with some liquour that diuine meate, to ser- σας, καὶ
ue the olde man with all , lying now panting τῷ πρεσ-
for desyre to be dimissed hence , and to haste βυτη κα-
him awaye to heauen, and powred it in to his μαῖος ἐπὶ
mowth . For that this old mannes mowth σάζαι,
and throte had long ben drye by force of his
sikenes, the priest, who had experience in
that case, prouidently gaue warning to moy-
ste the Sacramêt with some lequoure , and so
together to powre it in to his mowth. Which
was so done by the ladde, as *Dionysius* expres-
seth . Now if the forme of wine had then
also ben brought , by the ladde to be ministred, there had ben no nede of such circum-
stance , to procure the olde man a moisture
to swalloe downe that holy foode.

And that this was the maner of ministring
the Sacrament to old men at their departing, it appeareth by record of *Theodoritus*,
who wryteth in his accclesiastical storye, how
one

Baſſus an archeprieſt miniſtred vnto an olde man called Simeones of great fame for his holynes. *Baſſus* (ſayeth he) as he viſited his churches, chaunced vpon holy Simeones that woonder of the world lying ſicke , who through feblenes was not able to ſpeake nor moue. When *Baſſus* ſawe he ſhuld dye, he geueth him his rightes before . But after what ſorte, it is to be marked. *Spongia petita Simeoni os humeɛtat atque eluit, ac tum ei diuinum obtulit Sacramentum* . He calleth for a ſponge (ſayeth *Theodoritus*) and therewith moiſteth and waſheth Simeones mowth, and then geueth him the holye Sacrament . If at that tyme the receiuing of the ſacred cupppe had ben in vſe, ſuch procuring of moiſture of the better ſwallowing downe of the Sacrament vnder the one kynde, had ben needles.

Amphilochius that worthy biſhop of Iconium in *Lycaonia* , of whom mention is made in the article afore this , writeth in the life of ſaint Baſile, that a litle before he gaue vp his ghoſt, he receiued a portion of the holy Sacrament, which long before he had willed to be kepte , to the intent it might be put in his graue with him at his buriall . Which no man can cauille to be any other, then the forme of breade onely.

It hath ben a cuſtome in the latine churche from th'apoſtles tyme to our dayes , that on good Fridaye as well prieſtes as other

Chriſten

chtisten people receiue the Sacramét vnder the forme of bread onelye confecrated the daye before, called the daye of oure lordes supper, commonly Maunde thursdaye, and that not without signification of a singular mysterie. And this hath euer ben iudged a good and sufficient communion.

And that in the greke churche also euen in the tyme of *Chrysostóme*, the communion vnder the forme of breade onely was vsed and alowed, it appeareth by this notable storye of *Sozomenus* a greke writer, which because it is long, I will here rehearse it onely in english, remitting the learned to the greke.

Historia ecclesiast. lib.8.cap.5 in græco.

When Iohn otherwise named Chrysostóme gouerned the church of Constantinople very well, a certaine man of the Macedonian heresie, had a wife of the same opinion. Whé this man had heard Iohn in his sermon declare, how one ought to thinke of god, he praysed his doctrine, and exhorted his wife to conforme her selfe to the same iudgement also. But when as she was leadde by the talke of noble women, rather then by her husbandes good aduertisementes, after that he sawe counsell tooke no place: excepte, (quoth he) thou wilt beare me companie in thinges touching god, thou shalt hane no more to doo with me, nor lyue any further with me, The womá hearing this, promysing faynedly that she would agree vnto it, conferreth the

I   matter

matter with a woman seruant that she had, whom she estemed for trusty, and vseth her helpe to deceiue her husband. About the tyme of the mysteries, she holding fast that which she had receiued, stouped downe, making resemblāce to praye. Her seruāt standing by, geueth to her secretly that which she had brought with her in her hād. That, as she put her teeth to it to byte it, hardneth in to a stone. With that, the woman sore astoyned, fearing least some euil shuld happē vnto her therefore, which came by the power of of God: ranne forthwith to the bishop, ād bewraying her selfe, sheweth him the stone, hauing yet in it the printes of her bitte, representing a straunge matter, and a wonderouse colour: and so with teares of her eyes besought forgeuenes, promising her husband, she would cōsent and agree to him. If this seme to any incredible (sayeth *Sozomenus*) that stone is witnes, which to this daye is kepte among the iewelles of the churche of Constantinople. By this storye it is cleare, the Sacrament was thē ministred vnder one kynde onely. For by receiuing that one forme, this womā would haue persuaded her husband, that she had communicated with him, and with that holy bishop. Elles if bothe kyndes had then ben ministred, she shuld haue practised some other shifte for the auoyding of the cuppe. Which had not ben so easye.

The

The place of S. Basiles epistles *ad Cæsariam,* can not be auoyded by no shifte nor sophistrie of the gospellers. These be his wordes. All they which lyue the solitaire life in wildernes, where is no priest, keping the communion at home communicate them selues. And in *Alexadria* and in Egypte, eche one of the people for the most parte hath the communion in his house.

Here I might aske M. Iuell how they could kepe wine consecrated in small measures, as shuld serue for euery mannes housel a parte, in those countries of extreme heate, specially in wildernes, where they had neither priest nor deacon, as in that place S. Basile writeth. For lacke of whom, they kepte it in store a long tyme, that they might not be destitute of it, at neede. Agayne here I might aske him, whether it was the forme of bread only, or of wine also, which Christen men and specially women, were wont deuoutely to receiue of the priestes in their cleane lynnen or napkyns, to beare home with them, taking great heede, that no fragments of it fell downe on the grownde, as bothe Origen, and also S. Augustine doo witnesse. I thinke he will confesse, that lynnen cloth is not a very fytte thing to kepe liquour in.

Vide articulum priore.

Though I might bring a great number of other places for the vse of one kynde, which after the most common rule of the churche

I 2   was

was the forme of breade : yet here I will staye my selfe, putting the reader in mynde, that the comunion hath ben ministred to some persons vnder the forme of wine onlye, and hath ben taken for the whole Sacrament, specially to such, as for drynesse of their throte at their death could not swallow it downe vnder the forme of bread . Whereas it appeareth by S. Cyprian, and also by S. Augustine, that the sacrament was geuen to infantes in their tyme, we fynde in S. Cyprian, that when a deacon offred the cuppe of oure lordes bloude to a litle mayde childe, which through defaulte of the nource, had tasted of the sacrifices that had ben offered to deuilles : the childe tourned awaye her face by the instincte of the diuine maiestie (sayeth he) closed fast her lippes, and refused the cuppe. But yet when the deacon had forced her to receiue a litle of the cuppe, the yeax and vomite folowed, so as that sanctified drinke in the bloude of oure lorde, gowshed foorth of the polluted boilles. If the Sacrament had ben geuen to this infant vnder the forme of breade before, she would haue refused that no lesse then she dyd the cuppe, that deacon then would not haue geuen her the cuppe. And that this may seme the lesse to be wondered at, *Ioannes Teutonicus* that wrote scholies vpon Gratian, witnesseth, that euen in his tyme the custome was in some places, to geue

Serm.5. de lapsis.

De consec. distinct.4. can.4. si qui apud illos hæreticos.

to geue the Sacrament to infantes, not by
deliuering to them the bodye of Chrift, but
by powring the bloude in to theire mowthes: which cuftome hath ben vppon good
confyderation abrogated in the church of
Rome, and kepte in the greke church, as Ly-
re writeth vpon S. Ihon.

The fourth councell of *Carthago* decreed, Can.76.
if a man in ficknes (who was enioyned publike penaunce) do demaunde his houfel, and
er he dye fall in a phrenefie, or becûme fpea-
cheles: that the Sacrament be powred in to
his mowthe. To take this for the forme of wine, we ar moued by the decree of the eleuéth
councell Tolerane. Where it is fayde, that Can.11.
the weake nature of mã is wonte at the pointe of death to be fo farre oppreffed with
drowth, that it may be refrefhed by no meates, vnneth fufteined with comforte of drinke. Then it foloweth. Which thing we fee to
be fo at departing of many, who being very
defyroufe to receiue their viage prouifion
of the holy communion, when the Sacrament was geuen them, haue caft it vp agayne:
not that they dyd this through infidelitie,
but for that they were not able to fwallow
downe the Sacrament deliuered to them,
but onely a draught of oure lordes cuppe.
How fo euer this be taken, it is plaine by this
councell, as by many other aunciét coûcelles
and doctours, that the maner of the catholike
I 3   churche

churche hath ben to minister the Sacrament
to the sicke vnder one kinde.

Now where as some saye, that the Sacrament to be geuen vnder the forme of bread,
was first dipte in the bloude of oure lorde,
and would haue so vsed nowe also for the sicke, and that it is so to be taken for the whole and intiere Sacrament, as though the Sacrament vnder forme of bread were not of it
selfe sufficient: let them vnderstand, that this
was an olde errour condemned aboue twelue hundred yeres past by *Iulius* the first that
great defender of *Athanasius* who hereof in
an epistle to the bishoppes throught Egypte

De conse.
distinct. 2.
can. cum
omne cri-
men.

wrote thus. *Illud vero quod pro complemento
communionis intinctam tradunt Eucharistiam
populis, nec hoc prolatum ex Euangelio testimonium receperunt, vbi Apostolis corpus suum dominus commendauit & sanguiuem. Seorsum enim panis, & seorsum calicis commendatio memoratur.* Where as some delyuer to the people the sacrament dipte for the full and whole communió, they haue not receiued this testimonie pronounced out of the gospel, where our lorde gaue his body and his bloude.
For the geuing of the bread is recorded aparte by it selfe, and the geuing of the cuppe aparte lykewise by it selfe. And where as some
afterwarde in the tyme of *Vitellianus* would
haue brought in agayne this abrogated custome, it was in lyke maner condemned and
abolished

abolished, *in tertio Concilio Braccarensi. Can. 1.*

Now I referre me to the iudgement of the reader, of what opinion so euer he bee, whether for proufe of the communió vnder one kynde we haue any word, sentence, or clause at all, or no: and whether these wordes of M. Iuell in his sermon be true or no, where he sayeth thus: *it was vsed through out the whole catholike churche six hundred yeres after Christes ascension vnder bothe kyndes, with out exception*. That it was so vsed, yea six hundred yeres and long after, we denye not: but that it was so alwayes, and in euery place vsed, and with out exception, that we denye. and vpon what growndes we doo it, let M. Iuell him selfe be iudge. Fol. 16. in the ende

If some of our allegatiós may bee with violence wrested from our purpose, verely a great number of them can not, the auctoritie of the auncient fathers who wrote them, remayning inuiolated. Whereof it foloweth, that after the iudgement of these fathers, where as Christ instituted this blessed Sacrament, and commaunded it to be celebrated and receiued in remembraunce of his death: he gaue no necessary commaundement either for the one, or for both kyndes, (besyde and without the celebration of the Sacrifice) but lefte that to the determinatió of the churche. Now that the churche for th'auoyding of vnreueréce, periles, offences,

I 4   and

and other weighty and importãt causes, hath decreed it in two generall councelles to be receiued of the laye people vnder one kynde onely, we thinke it good with all humblenes to submitte our selues to the churche herein: which churche, Christ commaundeth to be heard and obeyed, saying, *he that heareth not the churche, let him be to the, as a heathen, and as a publican.* In doing whereof we weigh aduisedly with our selues the horrible danger that remaineth for them, who be auctours of schisme, and breakers of vnitie.

Matth.18.

Now for answere to M. Iuelles place alleaged out of *Gelasius*, which is the chiefe that he and all other the aduersaries of the churche haue to bring for theire purpose in this pointe, this much may be sayde. First, that he alleageth *Gelasius* vntruly, making him to sownde in English otherwise, then he doth in Latine. M. Iuelles wordes be these. *Gelasius an olde father of the Church and a bisshop of Rome, sayeth that to minister the communion vnder one kinde, is open sacrilege.* But where sayeth *Gelasius* so? this is no syncere handeling of the matter. And because he knewe the wordes of that father imported not so much: guilefully he reciteth them in Latine, and doth not English them: which he would not haue omitted, if they had so plainely made for his purpose. The wordes of *Gelasius* be these. *Diuisio vnius eiusdemq́ mysterij, sine grandi sacrilegio*

Gelasius his canon guilefully by M. Iuel alleaged, truly examined.

legio

legio non poteſt peruenire. The diuiſion of one and the ſame myſtery, can not come without great ſacriledge. Of theſe wordes he can not conclude *Gelaſius* to ſaye, that to miniſter the cōmuniō vnder one kinde, is opē ſacriledge. *Gelaſius* rebuketh and abhorreth the diuiſion of that high myſterie, which vnder one forme, and vnder bothe, is *vnum idémque*, one and the ſame, not one vnder the forme of breade, and an other vnder the forme of wine, not one in reſpecte of the bodye, and an other in reſpecte of the bloude: but *vnum idémque*, one and the ſelfe ſame. The wordes afore recited be taken out of a fragment of a Canon of *Gelaſius*, which is thus, as we ſynde in *Gratian*. *Comperimus autem quòd quidam sumpta tantum corporis sacri portione, à calice sa-crati cruoris abſtineant. Qui procul dubio(quo-niam neſcio qua ſuperſtitione docentur adſtringi) aut integra ſacramenta percipiãt, aut ab integris arceautur: quia diuiſio vnius eiuſdemq̃, myſterij, ſine grãdi ſacrilegio non poteſt peruenire.* Which may thus be Engliſhed. But we haue founde, that ſome hauing receiued onely the portion where in is the holy bodye, abſteine from the cuppe of the ſacred bloude : who with out doubte (for as much as I knowe not with what ſuperſtition they be taught to be tyed) either let them receiue the whole Sacramen-tes, or let them be kepte from the whole: be-cauſe the diuiſion of one and the ſame myſte-

De conſe-crat. diſtin. 2.can. com perimus.

I 5 　　ry, can

ry, can not comme without great sacriledge.

Here might be sayde to M. Iuell, shewe vs the whole epistle of *Gelasius*, from whence this fragment is taken, that we maye weigh the circunstance, and the causes why he wrote it, conferring that goeth before, and that foloweth, and we will frame you a reasonable answere. But it is not extant, and therfore your argument in that respecte, is of lesse force. But for auoyding of that our aduersaries would hereof conclude, it is to be vnderstanded, that this canon speaketh agaynst the heretikes named *Manichæi* : who in the tyme of *Leo* the first, about fourty yeres before *Gelasius*, went about to spredde their heresie in Rome, and in the parties of Italie. Their hereticall opinion was, that Christ tooke not our fleshe and bloude, but that he had a phātasticall bodye, and dyed not, ne rose agayne trulye and in dede, but by waye of phantasie. And therefore at the communion they absteined from the cuppe, and the better to cloke their heresie, came to receiue the Sacrament in the forme of breade with other catholike people. Against whom *Leo*

Serm.4.
de quadra-
gesima.

sayeth thus. *Abdicant enim se sacramento salutis nostræ, etc.* They dryue them selues awaye from the Sacrament of oure saluation. And as they denye, that Christ our lorde was borne in truth of our fleshe, so they beleue not that he dyed, and rose agayne truly.

truly. And for this cause they condemne the daye of our saluation and gladnes (that is the sunneday) to be their sadde fastinge daye.

And where as to cloke theire infidelitie, they dare to be at our mysteries: they temper thé selues so in the communion of the Sacramentes, as in the meane tyme they may the more safely kepe them priuye. With vnworthy mowth they receiue Christes bodye, but to drinke the bloude of our redemption, vtterly they will none of it. Which thing we would aduertise your holynes of, that bothe such men maye be manifested by these tokens vnto you, and also that they whose deuilish simulation and fayning is fownde, being brought to light, and bewrayed by the felowship of saintes, maye be thrust out of the churche, by priestly auctoritie. Thus farre be Leo hiswordes.

Gelasius that succeded fourty yeres after *Leo*, imployed no lesse diligence then he dyd, vtterly to vanquish and abolish that horrible heresie, of whom *Platina* wryteth, that he banished so many Maniches, as were fownde at Rome, and there openlye burned their bookes. And because this heresie shuld none elles where take roote and springe, he wrote an epistle to *Maioricus* and *Joannes* two bisshops, amongest other thinges warning thé of the same. Out of which epistle this fragment onely is také, whereby he doth bothe,
briefly

briefly shewe what the Maniches dyd for clo
king of their infidelitie, as Leo sayeth: and also in as muche as their opiniō was, that Christes bodye had not verye bloude, as being
phantasticall onely, and therefore supersti-
tiously absteined from the cuppe of that holy
bloude: geueth charge and commaundemēt,
that either forsaking their heresie they receiue the whole Sacramentes, to witte, vnder
bothe kyndes, or that they be kepte from
them wholy.

Here the wordes of Leo afore mentioned,
and this Canon of *Gelasius* conferred together, specially the storye of that tyme knowen: it may sone appeare to any man of iudgement, agaynst whom this fragment of *Gelasius* was written. Verelye not agaynst the
churche for ministring the communion vnder one kynde, but agaynst the detestable
Maniches, who going about to diuide the
mysterie of the body and bloude of Christ,
denying him to haue taken very flesh and
bloude, so much as in thē laye, loused Christ,
whereof S. Iohn speaketh: And would haue
made frustrat the whole worke of our redemption.

2.Ioan.4.

And therefore M. Iuell doth vs great wrōg
in wresting this canon against vs, for as much
as we do not diuide this diuine mystery, but
beleue stedfastly with harte, and confesse
openly with mowth, that vnder eche kynde
the

the very flesh and bloude of Chrift, and whole Chrift him felfe, is prefent in the Sacrament, euen as *Gelafius* beleued. Vpon this
occafion in the parties of Italie, where the
Maniches vttered their poyfon, the communion vnder both kyndes was reftored, and
commaunded to be vfed agayne: where as
before of fome the Sacrament was receiued
vnder one kynde, and of fome vnder bothe
kyndes. Elles if the communion vnder bothe kyndes had ben taken for a necellarie inftitution and commaundement of Chrift,
and fo generally and inuiolably obferued
euerye where, and alwayes without exception : what neded *Gelafius* to make fuch an
ordinaunce of receiuing the whole Sacramentes, the caufe whereof by his *parenthe-*
fis, (quoniam nefcio qua fuperftitione docentur
adftringi) plainely expreffeth? Agayne if it
had ben fo inuiolably obferued of all vntill
that tyme, then the Maniches could not haue couered and cloked theire infidelitie, as
Leo fayeth, by their receiuing the communion with other catholike people vnder one
kynde. For whiles the catholikes went from
churche contented with the onely forme of
breade, it was yncertaine, whether he that
came to receiue, were a Manichey, or a catholike. But after that for difcrying of them
it was decreed, that the people fhuld not forebeare the communion of the cuppe any
                                                      more:

more: the good catholike folke so receiued, and the Maniches by theit refusall of the cuppe, bewrayed them selues. Whereby it appeareth, that the communion vnder one kynde vsed before, by the commaundementes of *Leo* and *Gelasius* was forbydden, to th'intent thereby the Manicheis heresie might the better be espied, rooted out, and cleane abolished.

Thus because we doo not diuide the mystery of our Lordes bodye and bloude, but acknowledge, côfesse, and teache, that Christ tooke of the virgine Marye very fleshe and very bloude in dede, âd was a whole and perfite man, as also God, and deliuered the same whole fleshe to death for our redéption, and rose agayne in the same for our iustification, and geueth the same to vs, to be pattakers of it in the blessed Sacramét, to lyfe euerlasting, that decree of *Gelasius* can not seme against vs iustelye to be alleaged: much lesse may he seme to saye or méane, that to minister the communion vnder one kynde, is open sacrilege.

 Or that

Or that the people had their cōmon prayers then **Iuell**
in a straunge tonge, that they vnderstoode not.

Of the Church Seruice in learned tonges, vvhich
the vnlearned people in olde tyme, in sundry
places vndērstoode not.

ARTICLE III.

 F you meane Maister Iuel by
the peoples common prayers,
such as at that tyme they cōmonly made to God in priuate deuotion. I thinke, they vttered them in that tonge, which they vnderstoode, and so doo Christen people now for
the most parte, and it hath neuer ben reproued by any catholike doctour. But if by the
common prayers you meane the publike
Seruice of the churche, whereof the most
parte hath ben pronounced by the bishops,
priestes, deacons and other ecclesiasticall
ministres, the people to sundry partes of it
saying *Amen*, or otherwise geuing their assent: I graunt, some vnderstoode the language thereof, and some vnderstoode it not, I
meane, for the tyme you referre vs vnto,
euen of syx hundred yeres after Christes cō-
uersation here in earth. For about nyne hundred yeres past, it is certaine, the people in
some countries had their Seruice in an vnknowen tonge, as it shall be proued of our
owne countrie of England.

But

But to speake first of antiquitie, and of the compasse of your first syx hundred yeres, It is euident by sundry auncient recordes bothe of doctours and of conncelles, specially of the councell Laodicene in *Phrygia Pacatiana*, holden by the bishops of the lesser *Asia*, about the yere of our lord. 364. that the Greke churches had solemne Seruice in due order and forme, set forth with exacte distinction of psalmes and lessons, of houres, dayes, feastes and tymes of the yere, of siléce and opé pronoúcing, of geuing the kisse of peace to the bishop, first by the priestes, then by the laye people, of offering the Sacrifice, of the only ministers comming to the aulter to receiue the communion, with diuerse other semely obseruations.

As for the Latine churches, they had their prayers and Seruice also, but in such fixed order, long after the Grekes. For *Damasus* the Pope first ordeyned, that psalmes shuld be songe in the churche of Rome, *alternatim*, enterchaungeably, or by course, so as now we sing them in the quyere, and that in the ende of euery psalme, shuld be sayde, *Gloria Patri & Filio & Spiritui sancto, sicut erat* etc. Which he caused to be done, by counsell of *S. Hierome*, that the faith of the 318. bishops of the Nicene councell, might with like felowship be declared in the mowthes of the Latines. To whom *Damasus* wrote by *Bonifacius* the priest

In tescripto Hieronymi ad 2. epist. Damasi Papæ ad Hieronymum presbyterum.

prieſt to Ieruſalem, that Hierom would ſend
vnto him *pſallentiam Græcorum*, the maner
of ſynging of the Grekes, ſo as he had learned the ſame of *Alexander* the biſhop in the
Eaſt. In that epiſtle complayning of the ſimplicitie of the Romaine churche he ſayeth,
that there was in the Sunnedaye but one
epiſtle of the Apoſtle, and one chapter of the
Goſpell rehearſed, and that there was no ſynging with the voice hearde, nor the comely-
nes of hymnes knowen among them.

About the ſame tyme, *S. Ambroſe* alſo tooke order for the Seruice of his churche of
Millane, and made holy hymnes him ſelfe. In
whoſe tyme (as *S. Auguſtine* writeth) when Lib. Con-
Iuſtina the young Emperour Valentinians feſsionū.9.
mother, for cauſe of her hereſie, where with Cap.7.
ſhe was ſeduced by the Arianes, perſecuted
the catholike faith, and the people thereof
occupied them ſelues in deuoute watches
more then before tyme, ready to dye with
their biſhop in that quarell: it was ordeined,
that hymnes and pſalmes ſhuld be ſong in
the churche of Millane after the maner of
the eaſt parties : that the good folke thereby
might haue ſome comfort and ſpirituall re-
liefe, in that lamentable ſtate and continuall
ſorowes. Thereof the churches of the Weſt,
forthwith tooke exáple, and in euery coútrie
they folowed the ſame . In his ſecóde booke Cap.11.
of Retractations, he ſheweth that in his tyme

K   ſuch

such maner of synging began to be receiued in *Aphrica*. Before this tyme had *Hilarius* also the bishop of Poiters in Fraunce made hymnes for that purpose, of which. S. Hierom maketh mention.

In 2.prooe-mio com-mentariorū epistol. ad Galat.

Much might be alleaged for proufe of hauing Seruice in the Greke and in the Latine churches, long before the first syx hundred yeres were expired, which is not denyed. The thing that is denyed by M.Iuell, is this. That for the space of syx hundred yeres after Christ, any Christen people had their Seruice or common prayers in a tonge they vnderstoode not. Which they of his syde beare the world in hande to be a haynouse errour of the churche, and a wicked deceite of the papistes. And I saye, as I sayde before, that the Seruice was then in a tōge which some people vnderstoode, and some vnderstoode not. I meane, the Greke tonge and the Latine tonge. For that it was within the syx hundred yeres in any other barbarous or vulgare tonge, I neuer reade, neither I thinke M.Iuell, nor any the best learned of his syde, is able to prooue. To be better vnderstāded, I call all tonges barbarous and vulgare, besyde the Hebrewe, Greke and Latine.

Vsage of churche ser-uice in any vulgare tō-ge vvith in 600.yeres after Christ, can not be proued.

The gospell and the faith of Christ was preached and set forth in *Syria* and *Arabia* by Paul, in Egypte by Marke, in *Ethiopia* by Matthew, in *Mesopotamia*, Persia, *Media*

Bactra

Bactra, Hyrcania, Parthia and *Carmania*, by
Thomas, in *Armenia* the greater by Barthe-
lemew, in *Scythia* by Androw, and likewise in
other countries by Apostolike men, who were sent by the Apostles and theire nexte successours, as in Fraunce by Luke sent of Paul,
as *Epiphanius* sayeth côtra *Alogas heresi* 51.by
Martialis sent by Peter, by *Dionisius* sent by
Clemét, by Crescens, as a Clemét and b Hierome writeth, and by *Trophimus* S. Paules
scholer, and by Nathanael Christe disciple, of
whom he at Arelate, and this at Bourges and
Treueres preached the gospell, as some recorde. In our countries here of Britaine, by
Fugatius, Damianus, and others, sent by *Eleu-*
therius the Pope and Martyr, at the request of
king *Lucius,* as *Damasus* writeth in *Pontifica-*
li. Other countties where the Greke and Latine tonge was commonly knowen, I passe
ouer of purpose. Now if M. Iuel, or any of
our learned aduersaries, or any man lyuing
could shewe good euidence and proufe, that
the publike Seruice of the churche was then
in the Syriacall or Arabike, in the Egyptian,
Ethiopian, Persian, Armenian, Scythian,
Frenche or Britaine tonge: then might they
iustly clayme prescription against vs in this
Article, then might they charge vs with
the example of antiquitie, then might they
requyre vs to yelde to the maner and auctoritie of the primitiue churche. But that

a Constitutionū apostolicarum lib.7.c.46.
b Lib.de scriptori, ecclesiast.

Temporibus Antonini Comodi,anno do.182.

K 2   doubteles

doubteles can not appeare. Which if any could shewe, it would make much for the Seruice to be had in the vulgare tonge. Wherefore M. Iuell in his sermon, which he vttered in so solemne an audience, and hath set forth in print to the world, sayeth more then he is able to iustifie, where he speaketh

Folio. 16.

generally thus. *Before the people grewe to corruption*, (whereby he meaneth the first syx hundred yeres after Christ,) *all christen men through out the world made their common prayers, and had the holy communion in their owne common and knowen tonge*. This is sone spoken Syr, but it will not by you be so sone prooued. In dede we fynde, that where as holy Ephrem deacon of the churche of *Edessa* wrote many thinges in the Syriacall tonge, he was of so worthy fame and renome, that (as S. Hierome witnesseth) his writinges were rehearsed in certaine churches openly, *post lectionem scripturarum*, after the scriptures had ben reade. Where of it appeareth to *Erasmus*, that nothing was wont then to be reade in the churches, besyde the writinges of the Apostles, or at least of such men, as were of Apostolike auctoritie. But by this

Lib. de scriptori. eccle siast.

place of S. Hierome it semeth not, that Ephrems workes were vsed as a parte of the common Seruice: but rather as homilies or exhortations to be reade after the Seruice, which consisted in maner wholly of the scriptures

ptures. And whether they were tourned in to greke or no so sone, it is vncertaine.

Neither S. Hieromes translation of the scriptures in to the Dalmatical tonge (if any such was by him made at all) proueth, that the Seruice was then in that vulgare tonge. That labour may be thought to haue serued to an other purpose. But of the translation of the scriptures into vulgare tonges I shall speake hereafter, when I shall come to that peculiar Article. Verely the handeling of this present and of that, hath most thinges common to bothe. Thus that the people of any countrie had the churche Seruice in their vulgare and common tonge, besyde the Greke and the Latine tonge, we leaue as a matter stowtly affirmed by M. Iuell, but faintly proued, yea nothing at all proued.

Now concerning the two learned tonges Greke and Latine, and first the Greke. That the Seruice was in the greke tonge, and vsed in the greke churche, I graunt. And to shewe what is meant by the Greke churche, the learned doo vnderstad all the christen people of that countrie, which properly is called *Græcia*, of *Macedonia, Thracia,* and of *Asia* the lesser and the coutries adioyning. The prouinces that were allotted to the Patriarke of *Alexandria* in Egypte, and to the patriarke of *Antiochia* in *Syria*, are of the olde writers called sometyme, by the name of the Orietall

K 3   or East

or Eaſt churche, ſometyme, of the Greke
churche.

This much by vs bothe confeſſed M.Iuell
and agreed vpon: I ſaye, that if I can ſhewe,
that the people of ſome countries of the
Greke churche, which all had their common
prayers and Seruice in the Greke tonge, for
the more parte vnderſtoode not the greke
tonge, more then Engliſhe men now vnderſtand the Latine tonge: then I haue proued,
that I promyſed to proue:that ſome peoples,
I meane whole nations, vnderſtoode not
their Seruice, for that they had it in an vnknowen tonge.

Now how well I am able to proue this, I
referre it to your owne conſideration. The
leſſer *Aſia* being a principall parte of the greke churche, had then the Seruice in the greke tonge. But the people of ſundry regions
and countries of the leſſer *Aſia* then vnderſtoode not the greke tonge: *Ergo* the people
of ſundry regions and coūtries had then their
Seruice in an vnknowen tonge. The firſt
propoſition or *maior*, is confeſſed as mani-
feſt, no learned man will denye it, and if any
would, it may eaſely be proued. The ſecond
propoſition or *minor*, maye thus be proued.
Strabo who trauailed ouer all the coūtries of
Aſia for perfite knowledge of the ſame, neare
about the tyme of S. Paules peregrination
there, who alſo was borne in the ſame: in
his

All people
of the Greke churche
vnderſtoo-
de not the
greke ſer-
uice.

his 14. booke of Geographie writeth, that
where as within that *Cherronesus*, that is,
the ſtreight betwen ſea and ſea, there were
ſyxten nations by reporte of *Ephorus*: of
them all onely three were grekes, all the reſt
barbarous. Likewiſe Plinius in the ſyxth
booke natural. hiſtor. cap. 2. declareth, that
within the circuite of that land, were three
greke nations onely, *Dores, Iones, Eoles*, and
that the reſte were barbarous, amongeſt
whom the people of *Lycaonia* was one, who
in S. Paules tyme ſpake before Paul and Barnabas, in the Lycaonicall tonge.   Act.14.

 The ſcripture it ſelfe reporteth a diuerſitie of language there, and there about, as
it appeareth by the ſecond chapter of the
Actes. Where the Iewes gathered together
in Ieruſalem for keping of the feaſt of Pen-
tecoſte, wondering at the Apoſtles for their
ſpeaking with ſo many ſundry tonges, emonges other prouinces different in language,
they rekon *Pontus* and *Aſia*, *Cappadocia*,
Phrygia and *Pamphylia*. Which two prouinces are of all attributed vnto the leſſer
Aſia. Which maketh a good argument,
that all *Aſia* the leſſer had not one onely
the greke tonge, and therefore ſo many of
them as were of other language, hauing the
Seruice in Greke, had it in a tonge they vn-
derſtode not.

 They that will ſeme to ſerche the cauſe why

that land had so great diuersitie of languages, impute it to the often chaunge of conquestes, for that it was ouercomen and possessed of diuerse nations : of which euery one
coueted with enlarging their Empyre, to
bring into the coūtries subdued their lawes,
their customes, and their language. Now this
being proued by good and sufficient auctoritie, that in *Asia*, of xvi. nations three onely
were Grekes, it foloweth, that the other thir-
tene hauing their Seruice in greke, had it not
in their owne, but in a straunge tonge. For elles if they had all naturally spoken greke, why
shuld not they haue ben called grekes? Thus
we see it is no newe thing proceding of a generall corruption in the churche, some peoples to haue the Seruice in an vnknowen
tonge.

Here perhappes M. Iuell, or some other
for him, replyeth and sayeth, that the people
of *Asia* commonly besyde their owne proper
language, spake the greke tonge also, and alleageth for that purpose S. *Hierome*, who sayeth, *Galatas, excepto Sermone Græco, quo omnis
Oriens loquitur, propriam linguam eandem habere, quam Treuiros.* That the Galathians, besyde the greke language, which all the Orient
or the East speaketh, haue their owne peculiar tonge, the very same, that they of Treueres haue. Lo sayeth this replyer, S. Hierome
affirmeth all the Orient to speake the greke
tonge

In prooe-
mio 2. lib.
comment.
epist. ad Ga
latas.

tonge. *Ergo* the Seruice in greke to them was not straunge and vnknowen.

To this I answere, S. Hierome meaneth, that some of all countries of the Orient or East spake greke, as the learned men, gentle men, merchantes, all of liberall education, and such other, as had cause to trauaile those countries. To be shorte, it was without doubte very cōmon, as being their only learned tonge for all sciences, and the tonge that might best serue to trauaile with all frō countrie to countrie with in the East, right so as the Latine tonge serueth to the like intentes, for all nations of the West. And he meaneth not that all and singular persons, of what degree or condition so euer they were, all vplandish people, tillers of the grownde, herdmen and women, spake greke. For if it had ben so, then had they not had peculiar and pper tonges. For it is not for their simple headdes (for the most parte) to beare a waie two lāguages. In that S. Hierome calleth the Galatians tonge *propriam linguam*, a proper and peculiar tonge to that nation, he doth vs to vnderstād, the same to perteine to all in particular, that is, to euery one of that prouince, and the greke, to all in generall, in respecte of other nations there, so as not of necessitie it be vnderstanded of euery one.

S Augustine speaking of the title written by Pilate on the crosse, sayeth thus. It was in Tracta. in Ioan. 117.

Hebrew, Greke, and Latine, *Rex Iudæorum.*
For thefe three tonges were there in preeminence before al other. *Hebræa,propter Iudaos
in Dei lege gloriantes, Græca, propter gentium
Sapientes, Latina, propter Romanos multis ac
penè omnibus iam tunc gentibus imperantes.*

The Hebrewe, for the Iewes, that gloried in
the lawe of God, the greke, for the wife men
of the gentiles, the Latine, for the Romaines bearing rule at that tyme ouer many,and
almoft ouer all nations. Now where he
fayeth here, that the greke tonge was in preeminence, *propter gentium Sapientes*, for the
wife men of the gentiles: he difcuffeth fully
the doubte, that might feme to rife of S.
Hierómes faying, and fheweth, that the greke tonge was common, not to all the vulgare
people of the whole Orient, but to the wife
men onely,and that for the atteyning of learning. And for this it is to be noted, that the
fcripture reporteth the vulgare tong of the
Lycaonians to haue ben vttered in hearing
of Paul and Barnabas, not by the Magiftra-
tes, or other the chiefe, but by the vulgare
people. *Turbæ leuauerunt vocem fuam Lycao-
nicè dicentes,&c. Act.14.* And fo S.Hierome
is to be vnderftanded to fpeake in that place,
not of all men of the nations of the Eaft, but
rather of a great nûber, and of fome perfons
of all nations. For elles if all the Eaft had fpoken greke, the fouldiers that buried *Gordia-*
nus

nius the younger, Emperour, *apud Circeium Castrum,* at Circey castle, neare to the land of Persie: would not haue written his title of honour vpon his sepulchre, in greke and la-tine, in the Persians, Iewes, and the Egyptians tonges, *vt ab omnibus legeretur,* that it might be read of all, as *Iulius Capitolinus* writeth. Which is an argument, that all the East spake not ne vnderstoode not the greke tonge. As likewise that *Epiphanius* writeth where he sayeth thus. Most of the Persians after the persicall letters, vse also the Syrianes letters. As with vs many nations vse the greke let-ters, yea where as in euery nation in maner they haue letters of their owne. And others some much esteme the most profownde ton-ge of the Syrians, and the tonge that is about *Palmyra,* both the tonge it selfe, and also the letters of the same. Bookes also haue ben written of Manes in the Syrianes tonge. Agayne if all the East had spoken greke, sun-dry the holy fathers would not haue ben so enuiouse to the common weale of the chur-che, as to hyde their singular workes from the reading of all, which they wrote in barba-rouse and vulgare tonges, to the commodi-tie only of their brethren that vnderstoode the same. *Antonius,* that wrote seuen no-table epistles to diuerse monasteries, of apo-stolike sense and speache, as S. Hierome wit-nesseth, in the Egyptian tonge. Likewise holy

In Gordijs

Libr. 2. hæ-resi 66.

Lib. de Ec-clesiastis.

hóly Ephrem of *Edeſſa*, Bardeſanes of *Meſo-potamia*, who wrote very excellent workes in the Syriacall tonge. Euen ſo dyd *Iſaac* of *An-tioche*, and *Samuel* of *Edeſſa* prieſtes write many goodly workes againſt the ennemies of the churche in the ſame tonge, as *Gennadius* recordeth.

But what ſhall we ſpeake of all the Eaſt? neither all the leſſer *Aſia*, and the countries there adioyning, ſpake not greke one genera-tion before the comming of Chriſt. For if all had ſpoke greke, *Mithridates* that renoumed king of *Pontus*, had not neded to haue lear-ned two and twenty languages of ſo many na-tions he was king ouer, to make anſwere to ſuters, to appoint them orders and lawes, and in open audience to ſpeake to them in ſo ma-ny languages with out an interpreter, as Pli-nie writeth. Here if theſe 22. nations of 22. ſundry tonges, had alſo beſyde their owne lan guage ſpoken greke, and vnderſtanded the ſa-me: Plinie would not haue vttered that word, *ſine interprete*, without an interpreter. And li-kewiſe that king had take vaine labour in lear-ning thoſe tonges, where one might haue ſerued his tourne.

Neare to this kinges dominion in the ſho-re of the ſea *Euxinus*, in the lande of *Colchis*, there ſtode a citie named *Dioſcurias*, ſo much haunted of ſtraungers, that as Plinie writeth by recorde of *Thimoſtenes*, it was reſorted vnto

Natural. hiſt.lib. 7. cap. 24.

Li. 6. nat. hiſt. ca. 5.

vnto of three hundred nations of diſtinɛte
languages, and that the Romaines for the better expedition of their affaires there, had at
lenght lying in the ſame, cxxx. interpreters.
Now if all the Orient had ſpoken greke, as S.
Hieromes wordes ſeme to importe : the Romaines ſhuld not haue neded to haue maine-
teyned there to theire great charges ſo great a
number of interpreters, to be their agentes
there. But for proufe that all the Orient ſpake not greke, what neede we alleage prophane
wryters ? the knowen place of the Actes maketh mencion of ſundry nations there, that
had diſtinɛte languages, the Parthians, Me-
dians, and Elamites etc. Aɛt. 2.

To conclude, they that to maineteine their
ſtraunge opinion of the vniuerſall vnderſtanding of the Seruice vſed of olde tyme in the
Eaſt Churche, ſaye and affirme, that all the O-
rient ſpake greke: ſeme much to diminiſhe the
maieſtie, vtilitie, and neceſſitie of the miraculouſe gifte of tonges, which the holy
ghoſt gaue in the primitiue churche, for the
better furtherance of the goſpell. For if all
in thoſe parties had ſpoken greke, the gifte
of tonges had ben in that reſpecte nedeles.
Hytherto of the greke, and of the Seruice in
that language.

Now concerning the Latine tonge, which
is the learned tonge of the Weſt. That the
Latine churche, or the Weſt churche, for
                                        ſo it

ſo it is called, had the Seruice in Latine, I graunt. The chiefe Regions and countries of the Latine churche within the forſayd ſyx hundred yeres, were theſe: Italie, Aphrike, Illyrike, bothe Pannonies, now called Hungarie and *Auſtria*, *Gallia*, now Fraūce, and Spaine. The countries of Germanie, Pole, and Swethen, and thoſe north partes, receiued the faith long ſithens. The countries of Britaine here had receiued the faith in moſt places, but were dryuen from the open profeſſiō of it agàyne, by the cruell perſecution of Diocletian the Emperour, at which perſecution, S. Albane with many others ſuffered martyrdom.

After that theſe countries had ben inſtructed in the faith, as thinges grewe to perfection, they had their Seruice accordingly: no doubte ſuch, as was vſed in the churches, frō whēce their firſt Apoſtles and preachers were ſent. And becauſe the firſt preachers of the faith came to theſe Weſt partes from Rome, directed ſome from S. Peter, ſome from Clement, ſome others afterward from other biſhops of that See Apoſtolike: they planted and ſet vp in the countries by them conuerted, the Seruice of the churche of Rome, or ſome other very like, and that in the Latine tonge onely, for ought that can be ſhewed to the contrary. Wherein I referre me onely to the firſt ſyx hundred yeres. Now that ſuch

Seruice

Seruice was vnderstanded of those peoples, that spake and vnderstoode Latine, no man denyeth. For to some nations that was a natiue and a mother tonge, as the greke was to the Grecians.

M. Iuell alleaging for the hauing of the prayers and Seruice in a vulgare tonge (as for England in the English, for Ireland in the Irishe, for doucheland in the douche tonge, &c.) authorities and examples of the churche, where in the tyme of the primitiue churche the greke and latine tong was the vsuall and commō tonge of the people, bringeth nothing for proufe of that, which lyeth in controuersie. *Arnobius* (sayeth he) called the latine tonge, *sermonem Italum.* S. Ambrose in Millane, S. Augustine in Aphrike, S. Gregorie in Rome, preached in Latine, and the people vnderstoode them. What then? no man denyeth you this. S. Basile also speaketh of a sownde, which the men, women, and children made in their prayers to God, like the sownde of a wauestryking the sea bākes. What can you conclude of this necessaryly M. Iuell? All this may be vnderstanded of the sownding that one worde, *Amen*, answered at the prayers ende, which is done now by the quyer, and may be done by the people also in the lower parte of the churche. For S. Hierome leadeth vs so to thinke. Who commending the deuotion of the

people

M. Iuelles allegations soluted.

Hexaemeron. hom. 4

In 2. proœ-
mio com-
ment. ad
Galatas.

people of Rome, sayeth in like maner. *Vbi sic
ad similitudinem cœlestis tonitrui, Amen reboat,
& vacua idolorum templa quatiuntur?* Where
elles are the churches and the sepulchres of
Martyrs, with so feruent deuotion, and with
so great companie resorted vnto (which wordes go before) Where doth *Amen* geue so
lowde a sownde, like the thunder clappe out
of the ayer, so as the téples empted of idoles
shake with it, as at Rome?

The people speaketh with the priest at the
mysticall prayers, sayeth Chrysostome alleaged by M. Iuell. What then? So was it long
before, euen in the Apostles tyme, as we rea-

Constitut.
apostolica-
rum li. 8.
cap. 16
* In oratio
nibus my-
stagogicis.

de in Clement, and likewise in S. Cyprian, in
* *Cryillus Hierosolymitanus,* and many others,
so is it now. For he shall fynde in the olde fathers, that to *Per omnia secula seculorū* (which
Chrysostom speaketh of) to *Dominus vobiscum,* so light as they make of it, to *Sursum corda,* and to *Gratias agamus domino Deo nostro,*
the people answered, as now also they answere, *Amen, & cum Spiritu tuo, habemus ad dominum, dignum & iustum est.*

As for the place he alleageth out of S. Augustine vpon the psalmes, it maketh nothing
for this purpose. S. Augustines wordes be
these, other wise then he reporteth them.

In Psal. 16.
in exposi-
tione secun
da.

*Quid hoc sit, intelligere debemus, vt humana ra-
tione, non quasi auium voce cantemus. Nam &
merula, & psittaci, & corui, & picæ, & huiusmodi volucres*

*di volucres , sæpè ab hominibus docentur sonare, quod nesciunt.*Hauing prayed to God (sayeth *S. August.*)that he make vs cleane of our priuie synnes,&c.we ought to vnderstand, what this is , that we maye singe with mannes reason , not with voice , as byrdes doo. For owselles,popiniayes, rauens, and pyes,and such the like byrdes,oftétymes be taughte of men to sownde, they knowe not what. These wordes are to be také of th'vnderstanding of the sense , not the tonge which the Seruice is songe in . For the people of Hippo , where he was bishop, vnderstoode the latine tonge meanely . Which sense can not rightly and safely be atteined of the common people, but is better and more holesomly taughte by the preaching of the learned bishops and priestes.

The commaundement of Iustinian the Emperour which M.Iuell alleageth,that bishops and priestes shuld celebrate the holy oblation or Sacrifice which we call the Masse, not closely*but with vtterance and sownde of voice , that they might be heard of the people : maketh nothing for the Seruice to be had in the Englishe tonge, in the churche of England , or in any other vulgare tonge, in the churche of any other nation : but requireth onely of the bishops and priestes opé pronouncing , vocall not mentall speaking, not whispering with the breath onely in the celebration

De ecclesia sticis diuersis capitulis Cóstitutione 123. Greg. Haloandro interprete. Nam in veteri translatione nihil tale habetur.
* μετὰ φωνῆς.
Iustinianes ordinaúce truly declared.

L   celebration

celebration of the holy Sactifice and other Seruice. Wherein he agreeth with S. Augustine, who in his booke *de Magistro* sayeth, that when we praye, there is no nede of speaking, onlesse perhappes we doo as priestes doo. Who when they praye (in publike assemble) vse speaking for cause of signifying theyr mynde, that is, to shewe, that they praye not to th'intent God, but menne maye heare, and with a certaine consent through putting in mynde (by sownde of voice) maye be lyfted vp vnto God. This much S. Augustine there. And this is the right meaning of that Constitution. And thus he ordeined for the greke churche onely; and thereto only it is to be referred, for that some thought the Sacrifice shuld be celebrated rather with silence, after the maner of the churche of Rome, specially at the consecration. And as that constitutiō perteined to the Grekes, and not to the Latines, so was it not fownde in the Latine bookes, vntill *Gregorius Holoander* of Germanie of late yeres translated the place.

And where M. Iuell alleageth this commaundement of Iustinian against the hauing of the Seruice in a learned tonge, vnknowen to the common people: it is to be noted, how he demeaneth him selfe, not vprightly, but so as euery man may thereby knowe a scholer of Luther, Caluine and Peter Martyr. For whereas by th'allegation

of that

of that ordinance, he might seme to bring
somewhat, that maketh for the blessed Sacrifice of the churche commonly named the
Masse, he dissembleth the worde of the sacrifice, which Iustinian putteth expressely,
τὴν θείαν προσκομιδὴν, *id est, diuinam oblationem,*
the diuine or holy oblation : and termeth it
other wise, in his replyes, by the name of
common prayers, and in his Sermon, by the
name of *the wordes of the ministration,* refusing
the worde of the churche, no lesse, then he
refuseth to be a member of the churche.
Thus through fooysting and coggyng their
dye, and other false playe, these newe peri-
louse teachers deceiue many poore soules,
and robbe them of the suer simplicitie of
their faith.

And where was this commaundement geuen? In Constantinople the chiefe citie of
Grece, where the greke tonge was commonly knowen. That Emperour had dominion
ouer some nations, that vnderstoode not
the greke commonly. Yet no man can tell
of any constitution, that euer he made for
Seruice there to be had in their vulgare and
barbarous tonge. So many nations hauing
ben conuerted to the faith, the common people whereof vnderstoode neither greke nor
latine: if the hauing of the Seruice in their
vulgare tonge, had ben thought necessary to
their saluation: the fathers that stickte not to

bestowe

beſtowe their bloude for their flockes, would
not haue ſpared that ſmal paine and trauaile,
to put their Seruice in vulgare tōges. If it had
ben neceſſary, it had ben done: if it had ben
done, it had ben mentioned by one or other.

Pſal. 104.
Lib.1. con-
tra hæreſ.
hæreſi. 39.
Vide epiſt.
Athanaſij
& AEgypt.
pontif. ad
Marcum
papam.
In Tuſ-
cul.q.

It appeareth by *Arnobius* vpon the Pſalmes, by *Epiphanius* writing againſt hereſies,
and by S. *Auguſtine* in his bookes *De doctrina Chriſtiana*, that by accompte of th'antiquitie, there were 72. tonges in the worlde.
Cicero ſayeth that they be in number infinite. Of them all, neither M. Iuell, nor any one
of his ſyde is able to ſhewe; that the publike
Seruice of the churche in any natiō was euer
for the ſpace of ſyx hūdred yeres after Chriſt
in any other, then in greke and latine.

For further anſwere to the auctoritie of
Iuſtinianes ordinance, we holde well with it.
Good men thinke it meete, the Seruice be
vttered now alſo with a diſtincte and audible
voice, that all ſortes of people, ſpecially ſo
many as vnderſtād it, may the more be ſtirred
to deuotion, and thereby the rather be moued to ſaye *Amen*, and geue their aſſent to it,
through their obedience and credite they
beare to the churche, aſſuring them ſelues
the ſame to be good and helthfull, and to the
glory of God. And for that purpoſe we haue
commonly ſene the prieſt, when he ſpedde
him to ſaye his ſeruice, to ring the Sawnce
bell, and ſpeake out a lowde *Pater noſter*.

By

By which token the people were commaunded silence, reuerence, and deuotion.

Now to saye some what touching the common prayers or Seruice of the churches of *Aphrica*, where S. *Augustine* preached in Latine, as you saye, and I denye not, and thereof you seme to conclude, that the common people of that countrie vnderstoode and spake latine, as their vulgare tonge. That the Aphricane churches had their Seruice in Latine, it is euident by sundry places of S. *Augustine*, in his exposition of the Psalmes, in his bookes *De Doctrina Christiana*, and in his sermons, and most plainely in an epistle that he wrote to S. Hierome, in which he sheweth, that the people of a citie in *Aphrica* was greatly moued ād offended with their bishop, for that in reciting the scriptures for parte of the seruice to them, he read out of the fourth chapter of *Ionas* the Prophete, not *cucurbita*, after the olde texte which they had ben accustomed vnto, but *hedera*, after the newe translation of S. Hierome. Now as I graunt, that some vnderstoode it, so I haue cause to doubte, whether some others vnderstoode it or no. Nay rather I haue great probabilitie to tkinke, they vnderstoode it not. For the bewraying of Hanibals Ambassadours to the Romaines by their Punicall language, whereof *Titus Liuius* writeth: and likewise the conference

All people of the latine churche vnderstoode not the latine Seruice. Lib. 3. 2. belli punici.

L 3 betwixte

betwixte *Sylla* the noble man of Rome, and *Bocchus* kinge of *Numidia*, had by meane of interpreters adhibited of bothe parties, as Saluste recordeth *in bello Iugurtino*, declareth, that the tonge of *Aphrica* was the punicall tonge before the Romaines conqueste. Now the same people remaining there vntill S. Augustines tyme, what shuld moue vs to iudge, that they forgate their owne natiue and mother tonge, and learned a newe the latine tonge? I confesse that many vnderstoode and spake latine, by reason of the Romaines common resorte thyther, of their lawes there executed, of their garnisons there abyding, and specially of the great multitude of latine people thyther sent to inhabite, *deductis colonijs*, by August. the Emperour first, then by *Adrianus*, and afterward by *Comodus*, who would haue had the great citie *Carthago* newly reedified to be called after his owne name, *Alexandria Comodiana*, as *Lampridius* writeth. These Romaine colonies, that is to witte, multitudes of people sent to inhabite the countrie, placed them selues about the sea costes, in the chiefe cities, in *Carthago*, *Vtica*, *Hippo*, *Leptis*, *etc.* and thereabout. And by this meanes the Romaine or Latine speache spred abroade there, and became to be very common, as that which remained still amóg the inhabitátes, that were of the Romaine kynde, and was

learned

learned by long vſe and cuſtome of others dwelling amongeſt them, ſpecially in the cities where the Romaines bare the ſwea and gouernement. For theſe conſyderations, I thinke the Latine tonge was there very common. But that it was common to the inwarde partes of the countrie alſo, and to the vplandiſhe people, amongeſt whom the olde accuſtomed language is longeſt kepte, as experience teacheth: it is not likely. For though the nobilitie and cities chaunge their language, to be the more in eſtimation, yet the common and baſe people of the countrie, fall not ſo ſone to a chaunge. In this realme of England after William Conqueroures tyme, by occaſion of great reſortes of Frenchemen hyther, and of our countrie men in to Fraunce, alſo of the Frenche lawes, and ſpeciall fauour by the princes borne, and prefermentes beſtowed vpon thoſe that ſpake Frenche: the moſt parte of the nobilitie, lawyers, merchantes, capitaines, ſouldiers and welthy folke, had ſkill in the vnderſtāding and ſpeaking of the Frenche tōge, but yet the cōmon and vplandiſh people ſpake litle or nought at all. Whereof grewe this prouerbe in England of olde tyme, Iacke would be a gentilman, but Iacke can no frenche. The like may be thouht of the Latine tonge of *Aphrica.*

What ſhall we thinke of the yplandiſh people there, when as *Septimius Seuerus* the

Emperour,

Emperour, yea after the Apostles tyme, had not very good skill in the latine tonge, but in the punicall tonge, and that being borne at *Leptis?* of whom *Aurelius Victor* sayeth thus in *Epitome. Latinis literis sufficienter instructus, Punica lingua promptior, quippe genitus apud Leptim Prouinciæ Aphricæ.* Seuerus was learned in the latine ettres sufficiétly, but in the punicall tonge he was redyer, as being borne at *Leptis* within the prouince of *Aphri ca.* Here the Latine tonge is attributed to instruction and teaching, and the punicall tonge to nature. *Aelius Spartianus* writing the lyfe of this *Seuerus* to Diocletian, sheweth, that whem his syster a woman of *Leptis* came to Rome to him *vix latine loquens*, her brother the Emperoure was ashamed of her, and blushed at her, for that she could scantly speake Latine, and therefore commaunded her a waie home againe to her countrie, for these be the very wordes of *Spartianus*. Now if such noble parsonages lacke the latine speache in the chiefe parte of *Aphrica*, it is sone vnderstanded, what is to be demed of the common and vulgare people abroade in the countrie.

Let vs come downe lowgher euen to *S. Hieromes* tyme. S. Hierome writing to a noble young Romaine virgine called *Demetria* being in *Aphrica*, exhorting her to kepe her selfe in that holy state of virginitie, sayeth thus

thus. *Vrbs tua quondam orbis caput, etc.* Thy citie once the head of the world, is becomme the sepulchre of the Romaine people, and wilt thou take a banished husband thy selfe beyng a banished woman in the shore of *Libya*: what woman shalt thou haue there to bring thee too and fro? *Stridor Punica lingua procacia tibi fescennina cantabit* . The iartyng punical tonge shall sing thee bawdy songes at thy weddyng. Lo, in S. Hieromes tyme they of *Aphrica* spake the punicall tonge, and that by the sea syde, where the Romanes of long tyme had made their abode. Of this maye be gathered, that the latine speache was not in the farther partes within the countrie very common.

S. Augustine in sundry places of his workes sheweth, that the people of *Aphrica* called Punikes, spake the punicall tonge, acknowledging a likenes and coosynage as it were, to be betwen that and the Hebrew tonge. But most euident witnes for the punicall tonge, is to be fownde in his 44. epistle *ad Maximum Madaurensem*. In which he answereth him soberly for his scoffing and iesting at certaine punicall wordes in derogation of the Christianes . After wondering that he being an Aphricane borne, and writing to Aphricanes , shuld fynde faulte with the punicall names and wordes, and after commendation of the tonge , for that many thinges

De verbis domini secundū Luc. Serm. 35.

L 5 haue

haue right wisely ben commended to memorie by great learned men in bookes of the punicall language: at length concluded against him thus. *Pæniteat te certè ibi natum, vbi huiusmodi linguæ cunabula recalent.* In good sooth thou mayest be sorye in thy heart, that thou were borne there, where the cradelles of such a tonge be warme agayne. By which wordes he semeth to charge him with an vnnaturall griefe and repenting, that he was borne in that countrie, where they speake punike, er they creape out of their cradelles. Whereby it appeareth, the mother tonge of those partes of *Aphrica* which he speaketh of, to be the punical, and not the latine. To conclude, if they had all spoken latine, and not some the punicall tonge, *S. Augustine* would neuer haue wrytten,

Lib.1.de peccatorú meritis & remissione cap.24. *Punici Christiani baptismum, salutem, Eucharistiam, vitam vocant:* That those Christianes which speake the punicall tonge, call baptisme in their language, helth or Saluation, and the Eucharist, lyfe. Wherefore we see that there were Latine christianes, and punicall christianes in *Aphrica*, of whom all vnderstoode not the latine seruice.

And whereas *S. Augustine*, as you alleage him, without shewing the place (as your maner is, whereby you may easely deceiue the reader) hath these wordes in his sermons to the common people diuerse tymes: *Nunc loquar*

loquar latinè, *vt omnes intelligatis*, now will I
ſpeake latine, that you maye all vnderſtand
me: of that ſaying, if any ſuch be, may be gathered, that ſometymes he ſpake in the punicall tongė to the punicall Chriſtianes,
not vnderſtanding the latine : but now amóg
the Latine Aphricanes, that were of the Romaine kynde, and vnderſtoode not the punike, he would ſpeake latine, that all ſuch
ſhuld vnderſtand him.

Who ſo deſyreth further to be perſuaded,
that the people of *Aphrica* called *Pœni*, ſpake
and vnderſtoode theire owne punicall tonge, and not the latine tonge, as likewiſe the
people of Spaigne named *Iberi*, ſpake that
language which was proper to them : let him
reade *Titus Liuius de bello Macedonico*. For
there he recordeth, that whé thoſe of *Aphrica*, or of Spaigne and the Romaines came together for parle and talke, they vſed an interpreter.

And *Vlpianus* the Lawier a great officer
about *Alexander Seuerus* the Emperour at
the begynning of Chriſten Religió, writeth,
that *fidei commiſſa* maye be leſte in all vulgare tonges, and putteth for examples, the
Punicall and the Frenche, or rather Gallicall
tonge. In l.fidei-
commiſſa
ff.d. leg.3.

This much or more might here be ſayde
of the language of the people of *Gallia* now
called Fraunce, which them was barbarouſe
and

and vulgare, and not onely latine, and yet had they of that nation their Seruice then in Latine, as all the West churche had . That the common language of the people there was vulgare, the vse of the latine seruing for the learned, as we must nedes iudge: we haue first the authoritie of *Titus Liuius*. Who writeth, that a Galloes, or as now we saye, a French man of a notable stature, prouoked a Romaine to fight with him man for man making his chalenge by an Interpreter. Which had not ben done, in case the latine tõge had ben cõmon to that natiõ: Nexte, the place of *Vlpianus* before mentioned: Then, the recorde of *Aelius Lampridius*, who writeth, that a woman of the order of the *Druides* cryed out a lowde to *Alexander Seuerus Mammæa* her sonne the Emperour, as he marched foreward on a daye with his armie *gallico sermone*, in the gallical tonge, these wordes boding his death: which right so shortly after folowed: *Vadas, nec victoriam speres, ne militõ tuo credas* . Go thy waye, and looke not for the victorie, truste not thy souldier. Lastly, the witnes of S. Hierom, who hauing trauailed ouer that region, and therefore being skilful of the whole state thereof, acknowlegeth the people of Treueres and of that territorie, to haue a peculiar language diuerse from latine and greke.

    If all that I haue broughte here touching
this

Ad vrbe cõ dita. lib. 7.

In vita Alexandri Mammæe.

In procemio 2.comment. ad Galatas.

this matter be well weighed, it will seme pro-
bable, I doubte not, that all sortes of people
in *Aphrica* vnderstoode not the Seruice,
which they had in the latine tonge. And no
lesse maye be thought of *Gallia* and Spaigne.
And so farre it is proued against M. Iuelles
stowte assertion, that within his syx hundred
yeres after Christ, some Christen people had
their common prayers and Seruice, in a tonge they vnderstoode not.

And thus all his allegations broughte for
proufe of his saying in this behalfe, be answered, the place of S. Paul to the Corinthians
excepted. Which er I answer, I will according to my promise proue, that about nyne
hundred yeres past, yea a thousand also, and
therefore somedeale within his syx hundred
yeres, euen in S. Gregories tyme, the Seruice was in an vnknowen tonge in this lande
of England, then called Britaine, and begonne to be called England, at least for so much,
as sithens, and at these dayes, is called by the
name of England.

Beda an English man, that wrote the eccle
siasticall storye of the English nation, in the
yere of our lord 731. and of their comming
in to Britaine, about 285. recordeth, that S.
Augustine and his companie, who were sent
hyther to conuert the English people to the
faith of Christ, which the Britons here had
professed lōg before, hauing a safe conducte
graunted

The anti-
quitie of
the latine
Seruice in
the church
of Englād.

graunted them by kyng Ethelbert to preache the gospell, where they would: sayde and song their seruice in a churche buylded of olde tyme in the honour of S. *Martine* adioyning on the east syde of the head citie of Kent, whiles the Romaines dwelt in Britaine. The wordes of Beda be these. *In hac (ecclesia) conuenire primo, psallere, orare, missas facere, predicare & baptizare cœperunt*. In this churche they beganne first to assemble them selues together, to synge, to praye, to saye Masse, to preache and to baptise. It is plaine, that this was the Seruice. And no doubte they resorted to it, who beleued and were of them baptized, wondering (as Bede sayeth) at the simplicitie of their innocent lyfe, and swetnes of their heauenly doctrine. In English it was not, for they had no skille of that tonge, as Bede sheweth. *lib.1.cap.23.* And therefore er they entred the land, they tooke with them by commaundement of S. Gregorie, interpreters out of Fraunce. Which interpreters serued for open preachingh and priuate instruction, exhortation and teaching. In synging and saying the Seruice, there was no vse of thé. Whereas S. *Augustine*, after that the English nation had receiued the faith, and he had bé made Archebishop ouer them, hauing fownde, the faith being one, diuersitie of customes in diuerse churches, one maner of Masses in the holy Romaine

Lib.1. hist. ecclesiast. cap.16.

Lib.1.cap.23.

Romaine churche, an other in that of Fraunce: for this and certaine other purposes, sent two of his clergie Laurence and Peter to Rome, to be aduertised amongest other thinges, what order, maner, and custome of Masses it liked S. Gregorie, the churches of the English nation shuld haue: hereunto that holy father answered, that what he espyed either in the Romaine or French, or any other churche, that might be most acceptable to almighty god, he shuld choose out, and gather together, and commende the same to the churche of England, there to be lefte in custome to continewe. *lib.1.cap27.* If it had then ben thought necessary, the Seruice of the Masse to be in English, or if it had ben translated in to the English tonge: it is not to be thougth, that Bede, who declareth all thinges concerning matters of Religion so diligently, specially professing to write an ecclesiasticall storye, would haue passed ouer that in silence. And if the Masse had ben vsed in the English tonge, the monumentes and bookes so much multiplied among the churches, would haue remained in some place or other. And doubteles some mention would haue ben made of the tyme and causes of the hauing such kynde of Seruice, and of begynning the newe latine Seruice. As certaine of S. Gregories workes tourned in to English by Bede him selfe haue

ben

haue ben kepte, so as they remaine to this daye. S. Gregorie him selfe is a witnes of right good auctoritie vnto vs, that this land of England, which he calleth Britaine, in his tyme, that is almost a thousand yeres past: had the common prayers and Seruice in an vnknowen tonge, without doubte in Latine, much in like sorte, as we haue of olde tyme had til now. His wordes be these. *Ecce (om∣nipotens dominus) pené cunctarum iam gentium corda penetrauit, ecce in vna fide Orientis limi∣tem Occidentíq́, coniunxit. Ecce lingua Bri∣tanniæ, quæ nil aliud nouerat, quàm Barbarum frendere, iam dudum in diuinis laudibus Hebræ∣um cœpit Halleluia resonare.* Beholde our lord almighty hath now pearced the hartes al∣most of all nations. Beholde he hath ioyned the borders of the East and the West in one faith together. Beholde the tonge of Britai∣ne, that could nothing elles but gnashe bar∣barously, hath begonne now of late in diuine seruice to sownde the Hebrewe *Halleluia.*

Bede in the ende of his second booke she∣weth, that one Iames a deacō of the churche of Yorke, a very cunning man in songe, sone after the faith had ben spred abroade here, as the number of beleuers grewe, began to be a maister or teacher of synging in the churche after the maner of the Romaines. The like he writeth of one Eddi surnamed *Stepha∣nus,* that taught the people of Northumber∣land

Expositio∣nis in Iob li.27. ca.8.

land to sing the Seruice after the Romaine maner, and of *Putta* a holy man bishop of Rochester; commending him much for his great skille of synging in the churche after the vse and maner of theRomaines, which he had learned of the disciples of S. Gregorie.

These be testimonies playne and euident ynough, that at the begnning the churches of England had their diuine Seruice in Latine, and not in English. One place more I will recite out of Bede most manifest of all other for proufe hereof. In the tyme of Agatho the Pope, there was a reuerent man called Iohn, *Archicantor*, that is chiefe chaunter or synger of S. Peters churche at Rome, and Abbot of the monasterie of S. Martin there. Benedicte an abbot of Britaine, hauing buylded a monasterie at the mowth of the Riuer *Murus*, (Bede so calleth it) sued to the Pope for confirmations, liberties, fraunchesies, priuileges, &c. as in such case hath ben accustomed. Among other thinges he obteined this cunning Chaunter Iohn to come with him into Britaine to teache songe.

Because Bedes ecclesiasticall storye is not very common, I haue thought good here to recite his owne wordes thus englished. This Abbot Benedicte tooke with him the foresayd Iohn to bring him in to Britaine, that he shuld teache in his monastery the course of seruice for the whole yere, so as it was done

M   at S.

at S. Peters in Rome. Iohn dyd as he had cōmaundement of the Pope, both in teaching
the synging men of the sayde monastery the
order and rite of synging and reading with
vtterance of their voice, and also of writing
and prycking those thinges, that the compasse of the whole yere requyred in the celebration and keping of the holy dayes. Which
be kepte in the same monasterie till this daye,
and be copied out of many rownde about
on euery coste. Neither dyd that Iohn teache the brethren of that monastery onely,
but also many other made all the meanes
they could to gete him to other places, where they might haue him to teache. This farre
Bede. I trowe no mã will thinke, that this Romaine taught and wrote the order and maner of synging and pronouncing the Seruice
of the churches of this lande in the English
tonge.

If it had bē demed of the learned and godly gouernours of Christen people then a necessary pointe to saluation, to haue the seruice in the english tonge: no man had ben so
apte and fitte to haue translated it, as he, who
in those dayes had by speciall grace of God,
a singular gifte to make songes and sonets in
english meter to serue religion and deuotiō.
Cednom. His name was *Cednom*, of whom Bede writeth merueilouse thinges. How he made diuerse songes conteining matter of the holy
scripture

scripture with such exceding sweetenes, and
with such a grace, as many feeling their hartes compuncte and prickte with hearing and
reading of them, withdrewe them selues frō
the loue of the world, and were enkendled
with the desyer of the heauenly lyfe. Many
sayeth Bede of th'english nation attempted
after him to make religiouse and godly poe-
tries, but none could doo comparably to
him. For he was not (sayeth he alluding to
S. Paules wordes) taught of men, neither by Galat.1.
man, that arte of making godly songes : but
receiued from God that gifte freely. And
therfore he could make no wanton, tryfling,
or vaine ditties, but onely such, as perteined
to godly Religion, and might seme to procede of a head guyded by the holy ghoft. lib.4.
cap.24. This diuine poet *Cednom,* though he
made many and sundry holy workes, hauing
their whole argument out of holy scripture,
as Bede reporteh:yet neuer made he any piece of the Seruice to be vsed in the churche.
Thus the faith hath continewed in this land
among the English people from the 14. yere
of the reigne of *Mauritius* the Emperour The first
almoft these thousand yeres, and vntill the entrée of
late king Edwardes tyme the English Ser- theEnglish
uice was neuer heard of, at leaft waye neuer Seruice.
in the churche of England by publike auctoritie receiued and vsed.

Now touching the scripture by M. Iuell,

and by all them of that syde alleaged, for the
Seruice to be had in the vulgare tonge. In
the 14. chapter of the first epistle to the Corinthians, S. Paul treateth of the vse of tonges, so as it was in the primitiue churche a spe
ciall gifte. As the faithfull folke came together to pray and to heare Gods worde, some
one mã suddeinly stoode vp, and spake in the
congregation with tonges of many nations,
Spiritu insusurrante, as Chrysostom sayeth,
that is, by inspiration or prompting of the
spirite, so, as neither others that were present, neither him selfe after the opinion of
Chrysostome vnderstoode, what he sayd:
That gifte the Apostle dyd not forbyd. For
that euery gifte of God is good, and nothing by him done in vaine: but dehorted the
Corinthians from the vaine and ambitiouse
vse of it, and therefore dyd much extenuate
the same, and preferred prophecying, that is
the gifte to interprete and expounde scriptures, farre before it. It was not in the churche but in the Apostles tyme, or a very shorte while after them, and that all together by
miracle, the holy ghost being the worker
of it.

The place
of S.Paul
to the Co-
rinthians
maketh
not for the
Seruice in
theEnglish
tonge.

As concerning the order of the common
prayers and publike Seruice, in such sorte as
we haue now, and that age had not: S. Paul
mentioneth nothing, neither speaketh one
word in that whole chapter, but of the vse of
the

the miraculouse gifte, as is sayde before. And therefore his sayinges out of that chapter be not fittely alleaged of M. Iuel and the reste of our aduersaries, against the maner of prayers and Seruice of the churche now receiued and of long tyme vsed, which in the West is vttered in the latine tonge, not by waye of miracle or peculiar gifte, but according to the institution and ordinance of the churche. *Profecto enim cœlum Ecclesia tum fuit.* In very dede sayeth Chrysostome, the churche then was a heaue, when as the holy ghost administred all thinges, moderated al the headdes of the churche, caughte eche one with his spiration. As for now, we kepe but the steppes onely of those thinges. We speake two or three of vs, and that a sundre, and one holding his peace, an other begynneth. But these be but signes onely and memorials of thinges. And so when we haue begonne, (he meaneth *Dominus vobiscum*) *& cum spiritu tuo*, the people answereth: meaning to signifie thereby, that so in olde tyme they spake, not of their owne wisedome, but of the instincte of the spirite of God. This much Chrisostome of the heauenly maner of the primitiue churche in the Apostles tyme.

Now if in these dayes the maner were like, if it pleased the holy ghost to powre vpon vs the like abundance of grace, as to doo all

In 1.Cor. 14.ho.37.

thinges

thinges for vs, to rule the headdes of all faith
full people, to carrie eche one of vs with his
diuine inspiration, and when we came to
churche together for cōforte and edifying,
to geue in to our hartes and put in to our
mowthes by daily miracle, what we shuld
praye, and what we shuld preache, and how
we shuld hādle the scriptures : In this case no
catholike christen man would allowe the vn-
fruitefull speaking with straunge and vnknowen tonges without interpretation, to
the lette and hinderance of gods word to be
declared, and to the keping of the people
onely in gasing and wondering, from saying
Amen, and geuing their assent to the godly blessing and thankes geuing. But the order of the churche now is farre otherwise.
We haue not those miraculouse giftes, and
right well maye we doo with out them. For
the speaking with tonges, was in stede of a
signe or wonder, not to them that beleued,
but to the vnbeleuers. And signes be for the
vnfaythfull, the faythfull haue no neede of
them. In churches, I meane where auncient
order is kepte, whiles the Seruice is song or
sayd, the ministers doo not speake with tonges or with a tonge in such sorte as S. Paul
vnderstoode: but they doo reade ād rehearse
thinges set forth and appointed to them. S.
Paul rebuketh them, who speaking with tonges letted the preachers, so as the people
present

present might not be edifyed. The Latine Ser
uice is not so done in the churche, as the exposition of the scriptures be thereby excluded. In the Apostles tyme, they came to
churche, to th'intent they might profitably
exercise the giftes God gaue them, and by the
same, specially by the gifte of prophecying,
edifie one an other, and teache one an other.
Now adayes they come not to churche together one to teache an other; and to expounde the scriptures in common: but to praye, and to heare the opening of Gods word,
not one of an other with out order, but of
some one, to witte, the bishop, priest, curate,
or other spirituall gouernour and teacher.
And for as much as all the people can not
heare the priestes prayers at th'aulter (which
hath from the Apostles tyme hytherto euer
ben a place to celebrate the holy oblation
at) tourning him selfe for the most parte to
the East, according to Apostolike tradition,
in what tonge so euer they be vttered, for
distance of the place they remaine in: it is
no inconuenience, such admitted in to the
quyer, as haue better vnderstanding of that
is sayd or song: that the reste remaine in semely wise in the neather parte of the churche, and there make their humble prayers to
God by them selues in silence in that language they best vnderstand, conforming them
selues to the priestes blessing and tankes

geuing through faith ād obediēce with their
brethen in the quyer, and geuing assent to
the same, vnderstanding some good parte of
that is done, as declāred by often preaching,
and by holy outward ceremonies perceiuea-
ble to the senses of the simplest.

Fol. 15.

Where as you M. Iuell alleage S. Paul for
your purpose, and make him to saye thus, o-
therwise then he wrote: *If thou make thy pra-*
yer in the congregation with thy Spirite or noise
of straunge wordes, how shall the vnlearned man
thereunto saye amen? for he knoweth not what
thou sayest: you bombaste this texte with your
owne counterfeit stuffing. The trāslation auctorised by king Edward and his counsell, is
truer, and foloweth the greke nearer, wich
hath thus. *When thou blessest with the spirite,*
how shall he that occupieth the rome of the vnle-
arned, saye amen at thy geuyng of thankes, seing
he vnderstādeth not, what thou sayest? Here the
Apostle S. Paul speaketh of blessing or thankes geuing with the Spirite, which spirite
what it is, it is not easy to declāre after the
iudgement of your owne patriarke Iohn Caluine. S. Ambrose taketh it for the spirite we
haue receiued in baptisme; that doth incline
and moue vs to prayer. S. Thomas for the holy ghoste geuen to vs, for reason, and for the
power imaginatiue. *Erasmus* for the voice it
selfe. *Isidorus Clarius* for the power of pronouncing or vtterāce. some for the breath that
passeth

1. Cor. 14.

paſſeth the throte, ſome for the intention, S. *Auguſtine* very ſubtily, *pro apprehenſione quæ ideas toncipit & ſignarerum* . Caluine in his Inſtitutions, *De Oratione cap.* 15. for the ſownde of the mowth, that is cauſed of the breath of a mannes throte and rebownding of the ayer. Chryſoſtom for the ſpirituall gifte, or the gifte of the holy ghoſt to ſpeake with tonges . Which Caluine him ſelfe ſytting in iudgemét as it were vpon this doubtefull matter, alloweth beſt, and códemneth the mynde of all others, and alſo his owne, though vnwares, as it ſemeth: ád ſo he would condemne your noyſe of ſtraunge wordes likewiſe, if he heard it. This texte being ſo doubtefull of it ſelfe in ſenſe, ſo put out of tune by your noyſe of ſtraunge wordes, wherewith you deſcant vpon the worde *Spirite*, ſo violently applyed by your newe fangled expoſition, maketh litle to the condemnation of the latine Seruice in the latine churche: ſpecially ſeing that S. Paul meaneth by that miraculouſe ſpeaking with tonges, vſed or rather abuſed among the Corinthiás, a farre different maner of ſpeaking from that ſpeaking, whereby the prieſt vttereth the common Seruice.

The prieſt (I graunt) ſaying his Seruice to his pariſh, ſpeaketh with a tonge, but ſuch maner of ſpeaking is not that, which S. Paul meant. For the prieſt vnderſtandeth it for the

better parte, if he be learned, and the people
be not vtterly ignorant, because of often
preaching, long custome, solemne feastes
and sundry ceremonies. And therefore your
argument gathered out of that texte, concludeth nothing against hauing the Seruice in
the learned latine tonge not perfitely vnderstanded of the vnlearned people.

Verely if you admitte the exacte iudgemēt
of S. Augustine concerning this place of S.
Paul, then must you seeke for other scriptures and proufes of your English Seruice. For
as he discusseth this point learnedly, by the
tonge S. Paul meaneth not the Latine, Greke,
or Hebrewe among the vnlearned people, or
any other alien or straunge tonge: but onely,
and that by waye of metaphore, any maner of
vtterance, whereby the signes of thinges are
pronounced, before they be vnderstanded.
And by the *Spirite*, he vnderstandeth not
a noyse of straunge wordes, after your straunge interpretation, but, as it is here in a
certaine proper and peculiar maner taken a
power of the soule inferiour to the mynde,
which conceiueth the similitudes of thinges,
and vnderstandeth them not. And thinges so
vttered, be vttered with *the tonge* and *spirite*,
whether it be in Englishe or Latine, or any
other language.

And Syr, although the people vnderstand
not in most exacte wise, what the priest
sayeth

Vide Aug.
lib. 12. de
Genesi ad
literam c. 7
8. & 9 .to. 3

ſayeth in the Latine ſeruice, yet haue they cō-
moditie and profite therby, ſo farre as it plea
ſeth God to accepte the common prayer of
the churche, pronounced by the prieſt for
them.

But S. Paul (ſaye they) requyreth that the
people geue aſſent, conforme them ſelues
vnto the prieſt, by anſwering *Amen* to his
prayer made in the congregation. Verely in
the Primitiue churche this was neceſſary, whē
the faith was a learning. And therefore the
prayers were made then in a common tonge
knowen to the people, for cauſe of their further inſtruction: who being of late conuerted to the faith, and of paynimes made chriſtians, had nede in all thinges to be taught.
But after that the faithfull people was multiplied and increaced in great numbers, and
had ben ſo well inſtructed in all pointes of
Religion, as by their owne accorde they con
formed them ſelues to the miniſters at the
common prayers: in the Latine churche the
Seruice was ſet out in Latine, and it was
thought ſufficient, parte of the people in the
quyer to anſwere for the whole people. And
this hath ben eſtemed for a more expedite
and conuenient order, then if it were in the
vulgare tonge of euery nation.

I graunt they can not ſaye *Amē* to the bleſſing or thankeſ-geuing of the prieſt, ſo wel
as if they vnderſtoode the Latine tonge per-
ſitely.

fitely. Yet they geue assent to it, and ratifie it
in their hartes, and doo conforme them selues vnto the priest, though not in speciall,
yet in generall: that is to witte, though not in
euery particular sentence of praise and thankes geuing, or in euery seuerall petition, yet
in the whole. For if they come to churche
with a right and good intent, as the simple
doo no lesse then the learned: their desyre is
to réder vnto god glorie, praise and honour,
and to thãke him for benefites receiued, and
with all, to obteine of him thinges behofull
for them in this life, and in the life to come.
And without doubte this godly affection of
their myndes, is so acceptable to God, as no
vnderstanding of wordes may be compared
with it. This requysite assent and cóforming
of thé selues to the priest, they declare by sun
dry outward tokés and gestures: as by stãding
vp at the gospell and at the preface of the
Masse, by bowing thé selues downe and adoring at the Sacramét, by kneeling at other tymes, as when pardon and mercie is humbly
asked, and by other like signes of deuotion,
in other partes of the Seruice.

And whereas S. Paul semeth to disallowe
praying with tonges in the common assemble, because of want of edifying, and to esteme the vtterance of fyue wordes or sentences with vnderstanding of his meaning, that
the reste might be instructed thereby, more
then

then ten thousand wordes in a straunge and vnknowen tonge : all this is to be referred to the state of that tyme, which was much vnlike the state of the church we be now in. The tonge of the prayers which S. Paul speaketh of, was vtterly straunge and vnknowen, and serued for a signe to the vnbeleuers. The latine tonge in the latine churche is not all together straunge and vnknowen. For besyde the priest, in most places some of the reste haue vnderstanding of it, more or lesse, and now we haue no nede of any such signe. They needed instruction, we be not ignorant of the chiefe pointes of Religion. They were to be taught in all thinges, we come not to churche specially and chiefly to be taught at the Seruice, but to praye, and to be taught by preaching. Their prayer was not vaileable for lacke of fayth, and therefore was it to be made in the vulgare tonge, for increace of faith. Our faith will stand vs in better stede, if we geue our selues to deuout prayer. They for lacke of faith, had nede of interpretation, bothe in prayers, and also in preaching, and all other spirituall exercises. We hauing sufficiēt instruction in the necessary rudimentes of our faith, for the reste, haue more nede by earnest and feruent prayer to make sute vnto God for an vpright pure and holy lyfe, then to spende much tyme in hearing for knowledge. Concerning

Contra
Anomæos
homil. 3.

ning which thing, Chryfoſtome hath this
ſaying, *Profecto ſi orare cum diligentia in-
ſueſcas, nihil eſt quòd doctrinam tui conſerui
deſideres, quum ipſe Deus ſine vllo interprete
mentem abundè luce afficiat.* Verely if thou
vſe to praye diligently, there is nothing
why thou ſhuldeſt deſyre teaching of thy
felowe ſeruant, ſeing God him ſelfe doth
abundanly lighten thy mynde without any
interpreter.

I would not here that any man ſhuld laye
to my charge the defence of ignorance, as
though I enuyed the people any godly knowlege. I wiſh them to haue all heauenly knowledge, and to be ignorant of nothing neceſſary to their Saluation. Yea euen with my
very harte I wiſh with *Moſes. Quis tribuat
vt omnis populus prophetet, & det dominus illis
ſpiritum ſuum.* O that all the people could
prophecie, and were learned in gods holy
worde, and that our lord would geue them
his ſpirite. But all the common people to vnderſtand the prieſt at the Seruice, I thinke
wiſe and godly men iudge it not a thing ſo
neceſſary, as for the which the auncient order
of the churche with no litle offence, publike
and vniuerſall auctoritie not côſulted, ſhuld
be côdemned, brokê, and quite abrogated,
by priuate aduiſe of a fewe.

If defaulte were in this behalfe iuſtely
fownde, it is knowen, to whom the redreſſe
perteineth.

Num. ii.

perteineth. Concerning the state of Religiõ
in all ages the generall Councell representing the vniuersall churche, for all sores hath
ordeined holesom remedies. Where they be
not heard, of whom Christ sayde, *He that hea-* Luc. 10.
reth you, heareth me, and he that dißißeth you,
dißißeth me: it is to be feared, that cōcerning
the seruice, the newe learned boldnes is not
so acceptable to God, as the olde simple humilitie. It were good the people hauing hũble and reuerẽt hartes, vnderstode the Seruice, I denye not. Yet all standeth not in vnder-
stãding. S. Augustine sayeth notably, *Turbam* Cõtrà Ma-
non intelligendi viuacitas, sed credendi simplici- nichæos.
tas, tutißimam facit. That as for the common epist. Fun-
people, it is not the quiknesse of vnderstan- damenti.
ding, but the simplicitie of beleuing, that ma cap. 4.
keth them safest of all. And in an other pla- Ad Enodiũ
ce, *Si propter eos solos Christus mortuus est, qui* epist. 102.
certa intelligentia poßunt ista discernere, penè
frustrà in Ecclesia laboramus. If Christ (sayeth
he) dyed onely for them which can with certaine or sure vnderstanding discerne these
thinges (concerning God) then is the labour
we take in the churche, in maner in vayne.
God requyreth not so much of vs, how much
we vnderstand, as how much we beleue, and
through beleefe, how much we loue. And
when we shall all appeare before Christ in
that dreadfull daye of iudgemẽt, whe shall not
be requyred to geue an accõpte of our vnder
standing

The benefite of prayer vttered in a tonge not vnderstanded.

ding, but faith presupposed, of our charitie.

Now though the people knowe not the Latine tonge, and albeit it were better, they had the Seruice in their owne vulgare tonge, for the better vnderstanding of it: yet as it is, for as muche as it consisteth in maner all together of the scriptures; that great profite cometh bothe to the reader and to the hearer of it: Origen sheweth at large, in the twentith homilie vpon *Iosue*. Because it were ouer long to bring all that he sayeth there to this purpose, the summe of the whole may thus be abbridged.

First the heauenly powers and angelles of God, which be with vs, haue great liking in our vtterance of the wordes of the scripture. Though we vnderstand not the wordes we vtter with our mowth, yet those powers (sayeth he) vnderstand them, and thereby be inuited, and that with delite, to helpe vs. And speaking of the powers that be within vs, to whom charge of our soules and bodies is cōmitted, he sayeth, that if the scriptures be read of vs, they haue pleasure therein, and be made the stronger toward taking heede to vs, yea and that if we speake with tonges, and our spirite praye, and our sense be with out fruite. And there he alleageth to that purpose, the common place of S. Paul to the Corinthians, calling it merueilouse, and in maner a mysterie, shewing how the spirite prayeth.

prayeth, the sense being with out fruite. After
this he declareth the euill powers and our
ghostly ennemie the deuill, by our reading
and hearing of the scriptures, to be dryuen
from vs. As by enchauntements sayeth he,
snakes be stayed from doing hurte with their
venime, so if there be in vs any serpent of cōtrary power, or if any snake waite priuely to
mischiefe vs : by vertue of the holy scripture
rehearsed (so that for weerynesse thou tourne not awaye thy hearing)he is put awaye. S.
Augustine cōfirmeth the same doctrine, whe- In prologo
re he sayeth, *psalmus dæmones fugat, angelos in* Psalmoru.
adiutorium inuitat. The psalme (read deuoutly
or heard)putteth deuilles to flight, and pro-
uoketh angels to helpe. At léght Origen shewing how by meate or drynke we finde remedie for sore eyes, though we feele no benefite forthwith in eating or drynking (he cōclu-
deth his speciall parte of the cōparison with
these wordes) : In this wise we must beleue
also of the holy scripture, that it is profitable,
and doth good to the soule, *etiāsi sensus noster*
ad præsens intelligentiā nō capit, although presently our sense doo not atteine the meaning
and vnderstāding ; because our good powers
by these wordes be refreshed and fedde, and
the cōtrary, that is, our aduersarie powers, are
weakned ād put to flight. At léght makīg ob-
lection to him selfe on the behalfe of his hearers, as though they shuld laye this doctrine

to his

to his charge for excuse of taking further paynes in preaching and expounding the scriptures to them : therto he answereth and sayeth . No no , we haue not sayd these to you for that cause , neither haue we vttered these thinges to you for excuse , but to shewe you, *in Scripturis sanctis esse vim quandam , quæ legēti etiam sine explanatione sufficiat* : that in the holy scriptures there is a certaine power or strength which is sufficient for one that readeth it, yeaw ith out any expouding of it. This sufficiencie he referreth (I thinke) to the procuring of the good powers to helpe vs , and to the dryuing awaye the malice of the euill powers our ghostly enemies , that they hurte vs not.

I trust wise godly and stedfast men, who be not caryed about with euery wynde of doctrine , will be moued more with the auctoritie of Origen, a man allwayes in the iudgemnet of all the christen world accōpted most excellently learned , then with the scorning of Caluine , who speaking of the auncient latine Seruice vsed in England and Fraunce,

In Instituti-
onibus.
sayeth: *ad Ecclesiam ex sono non intellecto, nullus penitus fructus redit* : that of the sownde not vnderstanded no fruite at all retourneth to the churche : vsing that word of dispite, that might better be spoken by a mynstrell of his pype and taburrette, thē by a preacher of the diuine Seruice. Neither hereof with any milder

der

der spirite speaketh his disciple and submi-
nister Theodore Beza, the hote minister of
the deformed churches of Fraunce. *Quæcun-* Confessio-
que preces ab aliquo concipiuntur eo idiomate, nis.cap.4.
quod ipse non intelligat,pro Dei ludibrio sunt ha- Sectiōe.1:.
benda. What prayers so euer be made (sayeth
he) of any man in a tonge that he vnderstandeth not, they be to be taken for a mockery
of God. Who so euer here alloweth Caluine
and Beza condemned of the churche, must
condemne Origen, for this point neuer reproued nor touched of any, that haue not
spared him, where so euer they could charge
him with any errour. If all prayers made in
an vnknowen tonge be a mocking of God,
as Beza sayeth: then were the prayers vttered by miracle in the primitiue churche with
tonges (which the vtterers them selues vnderstoode not) after the mynde of Chrysostome) a mocking of god: for I see nothing,
whereby they are excluded from his generall saying and vniuersall proposition. Verely
this teaching of Beza is not sownde. I wene, if
he were out of the protectiō of his deformed
churches, and conuented before a catholike
Bishop to geue an accompte of this doctrine,
he would steppe backe and reuoke that rashe
saying agayne. For els he shuld seme to graūt,
that god gaue at the begynnig of the church,
the giftes of tonges to be mokte withall,
which were very absurde and blasphemouse.

N 2   S.Paul

Paul wisheth that all the Corinthians spake
with tōges, but rather that they prophecied.

If our newe maisters condemne the Latine Seruice in the Latine churche, for that the
people vnderstand it not, thereof must it folowe, that the English seruice so much of it
as consisteth of Dauides psalmes, which is
the most parte, be also condemned. The like
may be sayde of other nations. For how many
shall we fynde not of the people onely, but
also of the best learned men, that vnderstand
the meaning of them, in what tonge so euer
they be set forth ? S. Hilarie compareth the
booke of psalmes to a heape of keyes, that be
to open the dores of euery house of a great
citie, layed together. Among whom it is hard
to fynde which keye serueth which locke, and
without the right keye no dore can be opened. S. Augustine lykeneth the people of
Aphrica synging the Psalmes which they vnderstoode not, to owselles, popiniayes, raues,
pyes, and such other byrdes which be taught
to soude, they knowe not what, and yet they
vnderstoode the tonge they sang them in.
And therefore he exhorteth them to learne
the meaning of them at his preaching, least
they shuld syng not with humaine reason, (as
is before recited) but with voyce onely, as
byrdes doo.

The reste of the scriptures whereof the
Seruice cōsisteth, is, though not all together

so obscure as the psalmes, yet veryly darker and harder, then that the common peoples grosse and simple wittes may pearce the vnderstanding of it, by hearing the same pronounced of the minister in their mother tonge. And by this reason we shuld haue no Seruice at all gathered out of the scriptures, for defaulte of vnderstading. And whereas of the Seruice in the vulgare tonge the people will frame lewde and peruerse mea ning of their owne lewde senses: So of the La tine Seruice, they will make no constructions either of false doctrine, or of euill lyfe. And as the vulgare Seruice pulleth their mindes from priuate deuotion to heare, and not to praye, to litle benefite of knowledge, for the obscuritie of it: so the latine geuing them no such motion, they occupie them selues, whiles the priest prayeth for all, and in the person of all, in their priuate prayers, all for all, and euery one for him selfe.

The nations that haue euer had their Seruice in their vulgare tonge, the people thereof haue continewed in schismes, errours, and certaine Iudaicall obseruances, so, as they haue not ben reckened in the number of the catholike churche. As the Christians of *Moschouia*, of *Armenia*, of Prester Iohn his land in *Ethiopia*. *Bessarion* asking by waye of a question of the Grekes his countrie men, what churche that is, against the which hell

Such nations as vse churche Seruice in their owne tonge, continevve in schismes.
In epistola ad Græcos.

gates shall neuer preuaile : answereth him
selfe, and sayeth : *Aut Latina aut Greca
est Ecclesia, tertia enim dari non potest . Siquidem aliæ omnes hæresibus sunt plenæ, quas sancti
patres & generales Synodi condemnarunt .* Either it is the Latine, or the Greke churche,
for there is no thyrd, that can be graunted,
For all other churches be full of heresies,
which the holy fathers and generall councelles haue condemned. Wherefore of these churches no example ought to be taken
for Seruice in the vulgare tonge, as neither
of the churches of *Russia* and *Morauia*,
and certaine other, to whom aboue syx hundred yeres past it was graunted to haue the
Masse in the Sclauons tonge, through speciall licence thereto obteined of the See Apostolike by *Cyrullus* and *Methodius*, that first
conuerted them to the faith. Which maner of seruice, so many of them as be catholike, for good causes haue lefte, and vse the
Latine, as other Latine churches doo . Concerning the reste yet keping their Sclauon
tonge, besyde other errours and defaultes,
for which they are not herein to be estemed
worthy to be folowed:we maye saye of them,
the wordes of *Gregorie Nazianzene. Priuile-
gia paucorum, non faciunt legem communem:*
The priuileges of a fewe, make not a thing
laufull in common.

Wherefore to conclude, seing in syx hūdred
yeres

yeres after Chrift, the Seruice of the churche was not in any other, then in the Greke
and Latine tongel, for that any man is able to
fhewe by good proufe, and the fame not vnderftanded of all people : feing the auctorities by M.Iuell alleaged, importe no neceffary
argument nor directe cōmaundement of the
vulgare tonge, but onely of plaine and open
pronouncing, and that where the tonge of
the Seruice was vnderftāded: feing the churche of the Englifhe nation had their Seruice
in the Latine tonge to them vnknowen, well-
near a thoufand yeres paft: feing the place of
S.Paul to the Corinthians either perteineth
not to this purpofe, or if it be fo graunted,
for the diuerfitie of ftates of that and of this
our tyme, it permitteth a diuerfitie of obferuation in this behalfe, though fome likenes
and refemblance yet referued : feing great
profite cometh to the faithfull people hauing it fo as they vnderftand it not : Finally
feing the examples rehearfed herein to be
folowed, be of fmall auctoritie, in refpecte either of antiquitie, or of true Religion: As the
bolde affertion of M.Iuell is plainely difpro-
ued, fo the olde order of the Latine Seruice
in the Latine churche, whereof England is a
prouince, is not rafhly to be condemned: fpecially whereas being firft committted to the
churches by the Apoftles of our coūtrie, and
the firft preachers of the faith here, it hath

ben

ben auctorised by continuance almost of a thousand yeres without controll or gaynesaying, to the glory of God, the welth of the people, and procuring of helpe from heauen alwayes to this land.

And to adde hereuto this much last of all, though it might be graunted, that it were good, the Seruice were in the vulgare tonge, as in Englishe for our countrie of England: yet doubteles good men and zelouse kepers of the catholike faith, will neuer allowe the Seruice deuysed in king Edwardes tyme now restored agayne, not so much for the tonge it is in, as for the order it selfe and disposition of it, lacking some thinges necessary, and hauing some other thinges repugnant to the faith and custome of the catholike churche.

Or that

Or that the bishop of Rome was then called an vniuersal bishop, or the head of the vniuersall churche.

Of the Popes Primacie.

ARTICLE. 4.

BY what name so euer the bishop of Rome was called within syx hū-dred yeres after Christes ascension, this is cleare, that his Prima-cie, that is to say, supreme power and aucto-ritie ouer and aboue all bishops, and chiefe gouernement of all Christes flocke, in mat-ters perteining to faith and Christen religiō, was then acknowleged and cōfessed. Which thinge beinge so, whether thē he were called by either of those names that you denye, or no: it is not of great importance. And yet for the one of thē some what, and for the other, an infinite number of good authorities may be alleaged. But thereof hereafter.

Now concerninge the chiefe point of this article, which is the Primacie of the Pope, Peters successour. First, it hath ben set vp and ordeined by God, so as it standeth in force *Iure diuino*, by gods lawe, and not onely by mans lawe, the scriptures leadinge thereto. Nexte, commended to the worlde by decrees of coūcelles, ād cōfirmed by edictes of Chri-sten emperoures for auoidinge of schismes. Furthermore, confessed and witnessed by the

N 5   holy

5 holy fathers. Againe, fownde to be necessary
6 by reason . Finally, vsed and declared by the
euēte of thinges and practise of the church.
For proufe of all this, so much might easely
be sayde, as shuld serue to a whole volume.
But I in this treatise seeking to auoide prolixitie, hauing purposed to saye somewhat to
this number of the other Articles, and knowing this matter of the Primacie to be allready largely and learnedly hādeled of others :
will but trippe as it were lightly ouer at this
tyme, and not sette my fast footing in the
deepe debating and treating of it.

I.
The Popes
Primacie
not of
Man, but
of Gods
ordinance.
The first
proufe of
the Popes
primacie,
scripture
expoūded.
Matt.16.

First, as concerning the right of the Popes primacie by gods lawe, by these aunciēt
authorities it hath ben auouched. *Anacletus*
that holy bishop and martyr S. Peters scholer, and of him consecrated priest, in his e-
pistle to the bishops of Italie writeth thus. *In
nouo testamento post Christum, etc.* In the newe
testament the order of priestes beganne after
our lord Christ, of Peter, because to him
bishoprike was first geuen in the churche of
Christ, where as our lord saide vnto him: *
Thou art Peter, and vpon this rocke I will buylde my church, and the gates of hell shall not preuaile against it, and vnto thee I will geue the keies of the kingdome of heauen.* Wherfore this
Peter recieued of our lord first of all, power to binde and to lowse, and first of all,
he brought people to the faith by vertue
of

of his preaching. As for the other Apostles, they receiued honour and power in like felowſhip with him, and willed him to be their prince or chiefe gouernour.

In an other epiſtle to all biſhoppes, alleaging the ſame texte for the Primacie of the See of Rome, ſpeaking of the diſpoſition of churches committed to Patriarkes and Primates, he ſaith thus moſt plainely. This holy ad Apoſtolike church of Rome hath obteined the Primacie, not of the Apoſtles, but of our lord Sauiour him ſelfe, and hath gotten the preeminence of power ouer all churches, and ouer the whole flocke of Chriſten people, euen ſo as he ſaide to bleſſed Peter th'Apoſtle: *Thou art Peter, and vpon this rocke etc.*

S. Gregorie writing to *Mauritius* the Emperoure againſt Iohn the biſhop of Conſtantinople, ambitiouſly claiming and vſurping the name of an vniuerſall biſhop, proueth the biſhop of Rome ſucceding in Peters chaier, to be Primate, and to haue charge ouer all the church of Chriſt, by ſcriptures, thus. Lib.4.epiſt. *Cunctis euangelium ſcientibus, liquet etc.* It [32.] is euident to all that knowe the goſpell, that the cure and charge of the whole church hath bē committed by the worde of our lord to the boly Apoſtle Peter prince of all the Apoſtles. for to him it is ſayde, *Peter, loueſt* Ioan.21. *thou me? feede my ſheepe.* to him it is ſayd: Luc.22.

Beholde

Beholde Sathan hath desyred to syfte you, as it were wheate, and I haue prayed for thee Peter, that thy faith faile not. And thou being once **Matth. 26.** *conuerted, strengthen thy brethren.* To him it is saide: *Thou art Peter, and vpō this rocke I will buylde my church, and the gates of hell shall not preuaile against it. And vnto the I wil geue the keies of the kingdom of heauen. And what so euer thou byndest vpon earth, shalbe bounde also in heauen, and what so euer thou lowsest on earth shalbe lowsed also in heauen.* Beholde he recei-

Cura ei to- ueth the keies of the heauenly kingdome, *tius Eccle-* the power of bynding and lowsing is geuen *siæ & prin-* to him, the charge of the whole church and *cipatus cō-* principalitie is comitted to him. Thus farre *mittitur.* Gregorie. But because our aduersaries though without iuste cause, refuse the witnes of the Bishops of Rome in this article, as vnlawfull witnesses in their owne cause, were they ne-uer so holy martyrs or learned confessours: they may vnderstand, we are able to alleage sundry other authorities to the cōfirmation hereof, that be aboue all exception.

S. Cyprian declaring the contempte of the high Priest Christes Vicare in earth, to be cause of schismes and heresies, writeth thus to *Cornelius* Pope and Martyr. *Neque enim a-liunde hæreses obortæ sunt, etc.* Neither haue he-resies or schismes rysen of any other occasiō, then of that, the Priest of God is not obeied, ād that one Priest for the tyme in the church, and

and one iudge for the tyme in ftede of Chrift
is not thoughte vpon. To whom if the whole
brotherhed(that is, the whole nūber of Chri
ftē people which be brethrē together ād were fo called in the primitiue church) would
be obediēt according to gods teachinges: thē
no mā would make adoo againft the colledge
of prieftes, no man woulde make him felfe
iudge, nor of the bifhop nowe, but of God,
after gods iudgement, after the fauour of the
people declared by theire voices at the Ele-
ctiō, after the cōfent of his felowbifhops: no
man through breach of vnitie and ftrife,
would diuide the church of Chrift: no man
ftanding in his owne conceite and fwelling
with pride, would fette vp by him felfe abroade without the church, a newe herefie.

Secundum magifteria diuina.

Of all other authorities, that of *Athana-*
fius, and of the bifhops of Egypte and *Libya*
gathered together in a Synode at *Alexan-*
dria, is te be regarded. Who making humble
fute to *Felix* then bifhop of Rome, for aide
and fuccour againft the Arianes; through the
whole epiftle confeffing the fupreme auctoritie of that Apoftolike See, vtter thefe very
wordes. *Veftræ Apoftolicæ fedis imploramus auxi*
lium etc. We humbly befech you of the helpe
of your Apoftolike See. Becaufe (as verely we
beleue) God hath not defpifed the praiers of
his feruantes offered vp to him with teares,
but hath conftituted and placed you & yout
predeceffours,

In primo tomo Con-ciliorum.

predeceffours, who were Apoftolike Prelates, in the higheft tower or fupreme ftate, and
commaunded them to haue cure and charge
of all churches, to th' intent you helpe and
fuccour vs, and that defending vs (as to whõ
iudgement of bifhops is committed) you
forflowe not through negligence, to delyuer vs from our enemies.

In the margin: *In summi-*
tatis arce
conftituit.

Now if the Apoftolike church of Rome
hath obteined the Primacie and preeminence of power ouer all churches, and ouer the
whole flocke of Chrifté people, of our lord
Sauiour him felfe, as *Anacletus* faith: If it be
euident to all that knowe the gofpel, that the
cure and charge of the whole church, hath
ben committed to the holy Apoftle Peter
Prince of all the Apoftles by the worde of
our lord, as Gregorie witneffeth: If the
whole brotherhed (that is to fay all Chriften
folke) ought to obeye the one hygh Prieft
or bifhop of God, and the one Iudge that
is Chriftes Vicare, or in the fteede of Chrift
for the tyme, according to the preceptes and
teachinges of God, as Cyprian writeth: If
it be God, that hath placed and ordeined the
bifhop of Rome in the higheft ftate of the
church, as *Athanafius* with all the fathers
of that Alexandrine councell recordeth: If
this I fay be true: then is it eafely fene, vpon
how good grownde this doctrine ftandeth,
whereby it is affirmed, that the bifhop of
Rome

Rome his Primacie hath his force by Gods lawe, and not onely by mannes lawe, much leſſe by vniuſt vſurpation. The ſcriptures, by which as wel theſe, as all other holy and learned fathers were leadde to acknowledge and confeſſe the Primacie of Peter and his ſucceſſours, were partly ſuch, as *Anacletus* and Gregorie here alleageth, and Cyprian meaneth, as it appeareth by his third treatiſe *De ſimplicitate prælatorum*, and ſundry mo of the newe teſtament, as to the learned is knowen: of which to treate here largely and piththely, as the weight of the matter requyreth, at this tyme I haue no leiſure, neither if I had, yet myght I conueniently performe it in this treatiſe, which otherwiſe will amount to a ſufficient bignes, and that matter throughly hādeled, will fill a right great volume. Wherfore referring the readers to the credite of theſe worthy fathers who ſo vnderſtoode the ſcriptures, as thereof they were perſuaded the Primacie to be attributed to Peters ſucceſſour by God him ſelfe: I will procede, keeping my prefixed order.

Whereas the preeminence of power and auctoritie, which to the biſhop of Rome by ſpeciall and ſingular priuiledge God hath graunted, is commended to the worlde by many and ſundry councelles: for auoiding of tediouſneſſe I wil rehearſe the teſtimonies of a fewe. Amonge the canons made by the three

The 1. proufe, coūcelles.

vide episto-
las Athana-
sij & AE-
gypti Pon-
tificum ad
Marcū pa-
pā,& Mar-
ci ad eos-
dem de ex-
emplaribus
Niceni cō-
cilij:Itē Iu-
lij papæ re-
scriptū con
tra orienta-
tes.
Vide Fran-
cisc. Turri-
anum, lib.
4. charact.
dogmat.

thre hundred and eightē bishops at the Nicene Councell, which were in number 70.
and all burnt by heretikes in the East church
saue xx. and yet the whole number was kepte diligently in the church of Rome in the o-
riginall it selfe, sent to Syluester the bishop
there from the conncell, subscribed with the
said 318.fathers handes: the 44. canon which
is of the power of the patriarke ouer the Me-
tropolitanes and bishops, and of the Metropolitane ouer bishops, in the ende hath this
decree. *Vt autem cunctis ditionis sua nationibus
etc.* As the patriarke beareth rule ouer all nations of his iurisdiction, and geueth lawes to
them, and as Peter Christes vicare at the beginning sette in auctoritie ouer religiō, ouer
the churches, and ouer all other thinges perteining to Christ, was Maister and ruler of
Christen princes, prouinces, and of all nations: So he whose principalitie or chieftie is
at Rome, like vnto Peter, and equal in auctoritie, obteineth the rule and souerainetie
ouer all patriakes. After a fewe wordes it foloweth there. If any man repine against this sta-
tute or dare resist it, by the decree of the
whole conncell he is accursed.

Julius that worthy bishop of Rome not
long after the councell of Nice, in his epistle
that he wrote to the 90. Ariane bishops assembled in councell at Antioche against *A-
thanasius* bishop of *Alexandria*, reprouing
them

them for theire vniuſt treating of him, ſaith of the canons of the Nicene councell, then freſhe in their remembrance : that they com-maunde, *Non debere præter ſententiam Roma-ni pontificis vllo modo concilia celebrari, nec epiſ-copos damnari.* That without the auctoritie of the Biſhop of Rome, neither Councelles ought to be kepte, nor biſhops condemned. Againe, that nothing be decreed without the Biſhop of Rome. *Cui hæc & maiora eccleſia-rum negotia, tam ab ipſo domino, quàm ab omni-bus vniuerſorum conciliorum fratribus, ſpeciali priuilegio contradita ſunt.* To whom theſe and other the weighty matters of the churches be committed by ſpeciall priuiledge, as well by our lord him ſelfe, as by all oure brethren of the whole vniuerſall coūcelles. Among other principall pointes, which he reciteth in that epiſtle out of the Nicene councelles canons, this is one. *Vt omnes epiſcopi etc.* That all biſ-hops who ſuſteine wrōge, in weighty cauſes, ſo often as nede ſhall require, make their ap-peale freely to the See Apoſtolike, and flie to it for ſuccour as to their mother, that from thence they may be charitably ſuſteined, de-fended, and deliuered. To the diſpoſition of which See, the auncient auctoritie of th'A-poſties, and their ſucceſſours, and of the ca-nons, hath reſerued all weighty, or great ec-cleſiaſticall cauſes, and iudgementes of biſ-hops.

O *Athanaſius*

Athanasius and the whole companie of
bishops of Egypte, *Thebaida* and *Libya* af-
sembled together in councell at *Alexandria*,
complaining in their epistle to *Felix* the Pope of the great iniuries and griefes they susteined at the Arianes: alleageth the determination of the Nicene councell, touching the
supreme auctoritie and power of that See A-
postolike ouer all other bishops . *Similiter &*
à supradictis patribus est definitum consonanter
etc. Likewise (saie they) it hath bē determined
by common assent of the fore saide fathers
(of Nice) that if any of the bishops suspecte
the Metropolitane, or theire felowbishops of
the same prouince , or the iudges : that then
they make their appeale to your holy See of
Matt. 16. Rome, to whom by our lord him selfe, power
to binde and louse, by speciall priuiledge abo
ue other hath ben graúted. This much alleaged out of the canōs of the Nicene councell,
gathered partly out of *Iulius* epistle, who wro
te to thē that were present at the makīg of thē
(which taketh awaye all suspicion of vntruth)
and partly out of *Athanasius* and others, that
were a great parte of the same coūcell. For fur
ther declaration of this matter , it were easy
here to alleage the coūcell of *Sardica*, the coū-
Ca. 4. cs 9. cell of *Chalcedon*, certaine councelles of *A-*
phrica, yea some coūcelles also holden by heretikes , and sundry other , but such store of
auctorities cōmonly knowē, these may suffise.

The

The Christen princes that ratified and cōfirmed with their proclamations and edictes
the decrees of the canons cōcerning the Popes Primacie ; and gaue not to him first that
auctoritie, as the aduersaries doo vntruly
reporte, were Iustinian and *Phocas* the Emperours. The wordes of Iustinianes edicte be
these. *Sancimus secundum canonum definitio-*
nes, sanctissimum senioris Romæ Papam, primū
esse omnium sacerdotū. We ordeine according
to the determinations of the canons, that the
most holy Pope of the elder Rome, be for-
mest and chiefe of all priestes,

The 3.
proufe,
Edictes of
Empe-
rours.

In authēr.
de Ecclesi-
ast. Tit.

About three score and ten yeres after Iustinian, *Phocas* the Emperour in the tyme of
Bonifacius, to represse the arrogancie of the
bishop of Constantinople, as *Paulus Diaco-*
nus writeth, who vainely, and as Gregorie sayeth, contrary to our lordes teachinges, and
the decrees of the canons, and for that wickedly ; tooke vpon him the name of the vniuersall or œcumenicall bishop, and wrote
him selfe chiefe of all bishops : made the like
decree and ordināce, that the holy See of the
Romaine and Apostolike church shuld be
holden for the head of all churches.

Lib. 3. hi-
storiæ lon-
gobardicæ
cap. 36.

Of the doctours what shall I say ? vetely
this matter is so often and so cōmonly reported by thē, that their sayinges laide together
would scantly be cōprised within a great volume. The recitall of a fewe shall here gēue
a taste

The 4.
proufe, do-
ctours.

O 2   a taste

a taste as it were, of the whole, and so suffise.

Lib.3,c.3. *Ireneus* hauing much praised the church of Rome, at length vttereth these wordes, by which the souerainetie therof is confessed. *Ad hanc Ecclesiam propter potentiorem principalitatem, necesse est omnem conuenire ecclesiam, hoc est, eos qui vndique sunt fideles.* To this church (of Rome) it is necessary, all the church, that is to say, all that be faithfull any where, to repaire and come together, for the mightier principalitie of the same, that is to witte, for that it is of greater power and auctoritie, then other churches, and the principallest of all. Androw folowed our Sauiour before that Peter dyd, *& tamen primatum non accepit Andreas, sed Petrus:* and yet Androw receiued not the Primacie, but Peter, sayeth In 1. Corinth 12. S. Ambrose. In the epistle of *Athanasius* and the bishops of Egipte to *Liberius* the Pope, in which they sue for helpe against the oppressiõs of the Arianes : we fynde these wordes. *Huius rei gratia vniuersalis vobis à Christo Iesu cõmissa est ecclesia etc.* Euen for this cause the vniuersall church hath ben committed to you of Christ Iesus, that you shuld trauaile for all, and not be negligent to helpe euery one, for whyles the stronge man being armed Luc.11. kepeth his house, all thinges that he possesseth, are in peace.

De Trinita.lib.6. *Hilarius* speaking much to th'extolling of Peter and his successour in that See, sayeth.

Supremi-

Supereminentem beatæ fidei suæ eonfessione locum promeruit: that for the confession of his blessed faith, he deserued a place of preeminence aboue all other. S. Ambros confessing himselfe to beleue, that the largenesse of the Romaine Empire was by Gods prouidence prepared, that the gospell might haue his course, and be spredde abrode the better, sayeth thus of Rome: *Quæ tamen per Apostolici sacerdotij principatum, amplior facta est arce religionis, quàm solio potestatis.* Which for all that, hath ben aduaunced more by the chieftie of the Apostolike priesthod in the tower of Religion, then in the throne of temporall power.

Matt.16.

De vocatione gentium lib.2. cap.6.

Saint Augustine in his 162. epistle, sayeth: *In Ecclesia Romana semper apostolicæ cathedræ viguit principatus.* The primacie or principalitie of the Apostolike chaier, hath euermore ben in force in the Romaine church. The same saint Augustine speaking to *Bonifacius* Bishop of Rome, this care (sayeth he complaining of the Pelagians) is common to vs all, that haue the office of a bishop, albe it therein, thou thy selfe hast the preeminence ouer all, being on the toppe of the pastorall watchetower. In an other place he hath these wordes: *Cæterum magis vereri debeo, ne in Petrum contumeliosus existam. Quis enim nescit, illum Apostolatus principatum, cuilibet episcopatui præferendum?* But I ought rather to be afraied,

Lib.1.c8. tra 1.epistolas Pelagianorum ad Bonifaciū cap.1. Quamuis ipse in eo preeminenas celsiore fastigio spe culæ pasto ralis. Lib.2.de baptismo, cōtra Donatistas.

afraied, least I be reprocheful towarde Peter.
For who is he that knoweth not, that that
principalitie of Apostleship, is to be preferred before any bishoprike that is?

An other most euident place he hath in his
booke, *De vtilitate credendi, ad Honoratum.*

Cum tantum auxiliū Dei etc. Whereas (sayeth
he) we see so great helpe of God, so great profite and fruite, shall we stáde in doubte, whether we may hide our selues in the lappe of
that church, which (though heretikes barke
at it in vaine rownde about, códemned part-
Culmen ly by the iudgement of the people them sel-
auctorita ues, partly by the sadnes of Councelles, and
tis obti-
nuit. partly by the maiestie of miracles euen to the
Cui pri- confession of mankynde) from the Aposto-
mas dare like See by successions of bishops, hath ob-
nolle, vel teined the toppe or highest degree of aucto-
summæ
profecto ritie? to which church, if we will not geue
impietatis and graunt the Primacie, soothly it is a point
est, vel prę- either of most high wickednes, or of hedlóg
cipitis ar-
rogantiæ. arrogancie.
Cótra Lu- The notable saying of S. Hierome may not
ciferianos. be let passe. *Ecclesiæ salus à summi sacerdotis
dignitate pendet. Cui si non exors quædam & ab
omnibus eminens detur potestas, tot in ecclesijs
efficientur schismata, quot sacerdotes.* The saftie
of the church hangeth of the worship of the
high Priest (he meaneth the Pope Peters suc-
ceTour) to whó if there be not geué a power
peerelesse and surmonting al others in the
churches

churches we shall haue so many schismes, as there be priestes.

There is an epistle of *Theodoritus* bishop of *Cyrus* extant in greke, written to *Leo* bishop of Rome. Wherein we finde a worthy witnes of the Primacie of the See Apostolike. His wordes may thus be englished. If Paul (sayeth he) the preacher of truth, and trumpet of the holy ghoste, ranne to Peter, to bring from him a determination and declaration, for them who at Antioche were in argument and contention cōcerning lyuing after Moyses lawe, much more wee, who are but small and vile, shall runne vnto your throne Apostolike, that of you we may haue salue for the sores of the churches (there folowe these wordes. διὰ πάντα γὰρ ὑμῖν τὸ πρωτεύειν ἁρμόττει, id est, *per omnia enim vobis cōuenit primas tenere*, that is, to saye: For in all thinges (perteining to faith or religion (so he meaneth) it is meete, that you haue the chiefe dooinges, or that you haue the Primacie. For your high seate or throne is endewed with many prerogatiues and priuileges.

Now let vs see, whether this chiefe auctoritie may be fownde necessary by reason. That a multitude, which is in it selfe one, can not continewe one, onlesse it be conteined and holden in by one, bothe learned philosophers haue declared, and the common nature of thinges teacheth. For euery multitude

πολλοῖς
γὰρ ὁ ὑμε
τέρες θρό
νος κοσμεῖ
ται πλεο-
νεκτήμα-
σι

The 5,
proufe,
Reason.

4   of their

their owne nature goeth a sunder in to many: and from an other it cometh, that it is one, and that it contineweth one. And that whereof it is one, and is kepte in vnion or onenesse, it is necessary that it be one, elles that selfe also shall nede the helpe of an other, that it bee one. For which cause that saying of Homere was alleaged by Aristotle as most notable, *It is not good to haue many rulers, let one be ruler.* Whereby is meant, that pluralitie of soueraine rulers, is not fitte to conteine and kepe vnitie of a multitude of subiectes. Therefore sith that the churche of Christ is one, (for as there is one faith, one baptisme, one calling, so there is one churche, yea all we are one body, and membres one of an other, as S. Paul sayeth: and in our Crede we all professe to beleue one holy Catholike and Apostolike churche) therefore I saye, it hath nede of one prince and ruler, to be kepte ād holdē in. If it be other wise, vnitie must nedes forth with be sparkled and brokē a sunder. And therefore it behoued that the rule and gouernemēt of the churche, shuld be comitted to one.

And whereas these Gospellers saye, that Christ is the gouernour of the churches, and that he being one kepeth the churche in vnitie, we answere, that, although the churche be first and principally gouerned by Christ, as all other thinges are, yet gods high goodnes hath so ordeined, as eche thing may be prouided

ἐκ ἀγαθὸν πολυκοιρανίη, εἷς κοίρανος ἔϛω.

uided for, according to his owne condition
and nature. Therefore whereas mankynde
dependeth most of sense, and receiueth all
learning and institution of sensible thinges,
therefor it hath nede of a man to be a gouernour and ruler, whom it maye perceiue by
outward sense. And euen so the Sacrametes,
by which the grace of God is geuen vnto vs,
in consideration of mannes nature being so
made of God, as it is, are ordeined in thinges
sensible. Therefor it was behoofull this gouernement of the churche to be committed
to one man, which at the first was Peter, and
afterward eche successour of Peter for his
tyme, as is a fore declared. Neither can this
one man haue this power of any consent or
companie of men, but it is necessary he haue
it of God. For to ordeine and appointe the
vicare of Christ, it perteineth to none other,
then to Christ . For where as the churche,
and all that is of the chuch, is Christes, as
well for other causes, as specially for that we
are bought with a great price, euen with his
bloude as S.Paul sayeth: how can it perteine 1.Cor.3.
to any other then to him, to institute and appoint to him selfe a vicare, that is, one to doe
his steede? Wherefore to conclude, excepte
we would wickedly graunt, that gods prouidence hath lacked or doth lacke to his churche, for loue of which he hath geué his onely begotten sonne, and which he hath promi-
O 5   sed

fed neuer to forgete, fo as the woman cã not
forgete the chylde fhe bare in her wombe:
Reafon may fone enduce vs to beleue, that
to one man, one bifhop, the chiefe and higheft of all bifhops, the fucceffour of Peter,
the rule and gouernement of the church by
God hath ben deferred. For elles if God had
ordeyned, that in the church fhuld be fundry
heades and rulers, and none conftituted to
be ouer other, but all of equall power, ech
one among their people: then he fhuld feme
to haue fet vp fo many churches, as he hath
appointed gouernours. And fo he fhall appeare to haue brought in among his faithful
people that vnruly confufion, the deftructiõ
of all common weales, fo much abhorred of
princes, which the grekes call *Anarchian*,
which is a ftate for lacke of order in gouernours, without any gouernement at all.
Which thing, fith that the wife and politike
men of this worlde doo fhunne and deteft in
the gouernement of thefe earthly kingdo-
mes, as moft pernicioufe and hurtfull, to attribute to the high wifdome of God, and to
our lord Chrift, who is the auctour of the
moft ordinate difpofition of all thinges in
earth and in heauen: it were heynous and
prophane impietie. Wherefore if the ftate
of a kingdome can not continew fafe, onleffe
one haue power to rule, how fhall not the
church fpredde fo farre abroade be in dãger
of great

of great diforders, corruption, and vtter de-
ftruction, if, as occafion fhalbe geuen, among
fo great ftrifes and debates of mē, among fo
many fyerbrandes of difcord toffed to and
fro by the deuils, enemies of vnitie: there be
not one head and ruler, of all to be cōfulted,
of all to be hearde, of all to be folowed and
obeied? If ftrife and contention be ftirred a-
bout matters of faith, if controuerfie happē
to rife about the fenfe of the fcriptures, fhall
it not be neceffary, there be one fupreme
iudge, to whofe fentence the parties may ftā-
de? If nede require (as it hath ben oftē fene)
that generall councelles be kepte, how can
the bifhops, to whom that matter belongeth
be brought together, but by cōmaundemēt
of one head gouernour, whō they owe their
obediéce vnto? For elles being fummoned
perhappes they will not come. Finally how
fhall the contumacie, and pertinacie of mif-
cheuous pfones be repreffed, fpecially if the
bifhops be at diffefion with in thē felues: if
there be not a fupreme power, who towardes
fome may vfe the rodde, towardes other fome the fpirite of lenitie, with fuch difcrete
téperamét, as malice be váquifhed, right defended, and cōcorde procured, leaft, if the
fmall fparkes of ftrife be not quéched by auctoritie at the beginnīg, at légth a great flame
of fchifmes and herefies flafhe abrode, to the
great danger of a multitude? Therefore as
there

there is one body of Christ, one flocke, one church, euen so is there one head of that his mysticall body, one shepeherd and one chiefe seruant made steward, ouerseer, and ruler ouer Christes housholde in his absence, vntil his comming againe.

The 6. proufe, practise of the churche, syxfolde.

But here perhappes some wil saie, it cā not appeare by the euente of thinges and practise of the church, that the Pope had this supreme power and auctoritie ouer all bishops, and ouer all Christes flocke in matters touching faith, and in causes ecclesiasticall. Verely who so euer peruseth the ecclesiasticall stories, and vieweth the state of the church of all tymes and ages, can not but cōfesse this to be most euident. And here I might alleage first, certaine placēs of the newe testament, declaring that Peter practised this preeminēce among the disciples at the beginning, and that they yelded the same, as of right apperteining vnto him. As whem he first and onely moued them to choose one in the stede of Iudas, and demeaned him selfe, as the chiefe auctour of all that was done therein: whē he made answere for all, at what time they were gased and wondered at, and of some mockte, as being dronken with newe wine: for that in the fiftith day thei spake with tonges of so ma ny nations: when he vsed that dredfull seueritie in punishing the falshed, and hypocrisiē of *Ananias* and *Saphira* his wife: when variance

Act.1.

Act.2.

Act.5.

riance being risen about the obseruation of **Act.15.**
certaine pointes of Moyses lawe, he as chiefe and head of the rest, saide his mynde before all others. Among many other places lefte
out for breuitie, that is not of least weight,
that Paul being retourned to Damasco out
of *Arabia*, after three yeres wēt to Ierusalem **Galat.1.**
to see Peter, and abode with him fiftē dayes.

But because our aduersaries doo wreath
and wreste the scriptures (be they neuer so
plaine)by theire priuate and straunge cōstru-
ctions, to an vnderstanding quite contrary to
the sense of the catholike church. I will referre the reader for further proufe of this matter, to the stories bearing faithfull witnes of
the whole state and condition of the church
in all ages. In which stories, the practise of
the church is plainely reported to haue bēn
such, as thereby the Primacie of Peters successour may seeme to all men sufficiently declared. For perusing the ecclesiasticall stories
with writinges of the fathers, besyde many
other thinges perteinīg hereto, we finde these practises for declaration of this speciall auctoritie and power. First, that bishops of eue- **1**
ry nation haue made their appeale in their
weighty affaires to the Pope, and alwayes haue sued to the See Apostolike, as well for succour and helpe against violence, iniuries and
oppressiōs, as for redresse of other disorders.
Also, that the malice of wicked persons hath **2**
ben

ben repressed and chastised by that auctorf-
tie with excommunication, eiection, and ex-
pulsion out of their dignities and romes, and
3 by other censures of the church. Furthermore, that the ordinations and elections of
bishops of all prouinces, haue ben confir-
4 med by the Pope. Beside this, that the approuing and disalowing of councelles haue per-
5 teined to him. Item, that bishops wrongfully
condemned and depriued by councelles, by
6 him haue ben assoiled and restored to their
churches againe. Lastly, that bishops and patriarkes after longe strifes and contentions,
haue at length vpon better aduise ben reco-
1 ciled vnto him againe.

Appella-
tions to
the Pope.

First, for the appellation of bishops to the
See Apostolike, beside many other, we haue
the knowen examples of *Athanasius* that
worthy bishop of *Alexandria*, and lighte of
the worlde: who hauing susteined great and
sundry wronges at the Arianes, appealed first
to *Iulius* the Pope, and after his death, to *Felix*: of Chrisostome, who appealed to *Innocentius* against the violence of *Theophilus*: of
Theodoritus, who appealed to *Leo*. Neither
made bishops onely their appeale to the Pope by their delegates, but also in certaine cases, being cited, appeared before him in their
owne persons. Which is plainely gathered of
Theodoritus his ecclesiasticall storye, who writeth thus. *Eusebius* bishop of *Nicomedia* (who
was

Hist. Tri-
part.
Lib.4.c.6.

was the chiefe pillour of the Arianes) and
they that ioyned with him in that factiō, fal-
sly accused *Athanasius* to *Iulius* the B. of Rome. *Iulius* folowing the ecclesiasticall rule,
commaunded them to come to Rome, and
caused the reuerent *Athanasius* to be cited to
iudgement, *regulariter*, after the order of the
canons. He came. The false accusers wēt not
to Rome, knowing righte well that theire
forged lye might easely be deprehended.

In the cause and defence of Ihō Chrysostome, these bishops came from Constantinople to *Innocentius* the Pope, *Pansophus* B. of
Pisidia, *Pappus* of *Syria*, *Demetrius* of the second *Galatia*, and *Eugenius* of *Phrygia*. These
were suters for Chrysostome. He him selfe
treated his matter with *Innocentius* by writing. In his epistle among other thinges he
writeth thus: Least this outragious cōfusion
runne ouer all and beare rule euery where,
write (I pray you) and determine by your auctoritie, such wicked actes done in our absen
ce, and when we withdrewe not our selues
from iudgemēt, to be of no force, as by their
re owne nature truly they be voied and ve-
terly none. Furthermore who haue committed these euilles, put you them vnder the
censure of the church. And as for vs, sith that
we are innocent, neither conuicte, neither
sownde in any defaulte, nor proued gyltie of
any crime : geue commandement, that we
be resto-

Vide re-
scriptum
Iulij Papæ
contra oriē
tales pro
Athanasio
& cæteris.

be restored to our churches agayne, that we
may enioye the accustomed charitie and peace with our brethren. *Innocentius* after that
he vnderstoode the whole matter, pronoun
ced and decreed the iudgement of *Theophilus*, that was againſt Chryſoſtome, to be
voyed, and of no force. This whole tragedie
is at large ſet forth by *Palladius* B. of *Heleno-
polis, in vita Ioannis Chryſoſtomi*, who lyued at
that tyme. By this appeale of Chryſoſtome,
and by the whole handeling of the matter,
and ſpecially by the purporte of his epiſtle
to *Innocentius*, the ſuperioritie of the Pope,
is euidently acknowleged. And ſo is it plaine
ly confeſſed by *Athanaſius* and the biſhops of
Egipte, *Thebais* and *Libya* aſſembled in coun
cell at *Alexandria* by theſe wordes of their
epiſtle to *Felix*. *Veſtrum eſt enim nobis manum
porrigere, &c*. It is your parte (ſaie they) to
ſtretche forth your helping hande vnto vs,
becauſe we are cōmitted vnto you. It is your
parte to defende vs and deliuer vs, it is our
parte to ſeeke helpe of you and to obey your
commaundementes. And a litle after. For we
knowe that you beare the cure and charge
of the vniuerſall church, and ſpecially of biſhops, who in reſpecte of their cōtemplation
and ſpeculation are called the eyes of our
Lord, as alwaies the prelates of your See, firſt
the Apoſtles, then theire ſucceſſours, haue
done.

Theodo-

Theodoritus that learned B. of *Cyrus* besyde the epistle he wrote to *Leo* for succour and helpe in his troubles, in an other, that he wrote to *Renaius* a priest neare about *Leo*, sayeth thus. *Spoliærüt me sacerdotio, &c.* They haue violently robbed me of my bishoprike, they haue caste me foorth of the cities, neither hauing reuerenced myne age spente in religion, nor my hoare heares. Wherefore I beseche thee, that thou persuade the most holy Archebishop (he meaneth *Leo*) to vse his Apostolike auctoritie, and to commaunde vs to come vnto your councell or consistorie. For this holy See holdeth the rudther, and hath the gouernemēt of the churches of the whole worlde, partly for other respectes, but specially, for that it hath euermore continewed cleare from stintche of heresie, and that none euer sate in it, who was of contrary opinion, but rather hath euer kepte the Apostolike grace vndefyled. In which wordes of *Theodoritus* this is chiefly to be marked, that the holy See of Rome (as he sayeth) hath the gouernement of the churches of all the worlde most for this cause, that it was neuer infected with heresie, as all other churches fownded by the Apostles were.

For which cause that See hath euer hitherto of all christen nations and now also ought to be hearde and obeyed in all pointes of faith. For that *See* though it hath failed sometymes

P

metymes in charitie, and hath ben in case as it might truly saye the wordes of the gospell spoken by the foolishe virgins, *our lampes, be without lighte:* yet it neuer failed in faith, as *Theodoritus* witnesseth, and S. Agustine affirmeth the same. Which speciall grace and singulare priuiledge, is to be imputed vnto the prayer of Christ, by which he obteined of God for Peter and his successours, that their faith shuld not fayle. Therfore the euill lyfe of the bishops of Rome ought not to withdrawe vs from beleuing and folowing the doctrine preached and taughte in the holy churche of Rome.

For better credite hereof, that is earnestly to be considered, which S. Augustine writeth *epistola* 165. where, after that he hath rehearsed in order all the Popes that succeded Peter, euen to him that was Pope in his tyme, he sayeth thus. *In illum ordinem episcoporum etc.* In to that rewe of bishops, that reacheth from Peter him selfe to *Anastasius*, which now sitteth in the same chaier, if any traitour or deliuerer the latine is *traditor* (by which worde is meant such a one as in tyme of persecution for feare had deliuered to the paynimes the bookes of holy Scripture) had crepte in, it shuld nothing hurte the church, and the innocent Christen folke, ouer whom our lord hauing prouidence, sayeth of euill rulers: *what they saye vnto you, doo ye, but what*

Math.25.

Euill lyfe of the B. of Rome: ought not to seuer vs frō the faith of the churche of Rome.

what they doo, doo ye not, for they saye, and Matth. 23. *doo not*: to the intent the hope of a faithfull person may be certaine, and such, as being set not in mã, but in our lord, be neuer scattered abroade with tempest of wicked schisme. And in his 166. epistle, (he sayeth) our heauenly Maister hath so farre forewarned vs to beware of all euill of dissension, that he assured the people also of euill rulers, that for their sakes the Seate of holosom doctrine shuld not be forsaken, in which Seate, euen the very euill mẽ be compelled to saye good thinges. For the thinges which they saye, be not theires, but Gods, who in the Seate of vnitie, hath put the doctrine of veritie.

By this we are plainely taught, that albeit the successours of Peter Christes vicares in earth be fownde blameworthy for euill lyfe, yet we ought not to dissente from them in doctrine, nor seuer cur selues from them in faith. For as much as notwithstanding they be euill, by Gods prouidence for the suertie of his people, they be compelled to saye the thinges that be good, and to teache the truth, the thiges they speake not being theirs but Gods, who hath put the doctrine of veritie in the Seate or chaier of vnitie. Which singulare grace cometh specially to the See of Peter, either of the force of Christes prayer, as is sayde before, or in respecte of place

and

and dignitie, which the bishops of that See holde for Christ, as Balaā could be broughte by no meanes to curse that people, whō God would to be blessed. And Caiphas also prophecied, because he was high bishop of that yere, and prophecied truly, beīg a mā otherwise most wicked. And therfore the euill doinges of bishops of Rome make no argument of discrediting their doctrine. To this purpose the example of Gregorie Nazianzene may very fittely be applied, of the golden, syluerne, and leadden seale. As touching the valewe of metalles, golde and syluer are better, but for the goodnes of the seale, as wel doth leadde imprint a figure in waxe, as syluer or golde. For this cause, that the See of Rome hath neuer ben defyled with stinking heresies, as *Theodoritus* sayeth, and god hath alwaies kepte in that chair of vnitie, the doctrine of veritie, as Augustine writeth : for this cause (I saye) it sitteth at the sterne, and gouerneth the churches of the whole worlde, for this cause bishops haue made their appellations thither, iudgement in doubtes of doctrine, and determinatiō in all controuersies and strifes, hath ben from thence alwayes demaunded.

Now that the B. of Rome had alwayes cure and rule ouer all other bishops, specially of the East (for touching them of the West church it is generally confessed) besyde a hūdred

Num. 23.

Ioan.18.

dred other euident argumentes, this is one very sufficient, that he had in the East to doo his stede, three delegates or vicares, now cōmonly they be named Legates. And this for the commoditie of the bishops there, whose churches were farre distāt from Rome. The one was the bishop of Constantinople, as we finde it mēcioned *in epistola Simplicy ad Acha tium Constantinopolitanum*. The seconde was the bishop of *Alexandria*, as the epistle of *Bonifacius* the secōde to *Eulalius*, recordeth. The third was the bishop of *Thessalonica*, as it is at large declared in the 82.epistle of *Lea ud Anastasium Thessalonicēsem*. By perusing these epistles euery man may see, that al the bishops of Grece, *Asia,Syria,*Egipte, and to be shorte of all the Orient, rendred and dehibited their humble obedience to the B. of Rome, and to his arbitrement referred their doubtes, complaintes and causes, and to him onely made theire appellations.

Of the B. of Rome his punishing of offenders by censures of the church and otherwyse, as by excōmunications, eiectiō, exposition, and enioyning penance for transgressions: we haue more examples, then I thinke good to recite here. They that haue knowledge of the ecclesiasticall stories, may remēber, how *Timotheus* B. of *Alexandria* was excommunicated with Peter his deacō, by *Simplicius* the Pope: *Nestorius* B. of Cōstantino-

ple,

ple, by *Celestinus : Theophilus* B. of *Alexandria* with *Arcadius* the Emperour and *Eudoxia* the Emperesse, by *Innocentius*, for their wicked demeanour toward Chrysostome: How *Dioscorus* B. of *Alexandria* was deposed though the whole seconde Ephesine councell stoode in his defence : how Peter B. of Antioche was not onely put out of his bisho prike, but also of all priestly honour : How *Photius* was put out of the Patriarkeship of Constantinople, into which he was intruded by fauour of *Michaël* the Emperour at the sute of his wicked vnkle, by *Nicolaus* the first.

Lib. 3.
epist. 13.

For proufe of this auctoritie, the epistle of *Cyprian*, which he wrote to *Stephanus* Pope in his tyme against *Martianus* the B. of Arelate in *Gallia*, maketh an euident argument. For that this *Martianus* became a maineteyner of the heresie of *Nouatianus*, and therewith seduced the faithfull people, *Cyprian* hauing intelligence of it by *Faustinus* from Lions, aduertised *Stephanus* of it, and moued him earnestly to directe his letters to the people of Arles, by auctoritie of which *Martianus* shuld be deposed, and an other put in his rome, to th'intent (sayeth he there) the flocke of Christ, which hytherto by him scattered abroade and woonded is contemned, may be gathered together. Which S. Cypriā would not haue written, had the B. of Rome had no suche auctoritie.

For

For the Popes auctoritie concerning cōfirmation of the ordinations and elections of
all bishops, many examples might easely be
alleaged, as the request made to *Iulius* by the
90. Ariane bishops assembled in councell at
Antioche against *Athanasius*, that he would
vouchesafe to ratifie and cōfirme those that
they had chosen in place of *Athanasius, Pau-*
lus, Marcellus and others, whom they had cō-
demned and depriued. Also the earnest sute,
which *Theodosius* the Emperour made to
Leo for confirmation of *Anatolius*, and likewise that *Martianus* the Emperour made to
him, for confirmation of *Proterius* bothe
bishops of *Alexādria*, as it appeareth by their
letters written to *Leo* in theire fauour. And
as for *Anatolius*, *Leo* would not in any wise
order and cōfirme him, onlesse he would first
professe, that be beleued and helde the doctrine, which was conteined in *Leo* his epistle to *Flauianus*, and would further by writing witnesse, that he agreed with *Cyrillus*
and the other catholike fathers against *Ne-*
storius. For this, if nothing elles could be alleaged, the testimonie of holy Gregorie were sufficient to make good credite. Who vnderstanding that *Maximus* was ordered bishop of *Salone* a citie in *Illyrico*, without the
auctoritie and confirmatiō of the See Apostolike, standing in doubte least perhappes
that had ben done by commaundement of

Cōfirma-
tions by
the Pope.

Vide Leo-
nis epist.
13.

P 4   *Mauritius*

Mauritius the Emperour, who did many
other thinges wickedly: thereof writeth to
Cōstantina the Emperesse thus. *Salonitanæ ciuitatis episcopus me ac responsali meo nesciente,
ordinatus est. Et facta est res, quæ sub nullis an-
terioribus principibus euenit.* The bishop of
the citie of *Salona* (sayeth he) is ordeted, neither I, nor my depute made priuye to it. And
herein that thing hath ben done, which neuer happened in the tyme of any princes before our daies. Thus it appeareth, that before a thousand yeres past, bishops had their
ordination and election confirmed by the
See Apostolike.

4
The Po-
pes appro-
uing of
coūcelles.

Li.4.c. 19.

That the bishops of Rome by accustomed
practise of the church, had auctoritie to ap-
proue or disproue councelles, I nede to saye
nothing for proufe of it, seing that the ecclesiasticall rule (as we reade in the Tripartite sto
rie) coniaundeth, that no coūcell be celebrate and kepte without the aduise and auctoritie of the Pope. Verely the coūcelles holdē at
Ariminū, at *Seleucia*, at *Sirmiū*, at *Antiochia*,
and at the seconde tyme at *Ephesus*, for that
they were not summoned nor approued by
the auctoritie of the B of Rome, haue not bē
accōpted for laufull coūcelles: but as well for
that reiected, as also for their hereticall deter
minatiōs. The fathers assēbled in the coūcell
of Nice, sent their epistle to *Siluester* the Pope, beseching hī with his cōsēt to ratifie and
confir-

confirme, what so euer they had ordeined. *Isi-* ^Quas Ro-
dorus witnesseth that the Nicene coūcell had ^mana suf-
set forth rules, the which (sayeth he) the ^firmauit
church of Rome receiued and cōfirmed. The ^Ecclesia. In
secōd general councel holdē at Cōstātinople, ^præfatione
was like wise allowed and approued by *Dama-* ^Niceni cō-
sus specially requested by the fathers of the ^cilij.
same therto. So was the third councell holdē
at *Ephesus*, ratified and cōfirmed by *Celestinus*,
who had there for his vicares or deputes, *Cy-*
rillus the famouse B. of *Alexandria*, and one
Arcadius a bishop out of Italie. As for the fourth councell kepte at Chalcedon, the fathers thereof also in their epistle to *Leo* the
Pope, subscribed with the handes of 44. bishops, made humble requeste vnto him, to
establish, fortifie and allowe, the decrees and
ordinances of the same. This being fownde
true for the fower sirst chiefe councelles, we
nede not to say any thinge of the rest that folowed. But for the suer proufe of all this, that
chiefly is to be alleaged, that *Constantius* the
Arian Emperour made so importune and so
earnest sute to *Liberius* the Pope, tō confirme
the actes of the councell holden at Antioche
by the 90. Ariane bishops, wherein *Athana-*
sius was depriued, and put out of his bishoprike. For he beleued, as *Ammianus Marcel-* Lib. 15.
linus writeth, that what had ben done in that
councell, shuld not stande and take effecte,
onlesse it had ben approued and confirmed

by the auctoritie of the B. of Rome, which he termeth the eternall citie.

5
Absolutiōs from the Pope.

Now what auctoritie the bishops of Rome haue euer had and exercised in the assoiling of bishops vniustly cōdēned, and in restoring of them againe to their churches, of which they were wrongfully thruste out by heretikes, or other disorder: it is a thing so well knowen of all that reade the stories, in which the auncient state of the church is described, that I nede not but rehearse the names onely. *Athanasius* of *Alexandria*, and *Paulus* of Constantinople, depriued and thrust out of their bishoprikes by the violence of the Arianes assisted with the Emperour *Constantius*, appealed to Rome, to *Iulius* the Pope and bishop there, and by his auctoritie were restored to their romer againe. So *Leo* assoiled *Flauianus* the B. of Constantinople, excommunicated by *Dioscorus*. So *Nicolaus* the first restored *Ignatius* to the see of Constantinople, though *Michael* the Emperour wroughte all that he could against it. Many other bishops haue ben in all ages assoiled and restored to their churches by the auctoritie of the See Apostolike, who haue ben without deserte excommunicated, depriued, and put from all their dignities. But to haue rehearsed these fewe it may suffise.

6
Reconcilations to the Pope.

Concerning the reconciliation of the prelates of the church both bishops and patriarkes to

to the B. of Rome, wherby his primacie is acknowleged and confeſſed, I nede not ſay
much, the matter being ſo euidẽt. After that
the whole churches of *Aphrica* had continewed in ſchiſme; and withdrawen them ſelues
from the obedience of the See Apoſtolike,
through the entiſement of *Aurelius* archebiſhop of *Carthago*, for the ſpace of one hundred yeres, during which tyme by Gods pu-
niſhment they came in to captiuitie of the
Barbarous and cruell Vandales, who were
Arians at the length, when it pleaſed God of
his goodnes to haue pitie on his people of
that prouince, ſending thẽ *Belliſarius* the valiant capitaine, that vãquiſhed and deſtroyed
the Vãdales, and likewyſe *Eulalius* that godly
archebiſhop of *Carthago*, that brought the
churches home againe, and ioyned the diuided mẽbres vnto the whole body the catholike church: A publike inſtrument cõteining
the forme of their repentance and of their
humble ſubmiſſion, was offered and exhibited ſolemly to *Bonifacius* the ſecond thẽ Pope by *Eulalius* in the name of that whole pro
uince, which was ioyfully receiued, and he
thereupon forthwith reconciled. Of this reconciliation and reſtoring of the Affricane
churches to the catholike church, the myſticall body of Chriſt, *Bonifacius* writeth his
lettres to *Eulalius* biſhop of *Theſſalonica*,
requiring him with the churches there
about

about to geue almighty God thankes for it.

But here if I would shewe what bishops diuiding them selues through heresie, schisme,
or other enormitie, from the obedience of
the See of Rome, haue vpon better aduise
submitted them selues to the same againe,
and thereupon haue ben reconciled: I had a
large field to walke in. As inferiour bishops
of sundry prouinces haue done it, so haue
the great patriarkes done likewise. Among
them that to satisfie the malicioufe mynde
of *Eudoxia* the Emperesse, practisetd heir wic
ked cospiracie against Chrysostome, through
which he was deposed and caried awaye in
to banishment, *Alexander* B. of Antioche
and primate of the Orient, was one: who at
length strooken with repentance, for that he
had bé both a consenter and a promotour of
that wicked acte, submitted him selfe humbly to Innocentius the Pope, and by all meanes sought to be assoiled and reconciled. And
therfore sent his legates to Rome, to exhibite to *Innocentius* a solemne instrument of his
repentance and lowly submiffion, and to accepte what shuld be enioyned. By which
his humblenes *Innocentius* moued, graunted
to his petitions, receiued him in to the lappe
of the catholike church againe, and thus was
he reconciled. Sundry the like reconciliati-
ons of the patriarkes of *Alexandria* and Ie-
rusalé to the See of Rome in like cases might
easely

eafely be recited, which for auoiding of te-
dioufneffe I paffe ouer, as likewife of the pa-
triatkes of Conftantinople, which as we reade in aunciét ftories, haue forfaké the church
of Rome twelue tymes, and haue ben recon-
cilied to the fame againe.

Thus hauing declared the fupreme auctoritie and primacie of the pope by the cómon
practife of the churche I nede not to fhewe
further, how in all queftiós, doubtes, and có-
trouerfies touching faith and religió, the See
of Rome hath alwayes ben cófulted, how the
decifió of all doubtefull cafes hath ben referred to the iudgement of that See, and to be
fhorte, how all the worlde hath euer fetched
light from thence. For the proufe whereof
becaufe it can not be here declared briefly, I
remitte the learned reader to the ecclefiafti-
call ftoryes, where he fhal fynde this matter
amply treated.

Now for a briefe anfwere to M. Iuell, who
denieth that within fix hundred yeres after
Chrift, the bifhop of Rome was euer called
an vniuerfall bifhop, or the head of the vniuerfall church, and maketh him felfe very
fuer of it: Although it be a childifh thing to
fticke at the name any thing is called by, the
thing by the name fignified being fufficiétly
proued: yet to th'intent good folke may vnderftand, that al is not truth of the olde gofpell, which our newe gofpellers either affirme or

The Pope aboue a thousand yeres sithens called vniuersall bishop and head of the vniuersall churche. actione.3.

me or denie : I will bring good and sufficient witnes, that the B. of Rome was, then called both vniuersall bishop, or œcumenicall patriarke, which is one, to witte, bishop or principall father of the whole world, and also head of the church . *Leo* that worthy B. of Rome, was called the vniuersall Bishop and vniuersall patriarke, of syx hundred and thirty fathers assembled together from all partes of the world in generall councell at Chalcedon. Which is both expressed in that councel, and also clearly affirmed by S. Gregory in three sundry epistles , to *Mauritius* the Emperour, to *Eulogius* Patriarke of *Alexandria*, and to *Anastasius* Patriarke of Antioche. Thus that name was deferred vnto the Pope by the fathers of that great coucell, which by them had not ben done, had it ben vnlawfull. In very dede neither *Leo* him selfe , nor any other his successour euer called or wrote him selfe by that name , as S. Gregorie sayeth, much lesse presumed they to take it vnto thé. But rather vsed the name of humilitie, calling them selues ech one *Seruum seruorum Dei*, the seruant of the seruantes of God . Yet sundry holy martyrs bishops of Rome vsed to calle them selues bishops of the vniuersall church, which in effecte is the same , as the fathers of Chalcedon vnderstoode. So did *Sixtus* in the tyme of *Adrianus* the Emperour in his epistle to the bishops of all the world . So dyd
Victor

Victor writing to *Theophilus* of *Alexandria*. So dyd *Pontianus* writing to all that beleued in Chrift before 1300.yeres paft. So dyd *Stephanus* in his epiftle to all bifhops of all prouinces in the tyme of S.Cyprian.And all thefe were before Conftantine the great,and before the councell of Nice, which times our aduerfaries acknowledge and confeffe to haue ben without corruption. The fame title was vfed likewife after the Nicene councell, by Marke in his anfwer to *Athanafius* and all the bifhops of Egypte,by *Felix*,by *Leo*,and by diuerfe others, before the firft fix hundred yeres after Chrift were expired. Neither did the bifhops of Rome vfe this title and name onely them felues to theire owne aduaúncemét,as the aduerfaries of the churche charge them,but they were honoured therewith alfo by others:as namely *Innocétius* by the fathers affébled in councell at *Carthago*, and *Marcus* by *Athanafius* and the bifhops of Egypte.

Concerning the other name (Head of the church) I meruell not a litle, that M. Iuell denyeth, that the bifhop of Rome was then fo called. Either he doth contrary to his owne knowledge , wherin he muft nedes be condemned in his owne iudgement and of his owne confcience , or he is not fo well learned , as of that fyde he is thought to bee. For who fo euer traueileth in the reading of the auncient fathers,findeth that name

Head of the churche.

me

me almost euery where attributed to Peter

Peter and consequētly the Pope Peters successour called head of the church, both in termes equiualēt, and also expressely.
Matth.10.

the first B. of Rome, and consequently to the successour of Peter, that name (I saie) either in termes equiualent, or expressely. First, the scripture calleth Peter *primum*, the first amōg the Apostles. *The names of the twelue Apostles* (sayeth Matthew) *are these. Primus Simon, qui dicitur Petrus. First Simon, who is called Peter*. And yet was not Peter first called of Christ, but his brother Androwe before him as is before saide. *Dionysius* that auncient writer calleth Peter sometyme, *supremum decus*, the highest honour, for that he was most honorable of all the Apostles, sometime, *summum*, sometime, *verticalem*, the chiefest and the highest Apostle. Origen vpon the beginning of Iohn sayeth: Let no man thinke, that we set Iohn before Peter. Who may so doo? for who shuld be higher of the Apostles then he, who is, and is called the toppe of them? Cyprian calleth the church of Rome, in consideration of that bishops supreme auctoritie, *Ecclesiam principalem, vnde vnitas sacerdotalis exorta est*. The principall or chiefe church, from whence the vnitie of priestes is spronge. *Eusebius Cæsariensis* speaking of Peter sent to Rome by Gods prouidence, to vanquish *Simon Magus*, calleth him *potētissimum & maximum Apostolorum, & reliquorum omnium principem*: the mightiest of power and greatest of the Apostles, and prince af all the reste.

De diuinis nomini bus.c.3.

Lib.1. epistola 3.

hist.eccles. lib.2. cap.14.

teſte. Auguſtine commonly calleth Peter, *pri-* τὸν καρτὶ
mum Apoſtolorum , firſt or chiefe of the Apo- ἐὸν καὶ
ſtles. Hierome, Ambroſe, *Leo*, and other do- μέγαν
ctours, Prince of the Apoſtles. Chryſoſtome τῶν ἀκτ̄
vpon the place of Iohn *cap. 21. ſequereme,* fo- σόλων,
lowe me , among other thinges ſayeth thus. λοι πῶν
If any would demaunde of me , how Iames ἁπάντων
tooke the ſee of Ieruſalem, that is to ſaie, how πϱούγο-
he became biſhop there : I would anſwere, ἐ θ.
that this (he meaneth Peter) Maiſter of the Homil 87.
whole worlde , made him gouernour there.
And in an other place bringing in that God In Matth.
ſaide to Ieremie, *I haue ſet thee like an yron pil-* homil. 55.
lour, and like a braſen wall: But the father (ſa- Iere m.1.
yeth he) made him ouer one natiõ, but Chriſt
made this man (meaning Peter) ruler ouer
the whole world. etc.

And leaſt theſe places ſhuld ſeme to attribute this ſupreme auctoritie to Peter onely,
and not alſo to his ſucceſſours : it is to be remembred, that *Ireneus* and Cyprian acknowledge and call the churche of Rome , chiefe and principall . And *Theodoritus* in an
epiſtle to *Leo*, calleth the ſame in conſiderāti- τῆς οἰκ̄.
on of the biſhop of that See his primacie, *or-* μένης πϱο
bi terrarum præſidentem , preſident or bearing καθημέ-
rule ouer the worlde. Ambroſe vpon that ᵐ̄.
place of Paul, 1. *Timoth. 3.* where the church
is called *the pillour, and ſtaie of the truth,* ſaieth
thus. *Cum totus mũdus Dei ſit, eccleſia tamẽ do-*
mus eius dicitur, cuius hodie rector eſt Damaſus.

Q.   Where

Where as the whole world is Gods, yet the churche is called his howse, the ruler whereof at these daies is *Damasus*.

I would not weery and trouble the reader with such a number of allegations, were not that M. Iuell beareth the world in hande, we haue not one sentence nor clause for vs, to proue eitheir this, or any other of all his Articles.

But perhappes some one will replye and saye, yet I heare not the B. of Rome called *Head of the vniuersall churche*, What forceth it, whether that very terme be founde in any auncient writer or no? Other termes of the same vertue and power be oftentymes founde. Is it not one to saie, *Head of the vniuersall churche*, ād to saie ruler of Gods house, which Ambrose sayeth? whereof this argument may be made. The church, yea the vniuersall church is the house of God: but *Damasus* B. of Rome is ruler of the house of God, after Ambrose: *Ergo Damasus* is ruler of the vniuersal church, and by like right and title is the Pope, who is B. of Rome now also, ruler of the same. What other is it to call the church of Rome the principall churche, respecte had to the bishop there, and not otherwise (wherein a figure of speach is vsed) as *Iræneus* and Cyprian doo, and president or set in auctoritie ouer the whole world, as Leo doth : then to call the bishop of Rome, *Heade of the vniuersall*

vniuersall church? what meaneth Chrysostome calling Peter *totius orbis magistrum*, the
Maister and teacher of all the worlde, and
saying in an other place, that Christ made
Peter not ruler ouer one natiō, as the father
made Ieremie ouer the Iewes, but ouer the
whole worlde? what other (I saie) meaneth
he thereby, then that he is head of the whole
worlde, and therefor of the vniuersal church.

In locum
Ioā.11 ho-
mil 87.ex-
ponens il-
lud, seque
re me.
In Matth.
homil. 55.

But to satisfie these men, and to take awaye
occasion of cauille, I wil alleage a fewe places, where the expresse terme (*Head*) is attributed to Peter the first B. of Rome, and by
like right to his successours, and to the See
Apostolike. Chrysostome speaking of the ver
tue and power of Peter, ād of the stedfastnes
of the church, in the 55. Homilie vpon Ma-
thewe, hath these wordes amōg other. *Cuius
Pastor & caput, homo piscator, atque ignobilis
&c.* By which wordes he affirmeth, that the
pastour and head of the church, being but a
fisher, a mā, and one of base parétage, passeth
in firmnes the nature of the diamant. Againe
in an homilie of the praises of Paul, he sayeth
thus. Neither was this man onely such a one,
but he also which was the head of the Apostles, who oftentymes sayde, he was ready to
bestowe his life for Christ, and yet was full
sore afrayed of death. If he were head of the
Apostles, then was he head of the inferiour
people, and so *Head of the vniuersall churche.*

Peter and
his succes-
sour called
head of the
churche,
expressely

Hierome

Hierome writing aginst Iouinian , *sayeth, propterea inter duodecim vnus eligitur, vt capite constituto schismatis tollatur occasio* . For that cause amóg the twelue on is specially chosen out , that the Head being ordeined , occasion of schisme may be taken awaye . Whereby it appeareth that Peter was constituted head for auoiding of diuision and schisme . Now the danger of the inconuenience remaining still, yea more then at that tyme, for the greater multitude of the churche, and for sundry other imperfections : the same remedy must be thought to continewe , onlesse we would saye , that Christ hath lesse care of his church now , that it is so much encreaced , then he had at the beginning , when his flocke was smal . For this cause excepte we denye Gods prouidence toward his church , there is one Head for auoiding of schisme also now , as well as in the Apostles tyme. Which head is the successour of him, that was head by Christes appointement then, the B. of Rome sitting in the seate that Peter sate in.

Cyrillus, sayeth, *Petrus vt princeps, caputque cæterorum, primus exclamauit, tu es Christus filius Dei viui.* Peter as prince and Head of the reste , first cryed out , *thou art Christ the sonne of the liuing God .* Augustine also in a sermó to the people , calleth him head of the church, saying. *Totius corporis membrū in ipso capite cūrat ecclesia, & in ipso vertice componit omnium membrorum*

Serm. 124. de tépore.

membrorum sanitatem. He healeth the member of the whole body, in the Head it selfe of the church, and in the toppe it selfe he ordereth the helth of all the members. And in an other place, *Saluator quãdo pro se & Petro exolui iubet, pro omnibus exoluisse videtur. Qui sicut in saluatore erant omnes causa magisterij, ita post saluatorē in Petro omnes continentur, ipsum enim constituit Caput omnium*. Our sauiour sayeth Augustine, when as he cōmaundeth paiment (for the Emperour) to be made for him selfe and for Peter, he semeth to haue payde for all. Becauseas all were in our sauiour for cause of teaching, so after our sauiour all are conteined in Peter, for he ordeined him Head of all.

Lib. quæst.
vet & no.
testam. q.
75.

Prosper in his booke of verses *de ingratis*, hath thus.

> *Pestem subeuntem prima recidit*
> *Sedes Roma Petri: quæ pastoralis honoris*
> *Facta caput mũdo, quicquid non possidet armis,*
> *Relligione tenet.*

Rome the seat of Peter hath first cutte of this poison as it was rysing, (he meaneth the heresie of the Pelagians) which made head of the honour of pastorship, what so euer it hath not goten by armes, holdeth by religion.

Here haue these men the plaine and expresse terme Head of the rest, Head of the church, Head of all, Head of the world, and therefore Head of the vniuersall church. What will they haue more? Neither here

Q̃ j   CAB

can they saie, that although this auctoritie and title of the Head be geuen to Peter, yet it is not deriued and transferred from him to his successours. For this is manifest, that Christ instituted his churche so, as it shuld continewe to the worldes ende, according to the saying of Esaie the prophete. *Super solium Dauid &c. Vpon the seat of Dauid, and vpon his kingdome, shall Messias sitte to strengthen it, and to establish it in iudgemēt and righteousnes from this daye for euermore.* And thereof it is euident, that he ordeined those, who then were in ministerie, so as their auctoritie and power shuld be deriued vnto their aftercommers for the vtilitie of the church for euer, specially, where as he sayde, *Beholde I am with you all dayes vntill the ende of the worlde.* And therefore as *Victor* writeth in his storie of the persecution of the Vandales, *Eugenius B.* of *Carthago* conuented by *Obadus* a great capitaine of Hunerike king of the Vandales about a councell to be kepte in *Aphrica* for matters of the faith, betwixte the Arians supported by the king, and the catholikes: sayde in this wise. *Si nostram fidem &c.* If the kinges power desyre to knowe our faith, which is one and the true, let hym sende to his frendes. I will write also to my brethren, that my fellowebishops come, who may declare the faith, that is common to you and vs (there he hath these wordes)

Et

Cap. 9.

Matt. vlt.

Lib. 2.

*Et præcipuè ecclesia Romana, quæ Caput est om-
nium ecclesiarum*, and specially the church of
Rome, which is the Head of al the churches.
Naming the church of Rome, he meaneth
the bishop there, or his legates to be sent in
his stede.

In the councell of Chalcedō *actione prima*,
it is sayed of Leo the Pope, that he gouerned
the Apostolike seat, and there the Romaine
See is called *caput omnium ecclesiarum*, Head
of all churches. By report of Iustiniā the Emperour, *Sanctitas episcopi Romani caput est omnium sanctarum ecclesiarū.* The bishop of Rome his holynes is head of all holy churches.
In the epistle of *Athanasius* and the bishops
of Egypte to Marke the Pope for the copies
of the Nicen councell, the See of Rome is
called *Mater & caput omnium ecclesiarū.*The
mother and head of all churches. And in an
other of the bishops of Egypte, *Thebais* and
Libia assembled in a synode at *Alexādria, Felix*
the Pope is by them named, *princeps, doctor,
caputq́, omniū etc.* the chiefe, the teacher, and
the head of all faithfull and right beleuers.

Thus it is proued by good and aunciēt auctorities, that the name and title of the Head
ruler, president, chiefe and principall gouernour of the church, is of the fathers attributed not onely to Peter, but also to his successours, bishops of the See Apostolike. And
therefore M. Iuell may thike hi selfe by this
Q 4   charitably

charitably admonished, to remeber his promise of yelding and subscribing,

I will adde to all that hath ben hytherto
sayde of this matter, a saying of Martin Luther, that such as doo litle regarde the graui-
tie of auncient fathers of the olde church,
may yet somewhat be moued with the lightnes of the youg father Luther, Patriarke and
fownder of their newe churche. Lightnes I
may well call it, for in this saying which I
shall here rehearse, he doth not so soberly
allowe the Popes Primacie, as in sundry
other treatises he doth rashly and furiously
inueigh against the same. In a litle treatise intituled, *Resolutio Lutheriana super propositio-
ne sua. 13. de potestate Papæ*: his wordes be these, *Primum quod me mouet Romanum pontificem alijs omnibus, quos saltem nouerimus se pontifices gerere, superiorem, est ipsa voluntas Dei,
quam in ipso facto videmus. Neque enim sine voluntate Dei, in hanc monarchiam vnquam veni-
re potuisset Rom. Pontifex. At volūtas Dei quo-
quo modo nota fuerit, cum reuerentia suscipien-
da est, ideoque non licet temerè Romano pontifici in suo primatu resistere. Hæc autem ratio tanta est, vt si etiam nulla scriptura, nulla alia causa
esset, hæc tamen satis esset ad compescendam te-
meritatem resistentium. Et hæc sola ratione glo-
riosissimus martyr Cyprianus per multas episto-
lis confidentissimè gloriatur contrà omnes episcoporum quorumcunque aduersarios, sicut 3. Re-
gum*

The po-
pes pri-
macie ac-
knovvle-
ged by
Martin
Luther.

gum legimus, quòd decem tribus Israël disceṣṣe-
runt à Roboam filio Salomonis , & tamen quia
voluntate Dei siue auctoritate factum est, ratum
apud Deum fuit. Nam & apud theologos omnes
voluntas signi , quam vocant operationem Dei,
non minus quàm alia signa voluntatis Dei , vt
præcepta prohibitiua &c. metuenda est. Ideo non
video, quomodo sint excusati à schismatis reatu,
qui huic voluntati contrauenientes, sese à Roma
ni pontificis auctoritate subtrahunt. Ecce hæc est
vna prima mihi insuperabilis ratio, quæ me subij-
cit Romano pontifici, & Primatum eius confite-
ri cogit . The firſt thing that moueth me to
thinke the B. of Rome to be ouer all other,
that we knowe to be biſhops, is the very will
of God, which we ſee in the facte or dede it
ſelfe , for without the will of God, the B. of
Rome could neuer haue commen vnto this
monarchie . But the will of God , by what
meane ſo euer it be knowen, is to be receiued
reuerently . And therefore it is not lawfull
raſhly to reſiſte the B. of Rome in his primacie. And this is ſo great a reaſon for the ſame,
that if there were no ſcripture at all, nor
other reaſō: yet this were ynough to ſtay the
raſhnes of thē, that reſiſte . And through this
onely reaſon the moſt glorioſe martyr Cypriā in many of his epiſtles vaūteth him ſelfe
very boldly againſt all the aduerſaries of Biſhops, what ſoeuer they were. As in the thirde
booke of the kinges we read, that the ten tri-

bes of Israel departed from Roboam Salomons sonne. Yeat because it was done by the will or auctoritie of God, it stoode in effecte with God . For amõg all the diuines, the will of the signe , which they call the working of God, is to be feared no lesse, then other signes of Gods will, as cõmaundementes prohibitiue, etc. Therefore, I see not, how they may be excused of the gilte of schisme, which going agaiñst this will, withdrawe thē selues from the auctoritie of the B. of Rome. Lo this is one chiefe inuincible reason, that maketh me to be vnder the bishop of Rome and compelleth me to cõfesse his Primacie. This farre Luther.

Thus I haue briefly touched some deale of the scriptures, of the canons and councelles, of the edictes of Emperours , of the fathers sayinges, of the reasons, and of the manifolde practises of the church , whīch are wonte to be alleaged for the Popes Primacie and supreme auctoritie. With all, I haue proued that, which M. Iuell denyeth , that the B, of Rome within sixe hũdred yeras after Christ, hath ben called *the vniuersall bishop* of no small number of men of great credite , and very oftentymes *Head of the vniuersall church* both in termes equiualent, and also expressely.

Now to the nexte article.

Or that

Or that the people was then taught to beleue, Juell. *that Christes body is really, substantially, corporally, carnally, or naturally, in the Sacrament.*

Of the termes really, substantially, corporally, carnally, naturally, fovvnde in the doctours treating of the true being of Christes body in the blessed Sacrament.

ARTICLE. V.

Hristen people hath euer ben taught, that the body and bloud of *Iesus* Christ by the vnspeakeable working of the grace of God and vertue of the holy Ghoste, is present in this most holy Sacramét, and that verely and in dede. This doctrine is fownded vppó the pláine wordes of Christ, which he vttered in the institution of this Sacrament, expressed by the Euangelistes, and by S. Paul. As they were at supper (sayeth Matthewe) *Iesus tooke* Matth.26. *breade and blessed it, and brake it, and gaue it to his disciples, and sayeth: Take ye, eate ye, this is my body. And taking the cuppe, he gaue thankes, and gaue it to them, saying: Drynke ye all of this: For this is my bloude of the newe testament which shall be shedde for many in remission of synnes* . With like wordes almost Marke, Luke and Paul, doo describe this diui- Marc.14. ne institution. Neither sayde our lord onely, Luc.22. *This is my body* ; but least some shuld doubte 1.Cor 11. how his wordes are to be vuderstandéd:

for

Luc.22.

for a playne declaration of them, he addeth this further, (*Wich ys geuen for you.* Likewise of the cuppe he sayeth not onely, *This is my bloude.* But also, as it were to putte it out of all doubte: *Which shall be shed for many.*

Now as faithful people doo beleue, that Christ gaue not a figure of his body, but his owne true and very body in substāce, and like wise not a figure of his bloude, but his very pretiouse bloude it selfe at his passion and death on the crosse for our Redēptiō: so they beleue also, that the wordes of the institution of this Sacramēt admitte no other vnderstanding, but that he geueth vnto vs in these holy mysteries his selfe same body, and his selfe same bloude in truth of substance, which was crucified and shedde foorth for vs. Thus to the humble beleuers scripture it selfe ministreth sufficient argument of the truth of Christes body and bloude in the Sacrament against the sacramentaries, who holde opinion, that it is there but in a figure, signe, or token onely.

Againe, we can not fynde where our lord performed the promise he made in the sixth chapper of Iohn, *The bread which I wil geue, is my fleshe, which I will geue for the lyfe of the worlde:* but onely in his last supper, where if he gaue his fleshe to his Apostles, and that no ne other, but the very same, which he gaue for the lyfe of the worlde: it foloweth that in

the

the blessed Sacramēt is not mere bread, but thatsame his very body in substāce. For it was not mere bread, but his very body, that was geuen and offred vp vpon the crosse.

If the wordes spoken by Christ in S. Iohn of promise, that he performed in his holy supper, *The bread that I will geue, is my flesshe,* had ben to be také not as they seme to meane plainely and truly, but metaphorically, tropically, symbolically and figuratiuely, so as the truth of our lordes flesshe be excluded, as our aduersaries do vnderstand them: then the Capernaites had not had any occasion at all of their great offence. Thē shuld not they haue had cause to murmour againft Christ, as the Euangelist sheweth: *The Iewes* (sayeth S. Iohn) *Stroue among them selues, saying, how can he geue vs his flesshe to eate?* And much lesse his dere disciples, to whō he had shewed so many and so great miracles, to whom he had before declared so many parables and so high secretes, shuld haue had any occasion of offence. And doubteles if Christ had meant, they shuld eate but the signe or figure of his body, they would not haue sayde, *Durus est hic sermo, this is a hard saying, and who cā abyde to heare it?* For then shuld they haue done no greater thing, then they had done oftentymes before in eating the Easter lābe. And how could it seme a hard worde or saying, if Christ had meant nothing elles, but this, the

Cap.6.

bread

bread that I will geue, is a figure of my body, that shall cause you to remember me?

To conclude shortely. If Christ would so haue ben vnderstanded, as though he had meant to geue but a figure onely of his body, it had ben no nede for him to haue alleaged his omnipotencie and almighty power to his disciples, thereby the rather to bring them to beleefe of his true body to be geuē them to eate. *Hoc vos scãdalizat? doth this offende you, sayeth he, what if ye see the sonne of mã ascend where he was before? it is the Spirite that geueth lyfe, &c.* As though he had sayde : ye consyder onely my humanitie, that semeth weake and fraile, neither doo you esteme my diuine power by the great miracles I haue wrought. But when as ye shall see me by power of my godhed ascend into heauen whēce I came vnto you, will ye then also stand in doubte, whether ye may beleue, that I geue you my very body to be eatē? Thus by signifying his diuine power, Christ confownded their vnbeleefe, touching the veritie and substance of his body, that he promysed to geue them in meate.

VVhat occasioned the fathers to vse these termes really, substanially, corporally &c.

These places of the scripture, and many other reportig plainely that Christ at his supper gaue to his disciples his very body, euen that same which the daye folowing suffered death on the Crosse, haue ministred iust cause to the godly and learned fathers of the churche

churche to faye, that Chriftes body is prefent in this Sacrament really , fubftantially,
corporally, carnally, and naturally . By vfe of
which aduerbes they haue meant onely a
truth of being , and not a waye or meane of
being. And though this manner of fpeaking
be not thus expreffed in the fcripture , yet is
it deduced out of the fcripture. For if Chrift
fpake plainely, and vfed no trope, figure, nor
metaphore, as the fcripture it felfe fufficiëtly
declareth to an humble beleuer , and would
his difciples to vnderftand him, fo as he fpake in manifeft termes, when he fayde, *This is
my body, which is geuen for you* : Then may we
faye, that in the Sacrament his very body is
prefent, yea really, that is to faye in dede, fubftantially, that is, in fubftance, and corporally
carnally, and naturally : by which wordes is
meant, that his very body, his very flefhe and
his very humaine nature is there , not after
corporal, carnal , or natural wife, but inuifi-
bly, vnfpeably, miraculoufely, fupernaturally
fpiritually , diuinely , and by waye to him
onely knowen.

And the fathers haue ben driuë to vfe thefe termes for more ample and full declaration of the truth , and alfo for withftanding
and ftopping obiections made by heretikes.
And becaufe the catholike faith touching
the veritie of Chriftes body in the Sacramēt
was not impugned by any man for the fpace
of a

of a thousand yeres after Christes being in earth, and about that tyme *Berengarius* first beganne openly to sowe the wicked sede of the sacramentarie heresie, which then sone confuted by learned mē, and by the same first authour abiured and recāted, now is with no lesse wickednes, but more busely and more earnestly set forth againe: the doctours that sythens haue written in defence of the true and catholike faith herein, haue more often vsed the termes a fore mentioned, then the olde and auncièt fathers, that wrote within M. Iuelles syx hundred yeres after Christ, who doubteles would no lesse haue vsed thē if that matter had ben in question or doubte in their tyme. And albeit these termes were straunge and newe, as vsed within these fyue hūdred yeres onely, and that the people were neuer taught for syx hundred yeres after Christ, as M. Iuell sayeth more boldly then truly, and therefore more rashely then wysely: yet the faith by them opened and declared, is vniuersall and olde, verely no lesse olde, then ys our lordes supper, where this Sacrament was first instituted.

Here before that I bring in places of auncient fathers reporting the same doctrine, and in like termes as the catholike churche doth holde concerning this article: least our opinion herein might happely appeare ouer carnall and grosse: I thincke it necessary briefly to

fly to declare, what maner a true bodie and
bloud of Chriſt is in the Sacrament. Chriſt
in him ſelfe hath but one fleſhe and bloud in
ſubſtance, which his godhed tooke of the vir
gine Mary once, and neuer afterward lefte it The fleſhe
of. But this one fleſhe and bloud in reſpecte and bloud
of double qualitie, hath a double conſidera- of Chriſt
tion. For at what tyme Chriſt lyued here in ble confy-
earth among men in the ſhape of man, his deration.
fleſhe was thrall and ſubiecte to the frailtie
of mannes nature, ſynne and ignorance excepted. That fleſhe being paſſible vntil death,
the ſouldiers at the procurement of the Iewes crucified. And ſuch maner bloud was at
his paſſiõ ſhedde foorth of his body, in ſighte of thẽ which were then preſent. But after
that Chriſt roſe againe from the deade, his
body from that tyme forward euer remaineth immortall and liuely, in danger nõ more of any inſirmitie or ſuffering, much leſſe of
death: but is become by diuine giftes and
endowmētes, a ſpirituall and a diuine body,
as to whõ the godhed hath cõmunicated diuine and godly properties and excellencies,
that ben aboue all mannes capacitie of vnderſtanding. This fleſhe and body thus con-
ſidered, which ſundry doctours call *corpus ſpi*
rituale & deificatum, a ſpirituall and deified
body, is geuen to vs in the bleſſed Sacramēt.

This is the doctrine of the church vttered
by S. Hierome in his commentaries vppon

Lib.1.ca.1. th'Epiſtle to the Epheſiãs, where he hath the
ſe wordes. *Dupliciter verò ſanguis et caro intelligitur, vel ſpiritualis illa atque diuina, de qua ipſe
dixit, Caro mea vere eſt cibus , & ſanguis meus
verè eſt potus : &, niſi manducaueritis carnem
meam, & ſanguinem meum biberitis , non habebitis vitam æternam : vel caro, quæ crucifixa eſt,
& ſanguis, qui militis effuſus eſt lancea* . that is.
The bloud and fleſhe of Chriſt is vnderſtanded two waies , either that it is that ſpiritual
and diuine fleſhe, of which he ſpake him ſelfe, *My fleshe is verely meate , and my bloud is
verely 'drinke* , And , *excepte ye eate my fleſhe
and drinke my bloud ye ſhall not haue lyfe in you:*
Or, that fleſhe, which was crucified, and that
bloud, which was ſhedde by pearcing of the
ſouldiers ſpeare . And to the intent a man
ſhuld not take this difference according to
the ſubſtance of Chriſtes fleſhe and bloud,
but according to the qualitie onely: S. Hiero
me bringeth a ſimilitude of our fleſhe, as of
which it hath ben in double reſpecte ſayde:
Iuxta hanc diuiſionem & in ſanctis etiam diuer
Luc.3. *ſitas ſanguinis & carnis accipitur, vt alia ſit caro*
1.Cor.15. *qua viſura eſt ſalutare Dei, alia caro & ſanguis,*
quæ regnum Dei non queant poſſidere.
According to this diuiſiõ diuerſitie of bloud
and fleſhe is to be vnderſtanded in ſainctes
alſo , ſo as there is one fleſhe which ſhal ſee
the ſaluacion of God, and an other fleſhe and
bloud , which may not poſſeſſe the kingdom
of

of God . Which two states of flesh and bloud, seme (as it appeareth to the vnlearned)quite contrarie.

But Saint Paul dissolueth this doubte , in the fiftenth chapter of his first epistle to the Corinthians, saying, that fleshe of such sorte as we beare about vs in this lyfe,earthly,mortal,fraile,and bourthenouse to the soule,can not possesse the kingdom of God , because corruption shal not possesse incorruption. But after resurrection we shal haue a spirituall,gloriouse,incorruptible and immortall flesh , and like in figure to the gloriouse body of Christ,as S.Paul sayeth : *This corruptible body must putte on incorruptiō,and this mortail,immortalitie,*Then such flesh,or our flesh he of that maner and sorte,shall possesse the kingdom of God,and shal beholde God him selfe . And yet our fleshe now corruptible, and then incorruptible , is but one fleshe in substāce, but diuerse in qualitie and propertie.Euen so it is to be thought of our lordes fleshe as is afore sayde.The due weighing of this differéce,geueth much light tothis matter, and ought to staye many horrible blasphemies wickedly vttered against this most blessed Sacrament.

Now whereas M . Iuell denyeth that Christé people were of olde tyme taught to beleue, that Christes body is really, substātially,corporally,carnally,or naturally in the Sacrmét,

I doo plainely affirme the contrarie. Yet I acknowledge, that the learned fathers which
haue so taught, would not thereby seme to
make it here outwardly sensible or percepti-
ble.

Hom. 83.
in Matt. &
60. ad po-
pul. Antio-
chen.
For they confesse all with Saint Chrysostome, that the thing which is here geuen vs, is
not sensible, but that vnder visible signes, inuisible thinges be delyuered vnto vs. But
they thought good to vse the aforesayed termes, to put awaye all doubte of the being of
his very body in these holy mysteries, and to
exclude the onely imagination, phantasie, figure, signe, toke, vertue, or signification there of.

For in such wise the Sacramentaries haue
vttered their doctrine in this pointe, as they
may seme by their manner of speaking and
wryting, here to represent our lordes body
onely, in deede being absent, as kinges ofte-
tymes are represented in a Tragedie, or
meane persones in a Comedie. Verely the
maner and waye by which it is here present
and geuen to vs, and receiued of vs, is secrete: not humaine ne naturall, true for all that.
And we doo not atteine it by sense, reason, or
nature, but by faith. For which cause we doo
not ouer basely consyder and attende the visible elementes, but as we are taught by the
councell of Nice, lifting vp our mynde and
spirite, we beholde by faith on that holy table

ble put and layde(fo for the better fignifica-   *κτίσθαι*
tion of the real prefence their terme fown-
deth)*the Lambe of God, that taketh awaye the
fynnes of the worlde.*And here (faye they) we
receiue his pretioufe body and bloude, *ἀλη-
θῶς* that is to faye, verely and in deede, which
is no other wife , nor leffe, then this terme
really importeth.

And touching thefe termes, fyrft Verely,
or which is all one Really , and fubftantially:
me thinketh M. Iuell fhuld beare the more
with vs for vfe of the fame , fith that Bucer
him felfe one of the greateft learned men of
that fyde hath allowed them:yea and that after much writing againft Luther in defence
of *Zuinglius* and *Oecolampadius* by him fet
forth,and after that he had affured him felfe
of the truth in this article by diuine infpira-
tion , as moft conftantly he affirmeth with
thefe wordes: *Hæc non dubitamus diuinitus no*   In refpon-
bis,& per fcripturam reuelata de hoc Sacramen   fione ad
*to.*We doubte not(fayeth he)but thefe thin-   Lutherũ.
ges concerning this Sacrament , be reueled
vnto vs frõ God,and by the fcripture. If you
demaunde where this may be fownde:in the
actes of a Councell holden betwen the Lutheranes and Zuinglianes for this very purpofe in Martine Luthers houfe at Wittenberg, in the yere of our lord: 1 5 3 6.you fhal
fynde thefe wordes. *Audiuimus D. Bucerum
explicantem fuam fententiã de Sacramento cor-*

R 3   *poris*

poris & sanguinis Domini hoc modo. Cum pane & vino verè & substantialiter adest, exhibetur & sumitur corpus Christi & sanguis. Et Sacramentali vnione panis est corpus Christi, & porrecto pane verè adest & verè exhibetur corpus Christi. We haue heard M. Bucer declare his mynde touching the Sacrament of the body and bloud of our Lord, in this sorte. With the bread and wyne the body of Christ and his bloud is present, exhibited, and receiued verely and substantially. And by Sacramental vnion the breade is the body of Christ, and the breade being geuen, the body of Christ is verely present, and verely deliuered.

Though this opinion of Bucer, by which he recanted his former Zuinglian heresie, be in sundry pointes false and hereticall, yet in this he agreeth with the catholike churche against M. Iuelles negatiue assertion, that the body and bloud of Christ is present in the Sacrament verely, that is, truly, and really or in dede, and substantially. Where in he speaketh, as the auncient fathers spake long before a thousand yeres past.

Let Chrysostome for proufe of this be in stede of many that might be alleaged. His wordes be these. *Nos secum in vnam (vt ita dicam) massam reducit, neque id fide solum, sed re ipsa nos corpus suum efficit.* By this Sacrament (sayeth he) Christ reduceth vs (as it were)

In 26. ca. Mat. hom. 83.

were) in to one loumpe with him selfe , and
that not by faith onely , but he maketh vs
his owne body in very dede, *reipsa*, which is
no other to saye, then Really. The other aduerbes Corporally, Carnally, Naturally, be
fownde in the fathers not seldom , specially
where they dispute against the Arianes. And
therefore it had ben more côuenient for M.
Iuell to haue modestly interpreted them,
then vtterly to haue denyed them.

The olde fathers of the Greke and Latine
churche denye that faithfull people haue an
habitude or disposition, vniô or coniunction
with Christ onely by faith and charitie, or
that we are spiritually ioyned and vnited
to him onely by hope , loue , religion , obediéce, and will: yea further they affirme, that
by the vertue and efficacie of this Sacrament
duely and worthely receiued Christ is really
and in dede communicated by true commu-
nication and participation of the nature and
substance of his body and bloud, and that he
is and dwelleth in vs truly, becaufe of our receiuing the same in this Sacrament. The benefite where of is such, as we be in Christ and
Christ in vs, according to that he sayeth, *Qui* Ioan.6.
manducat meam carnem, manet in me, & ego in
illo . *Who eateth my flesshe, he dwelleth in me,*
and I in him . The which dwelling vnion
and ioinyng together of him with vs, and
of vs with him , that it might the better be
R 4   expressed

expreſſed.and recommended vnto vs : they thought good in their writinges to vſe the aforeſayde aduerbes.

Hilarius writing againſt the Arianes alleaging the wordes of Chriſt. 17. Iohn . *Vt omnes vnum ſint,ſicut tu pater in me,& ego in te,vt & ipſi in nobis vnum ſint*,that al maye be one, as thou father art in me , and I in thee , that they alſo may be one in vs : going about by theſe wordes to ſhewe that the ſonne and the father were not one in nature and ſubſtance,but onely in cócord and vnitie of will amóg other many and lóg ſentéces for proufe of vnitie inſubſtáce,bothe betwen Chriſt and the father , and alſo betwen Chriſt and vs,hath theſe wordes.*Si enim veré verbũ caro factum eſt,& nos veré verbum carnem cibo Dominico ſumimus, quomodo nõ naturaliter manere in nobis exiſtimandus eſt , qui & naturã carnis noſtrae iam inſeparabilem ſibi homo natus aſſumpſit,et naturam carnis ſuae ad naturam aeternitatis ſub Sacramento nobis communicandae carnis admiſcuit:*If the word be made fleſhe verely, and we receiue the word being fleſhe in our lordes meate verely : how is he to be thought not to dwell in vs naturally , who bothe hath taken the nature of our fleſhe now inſeparable to him ſelfe, in that he is borne mã,and alſo hath mengled the nature of his owne fleſhe to the nature of his euerlaſtingneſſe vnder the Sacramét of his fleſhe

De Trinitate lib .8.

to be

to be receiued of vs in the communiõ? There afterwarde this word *naturaliter*, in this sense that by the Sacrament worthely receiued Christ is in vs, and we in Christ naturally that is in truth of nature, is sundry tymes put and rehearsed. Who so listeth to reade further his eight booke de *Trinitate*, he shall fynde him agnise *manentem in nobis carnaliter filium*, that the sonne of God (through the Sacrament) dwelleth in vs carnally, that is in truth of fleshe; and that by the same Sacrament we with him, and he with vs are vnited and knitte together *corporaliter*, *& inseparabiliter*, corporally and inseparably, for they be his very wordes.

Gregorie Nyssene speaking to this purpose sayeth, *Panis qui de cœlo descendit, non incorporea quædam res est, quo enim pacto res incorporea corpori cibus fiet? res verò quæ incorporea non est, corpus omnino est. Huius corporis panem non aratio, non satio, non agricolarum opus effecit, sed terra intacta permansit, & tamen pane plena fuit, quo famescentes, mysterium virginis perdocti, facile saturantur.* In lib.de vita Mosis Which wordes reporte so plainely the truth of Cristes body in the Sacrament, as al maner of figure and signification must be excluded. And thus they may be englished. The bread that came downe from heauen, is not a bodilesse thing. For by what meane shall a bodilesse thing be made meate to a body? And

R 5　　the

the thing which is not bodyleſſe, is a body
without doubte. It is not earing, not ſowing,
not the worke of tillers, that hath brought
forth the bread of this body, but the earth
which remained vntouched, and yet was full
of the bread, whereof they that waxe húgry,
being thoroughly taught the myſterie of the
virgine, ſone haue their fylle. Of theſe wordes may eaſely be inferred a concluſion, that
in the Sacrament is Chriſt and that in the ſame we receiue him corporally, that is, in veri-
ite and ſubſtance of his body, for as much as
that is there, and that is of vs receiued,
which was brought forth and borne of the
virgine Mary.

    Cyrillus that auncient father and worthy
biſhop of *Alexandria*, for confirmation of
the catholike faith in this point, ſayeth thus.
Non negamus recta nos fide charitateque ſyn-
cera Chriſto ſpiritaliter coniungi : ſed nullam
nobis coniunctionis rationem ſecundum carnem
cum illo eſſe, id profecto pernegamus, idque à di-
uinis ſcripturis omnino alienum dicimus. We
denye not but that we are ioyned ſpiritually
with Chriſt by right faith and pure charitie : but that we haue no maner of ioyning with him according to the fleſhe
(which is one as to ſaye *Carnaliter* carnally) that we denye vtterly, and ſaye, that
it is not aggreable with the ſcriptures. A-
gaine leaſt any man ſhuld thinke this ioyn-
ning

In Ioan.
lib. 10.
cap. 13.

ioyning of vs and Chriſt together to be by
other meanes then by the participation of his
body in the Sacrament, in the ſame place afterward he ſayeth further. *An fortaſſis putat
ignotam nobis myſticæ benedictionis virtutē eſſe?
Quæ cum in nobis fiat, nonne corporaliter quoquè
facit communicatione corporis Chriſti Chriſtum
in nobis habitare?* what troweth this Ariane
heretike perhappes, that we knowe not the
vertue of the myſticall bleſſing? (whereby
is meant this ſacrament) which when it is
become to be in vs, doth it not cauſe Chriſt
to dwell in vs corperally by receiuing of
Chriſtes body in the communion? And after
this he ſayeth as plainely, that Chriſt is in vs,
*non habitudine ſolum quæ per charitatem intel-
ligitur, verumetiam & participatione naturali.*
not by charitie onely, but alſo by naturall
participation.

The ſame Cyrill ſayeth in an other place,
that through the holy communion of Chriſtes body, we are ioyned to him in naturall
vnion. *Quis enim eos, qui vnius ſancti corporis
vnione in vno Chriſto vniti ſunt, ab hac naturali
vnione alienos putabit?* who will thinke (ſayeth
he) that they, wich be vnited together by
the vnió of that one holy body in one Chriſt,
be not of this natural vnion? He calleth this
alſo a corporall vnion in the ſame booke,
and at length after large diſcuſſion how
we

Lib. in Io-
an. 11, cap.
26.

we be vnited to Chrift, not onely by charitie and obedience of religion, but alfo in fubftance, concludeth this. *Sed de vnione corporali fatis*. But we haue treated ynough of the corporall vniō. Yet afterward in diuerfe fentences he vfeth thefe aduerbes (for declaring of the veritie of Chriftes body in the facrament) *naturaliter, fubftantialiter, fecundum carnem* or *carnaliter, corporaliter*, as moft manifeftly in the 27. chapter of the fame booke. *Corporaliter filius per benedictionem myfticam nobis vt homo vnitur, fpiritualiter autem vt Deus.* The fonne of God is vnited vnto vs corporally as man, and fpiritually as God.

Agayne where as he fayeth there : *Filium Dei natura Patri vnitum corporaliter fubftantialiterqne accipientes, clarificamur, glorificamurque, &c.* We receiuing the fonne of God vnited to the father by nature corporally and fubftantially, are clarified and glorifyed or made glorious, being made partakers of the fupreme nature: The like faying he hath. lib. 12. cap. 58.

Now this being and remayning of Chrift in vs, and of vs in Chrift naturally and carnally, and this vniting of vs and Chrift together corporally, prefuppofeth a participation of his very body, which body we can not truly participate, but in this bleffed facrament. And therefor Chrift is in the Sacramēt naturally, carnally, corporally, that is to faye,

according

acccording to the truth of his nature, of his fleshe, and of his body. For were not he so in the Sacrament, we could not be ioyned vnto him, nor he and we could not be ioyned and vnited together, corporally,

Diuerse other auncient fathers haue vsed the like manner of speach, but none so much as *Hilarius* and *Cyrillus*, whereby they vnderstand, that Christ is present in this sacrament as we haue sayde, according to the truth of his substace, of his nature, of his fleshe, of his body and bloud. And the catholike fathers that sithens the tyme of *Berengarius* haue written in defence of the truth in this point, vsing these termes sometymes for excluding of metaphores, allegories, figures, and significations onely, whereby the sacramentaries would defraude faithfull people of the truth of Christes pretiouse body in this Sacrament: doo not thereby meane that the maner, meane, or waye of Christes presence, dwelling, vnion and coniunction with vs, and of vs with him, is therefor naturall, substanciall, corporall, or carnal: but they and all other catholike men confesse the contrarie, that it is farre higher and worthier, supernaturall, supersubstantiall, inuisible, vnspeakeable, speciall and propre to this sacrament, true, reall, in and deede notwithstanding, and not onely tropicall, symbolicall, metaphoricall, allegoricall, not spirituall onely, and yet spirituall,

not

not figuratiue or significatiue onely. And likewise concerning the maner of the presence and being of that body and bloud in the sacramēt, they and we acknowledge and confesse, that it is not locall, circumscriptiue, diffinitiue, or subiectiue, or naturall, but such, as is knowen to God onely.

Iuell.

Or that his body is or may be in a thousand places, or mo, at one tyme.

Of the being of Christes body in many places
at one tyme.

ARTICLE. VI.

Mong the miracles of this blessed Sacrament, one is, that one and the same body maye bee in many places at once, to witte, vnder all consecrated hostes. As for God, it is agreable to his Godhed to be euery where, *simpliciter & proprie*. But as for a creature, to be but in one place onely. But as for the body of Christ, it is after a maner betwen bothe. For where as it is a creature, it ought not to be made equall with the Creatour in this behalfe, that it be euery where. But where as it is vnited to the Godhed, herein it ought to excelle other bodyes, so, as it maye in one tyme bee in mo places vnder this holy Sacrament. For the vniting of Christes naturall body vnto the almighty Godhed duly considered, bringeth a true Christen man in respecte of the same, to forsake reason, and to leane to faith,

to put

to put aparte all doubtes and difcourfes of humaine vnderftanding, and to reft in reuerent fimplicitie of beleefe.

Thereby through the holy ghoft perfuaded he knoweth, that although the body of Chrift be naturall and humaine in dede, yet through the vnion and coniunction, many thinges be poffible to the fame now, that to all other bodies be impoffible: as to walke vpon waters, to vanifhe awaye out of fight, to be trāsfigured and made bright as the funne, to afcende vp through the clowdes: and after it became immottall, death being cōquered, to ryfe vp againe out of the graue, and to entre through doores faft fhutte. Through the fame faith he beleueth and acknowlegeth, that accordīg vnto his worde, by his power it is made prefēt in the bleffed facramēt of th'aulter vnder the forme of bread and wyne, where fo euer the fame is duly cōfecrated according vnto his inftitutiō in his holy fupper, and that not after a groffe or carnall maner, but fpiritually, and fupernaturally, and yet fubftātially, not by locall, but by fubftantiall prefence, not by maner of quantitie, or fylling of a plaor by chaunging of place, or by leauing his fitting on the right hāde of the father, but in fuch a maner, as God onely knoweth, and yet doth vs to vnderftand by faith the truth of this very prefence, farre paffing all mannes capacitie to comprehend the maner how.

Matt.14.
Luc.24.
Matt.17.
Luc.24.
Act. 1.
Matt.28.
Ioan.20.

Where

Where as some against this pointe of be-leefe doo alleage the article of Christes Ascension, and of his being in heauen at the right hande of God the father, bringing certaine textes of scriptures perteining to the same, and testimonies of auncient doctours signifying Christes absence from the earth: it may be rightly vnderstanded, that he is verely bothe in heauen at the right hande of his father in his visible and corporal forme, very God and man, after which maner he is there, and not here, and also in the Sacrament inuisibly, and spiritually, bothe God and Man in a mysterie, so as the graunting of the one may stande without denyall of the other, no contradiction fownde in these beinges, but onely a distinction in the waye and maner of being.

And how the auncient fathers of the churche haue confessed and taught bothe these beinges of Christ in heauen and in the sacrament together, contrarie to M. Iuelles negatiue, by witnes of their owne wordes we may perceiue. Basile in his liturgie, that is to saye seruice of his Masse, sayeth thus in a prayer. Looke downe vppon vs lord Iesus Christ our God from thy holy tabernacle, and from the throne of glorie of thy kingdom, and come to sanctifie vs, which sittest aboue with thy father, and art conuersant here inuisibly: And vouchesaufe to imparte vnto vs thine vnde-

fyled

(marginal notes:)
Christes being in heauē and in the Sacrament at one tyme, implyeth no contradiction.

Qui suprà cum patre sedes, & hic inuisibiliter ver- saris.

fyled body, and precrouse bloude, and by vs
to all thy people. S. Chrisostome prayeth
with the very same wordes also in his Liturgie or Masse. Where we read further that the
priest and the deacon doo adore and worship
saying three tymes secretly, *God be merciful to* Et popu-
me a synner, and that the people doo all like- lus simili-
wise deuoutly adore. Now sith he will adora- ter omnes
tiō to be made, he acknowlegeth Christ pre- cum pieta-
sent, whom he graunteth to be also at the sa- te adorant.
me tyme in heauen. Which he vttereth more
plainely in these wordes *O miraculum, O Dei* Chrysost.
benignitatem, &c. O miracle, O the goodnes de Sacer-
of God, who sytteth aboue with the father, at dotio.lib.
that very instant of tyme, is handeled with 3.
the hādes of all, and geueth him selfe to those that will receiue and imbrace him. And
that is done by no crafty sleightnes, but opē-
ly in the sight of all that stande about. How
sayest thou, seme these thinges to thee no bet
ter then to be condemned and despysed? By
which words of S. Chrysostome we may see,
that Christes being in heauen, maketh no
proufe that he is not in earth, sith both these
verities may well stande together.

The same father confesseth the body of Christes
Christ to be in diuerse places likewise in his body in
homilies *ad populū Antiochenum* most plaine- many pla-
ly alluding to *Elias, Elias* (sayeth he) *melotem* ces at once
quidem discipulo reliquit, filius autem Dei ascen- Hom. 2.
dēs suam nobis carnem dimisit: sed Elias quidem
S   *exutus*

exutus, Christus autē & nob is reliquit, & ipsam habēs ascendit. Elias (when he was caried vp in the fyery chariot) lefte to his disciple *Elisus* his mantell of sheepes skynnes: but the sonne of God whē he ascended, lefte to vs his fleshe: but *Elias* dyd put of his mantel , and Christ bothe lefte his flesshe to vs, and also ascended hauing it with him . Nothing can be spoken more plainely, whereby to shewe that we haue the same flesshe here in earth , that was receiued into heauen, which Christ hath not put of to geue it to vs . By which doctrine of S. Chrysostome we are taught to beleue , that Christes flesshe or his body is bothe in heauē and also in the earth, in how many places to euer this blessed Sacrament is rightely celebrated.

And whereas many measuring all thinges by the common order and lawes of nature, beleue nothing can be done aboue nature, and therefor thinke that the body of Christ, for as much as it is of nature finite, cā not by power of God be in many places at once : of which opinion. M Iuell semeth to be him selfe: it shall not be besyde the purpose, though the places alredie alleaged proue the cōtrarie to receite the testimonies of an olde doctour or two, wherei they cōfesse most plainely that which by this article is most vntruly denyed.

In Psal 38.   Saint Ambrose hath these wordes . *Et si Christus nunc nō videtur offerre, tamē ipse offertur in sur in terris, quando Christi corpus offertur. Imd ipse offerre manifestatur in nobis, cuius sermo sanctificat sacrificium quod offertur.* If Christ now be not sene to offre, yet he is offered in earth, when the body of Christ is offered, yea it is manifest that him selfe offereth in vs, whose worde sanctifieth and consecrateth the sacrifice, that is offered. Now if Christes body be offered in earth, as this father affirmeth, and that by Christ him selfe, in respecte that the sacrifice which is offered, is by his word consecrated, then it foloweth Christes bodie to be in so many places, as it is offered in. Where by the waye this may be noted, that the sacrifice of the churche is not thankes geuing (as our newe Maisters doo teache) but the body of Christ it selfe, which of the fathes is called an vnbloudy and quikning or life geuing sacrifice. We finde in Chrysostome a most manifest place for the being of Christes body in many places at once, so as though he be offered in many places, yet is he but one Christ, not many Christes, his wordes be these. *Unu̅ est hoc sacrificiu̅, alioquin hac ratione quonia̅ multis in locis offertur, multi Christ sunt? nequaqua̅: sed vnus vbique est Christus, et hic plenus exist es & illic plenus. Vnum corpus. Sicut enim qui vbique offertur vnum corpus est, & non multa corpora: ita etiam & vnum sacrificium.* This sacrifice is one, elles by this reason, sith it is offered in many places, bee there many

Sacrificiu̅ incruentu̅ & viuificu̅

In epist. ad Heb. homil. 17.

S 2   Christes?

Christes? Not so, but there is but one Christ euery where, being both here fully, and there fully also, one body. For as he that is offered euery where, is but one body, and not many bodies, so likewise it is but one sacrifice. By this place of Chrysostome we see, what hath ben the faith of the olde fathers touching this article, euen the same, which the catholike church professeth at these dayes, that one Christe is offered in many places, so as he be fully and perfitely here, and fully and perfitely there. And thus we perceiue, what force their argumentes haue in the iudgement of the learned fathers, by which they take awaie from Christ power to make his body present in many places at once.

Sermon. in cœna Domini. S. Bernard vttereth the faith of the church in his tyme agreable with this, in these wordes. *Sed vnde hoc nobis pijssime Domine, vt nos vermiculi reptantes &c.* From whence commeth this most louing lord, that we seely wormes creeping on the face of the earth, yea we, that are but duste and asshes, be admitted to haue thee present in our handes, and before our eyes, which all and whole sittest at the right hãde of thy father, which also arte present to all in one moment of tyme from the eaft to the weft, from the north to the sowth, one in many, the same in diuerse places? from whence (I saye) commeth this? soothly not of our dutie or deserte, but of thy good will,

and

and of the good pleasure of thy swetnesse, for thou hast prepared in thy swetnesse for the poore one O God. In the same sermō exhorting the churche to reioise of the presence of Christ, he sayeth , *In terra spōsū habes in Sacramēto, in cœlis habitura es sine velamēto: & hic & ibi veritas. sed hic palliata, ibi manifestata.* In the earth thou hast thy spouse in the sactamēt, in heauē thou shalt haue hī without vaile or couerīg, both here and also there is the truth(of his presēce) but here couered , there opened.

Thus all these fathers as likewise the rest, cōfesse as it were with one mowth, that Christ sitteth at the right hande of his father, and is here present in the sacrament the same tyme that he is in heauen and in earth at once , in many and diuerse places one , and that the same is euery where offered , the one true sacrifice of the churche . And this article is by them so clearely and plainely vttered, that figures, significations , tropes , and metaphores can fynde no appearaunce nor colour at all. Whereby the new Maisters reasons seme very peeuish : Christ is asended , *Ergo* he is not in the sacrament. Christ is in heauen sitting at the right hande of his father , *Ergo* he is not in earth . Christes body is of nature finite , *Ergo* it is conteined in a place circunscriptiuely , *Ergo* it is not in many places . In making of which slender argumētes, they will not seme to acknowledge whose body it is,

S 3   euen

euen that, which is proper to God, whose power is ouer all, and to whõ all thinges obeye.

But becaufe M. Iuell and they of that secte, feme to fet litle by thefe fathers, though very auncient, S. Bernard excepted, and of the churche holdē for Saintes, I will bring forth the auctoritie of Martin Bucer, a late doctour of their owne fyde, though not canonizate for a fainte as yet, for that I knowe. This newe father whom they efteme fo much, and was the reader of diuinitie in Cambridge in kyng Edwardes tyme, very vehemently, and for fo much truly, affirmeth the true reall prefence of Chriftes body in the facrament. For he fayeth. Chrift fayde not, *This in my fpirite, this is my vertue, but this is my body*: wherefore we muft beleue fayeth he, Chriftes body toj be there, euen the fame that dyd hang vpon the croffe, our lord him felfe. Which in fome parte to declare, he vfeth the fimilitude of the funne for his purpofe, contrary to M. Iuelles negatiue, to proue Chriftes body prefent, and that really and fubftantially, in what places fo euer the facrament is rightly miniftred. His wordes be thefe. *Vt fol verè vno in loco cæli vifibilis circunfcriptus eft, radijs tamen fuis præfens verè & fubftantialiter exhibetur vbilibet orbis: Ita Dominus, etiam fi circumferibatur vno loco cæli, arcani & diuini, id eft gloriæ Patris, verbo tamẽ fuo, & facris fymbolis verè & totus ipfe Deus et homo præfẽs exhibetur in facra cœna,*

Truth cõ-
feffed by
the enemie
of truth.

In cõmet.
in 16. cap.
Matthæi.

cœna, eóque substantialiter, quam præsentiam no
minus certò agnoscit mens credens verbis his Do
mini & symbolis, quàm oculi vident & habent
solem præsentem demonstratū & exhibitum sua
corporali luce. Res ista arcana est, & noui testa-
menti, res fidei, non sunt igitur huc admittendæ
cogitationes de præsentatione corporis, quæ cōstat
ratione huius vitæ etiam patibilis & fluxæ. Ver-
bo Domini simpliciter inhærendum est, & debet
fides sensuum defectui præhere supplementum.
Which may thus be englished.

As the sunne is truly placed determinatly
in one place of the visible heauen, and yet is
exhibited truly and substantially by his bea-
mes euery where abroade in the worlde : So
our lord although he be conteined in one
place of the secret and diuine heauen, that is
to witte, the glorie of his father : yet for all
that by his word and holy tokens, he is exhibited preset in his holy supper truly and him
selfe whole God and mā, and therefore substātially or in subštance. Which presence the
mynde geuing credite to these our lordes
wordes and tokens, doth no lesse certainely
acknowledge, then our eyes see and haue the
sunne present shewed and exhibited with his
corporall light. This is a secrete matter, and
of the newe testamēt, a matter of faith, there
forherei thougthes be not to be admitted of
such a presentatiō of the body, as cōsisteth in
the maner of this lyfe passible and trāsitorie.

S 4   We

We muſt ſymply cleaue to the word of our
lord, and where our ſenſes faile, there muſt
faith helpe to ſupplie. Thus we ſee, how Bucer in ſundry other pointes of faith bothe
deceiued and alſo a deceiuour, confirmeth
the truth of this article pyththely and playnely. Such is the force of truth, that oftentymes
it is confeſſed by the very enemies of truth.

Fight not with the churche M. Iuell, but
fight with the enemie of the churche, fight
with him, whom you haue folowed in departing from the churche, who neuer the leſſe
by force of truth, is driuen againſt you to cō-
feſſe the truth in thoſe moſt plaine wordes,
*Verè & totus ipſe Deus & homo præſens exhibe-
tur in ſacra cœna, eóque ſubſtantialiter*. In this
holy ſupper him ſelfe God and Man is exhibited preſent truly and whole, and therefore
ſubſtantially.

Now to be ſhorte, where as the chiefe argumentes that be made againſt the being of
Chriſtes body in many places at once, be deduced of nature, in reſpecte that this article
ſemeth to them to aboliſh nature, it maye
pleaſe them to vnderſtand, that God who is
auctour of nature, cā by his power doo with
a body that, which is aboue the nature of a
body, nature not deſtroyed, but kepte and
preſerued whole. Which Plato the hethen
philoſopher would ſone haue ben induced
to beleue, if he were alyue. Who aſked what

God vvor-
king abo-
ue nature
deſtroyeth
not nature

was

was nature, answered, *quod Deus vult*, that which God will.

And therefore we beleeue, that *Enoch* and *Elias* yet mortal by nature, doo by power of God lyue in body, and that aboue nature. *Abacuc* was by the same power caught vp, and in a moment caried from Iewrie to Babylon, his nature reserued whole. Saint Peter by God according to nature walked on the earth, the same by God besyde nature, walked vpon the waters. Christ after condicion of nature assumpted, suffred death in body, the same Christ by his diuine power entred with his body in to his disciples through dores closed. Christ at his last supper according to nature sate downe with his twelue disciples, and among them occupied a place at the table visibly, by his diuine power there he helde his body in his handes inuisibly. For (as *S.*Augustine and also *Prosper* sayeth) *Ferebatur in manibus suis*, he was borne in his owne handes, where nature gaue place, and his one body was in mo places then one. Verely *non est abbreuiata manus domini*, the hande of our lord is not shortened, his power is as great, as euer it was. And therefore let vs not doubte, but he is able to vse nature finite infinitely, specially now the nature of his body being glorified after his resurrection from the dead. And as the lyuing is not to be sought among the dead, so the

Daniel.14.

Mat.14.
Ioan.20.
In Psal.
33. cōcione prima.
Portatus *
est quippe
& Iesus
Dominus
in manibus suis
dum suum
corpus in
sanctificato
pane ge-
stans ma-
nibus suis,
dixit: Hoc
est corpus
meū quod
pro vobis
tradetur
Prosper
part.2.de
promiss. &
prædict.
Dei.ca.25,

S 5   thinges

thinges that be done by the power of God aboue nature, are not to be tryed by rules of nature.

And that all abfurdities and carnall grofnes be feuered from our thoughtes, where true Chriften people beleue Chriftes body to be in many places at once, they vnderftãd it fo to bee in a myfterie. Now to be in a myfterie,is not to be comprehended in a place, but by the power of God to be made prefent in forte and maner,as him felfe knowerh verely fo,as no reafon of man can atteine it, and fo,as it may be fhewed by no examples in nature . Whereof that notable faying of S. Auguftine may very well be reported, *O homo ſi rationem à me pafcis , non erit mirabile: exemplum quaritur, non erit ſingulare,* that is, O man if(herein)thou require reafon,it fhal not be marueilloufe, feeke for the like example,and then it fhall not be finguler.If Goddes working be comprehended by reafon (fayeth holy Gregorie) it is not wonderoufe:neither faith hath meede,whereto mannes reaſon geueth proufe.

Being in a myſterie.

Aug.epiſt. ad voluſianum.Itẽ Ser.159.de tempore.

Gregorius in homil.

Or that

Or that the priest did then holde vp the Sa- Iuell.
crament ouer his head.

Of the Eleuation or lyfting vp the Sacrament.

ARTICLE. VII.

F what weight this ceremonie is
to be accompted, catholike Chriſten men, whom you call your aduerſaries M. Iuell, knowe no leſſe
then you . Verely whereas it pleaſeth you
thus to ieſte, and like a Luciã to ſcoffe at the
Sacramentes of the church, and the reuerent
vſe of the ſame, calling al theſe articles in generall the higheſt myſteries , and greateſt
keyes of our religion, without which our doctrine can not be maineteined and ſtand
vpright: vnderſtand you that this , as ſundry
other articles which you denye and requyre
proufe of, is not ſuch, ne neuer was ſo eſtemed . The prieſtes lifting vp or ſhewing of
the Sacrament, is not one of the higheſt myſteries or greateſt keyes of our Religion: and
the doctrine of the catholike churche may
right well be maineteined and ſtáde without
it. But it appeareth, you regarde not ſo much
what you ſaye, as how you ſaye ſomewhat for
colour of defacing the churche : which whiles you go about to doo, you deface your ſelfe more then you ſeeme to be ware of, and
doo that thing, whereby among good Chriſten men ſpecially the learned, you may be a
ſhamed to ſhewe you r face . For as you haue
ouer

ouer rashely, yea I maye saye wickedly, affirmed the negatiue of sundry other articles,
and stowtely craked of your assuráce thereof,

so you haue likewise of this. For perusing the
auncient fathers writinges, we synde record
of this Céremonie vsed euen from the Apostles tyme foreward.

Saint Dionyse, that was S. Paules scholer,
sheweth, that the priest at his tyme after the
consecration was wont to holde vp the dredfull mysteries, so as the people might beholde them. His wordes be these according to

the Greke. *Pontifex diuina munera laude pro-
secutus, sacrosancta & augustissima mysteria. có-
steit, & collaudata in conspectum agit per symbo-
la sacré proposita*. The bishop after that he
hath done his seruice of praising the diuine
giftes, consecrateth the holy and most worthy mysteries, and bringeth them so praysed
in to the sighte of the people by the tokens
set forth for that holy purpose. On which
place the auncient Greke writer of the scholies vpō that worke, sayeth thus. Ἰδὺ κουφισμὸν
καὶ Ἰην ὑ Ἰοσιν τῆς μιᾶς εὐλογίας τοῦ θείου ἄ ₴ ου
φηοὶ, ὂς ὑ ᕱει ἱερᵱὺς λέγων, τά ἄγιαῖοις ἁγίοισ. *Loquitur de vnius benedictionis, nimirum panis diuini eleuatione, quem Pontifex in sublime attoll-
lit, dicens, Sancta sanctis*. This father speaketh
in this place, of the lifting vp of the one blessing, (that is to saye of the one forme or kynde of the Sacrament) euen of that diuine
breade

breade, which the bishop lifteth vp on high, saying, holy thinges for the holy. In saint Basiles and Chrysostomes Masse we finde these wordes. *Sacerdos eleuans sacrum panem, dicit, Sancta sanctis.* The priest holding vp that sacred bread, sayeth : Holy thinges for the holy. In Saint Chrysostomes Masse we reade, that, as the people is kneeling downe after th'example of the priest and of the deacon, the deacon seing the priest stretching forth his handes , and taking vp that holy bread, πρὸς τὸ ποιῆσαι τὴν ἁγίαν ὕψοσιν, ἐκφωνεῖ, πρόσχωμεν, *ad sacram eleuationem peragendam, palam edicit, attendamus,* to doo the holy eleuation, speaketh out a lowde, let vs be attēt, and (thē) the priest sayeth (as he holdeth vp the Sacrament) holy thinges for the holy.

Amphilochius, of whom mention is made afore, in the lyfe of S. Basile speaking of his wonderouse celebrating the Masse , among other thinges sayeth thus . *Et post finem orationum, exaltauit panem, sine intermissione orās, & dicens: Respice domine Iesu Christe, etc.* And after that he had done the prayers of consecration, he lyfted vp the bread, without ceasing praying and saying, Looke vpon vs lord Iesus Christ etc. The same saint Basile meant likewise of the Eleuation and holding vp of the Sacrament after the custome of the Occidentall churche, in his booke *dè spiritu sancto,* where he sayeth thus . *Inuocationis verba,* Cap.27. *dum*

dum oſtenditur pænis Euchariſtiæ & calix bene-
dictionis , quis ſanctorum nobis ſcripto reliquit?
Which of the ſainctes hath lefte vnto vs in
writing the wordes of Inuocatiō , whiles the
bread of *Euchariſtia*(that is to witte the blef-
ſed Sacrament in forme of bread)and the cōſecrated chalice, is ſhewed in ſight? He ſpeaketh there of many thinges that be of great
auctoritie and weight in the church, which
we haue by tradition onely , and can not be
auouched by holy ſcripture. Of ſhewing the
holy myſteries to them that be preſent in the
ſacrifice,the olde doctours make mentiō not
ſildom. S. Chryſoſtom declareth the maner
of it ſaying,that ſuch as were accompted vnworthy and heynouſe ſynners were put forth
of the churche, whiles the ſacrifice was offered,whiles Chriſt and that lambe of our lord
was ſacrificed . Which being put out of the
churche,then were the vailes (of the aulter)
taken awaie, to th'entent the holy myſteries
might be ſhewed in ſight,doubteles to ſtyrre
the people to more deuotion,reuerence,and
to the adoration of Chriſtes bodie in them
preſent.And thus for the Eleuation
or holding vp of the Sacrament,we haue ſayde
ynough.

In Epiſt.
ad Epheſ.
Sermo.3.
in moral.

Or

Or that the people did then fall downe, and 　*Iuell.*
worship the Sacrament with godly honour.

Of the vvorshipping or adoration of the Sacrament.

ARTICLE. VIII.

F the blessed Sacramēt of the aulter were no other, then M . Iuell
and the rest of the Sacramentaries
thinke of it: then were it not well
done the people to bowe downe to it, and to
worship it with godly honour. For then were
it but bare bread and wyne, how honorably
so euer they speake of it, calling it symbolicall, that is, tokening, and Sacramētal bread
and wyne . But now this being that very
bread, which God the father gaue vs frō heauen, as Christ sayeth : This bread being the 　Ioan.6.
fleshe of Christ, which he gaue for the life of
the world : this being that bread and that 　1.Cor.11.
cuppe, whereof who so euer eateth or drinketh vnworthely, shall be gylty of the body
and bloud of our lord : in this Sacrament
being conteined the very reall and substantiall body and bloud of Christ, as him selfe
sayeth expressely in the three first Euangelistes, and in Saint Paul : this being that holy *Eucharistia*, which *Ignatius* calleth the
fleshe of our Sauiour *Iesus* Christ that hath
suffered for our synnes, which the father
by his goodnes hath raysed vp to life againe : This being not common bread, but the
Eucharistia, after consecration consisting
　　　　　　　　　　　of

In Episto-
la quadam
ad Smyr-
nenses, vt
citatur à
Theod.

of two thinges, earthly and heauenly, as *Jreneus* sayeth, meaning by the one, the outward formes, by the other, the very body and bloud of Christ, who partely for the godhed inseparably thereto vnited, and partely for that they were conceiued of the holy ghoste in the most holy virgine Mary, are worthely called heauély: This being that bread, which of our lord geuen to his disciples, not in shape, but in nature chaunged by the almighty power of the word, is made fleshe, as S. Cyprian termeth it: This being that holy mysterie, wherein the inuisible priest tourneth the visible creatures (of bread and wyne) in to the substance of his body and bloud, by his word with secrete power, as *Eusebius Emisenus* reporteth: This being that holy foode, by worthy receiuing where of Christ dwelleth in vs naturally, that is to witte, is in vs by truth of nature, and not by concorde of will onely, as *Hilarius* affirmeth: Againe this being that table, whereat in our lordes meate we receiue the worde truly made fleshe of the most holy virgine Mary, as the same Hilarie sayeth: This being that bread which neither earing nor sowing nor worke of tyllers hath brought forth, but that earth which remained vntouched, and was full of the same, that is the blessed virgine Mary, as Gregorie Nyssene describeth: This being that supper, in the which Christ sacrificed hi selfe

Theodorito in Polymorph.
Lib.4. cō-
trā hæreses
cap.34.

In Ser. de
cœna Do.

Homil. 5.
de Pascha.

Lib.8.de
Trinitate.

as

as *Clemens Romanus*, and as *Hesychius* de- Lib.de vita
clareth: Who furthermore in an other place Mosis.
writeth most plainely, that these mysteries, cap.48.
meaning the blessed Sacrament of th'aulter, Côstitut.
are *sancta sanctorū*, the holiest of all holy thin li.8.ca.vlt.
ges, because it is the body of him selfe, of In Leuit.
whom *Gabriel* sayd to the virgine, *the holy* lib.1. ca.4.
ghost shall come vpon the, and the power of the
highest shall ouershaddowe the, therefore that ho Luc,1.
ly thing which shall be borne of the, shall be cal-
led the sonne of God, and of whō also *Esaie* spake, *Holy is our lord, and dwelleth on high*, verely euen in the bosome of the father: On the
holy table where these mysteries are celebra
ted, the lambe of God being layed and sacrificed of priestes vnbloudely, as that most aun
cient and worthy coūcell of Nice reporteth:
Briefly in this highest Sacrament vnder visible shape inuisible thinges, soothly the very
true, reall, naturall and substantiall body and
bloude of our Sauiour Christ being conteined, as the scriptures, doctours, councelles,
yea and the best learned of Martin Lutheres
schoole doo most plainely and assuredly affirme: This (I saye in conclusion) being so, as
it is vndoubtedly so : we that remaine in the
catholike churche, and can by no persecutiō
be remoued from the catholike faith, whom
it liketh M. Iuell and his felowes to call papistes, beleue verely, that it is our bownden
duetie to adore the Sacrament, and to wor-

T   ship

hip it with all godly honour. By which word Sacrament notwithstanding in this respect, we meane not the outward formes, that properly are called the Sacramēt, but the thing of the Sacrament, the inuisible grace and vertute therein conteined, euen the very body and bloud of Christ.

And when we adore and worship this blessed Sacrament, we doo not adore and worship the substance it selfe of bread and wine, because after consecration none at all remaineth. Neither doo we adore the outward shapes and formes of bread and wine which remaine, for they be but creatures that ought not to be adored: but the body it selfe and bloud of Christ, vnder those formes verely and really conteined, lowly and deuoutly doo we adore. And therefore to speake more properly, and according to skill, least our aduersaries might take aduantage against vs through occasion of termes, whe-re right sense onely is meant: we proteste and saye, that we doo and ought to adore and worship the body and bloud of Christ in the Sacrament.

And here this much is further to be sayde, that in the Sacrament of the aulter, the body of Christ is not adored by thought of mynde sundred from the word, but being inseparably vnited to the word. For this is specially to be considered, that in this most

holy

VVhat Christen people adore in the Sacrament.

holy Sacramét, the body and bloud of Chriſt
are not preſent by them ſelues alone, as beig
ſeparated from his ſoule and from the Godhed : but that there is here his true and lyuing fleſhe and bloud ioyned together with
his Godhed inſeparably, and that they be as
him ſelfe is, perfite, whole and inſeparable.
Which is ſufficiently confirmed by ſundry
his owne wordes in S.Iohn. *I am*(ſayeth he)
*the bread of lyfe.*Againe, *this is bread comming
downe from heauen, that if any eate of it, he dye
not.ƒ am the liuely bread that came downe from
heauen, if any eate of this bread, he ſhall lyue
euerlaſtingly*. And to ſhewe what bread he
meant, he concludeth with theſe wordes:
*And the bread which I ſhall geue, is my fleſhe,
which I ſhall geue for the life of the world*. By
which wordes he aſſureth vs plainely, that
his fleſhe which he geueth vs to eate, is full
of lyfe, and ioyned with his Godhed, which
bringeth to the worthy receiuers thereof im
mortalitie as well of body as of ſoule. Which
thing fleſhe and bloud of it ſelfe could not
perforime, as our lord hi ſelfe declareth plainely, where he ſayth, as there it f loweth:*ƒt is
the ſpirite that quikneth or geueth lyfe, the fleſhe
proſiteth nothig. The wordes which ƒ haue ſpoké
ta you bee ſpirite and life.*As though he had ſayde thus.The fleſhe of it ſelfe ꝓfiteth nothig,
but my fleſhe which is full of Godhed and
ſpirite, bringeth and worketh immortalitie

T 2   and

and life euerlasting to them that receiue it worthely. Thus we vnderstãd in this blessed Sacrament not onely the body and bloud of Christ, but all and whole Christ, God and man, to be present in substance, and that for the inseparable vnitie of the persõ of Christ: and for this cause we acknowledge our selues bownden to adore him, as very true God and man.

For a clearer declaration hereof, I will not let to recite a notable sentence out of S. Augustine, where he expoundeth these wordes of Christ: *Then if ye see the sonne of man go vp, where he was before.*. There had ben no question (sayeth he) if he had thus sayde: if ye see the sonne of God go vp, where he was before. But whereas he sayde, *the sonne of man go vp, where he was before*, what was the sonne of man in heauen, before that he beganne to be in earth? Verely here he sayde, where he was before, as though thẽ he were not there, when he spake these wordes. And in an other place he sayeth, *No man hath ascended in to heauen, but he that discended from heauen, the sonne of man, which is in heauen*. He sayde not was, but *the sonne of man* sayeth he, *which is in heauẽ*. In earth he spake, and sayde him selfe to be in heauen. To what perteineth this, but that we vnderstand Christ to be one person. God and man, not two, least our faith be not a trinitie, but a quaternitie ? Wherefore

Christ

In Ioan. tractat.27.

Chriſt is one, the worde, the ſoule and the fleſhe, one Chriſt:the ſonne of God, and the ſonne of man, one Chriſt. The ſonne of God euer, the ſonne of mã in tyme :yet one Chriſt according to th'vnitie of perſon was in heauen, when he ſpake in earth. So was the ſonne of man in heauē, as the ſonne of God was in earth. The ſonne of God in earth fleſhe taken, the ſonne of man in heauen in vnitie of perſon. This farre Saint Auguſtine.

Herevpon he expoundeth theſe wordes, *It is the ſpirite that quikneth or geueth life, the fleſhe auaileth nothing*, thus: The fleſhe profiteth nothing, but the onely fleſhe. Come the ſpirite to the fleſhe, and it profiteth very much. For if the fleſhe ſhuld profite nothing the word ſhuld not be made fleſhe to dwell amongeſt vs. For this vnitie of perſon to be vnderſtanded in bothe natures (ſayeth the great learned father Leo) we reade that bothe the ſonne of man came downe from heauen, when as the ſonne of God tooke fleſhe of that virgine, of whom he was borne : and againe, it is ſayde, that the ſonne of God was crucified and buryed, whereas he ſuffered theſe thinges not in the Godhed it ſelfe, in which the onely begoten is coeuerlaſting and conſubſtantiall with the father, but in the infirmitie of humaine nature. Wherefor we confeſſe all in the Crede alſo, the onely begoten ſonne of God crucified and buryed,

Epiſt. ad Flauianū Conſtan-tinopoli-tanū epiſ. cap.5.

T 3   according

according to that saying of th'apostle : *For if*
they had knowē, they would neuer haue crucified
the lord of maiestie.

1.Cor.2.

In Iohan.
li.4.ca.15.

According to this doctrine *Cyrillus* writing vpon S.Iohn, sayeth, he that eateth the
fleshe of Christ hath lyfe euerlasting. For this
fleshe hath the word of God, which naturally
is lyfe. Therefore he sayeth : *I wil rayse him*
againe in the last daye. For I, sayde he, that is,
my body, which shall be eaten, will raise him
againe. For he is not other, then his fleshe. I
saye not this because by nature he is not
other, but because after incarnatiō he suffereth not hī selfe to be diuided in to two sonnes. By which wordes he reproueth the heresie of wicked *Nestorius,* that went about to
diuide Christ, and of Christ to make two sonnes, the one the sonne of God, the other the
sonne of Marye, and so two persones. For
which *Nestorius* was condemned in the fitst
Ephesine councell, and also specially for that
he sayde, we receiue in this Sacrament onely
the fleshe of Christ in the bread, and his
bloud onely in the wine without the Godhed, because Christ sayde, *he that eateth my*
fleshe, and sayde not, he that eateth or drinketh my Godhed, because his Godhed cā not

Vide Ana-
thematis-
mum.11.
Item ad

be eatē, but his fleshe onely. Which heretical
cauille *Cyrillus* doth thus auoyd. Although
(sayeth he) the nature of the Godhed be not
eaten, yet we eate the body of Christ, which
verely

verely may be eatē. But this body is the Wor Theodo∫.
des owne proper body, which quikneth al de recta
thinges, and in as much as it is the body of li fide. & lib.
fe, it is quikning or lyfe geuing. 2. ad Regi
nas, de rē
Now he quikneth vs or geueth vs lyfe, as cta fide.
God, the onely fonteine of lyfe. Wherefore
∫uch ∫peaches vttered in the ∫criptures of
Chri∫t, whereby that appeareth to be attributed to the one nature, which apperteineth
to the other, and contrary wi∫e: according to
that incōprehen∫ible and vn∫peakeable coniunction and vnion of the diuine and humaine nature in one per∫on, are to be taken of
him in∫eparably, in as much as he is both
God and man: and not of this or that other
nature onely, as being ∫euered frō the other.
For through cau∫e of this in∫eparable vnion,
what ∫o euer is apperteining or peculiar to
either nature, it is rightly a∫cribed, yea and
it ought to be a∫cribed to the whole per∫on.
And this is done, as the learned diuines termé it, *per communicationem idiomatum*. And
thus *Cyrillus* teacheth, how Chri∫t may be eaten, not according to the diuine, but humaine nature, which he tooke of vs, and ∫o likewi∫e he is of Chri∫ten people adored in the
Sacrament according to his diuine nature.
And yet not according to his diuine nature
onely, as though that were ∫eparated from
his humaine nature, but his whole per∫on together God and mā. And his pretious fle∫he

and bloud are adored for the inseparable cõ-
iunction of bothe natures into one person,
which is Iesus Christ God and man. *Whom
God hath exalted,* (as S. Paul sayeth) *and hath*
Philip.2. *geuen him a name, which is aboue all name, that*
in the name of Iesus euery knee be bowed of the
heauenly and the earthly thinges, and of thinges
beneathe, and that euery tonge confesse, that our
lord Iesus Christ is in glory of God the father,
that is, of equal glory with the father. *And*
Heb.10. *when God* (sayeth S. Paul) *bringeth his first be-*
Psal.96. *gotẽ in to the world, he sayeth, and let all the An-*
gelles of God adore him. S. Iohn writeth in his
reuelation, that he heard all creatures saye,
Apoc.5. *blessing honour, glory and power be to him which*
sitteth in the throne, and to the lambe for euer.
And the foure and twentie elders fell downe
on their faces, and adored him that lyueth vntill
worldes of worldes.

But it shall be more tediouse then nedefull, to recite places out of the scriptures for
proufe of th'adoration of Christ, there may
of them be fownde so great plentie. Yet be-
Contra- cause Luther was either so blinde or rather
rietie in so deuilish, as to denye th'adoration, where
the first notwithstanding he confessed the presence
diuisers of of Christes true and natural body in the Sa-
the nevve crament: I will here recite what the Sacramẽ-
gospell. taries of Zurich in Latin called *Tigurum,* haue written against him therefore. What (saye
they) is the bread the true and natural body
of

of Chrift, and is Chrift in the fupper (as the Pope and Luther doo teache)prefent? Whe refore then ought not the lord there to be adored, where ye faye him to be prefet? Why fhall we be forbydden to adore that, which is not onely Sacramentally, but alfo corporally the body of Chrift? *Thomas* toucheth the true body of Chrift rayfed vp from the dead, and falling downe on his knees adoreth faying: *My God and my lord*. The difciples adore the lord as well before as after his Afcenfion. Matth. 28. Act. 1. And the lord in Ioan.9. S. John fayeth to the blinde mã, *beleueft thou in the fonne of God?* and he anfwered hĩ faying, *Lord who is he, that I may beleue in him? And Iefus fayed to him: Thou haft both e fene him, and who fpeaketh with thee, he it is. Then he fayeth, lord I beleue, and he adored him*. Now if we taught our lordes bread to be the natural body of Chrift, verely we would adore it alfo faithfully with the papiftes. This much the Zuinglians againft Luther. Whereby they prooue fufficiently th'adoration of Chriftes body in the Sacrament, and fo confequently of Chrift him felfe God and man, becaufe of the infeparable coniunction of his diuine and humaine nature in vnitie of perfone, fo as where his body is, there is it ioyned and vnited alfo vnto his Godhed, and fo there Chrift is prefent perfitely, wholly, and fubftantially, very God and man.

T 5   For

For the cleare vnderstanding whereof the
better to be atteined, the scholastical diuines
haue profitably deuised the terme *Concomi-*
tantia, plainely and truly teaching that in this
Sacrament after consecration vnder the forme of breade is present the body of Christ,
and vnder the forme of wine his bloud *ex vi*
Sacramenti, and with the body vnder forme
of bread also the bloud, the soule, and Godhed of Christ, and likewise with the bloud,
vnder the forme of wine, the body, soule, and
Godhed, *ex concomitantia*, as they terme it, in
shorter and playner wise vttering the same
doctrine of faith, which the holy fathers dyd
in the Ephesine councell against *Nestorius.*
Whereby they meane, that where the body
of Christ is present, by necessary sequell, because of the indiuisible copulation of bothe
natures in the vnitie of person, (for as much
as the Word made flesshe neuer lefte the humaine nature) there is also his bloud, his sou
le, his Godhed, and so whole and perfite
Christ God and mã. And in this respecte the
terme is not to be missliked of any godly lear
ned man, though some newe Maisters scoffe
at it, who fill the measure of their predeces-
sours, that likewise haue bē offēded with ter
mes for the apter declaratiõ of certaine necessary articles of our faith, by holy and learned fathers in general councelles holesomly
deuised. Of which sorte ben these, *homousion,*
humanatie

humanatio, incarnatio, tranſubſtantiatio, &c.
Now here is to be noted, how the Zuinglians, whom M, Iuell foloweth, in th'article of
adoration confute the Lutherans, as on the
other ſyde, the Lutherans in th'article of the
preſence, confute the Zuinglians. As
though it were by Gods ſpeciall prouidence
for the better ſtaye of his churche ſo wrought
that bothe the truth ſhuld be confeſſed by
the enemies of truth, and alſo for vttering
of vntruth, the one ſhuld be condemned of
the other, that by the warre of heretikes the
peace of the churche might be eſtabliſhed,
and by their diſcorde the catholike people
might the faſter greowe together in concorde.

Now hauing ſufficiély proued by the ſcriptures, and that with the Zuinglians alſo,
adoration and godly honour to be due vnto
Chriſtes body, where ſo euer it pleaſe his maieſtie to exhibit the ſame preſent: let vs ſee,
whether we can finde the ſame doctrine affirmed by the holy and auncient fathers.

What the Apoſtles taught in their tyme
concerning this Article, we may iudge by
that we reade in *Dioniſius*, that was S. Paules ſcholer, and for that is to be beleued. He
adoreth and worſhippeth this holy myſterie
with theſe very wordes. *Sed ò diuinum pe-* Eccleſiaſ.
nitus ſanctumque myſterium, &c. But ô diui- hierarch.
ne and holy myſterie, which vouchesafeſt to cap. 3.

open

open the cooueringes of signes layd ouer the, vtter thy light to vs openly and plainely, and fill our spirituall eyes with the singular and euident brightnes of thy light.

Orige teacheth vs how to adore and worship Christ in the Sacrament, before we receiue it, after this forme of wordes. *Quando sanctum cibum, &c.* when thou receiuest the holy meate and that vncorrupt banket, when thou enioyest the bread and cuppe of lyfe, thou eatest and drinkest the body and bloud of our lord : then our lord entreth in vnder thy roofe. And therefor thou also humbling thy selfe folowe this Centurion or captaine, and saye : *Lord I am not worthy that thou enter vnder my roofe.* For where he entreth in vnworthely, there he entreth in to the condemnation of the receiuer.

Hom. 5. in diuersos Euangelij locos.

What can be thought of S. Cyprian, but that he adored the inuisible thing of his Sacrament, which is the body and bloud of Christ, seing that he confesseth the Godhed to be in the same, no lesse then it was in the person of Christ, which he vttereth by these wordes. *Panis iste quem dominus discipulis porrigebat, &c,* This bread which our lord gaue to his disciples, chaunged not in shape, but in nature, by the almighty power of God is made fleshe. And as in the person of Christ the manhode was sene, and the godhed was hydden, euen so the diuine essence hath vnspeakeably

In Ser de cœna do.

keably infused it selfe into the visible sacrament.

Chrysostom hath a notable place for the adoration of Christes body in the Sacramét, in his commentaries vpon S. Paul, where he affirmeth also the real presence and the sacrifice. Let vs not (sayeth he) be willing impudently to kill our selues. And when thou seest that body set forth, saye with thy selfe, for cause of this body I am no lenger earth and ashes, no lenger captiue, but free. This body fastened (on the Crosse) and beaten, was not ouercome with death. After this he exhorteth all to adore and worship our lordes body in the Sacrament. This body (sayeth he) the wise men worshipped in the stalle, and hauing taken a long iourney, being bothe wicked and aliantes, with very great feare and trembling adored him. Wherefore let vs folowe at least those aliants, vs I saye, that are citizens of heauen. For they, whereas they sawe but that stalle and cabben onely, and none of all the thinges thou seest nowe, came notwithstanding with the greatest reuerence and feare, that was possible. But thou seest it not in a stalle of beastes, but on the aulter, not a woman to holde it in her armes, but a priest preset, and the holy ghoste plentyfully spred de vpon the sacrifice. This father in his Masse maketh a prayer in presence of the blessed Sacrament, almost with the same wordes, that

In 10.cap. prioris ad Corinth.

S.Basile

S.Basile did. *Attende domine Iesu Christe Deus nofter,&c.*Looke vpon vs O lord Iesus Christ our God, from thy holy habitacle, and from the throne of the glory of thy kingdom, and come to sanctifie vs, who sitteft on high with the father, and art here inuisibly with vs, and make vs worthy by thy mighty hande, that we may be partakers of thy vnspotted body and pretioufe bloude, and through vs all the people.

In the fame Chryfoftomes liturgie or Maffe, a moft euident teftimonie of adoration of the Sacramet is thus vttered. *Sacerdos adorat, et diaconus in eo in quo eft loco, ter fecretò dicētes: Deus propitius efto etc.*The prieft adoreth,and the deacon likewife in the place he ftādeth in, faying three tymes fecretly:*God be mercifull to me a fynner*.So the people, and likewife all ma ke their adoration deuoutely and reuerently.

In the fame father is an other prayer,which the greke prieftes doo vfe to this daye at their adoration of Chriftes body in the Sacrament, and it is expreffed in thefe wordes. *Domine non fum dignus &c.* Lord I am not worthy that thou enter vnder the filthy roofe of my foule. But as thou tookeft in good parte to lye in the denne and ftall of brute beaftes, and in the houfe of Simon the leproufe, receiuedft alfo a harlot and a fynner like me comming vnto thee: vouchefafe alfo to enter into the ftalle of my foule voyde of rafon,

A prayer to befayde in the vvorfhip of the Sacrament before it be receiued.

reaſon; and into my ſylthy body being dead and leprouſe. And as thou dydſt not abhorre the fowle mowth of a harlot, kiſſing thyne vndefyled feete: So my lord God abhorre not me though a ſynner, but voucheſafe of thy goodneſſe and benignitie, that I maye be made partaker of thy moſt holy body ãd bloude.

S. Ambroſe after long ſerche and diſcuſſion, how that ſaying of the prophete might be vnderſtanded, *Adore and worſhip ye his footeſtoole, becauſe it is holy* : At length concludeth ſo, as by the footeſtoole he vnderſtandeth the earth, becauſe it is written, *Heauen is my ſeate, and the earth is my footeſtoole* : And becauſe the earth is not to be adored, for that it is a creature, by this earth he vnderſtandeth that earth, which our lord Ieſus tooke in the aſſumption of his fleſhe of the virgine Marye, and hereupon he vttereth thoſe plaine wordes for teſtimonie of the adoration. *Itaq; per ſcabellum terra intelligitur, per terrã autem caro Chriſti, quã hodie quoq; in myſterys adoramus, et quã Apoſtoli in domino Ieſu adorarũt.* And thus by the footeſtoole earth may be vnderſtãded, and by earth the fleſhe of Chriſt, which euen now adayes alſo we adore in the myſteries, and the Apoſtles adored in our lord Ieſus.

S. Auguſtines learned hãdling of this place of the pſalme, *adore ye his footeſtoole, becauſe it is holy*: maketh ſo euidẽtly for this purpoſe, that of all other auctorities, which in great number

De ſpiritu ſanĉto. lib. 3. cap. 12. Pſal. 96.

Eſa. 66.

number might be brought for proufe of the same, it ought leaſt to be omitted. The place being long, I will recite it in Engliſh onely.

In Pſal.98. His wordes be theſe. *Adore ye his footeſtoole, becauſe it is holy.* See ye brethren, what that is, he byddeth vs to adore. In an other place the

Eſa.66. ſcripture ſayeth : *heauen is my ſeate, and the earth is my footeſtoole.* What doth he the bydde vs adore and worſhip the earth, becauſe he ſayde in an other place, that it is the footeſtoole of God? And how ſhall we adore the earth, whereas the ſcripture ſayeth plainely

Deut.6.10. *Thou ſhalt adore thy lord thy God*, and here he ſayeth, *adore ye his footeſtoole?* But he expoundeth to me, what his footeſtoole is, and ſa-

Matth.4. yeth *And the earth is my footeſtoole.* I am made doubtefull, afrayed I am to adore the earth, leaſt he damne me, that made heauen and earth. Againe I am afrayed not to adore the footeſtoole of my lord, becauſe the Pſalme ſayeth to me, *Adore ye his footeſtoole.* I ſeeke what thing is his footeſtoole, and the ſcripture tellleth me, *The earth is my footeſtoole.* Being thus wauering, I tourne me to Chriſt, becauſe him I ſeeke here, and I ſynde how without impietie the earth may be adored. For he tooke of earth, earth, becauſe fleſhe is of earth, and of the fleſhe of Marye, he tooke fleſhe. And becauſe he walked here in fleſhe, and that very fleſhe he gaue vs to eate to Saluation, and no man eateth that fleſhe, excepte

firſt

first he adore it: it is fownde out how such a footestoole of our lord may be adored, and how we not only synne not by adoring, but synne by not adoring. Doth not the fleshe quicke and geue lyfe? Our lord him selfe sayde, when he spake of the commendation it selfe of that earth: *it is the spirite that quikneth, but the fleshe profiteth nothing.* Therfore when thou bowest thy selfe and fallest downe to euery such earth, beholde it not as earth, but that holy one, whose footestoole it is, that thou doest adore, for because of him thow doest adore. And therefore here he added: *Adore ye his footestoole, because it is holy.* Who is holy? he for whose loue thou adorest his footestoole. And when thou adorest him, remaine not by cogitation in fleshe, that thou be not quikned of the spirite. For *the spirite (*sayeth he)*quikneth, and the fleshe profiteth nothing.* And then when our lord commended this vnto vs, he had spoken of his fleshe, and had sayde: *Excepte a man eate my fleshe, he shall not haue in him lyfe euerlasting.*

Againe S. Augustine sheweth the maner and custome of his tyme touching the adoration of Chrift in the Sacrament, writing thus *ad Honoratum,* vpon the verse of the xxj. psalme, *Edent pauperes & saturabuntur,* that is, the poore shall eate and be filled, and vpon that other, *Manducauerunt omnes diuites terræ,* all the riche of the earth haue eaten and

V   adored.

Ioan.6.

Epift. 120.
cap.21.

adored. It is not without cause (sayeth he) that the riche and the poore be so distincted, that of the poore it was sayde before, *the poore shall eate and be fylled:* and here (of the riche) *they haue eaten and adored all that be the riche of the earth.* For they haue ben brought to the table of Christ, and do take of his body and bloud, but they doo adore onely, and be not also fylled, for as much as they doo not folowe him.

In Psal. 21.   Likewise in his expositiō vpō that Psalme: All the riche also (sayeth he there) of the earth haue eaten the body of the hūblenes of their lord, neither haue they bē fylled as the poore vntill the folowing. But yet they haue adored and worshipped it, that is by adoratiō they haue acknowleged Christ their lord there psent,

Furthermore writing against *Faustus* the heretike of the Maniches secte, amōgest other thiges he sheweth, how the Ethnikes thought that christen people for the honour they dyd before the blessed Sacrament, that is of the bread and wyne consecrated, dyd honor *Bacchus* and *Ceres*, which were false goddes honoured of the Gentiles for the inuention of wyne and corne. Whereof may iustly be gathered an argumēt, that in those dayes faithfull people worshipped the body and bloud of Christ in the Sacrament, vnder the formes of bread and wyne. For elles the infidelles could not haue suspected them of doing idolatrie to *Bacchus* and *Ceres*.

One

One other moſt euident place touching this honour and adoration, we fynde in him rehearſed by *Gratiã, lib.Sēt.Proſperi.* We doo honour(ſayeth he)in forme of bread and wyne which we ſee, thinges inuiſible, that is to ſaye,fleſhe and bloud.Neither take we likewiſe theſe two formes,as we tooke them before conſecration.Sith that we doo faithfully graunt, that before conſecration it isbread and wyne which nature hath ſhapte, but after cõſecration, fleſhe, and bloud of Chriſt, which the bleſſing (of the prieſt) hath conſecrated.

De conſecrat. diſt.2. can. Nos autem.

Leauing a number of places that might be alléaged out of the auncient fathers for the confirmation of this matter to auoyde tediouſnes, I will conclude with that moſt plaine place of *Thedoritus.* Who ſpeakig of the outward ſignes of the Sacrament ſayeth, that notwithſtanding they remaine after the myſticall bleſſing.in the proprietie of their former nature,as thoſe that may be ſene and felte noleſſe then before: yet they are vnderſtanded and beleued to be the thinges,which they are made by vertue of conſecration,and are worſhipped with godly honour.His wordes be theſe.*Intelliguntur ea eſſe, quæ facta ſunt. & creduntur,& adorantur, vt quæ illa ſint.quæ, creduntur.* Theſe myſticall ſignes (ſayeth he) are vnderſtanded to be thoſe thinges which, they are made, and ſo they are beleued, and, are adored, as being the thinges which they

Dialogo.2.

are

are beleued to be. With which wordes *Theo-doritus* affirmeth bothe the reall presence, and also the adoration. The reall presence, in that he sayeth these outward signes or tokés after consecration to be made thinges, which are not sene, but vnderstanded and beleued, whereby he signifieth the inuisible thing of this Sacramét, the body and bloud of Christ. Adoration he teacheth with expresse termes, and that becaufe through power of the my-sticall blessing the signes be in existence and in dede the thinges which they are beleued to be, soothly the body and bloud of Chríst. For otherwise God forbydde, that christén people shuld be taught to adore and worship the insensible creatures bread and wyne. Of which he sayeth, that they are adored not as signes, not so in no wise, but as being the thin-ges which they are beleued to be. Now I re-porte me to the Christen reader, whether this Adoration of the Sacrament, whereby we meane the godly worship of Chriltes bo-dy in the Sacrament, be a newe deuise or no, brought into the church but lately, about three hundred yeres past, as M. Iuell maketh him selfe sure of it in his sermon. And whe-reas vtterly to abolishe this adoration, he al-leageth great danger of idolatrie, in cafe the priest do not truly consecrate: thereto may be answered, that Iacob stoode in no danger of conscience, for that by the procurement

of

Fol. 20.

Fol. 26.

Gen. 29.

of *Laban*, he laye with Lya in stede of Rachel,
neitheir for the same was he to be charged
with aduowtrie, becaule he meāt good faith,
and thought him selfe to haue had the companie of his wyfe Rachel : So idolatrie is not
to be imputed vnto him, that worshippeth
Christ with godly honour in the bread not
confecrate, which of good faith he thinketh to be confecrate. Touching this cafe S.
Auguftine hath this notable saying. We haue Enchi.*de.*
nede (fayeth he) to put a difference in oure
iudgement, and to knowe good from euyll,
for as much as Sathan chaunging his shape,
sheweth him selfe as an angell of light, leaſt
through deceite he leade vs a fyde to fome
pernitioufe thiges. For whē he deceiueth the
fenfes of the bodye, and remoueth not the
mynde frō true and right meaning wherein
ech mā leadeth a faithfull lyfe: there is no perill in religiō. Or if whē he fayneth him felfe
good, and doth or fayeth those thiges, that of
cōgruēce perteine to good angels, although
he be thought to be good, this is not a peri-
loufe or fickely errour of Chriftian faith. But
whē as by thefe thinges he begynneth to brig
vs to thinges quite contrarie, then to knowe
him frō the good Spirite, and not to go after
him, it ftādeth vs much vpō diligētly to watche and take heede. Thus S. Auguftine. This
much for th'adoration of the Sacrament, or
rather of Chrift in the Sacramēt, maye fuffife.

Or that the Sacramēt was then, or now ought,
to be hanged vp vnder a Canopie.

Of the reuerent hanging vp of the Sacrament vnder
a Canopie.

ARTICLE IX.

I F M. Iuell would in plaine termes denye the reseruation and keping of the blessed Sacramēt, for which purpose the Pyxe and Canopie serued in the Churches of England, as of the professours of this newe gospell it is bothe in word and also in dede denyed : it were easy to proue the same by no small number of auctorities, such as him selfe can not but allowe for good and sufficient. But he knowing that right well, guilefully refraineth from mention of that principall matter, and the better to make vp his heape of Articles for some shewe against the Sacrament, by denyall reproueth the hanging vp of it vnder the Canopie, thereby shewing him selfe like *Momus*, who espying nothing reproueable in fayer *Venus*, fownde faulte with her slypper. Whereto we saye, that if he with the rest of the Sacramentaries would agree to the keping of the Sacrament, then would we demaunde, why that maner of keping were not to be liked. And here vpon proufes made of defaulte in this behalfe and a better waye shewed, in so small a matter conformitie

mitie to the better would fone be perfuaded.

In other Chriften countries (we graunt) it is kepte otherwife, vnder locke and keye, in fome places at the one ende or fyde of the aulter, in fome places in a chappell buylded for that purpofe, in fome places in the veftrie or in fome inward and fecrete Rome of the churche, as it was in the tyme of Chryfoftõ at Conftantinople. In fome other places we reade, that it was kepte in the bifhoppes palais neare to the churche, and in the holy dayes brought reuerently to the churche and fette vppon th'aulter, which for abufes cõmit ted was by order of councelles abrogated. Thus in diuerfe places diuerfely it hath ben kepte, euery where reuerently and furely, fo as it might be fafe from iniurie and villainie of mifcreantes and difpyfers of it. The hanging vp of it on high hath ben the maner of England, as Lindewode noteth vpon the cõftitutions prouinciall: on high, that wicked difpite might not reache to it, vnder a Canopie, for fhewe of reuerence and honour.

If princes be honored with cloth of eftate, bifhops with folemne thrones in their churches, and deanes with Canopies of tapiftrie, fylke and arras (as we fee in fundry cathedrall churches) and no man finde faulte with it: why fhuld M. Iuell miflike the Canopie that is vfed for honour of that bleffed Sacrament, wherein is conteined the very body of

Diuerfe maners of keping the bleffed Sacrament.

In epiftola ad Innocentium.

In Cõcil. Braccarẽ. 3. Can. 5.

V 4   Chrift

Chrift, and through the inseparable ioyning
together of bothe natures in vnitie of perſo,
Chriſt him ſelfe very God and man? With
what face ſpeaketh he againſt the Canopie
vſed to the honour of Chriſt in the Sacramēt, that ſytting in the biſhoppes ſeate at Sa-
leſburie, can abyde the ſyght of a ſolēne canopie made of painted bourdes ſpredde
ouer his head? If he had ben of coūſell with
Moſes, *Dauid* and *Salomõ*, it is lyke he would
haue reproued their iudgementes for the
great honour they vſed and cauſed ſo to be
continewed towardes the Arke, wherein was
conteined nothing but the tables of the lawe, Aarõs rodde, and a potte full of *Manna*.

2.Reg.7.   King *Dauid* thought it very vnſitting, and
felte great remorſe in heart, that he dwelte in
a houſe of Cedres, and the Arke of God was
putte in the myddes of ſkynnes, that is, of
the tabernacle: whoſe outward partes were
couered with beaſtes ſkynnes. And now there is one fownde among other monſtrouſe
and ſtraunge formes of creatures, maners
and doctrines, who beig but duſte and aſhes,
as *Abraham* ſayde of him ſelfe, promoted to
the name of a biſhop, and not choſen (I wene) to doo high ſeruice of a man according
to Gods owne hearte, as *Dauid* was: thinketh
not him ſelfe vnworthey to ſytte in a biſhops
chaver vnder a gorgeouſe teſture or Canopie
of gilted bourdes, and can not ſuffer the pretiouſe

tiouſe body of Chriſt, whereby we are rede-
med, to haue for remembraunce of honour
done of our parte , ſo much as a litle Cano-
piè, a thing of ſmall price . Yet was the Arke
but a ſhadowe, and this the body, that the figure, this the truthe , that the type or ſigne,
this the very thing it ſelfe . As I doo not enuie M. Iuell that honour , by what right ſo
euer he enioyeth it , So I can not but blame
him for bereuing Chriſt of his honour in
this bleſſed Sacrament.

Now concerning this article it ſelfe, if it
may be called an article , wherein M. Iuell
thinketh to haue great aduantage againſt vs,
as though nothing could be brought for it
(though it be not one of the greateſt keyes
nor of the higheſt myſteries of our Religion
as he reporteth it to bee the more to deface
it)of the Canopie what may be fownde, I lea
ue to others , neither it forceth greatly . But
of the hanging vp of the Sacrament ouer the
aulter, we fynde plaine mention in S. Baſiles
lyfe written by *Amphilochius* that worthy
biſhop of *Iconium* . Who telleth that S. Baſile at his Maſſe hauing diuided the Sacramēt
in three partes , dyd put the one in the goldē
dooue (after which forme the Pyxe was then
commonly made) hanging ouer the aulter.
His wordes be theſe , *Impoſuerit colūba aurea
pendenti ſuper altare.* And for further euidēce
that ſuch pyxes made in forme of a dooue

Hanging
vp of the
Sacrament
in a pyxe
ouer the
aulter is
auncient.

V 5   in rein remembraunce of the holy ghost, that appeared like a dooue, were hanged vp ouer th'aulter, we synde in the actes of the general councell holdé at Côstâtinople, that the clergie of Antioche accused one *Seuerus* an heretike, before Iohn the patriarke and the councel there, that he had ryfied, and spoyled the holy aulters, and molted the consecrated vessels, and had made awaye with some of them to his companions, *Præsumpsisset etiã columbas aureas & argenteas in formam Spiritus sancti super diuina lauacra & altaria appensas vna cum alijs sibi appropriare, dicens: Non oportere in specie columbæ Spiritũ sanctum nominare.* Which is to saye, that he had presumed also to côuerte to his owne vse besyde other thinges, the golden and syluerne dooues made to represent the holy ghoste, that were hanged vp ouer the holy fontes and aultres, saying that no man ought to speake of the holy ghoste in the shape of a dooue.

Neither hath the Sacrament ben kepte in all places and in all tymes in one maner of vessels. So it be reuerently kepte for the viage prouision for the sicke, no catholike man will maineteine strife for the maner and order of keping. *Symmachus* a very worthy bishop of Rome in the tyme of *Anastasius* the Emperour, as it is writté in his lyfe, made two vessels of syluer to reserue the Sacramét in, and set them on the aulters of two churches

113

in Rome, of S. Syluefter, and of S. Androw. Thefe veffelles they call commonly, *Ciboria*. We fynde likewife in the lyfe of S. Gregorie, that he alfo like *Symmachus* made fuch a veffell which they call *Ciborium* for the Sacrament, with four pillours of pure fyluer, and fet it on the aulter at S. Petres in Rome.

In a worke of *Gregorius Turonenfis* this veffell is called, *Turris in qua myfterium dominici corporis habebatur*, a tower wherein our lordes body was kepte. In an olde booke *de pœnitentia* of *Theodorus* the Greke of *Tarfus in Cilicia*, fometyme archbifhop of Cantorbury before Beda his tyme, it is called *pixis cũ corpore Domini ad viaticum pro infirmis*. The pyxe with our lordes body for the viage prouifiõ for the ficke. In that booke in an admonition of a bifhop to his clergie in a fynode, warning is geuẽ, that nothing be put vppõ th'aulter in tyme of the Sacrifice, but the cofer of Relikes, the booke of the four Euangeliftes, and the pyxe with our lordes body.

Thus we fynde that the bleffed Sacramẽt hath alwaies ben kepte in fome places in a pyxe hanged vp ouer the aulter, in fome other places otherwife, euery where and in all tymes fafely and reuerently, as is declared, to be alwaife in readynes for the viage prouifiõ of the ficke. Which keping of it for that godly purpofe, and with like due reuerẽce, if M. Iuell and the Sacramentaries would admitte
ne

no man will be either so scrupulouse or so contentiouse, as to stryue with them either for the hanging vp of it, or for the Canopie.

Or that in the Sacrament after the wordes of Consecration there remayneth only the accidentes and shewes without the substance of breade and wyne.

Of the remaining of the Accidentes vvithout their substance in the Sacrament.

ARTICLE. X.

I N this Sacrament after consecration, nothing in substance remayneth that was before, neither breade nor wine, but onely the accidentes of breade and wine : as their forme and shape, sauour, smell, colour, weight, and such the like, which here haue their being miraculously without their subiecte : for as much as after consecration, there is none other substance, then the substäce of the body and bloud of our lord, which is not affected with such accidentes, as the scholasticall doctours terme it: Which doctrine hath alwayes though not with these precise termes, ben taught and beleued from the begin ning, and depédeth of the Article of Trásubstantiation. For if the substäce of bread and wyne be chaunged in to the substance of the body and bloud of our lord (which is cóstätly affirmed by all the learned and auncièt fathers of the churche) it foloweth by a necessary

Iuell.

Transub-stantiatió affirmed.

sary

fary fequell in nature and by drifte of reafon,
that then the accidentes onely remaine. For
witnes and proufe whereof, I will not let to
recite certaine moft manifeft fayinges of the
olde and beft approued doctours.

S. Cyprian that learned bifhop and holy
martyr fayeth thus *In fermone de cœna Domi-
ni.Panis ifte quem Dominus difcipulis porrigebat,non effigie,fed natura mutatus , omnipoten-
tia verbi factus eft caro.*This bread which our
lord gaue to his difciples,chaūged not in fha
pe, but in nature, by the almighty power of
the word(he meaneth Chriftes word of Cō-
fecratiō)is made flefhe. Lo he confeffeth the
breade to be chaūged not in fhape or forme,
for that remayneth, but in nature , that is to
faye,in fubftance. And to fignifie the chaūge
of fubftance, and not an accidentarie chaūge
onely,to witte, from the vfe of commō breade to ferue for Sacramentall bread , as fome
of our newe Maifters doo expounde that pla
ce for a fhifte:he addeth great weight of wor
des,whereby he farre ouerpeifeth thefe mennes light deuife , faying that by the almighty
power of our lordes word , it is made flefhe.
Verely they might confyder , as they would
feme to be of fharpe iudgement , that to the
performance of fo fmall a matter, as their Sa
cramenfal chaunge is,the almighty power of
Gods worde is not nedefull. And now if here this worde, *Factus eft* may fignifie an ima-
                                    ginatiue

ginatiue making, then why may not *verbum caro factum est*, likewise be expounded to the defence of sundry olde haynouse heresies against the true manhod of Christ? Thus the nature of the bread in this Sacrament being chaunged, and the forme remayning, so as it seme breade, as before consecratio, and being made our lordes fleshe by vertue of the word the substace of bread changed into that most excellent substance of the fleshe of Christ: of that which was before, the accidentes remaine onely, *without the substace of breade*. The like is to be beleued of the wyne.

De conse-
crat. dist.2.
ca.omnia
quæcūque Nothing can be playner to this purpose, then the sayinges of S. Ambros . *Licet figura panis & vini videatur, nihil tamen aliud, quam caro Christi & sanguis post consecrationem credendum est.* Although (sayeth he) the forme of bread and wyne be sene, yet after consecration we must beleue, they are nothing elles, but the fleshe and bloud of Christ. After the opinion of this father the shewe and figure of breade and wyne are sene, and therefore remaine after consecration . And if we must beleue that which was breade and wyne before, to be no other thing, but the fleshe and bloud of Christ: then are they no other thing in dede. For if they were, we might so beleue . For beleefe is grownded vpon truth, and what so euer is not true, it is not to be beleued. Hereof it foloweth, that after

consecra-

consecration the accidentes and shewes onely remayne without the substance of breade
and wyne. In an other place he sayeth as *De Sacra-*
much. *Panis iste,&c.* This bread before the *métis lib.*
wordes of the Sacramentes, is bread, as sone *4.cap.4.*
as the consecratió commeth, of bread is made the body of Christ. Againe in an other
place he sayeth most plainely.That the power *De ijs qui*
of consecration is greater then the power *initiantur.*
of nature, because nature is chaunged by
consecration. By this father it is euident,
that the nature, that is to saye; the substance
of breade and wyne by consecration being
chaúged into the body and bloude of Christ,
their natural qualities, which be accidentes
contynewing vnchaunged for performance
of the Sacrament, remayne without the substance of bread and wyne.

According vnto the which meaning *Theo-* *Dialog.1.*
doritus sayeth,*Videri et tangi possunt sicut prius,*
Intelliguntur autem ea esse,quæ facta sunt,& cre-
duntur. The breade and wyne may be sene
and felte as before consecration,but they are
vnderstanded to be the thinges, which they
are made, and beleued. We do not in like
forte(sayeth S.Augustine)take these two for- *In lib.Sé-*
mes of breade and wyne after consecratió, as *tent Pro-*
we tooke them before. Sith that we graunt *speri.de*
faithfully that before consecratió it is bread *côse.dict.*
and wyne that nature hath shapte, but after *1.ca.Nos*
consecratió, that it is the flesshe and bloud of *autem.*
                                        Christ,

Chrift, that the bleſſing hath conſecrated. In an other place he ſayeth, that this is not the bread which goeth in to the body (meaning for bodily ſuſtenance) but that bread of life, *Qui animæ noſtræ ſubſtantiam fulcit*, which ſuſteineth the ſubſtance of our ſoule.

No man can ſpeake more plainely hereof then *Cyrillus Hieroſolymitanus* an olde auctor who wrote in Greke, and is extant, but as yet remayning in written hande, and comen to the ſighte of fewe learned men. His wordes be not much vnlike the wordes of the ſcoledoctoures. *Præbetur corpus* ἐν τύπῳ ἄρτου. i. *in ſpecie ſiue figura panis. Item præbetur ſanguis* ἐν τύπῳ οἴνου. Chriſtes body (ſayeth he) is geuen vs in forme or figure of bread. Againe his bloud is geuen vs in forme of wine. A litle after theſe wordes he ſayeth thus. μὴ πρόσεχε νοῦν ὡς ψιλοῖς τῷ ἄρτῳ καὶ τῷ οἴνῳ, etc. *Neme tem adhibeas quaſi pani & vino nudis, ſunt enim hæc corpus & ſanguis, vt Dominus pronunciauit. Nā tametſi illud tibi ſenſus ſuggerit, eſſe ſcilicet panē & vinū nudum, tamen firmet te fides, & ne guſta tu rem diiudices, quin potius pro certo ac comperto habe, omni dubitatione relicta, eſſe tibi impartitum corpus & ſanguinem Chriſti.* Cōſider not (ſayeth this father) theſe as bare bread and wyne. For theſe are his body and bloud, as our lord ſayde. For although thy teſe reporte to thee ſo much, that it is bare bread and wyne, yet let thy faith ſtaye thee, and iudge not

thereof

thereof by thy taſte, but rather be right well
aſſured all boubte put a parte, that the body
and bloud of Chriſt is geuen to thee. Againe
ne he ſayeth thus in the ſame place. *Hec cum
ſcias, & pro certo & explorato habeas, qui videtur
tur eſſe panis, nõ eſſe, ſ̃d corpus Chriſti, it̃m quod
vid̃tur vinum, non eſſe, quanquam id velit ſenſus,
ſus, ſed ſanguinẽm Chriſti, ac de eo prophetã dixiſſe,
xiſſe, panis cõr hominis cõſirmat. firma it ſe cor,
ſũmpto hoc pane, vtpote ſpirituali.* Where as
thou knoweſt this for a very certainetie, that
that, which ſemeth to be wyne, is not wyne,
albeit the ſenſe maketh that accompte of it,
but the bloud of Chriſt, and that the prophete
te thereof ſayde, *bread ſtrengthneth the hart of* Pſal. 103.
man: ſtrengthẽ thou thy ſelfe thy harte by taking
king this bread which is ſpiritual. And in 3.
Catecheſi this father ſayeth, *Panis Euchariſtiæ
poſt inuocationem ſanĉti ſpiritus non ampliꝰ eſt
panis nudus & ſimplex, Sed corpus &c.* The
bread of the Sacrament after prayer made to
the holy ghoſt, is not bare and ſimple bread,
but the body of Chriſt.

Now ſith that by this doĉtours plaine declaration
claration of the catholike faith in this point,
we ought to beleue, and to be verely aſſured,
that the bread is no more bread after conſecration,
cration, but the very body of Chriſt, and
the wyne no more wyne, but his pretiouſe
bloud, though they ſeme to the eye otherwiſe,
ſe, though taſte and feeling iudge otherwiſe,

     X and

and to be shorte, though al senses reporte the contrary, and all this vpon warrant of our lordes word, who sayde these to be his body and bloud: an I that (as he teacheth) not in the bread and wyne: And further sith we are taught by *Eusebius Emisenus* in his homilies of Easter, to beleue, *terrena comutari & transire*, the earthly thinges to be chaunged and to passe, againe, *creaturas conuerti in substantiã corporis Christi*, the creatures of bread and wyne to be tourned in to the substãce of our lordes body and bloud, which is the very trãsubstantiation: And sith Chrysostõ sayeth *Panẽ absumi*, that the bread is consumed awaie by the substance of Christes bodye: And Damascen, bread and wine *transmutari supernaturaliter*, to be chaunged aboue the course of nature: and Theophylact, the bread *transelemẽtari in carnem domini*, to be quite tourned by chaunging of the elementes, that is the matter or substance it cõsisteth of, into the fleshe of our lorde: and in an other place, *ineffabili operatione transformari, etiamsi panis nobis videatur*, that the bread is transformed or chaunged into an other substantiall forme (he meaneth that of our lordes body) by vnspeakeable working, though it seme to be bread.

Finally, sith that the greke Doctours of late age affirme the same doctrine, among whom *Samona* vseth for persuasion of it the similitude, which Gregorie Nyssene and *Damascen*

Transubstantiation. In Liturgia Lib. 4 de orthodoxa fi. c 14. In Mar. 14.

In Matth. 26.

The treatises of these greke vvriters haue ben set forth of late by one Claudius de Sainctes.

Damascen for declaration of the same vsed
before:which is, that in cōsecration such maner transubstantiatiō is made, as is the cōuer-
sion of the bread in nourrishing, in which it
is tourned into the substance of the nourri-
shed: *Methonensis*, like *S. Ambrose*, would not
men in this matter to looke for the order of
nature, seing that Christ was borne of a virgine besyde all order of nature, and sayeth,
that our lordes bodye in this Sacramēt, is receiued vnder the forme or shape of an other
thing, least bloud shuld cause it to be horrible : *Nicolaus Cabasila* sayeth that this bread Cap.17.
is no more a figure of our lordes bodye, neither a gifte bearing an image of the true gifte, nor bearing any discription of the passions
of our Sauiour him selfe as it were in a table,
but the true gifte it selfe, the most holy bodye of our lord it selfe, which hath truly receiued reproches, cōtumelies, stripes, which
was crucified, which was kylled : *Marcus
Ephesius* though otherwise to be reiected, as
he that obstinatly resisted the determination
of the Councell of Florence concerning the
proceding of the holy ghost out of the sonne, yet a sufficient witnes of the Greke churches faith in this point, affirming the thinges
offered to be called of *S. Basile antitypa*, that
is, the saplers and figures of our lordes bodye
because they be not yet perfitely cōsecrated,
but as yet bearing the figure and image, re-
X 2   ferreth

ferreth the chaunge or transubstantiation of
them to the holy ghost, *donec spiritus sanctus
adueniat, qui ea mutet* these giftes offered (sayeth he)be of *S. Basile* called figures, vntill the
holy ghost come vpon them, to chaunge thé.
Whereby he sheweth the faith of the Greke
church, that through the holy ghost in consecration the bread and wine are so chaůged,
as they maye no more be called figures, but
the very bodye and bloud of our lord it selfe,
as into the same chaunged by the comming
of the holy ghost. Which chaunge is a chaun-

Transub-
ge in substance, and therefore it may rightly
ftátiation.
be termed transubstátiatió, which is nothing
elles, but a tourning or chaunging of one
substance into an other substance: Sith for
this point of our religion, we haue so good
auctoritie, and being thus assured of the infal-
lible faith of the churche declared by the testimonies of these worthy fathers of diuerse
ages and quarters of the worlde: we may well
saye with the same churche against M. Iuell,
that in this Sacrament after cósecration there remayneth nothing of that which was before, but onely the accidentes and shewes,
without the substance of bread and wyne.

And this is a matter to a Christen man not
hard to beleue. For if it please God the al-
mightie Creatour, in the condition and state
of thinges thus to ordeine, that substances
created beare and susteine accidentes, why
may

may not he by his almighty power conserue
and kepe also accidentes without substance,
sith that the very hethen philosophers repute
it for an absurditie to saye, *primam causam
non posse id præstare solam, quod possit cum secunda*, that is to saye, that the first cause (whereby
they vnderstand God) can not doo that alone, which he can doo with the second cause,
where by they meane a creature?

And that this being of accidentes without
substance or subiecte in this Sacrament, vnder which, the bread not remaining, the bodye of Christ is present, maye the rather be
beleued: it is to be cōsydered, that this thing
tooke place at the first creation of the world,
after the opinion of some Doctoures. Who Basilius
do affirme that that first light, which was at hexaeme
the begynning vntill the fourth daye, was rō.hom. 6.
not in any subiecte, but susteined by the po- 2. cap.7.
wer of God, as him lyked. For that first light Paulus
and the sunne were as whitenesse and a body Burgensis.
whithed, sayeth S. Basile. Neither then was Gene.1.
Wiclef yet borne, who might teache them,
that the power of God can not put an accidēt
without a subiect. For so he sayeth in his boo Lib.2.historstor.hussi-
ke *de apostasia cap. 5.* as *Cochlæus* reporteth. tarum.
Hereof it appeareth, out of what roote the
Gospellers of our countrie spring. Who
smatching of the sape of that wicked tree, and
hereby shewing theire kinde, appoint bowndes and borders to the power of God, that

X 3 is

is infinite and incōprehenſible. And thus by
thoſe fathers we maye conclude, that if God
can ſuſteine and kepe accidentes with ſubſtance, he can ſo doo without ſubſtance.

Iuell.

*Or that the prieſt then diuided the Sacramēt
in three partes, and afterward receiued him ſelfe all alone.*

Of diuiding the Sacrament in three partes.
ARTICLE. XI.

F the prieſtes receiuing the Sacrament him ſelfe alone, ynough hath
ben ſayde before. This terme *All*,
here ſmatcheth of ſpite. For if any
deuout perſon require to be partetaker
with the prieſt, being worthely diſpoſed and
examined, he is not tourned of, but with all
gētlenes admitted. And in this caſe the prieſt
is not to be charged with receiuing all alone.
Albeit reſpecte had to the thing receiued,
how many ſo euer receiue, it is all of all, and
all of euery one receiued. Concerning the
breaking of the Sacrament, and the diuiding
of it in three partes, firſt, it is broken by the
prieſt, that we may knowe our lord *in fractione panis*, in the breaking of the breade, as the
two diſciples acknowleged him, to whom Ie-
Luc.24.
ſus appeared in the daye of his Reſurrection,
as they were going to *Emaus*. And alſo that
thereby the paſſion of Chriſt may be repreſented to our remembraunce, at which his
pretiouſe body was for our ſynnes broken,
rent and torne on the croſſe. And this maner
was

was vsed at the Sacrifice in the Apostles tyme, as it is witnessed by Dionysius S . Paules
scoler . *Opertum panem Pontifex aperit, in fru-*   Ecclesiaf.
stra cocidens &c. The bishop (sayeth he) ope-   hierarch.
neth the couered breade , diuiding it in pie-   cap.3.
ces etc.Now touching the diuiding of the Sa-   The diui-
crament in three partes,it may appeare to be   ding of the
a Tradition of the Apostles , or otherwise a   Sac.in
custome very auncient,for as much as *Sergius*   three par-
the bishop of Rome,who lyued within lxxx.   tes,a tradi-
yeres of the syx hundred yeres after Christ,   tion of the
that M. Iuell referreth vs vnto, wrote of the   Apostles.
mysterie of that breaking or diuiding the
outward forme of bread , and declareth the
signification of the same.

It is no small argument of the antiquitie
of this obseruation,that S.Basile, as *Amphi-*
lochius writeth of him, diuided the Sacramet
in three partes at his Masse , as is aboue re-
hearsed.And where as *Sergius* sayeth,that the   De conse-
portion of the hoste which is put in to the   crat.dist.2.
chalice , betokeneth the body of Christ that   can.Tri-
is now risen againe,and the portion which is   forme.
is receiued and eaten , sheweth his body yet
walking on the earth, and that other portion
remayning on the aulter signifieth his body
in the sepulchre : what I praye you is there
herein, that any man shuld be offended with
al?I acknowledge that the mysterie hereof is
otherwise of some declared,and of all to this
ende to put vs in mynde of the benefites pur

X 4   chaced

chaced to vs by Christ in his bodye . Now that this custom or mysticall ceremonie was not first ordeined by *Sergius* , for ought that câ be gathered, but of hî expouded onely touching the mysterie of it, as vsed before his tyme from the beginning of the churche , no one auncièt councell or authour sownde vppon whom it may be fathered , of good reason , sith it hath generally ben obserued , we may referre the first institution of it to the Apostles: and that according to the rule of S. Augustine, whose notable saying for that behalfe is this. *Quod vniuersa tenet Ecclesia, nec in concilijs constitutum, sed semper retentum est, non nisi auctoritate Apostolica traditum rectissimè creditur.* What (sayeth he) the vniuersall churche kepeth , neither hath ben ordeined in coûcelles, but hath alwaies ben obserued: of good right we beleeue it hath ben delyuered(to the church) as a Tradition by the auctoritie of the Apostles.

To conclude, if any sparke of godlynes remaine in our deceiued countrie mê and brethren , they will not scorne and dispyse this auncient ceremonie of diuiding the Sacramêt in three partes at the blessed Sacrifice of the Masse, whereof any occasiô of euill is not onely not ministred , but rather côtrarywise, whereby we are admonished and stirred to têder our owne soule helth, and to rêdre thâkes to God for the great benefite of our redêptiô

Or that

Or that whoſo euer had ſayed the Sacrament Iuell. *is a figure, a pledge, a token , or a remembraunce of Chriſtes bodye, had therefor ben iudged for an heretike.*

Of the termes figure, ſigne, token, &c. by the fathers applyed to the Sacrament.

ARTICLE. XII.

N this article we doo agree with M . Iuell in ſome reſpecte. For we confeſſe, it can not be auouched by ſcripture, auncient councell, doctour or exáple of the primitiue church, that who ſo euer had ſayde, the Sacramét is a figure, a pledge, a token, or a remembraúce of Chriſtes body, had therefore bé iudged for an heretike. No má of any learning euer wrote ſo vnlearnedly. Much leſſe to impute hereſie to any man for ſaying thus, hath ben any of the higheſt myſteries or greateſt keyes of our Religion, with which vntruth M. Iuell goeth abowt to deface the truth . Wherefore this article ſemeth to haue ben put in either of malice toward the church, or of ignorance, or onely to fill vp the héape , for lacke of better ſtuffe. Peruſing the workes of the auncíét and learned fathers we ſynde , that oftentymes they call the Sacrament a figure , a ſigne, a token, a myſterie, a ſampler . The wordes of them vſed to this purpoſe in their learned tonges,

X 5　　　are

are thefe *Figura, Signum, Symbolum, Mysteriũ, Exẽplar,* ἀντίτυπον, *Imago,* & *c.* By which they meane not to diminiſh the truth of Chriſtes body in the Sacrament, but to ſignifie the ſecrete maner of his being in the ſame.

For the better vnderſtanding of ſuch places, where theſe termes are vſed in the matter of the Sacrament, the doctrine of S. Auguſtine *in ſentẽtijs Proſperi,* may ſerue very wel. Which is thus. *Hoc eſt qnod dicimus, quod omnibus modis approbare contẽdimus, ſacrificiũ Eccleſiæ duobus conſſci, duobus conſtare, viſibili elemento rum ſpecie,* & *inuiſibili Domini noſtri Jeſu Chriſti carne* & *ſanguine: Sacramẽto, (id iſt externo ſacro ſigno)* & *re ſacramenti, id eſt, corpore Chriſti,* & *c.* This is that we ſaye (ſayeth he) which by all meanes we go about to proue, that the Sacrifice of the church is made of two thinges, and conſiſteth of two thinges, of the viſible ſhape of the elementes (which are breade and wine) and the inuiſible fleſh and bloude of our lord Ieſus Chriſt, of the Sacrament, (that is the outward ſigne) and the thinge of the Sacramẽt, to witte, of the body of Chriſt, &c. By this we vnderſtãd, that this word (*Sacrament*) is of the fathers two waies taken. Firſt, for the whole ſubſtãce of the Sacramẽt, as it conſiſteth of the outward formes, and alſo with all of the very body of Chriſt vetely preſent, as ſaint Auguſtine ſayeth the Sacrifice of the Church to conſiſt of theſe two.
Secondly,

De conſecrat diſt. 2. can. hoc eſt quod dicimus:

Secondly, it is taken so as it is distincte from that hydden and diuine thing of the Sacrament, that is to saye, for the outward formes onely, which are the holy signe of Christes very body present vnder them conteined. Where of we must gather, that when so euer the fathers doo call this most excellent Sacrament a figure, or a signe, they would be vnderstanded to meane none otherwise, then of those outward formes, and not of Christes body it selfe, which is there present not typically, or figuratiuely, but really and substantially. onlesse perhaps respecte be had not to the body it selfe present, but to the maner of presence, as sometymes it happeneth.

Hovv the fathers are to be vnderstanded calling the Sacrament a figure, signe, token, &c.

So is Saint Basile to be vnderstanded in *Liturgia*, calling the sacramét *Antitypon*, that is, a sampler or a figure, and that after consecration, as the copies that be now abroade, bee founde to haue. So is *Eustathius* to be taken that great learned father of the Greke churche, who so constantly defended the catholike faith against the Arians, cited of *Epiphanius in 7 .Synodo*. Albe it concerning S. Basile, Damascé and *Euthymius*, likewise *Epiphanius* in the second Nicene councel *Actione 6*. and *Marcus Ephesius*, who was present at the councell of Florence, would haue that place so to be taken before consecration. As S. Ambrose also, calling it a figure of our lordes body

Li.4.c.14. in caput Matth. 26.

body and bloud.*lib.*4.*de Sacram. cap.* 5. And
if it appeare ſtraunge to any man, that S.Baſi-
le ſhuld call thoſe holy myſteries *Antitypa*
after conſecration, let him vnderſtand, that
this learned father thought good by that
word to note the great ſecrete of that myſterie, and to ſhewe a diſtincte condition of preſent thinges, from thinges to come. And this
conſideratiõ the church ſemeth to haue had,
which in publike prayer after holy myſteries

Sabba᷑o.4.
temporum
mēſis Sep-
temb.

receiued, maketh this humble petiition, *Vt
quæ nunc ſpecie gerimus, certa rerum veritatę ca-
piamus*: that in the lyfe to come we may take
that in certaine truth of thinges, which now
we beare in ſhape or ſhewe. Neither doo theſe wordes importe any preiudice againſt the
truth of the preſence of Chriſtes body in the
Sacramēt: but they ſignifie and vtter the moſt
principall truth of the ſame, when as all outward forme, ſhape, ſhewe, figure, ſampler and
couuer taken awaie, we ſhall haue the fruitiõ
of God him ſelfe in ſight face to face, not as it
were through a glaſſe, but ſo as he is, in truth
of his Maieſtie. So this word *Antitypon* thus
takē in S. Baſile, futthereth nothing at all the
Sacramētaries falſe doctrine againſt the truth
of the preſence of Chriſtes body in the Sacrament.

And becauſe our aduerſaries doo much
abuſe the ſimplicitie of the vnlearned, bearing them in hand, that after the iudgement
and

and doctrine of th'auncient fathers the Sacrament is but a figure, a signe , a token, or a badge , and conteineth not the very body it selfe of Christ , for proufe of the same alleaging certaine their sayinges vttered with the same termes: I thinke good by the recitall of some the chife such places to shewe, that they be vntruly reported , and that touching the veritie of the presence in the Sacramēt, they taught in their dayes the same faith , that is taught now in the catholike churche.

Holy *Ephrem* in a booke he wrote to those that will serch the nature of the sonne of God by mannes reason, sayeth thus: *Inspice di-* Cap.4. *ligenter, quomodo sumens in manibus panem, benedicit ac frangit in figura immaculati corporis sui, calicemá, in figura pretiosi sanguinis sui benedicit, & tribuit discipulis suis.* Beholde (sayeth he)diligently, how taking bread in his hādes he blesseth it and breaketh it in the figure of his vnspotted body , and, blesseth the cuppe in the figure of his pretiouse bloude, and geueth it to his disciples . By these wordes he sheweth the partition, deuision, or breaking of the Sacrament , to be done no otherwise, but in the outward formes , which be the figure of Christes body present and vnder thē conteiued. Which body now being gloriouse, is no more broken nor parted, but is indiuisible, and subiect no more to any passion, and after the Sacrament is broken , it remaineth

neth whole and perfite vnder ech portion. Agayne, by the same wordes he signifieth, that outward breaking to be a certaine holy figure and representation of the crucifying of Christ and of his bloude shedding. Which thing is with a more clearnes of wordes set forth by saint Augustine *in Sententijs Prosperi.*

De conse-
crat.dist.2.
ean.dum
frangitur.

Dum frangitur hostia, dum sanguis de calice in ora fidelium funditur, quid aliud quàm Domini ci corporis in cruce immolatio, eiusque sanguinis de latere effusio designatur? Whiles the hoste is broken, whiles the bloud is powred in to the mowthes of the faithfulles, what other thing is thereby shewed and set forth, then the sacrificing of Christes body on the crosse, and the shedding of his bloud out of his syde? And by so dooing the cōmaundemēt of Christ is fulfylled, *Doo this in my remēbraūce.*

That it may further appeare, that these wordes, figure, signe, image, token, and such other the like sometymes vsed in anciēt writers, doo not exclude the truth of thinges exhibited in the Sacrament, but rather signifie the secrete maner of th'exhibiting: amongest all other, the place of Tertulliā in his fourth booke *contrâ Marcionem*, is not to be omitted, specially being one of the chiefe and of most appearaunce, that the Sacramentaries bring for proufe of their doctrine. Tertullianes wordes be these. *Acceptum panem & distributum discipulis suis, corpus suum illum facit, fæcit, hoc esse corpus meum dicendo, id est, signra corporis mei.* The breade that he tooke and gaue to his disciples, he made it his body, in saying, *this is my body*, that is, the figure of my body.

The double taking of the worde *Sacramēt* afore mentioned remembred, and consideration had, how the sacramentes of the Newe testament comprehend two thinges, the outward visible formes, that be figures, signes and tokens, and also, and that chiefly a diuine thinge vnder thē according to Christes promisse couertly conteined, specially this being weyed, that this most holy Sacrament consisteth of these two thinges, to witte, of the visible forme of the outward elemétes, and the inuisible fleshie and bloud of Christ, that is to saye, of the Sacramēt, and of the thing of the sacramēt. Tertulliā may seme to speake of those two partes of the sacrament ioyntly in this one sētéce. For first, he speaketh most plainely of the very body of Christ in the Sacramēt, and of the maruelouse tournīg of the breade into the same, the breade (sayeth he) that he toke and gaue to his disciples, he made it his body. Which is the diuine thing of the sacramēt. Thē forthwith he sayeth, that our lord dyd it by saying. *This is my body*. i. the figure my body. By which wordes he sheweth the of other parte, the sacrament onely, that is to saye, that holy outward signe of the forme of breade,

breade, vnder which forme Chriftes body, into the which the breade by Gods power is tourned, is conteined:which outward forme is verely the figure of Chriftes body prefent, which our lord vnder the fame cōteined delyuered to his difciples , and now is likewife at that holy table to the faithfull people delyuered ; where the order of the catholike church is not broken.

That Tertulliā in this place is fo to be vnderftanded , we are taught by the great learned bifhop Saint Auguftine, and by *Hilarius*, who was bifhop of Rome nexte after Leo the firft. Saint Auguftines wordes be thefe. *Corpus Chrifti & veritas,& figura eft.Veritas dum corpus Chrifti & fanguis in virtute Spiritus fancti ex panis & vini fubftantia efficitur. Figura verò eft , quod exterius fentitur*. The body of Chrift is both the truth , and the figure.The truth , whiles the body of Chrift and his bloud by the power of the holy ghoft, is made of the fubftance of bread and wine. And it is the figure , that is with outward fenfe perceiued.

Where S.Auguftine here fayeth,the body and bloude of Chrift to be made of the fubftance of bread and wine, beware thou vnlearned man,thou thinke not them thereof to be made,as though they were newely created of the matter of bread and wine, neither that they be made of breade and wine,as of a

matter

De confec. dift.2.canon vtrū fub figura.

matter : but that where bread and wine were before, after confecration there is the very body and bloud of Chriſt borne of the virgine Mary, and that in ſubſtance, in ſorte and maner to our weake reaſon incōprehenſible.

The wordes of *Hilarius* the Pope vtter the ſame doctrine. *Corpus Chriſti quod ſumitur de altari, figura eſt, dum panis & vinū videtur extrà: Veritas autem, dum corpus Chriſti interius creditur.* The body of Chriſt which is receiued from the aulter, is the figure, whiles bread and wine are ſene outwardly: And it is the truth, whiles the body and bloud of Chriſt are beleued inwardly.

Diſt. 2. ca-no. corpus Chriſti.

Thus the fathers call not onely the ſacrament, but alſo the body and bloud of Chriſt it ſelfe in the ſacramēt, ſometymes the truth, ſometymes a figure: the truth, that is to witte, the very and true body and bloud of Chriſt, a figure, in reſpecte of the maner of being of the ſame there pſent, which is really and ſubſtantially, but inuiſibly, vnder the viſible forme of the outward elementes. And ſo Tertullian meaneth by his, *that is the figure of my body*, as though Chriſt had ſhewed by the word (*Hoc*) that which was viſible, which verely is the figure of the body, right ſo as that which is the inuiſible inward thing, is the truth of the body. Which interpretation of Tertullian in dede is not according to the right ſenſe of Chriſtes wordes, though his
Y meaning

meaning swarue not from the truth. For where as our lord sayde, *this is my body*, he meant
not so as though he had sayde, the outward
forme of the Sacrament, which here I delyuer to you, is a figure of my body vnder the
same conteined, for as much as by these wordes, *Hoc est*, he shewed not the visible forme
of breade, but the substance of his very body,
in to which by his diuine power he tourned
the bread. And therefore none of all the fathers euer so expownded those wordes of
Christ, but cotrary wise, namely Theophylacte, and Damascen. He sayd not (sayeth

In Matth. Theophylact) This is a figure, but *this is my*
cap.26. *body*. The bread, nor the wyne (meaning
Lib.4. cap. their outward formes) sayeth Damascen is
14. not a figure of the body and bloud of Christ:
Not so, in no wise. But it is the body it selfe
of our lord deificated, sith our lord him selfe
sayeth, *This is my body*, not the figure of my
body, but my body, and not the figure of my
bloud, but my bloud &c.

And the cause why Tertullian so expownded these wordes of Christ, was, that thereby
he might take aduatage against Marcion the
heretike, as many tymes the fathers in heate
of disputation doo handle some places, not
after the exacte signification of the wordes,
but rather folowe such waye, as serueth them
best to cofute their aduersarie. Which maner
not reporting any vntruth, S. Basile doth excuse

cuse in the setting forth of a disputation, not
in prescribing of a doctrine. As he defendeth Epist. 64.
Gregorius Neocæsariensis against the Sabellia-
nes, for that in a contention he had with
Ælianus an Ethnike, to declare the mysteries
of the trinitie, he vsed the word ὑπόϛασις in
stede of ἐϛία. And the learned men that be
well sene in the fathers, knowe they must vse
a discretion and a sundry iudgement betwen
the thinges they write agonisticῶs, that is to
saye, by waye of contention or disputation,
and the thinges they vtter dogmaticῶs, that
is by waie of setting forth a doctrine or matter of faith. Neither in that cõtentiõ dyd Tet-
tullian so much regard the exacte vse of wordes, as how he might wynne his purpose, and
driue his aduersarie denying that Christ tooke the true body of man, and that he suffered
death in dede, to confesse the truth, which he
thought to brĩg to passe, by deducĩg an argu-
mét from the figure of his body, which cõsisteth in that which is visible in the sacramét,
to proue the veritie of his body, and therefore in framing his reason by waie of illatiõ he
sayeth, *Figura autẽ nõ esset nisi veritatis esset cor-*
pus. There were not a figure, onlesse there were a body of truth or a very body in dede.

And whereas Tertullian vseth this word figure in this place, it is not to be vnderstãded
to be such, as the figures of the olde testamét
bee, as though it signified the shewing of

The wor-
des figure,
signe, tokẽ,
&c. exclude
not the
truth.

Y 2   a thing

a thing to come, or of a thing absent, which
is wonte to be set against the truth as cōtraly
to the same : but it is such a kynde of figure,
as doth couer the truth present, and so as it
were ioyned with the truth, as it is wōte to be
taken in the newe testamēt, where it sheweth
rather the maner of a thing to be exhibited,
then that it taketh away the truth of presence
of the thing which is exhibited. For elles con-
cernīg the truth of Christes body in the Sacrament, if any man doubte what opinion he
was of, he sheweth him selfe plainely so to
iudge of it, as euer hath ben taught in the catholike churche. Whereof he geueth euidence in many other places, but specially in
his second booke to his wife, exhorting her
not to marie againe to an infidell, if she ouer-
lyued him, least if she dyd, she should not
haue oportunitie to obserue the Christen
Religion, as she would. Speaking of the blessed Sacrament, which was then commonly
kepte of deuout men and womē in their houses, and there in tymes of persecution receiued before other meates, when deuotion
styrred them, he saeyth thus. Will not thy
husband knowe, what thou eatest secretly
before other meat? And if he knowe it, he
wil beleue it to be bread, not him who it is
called. the latine is recited before. I omitte
many other places, which shewe him to acknowledge Christes body in the Sacramēt, be-
                                          cause

eause I would not be tediouse, which veryly
by no wresting can be drawen to the significatiō of a mere figure. The like answere may
be made to the obiection brought out of S.
Augustine *contrà Adimantum Manichæum,
cap. 13. Non dubitauit dominus dicere, Hoc est
corpus meum, cum tamen daret signum corporis
sui.* our lord stickte not to saye, *This is my
body,* when notwithstāding he gaue the signe
of his body. For this is to be consydered, that
S. Augustine in fighting against the Maniches
oftētymes vseth not his owne sense and meaning, but those thinges, which by some meane, how so euer it were, might seme to geue
him aduantage against them, so as he might
put thē to the worst: as he witnesseth him selfe in his booke *de bono perseueratiæ ca. 11 et 12.*

*Gregorie Nazianzene oratione 4. in sanctum
Pascha,* shewing difference betwen the passeouer of the lawe, which the Iewes dyd eate,
and that which we in the Newe testament
doo eate in the mysterie of the Sacrament,
and that which Christ shall eate with vs in
the lyfe to come in the kingdō of his father,
vttereth such wordes, as whereby he calleth
that we receiue here, a figure of that shall be
receiued there. *Cæterum iam Pascha fiamus
participes, figuraliter tamen adhuc, etsi Pascha
hoc veteri sit manifestius. Siquidem Pascha
legale, audenter dico, figuræ figura erat obscurior:
at paulò post illo perfectius & purius fruemur, cū*

verbum

Verbum ipsum biberit nobiscum in regno patris nouum, detegens & docens, quæ nunc mediocriter oftendit . Nouum enim femper exiftit id, quod nuper eft cognitum. But now (fayeth he) let vs be made partetakers of this paffeouer, and yet but figuratiuely as yet albeit this paffeouer be more manifeft, then that of the olde lawe. Fór the paffeouer of the lawe (I fpeake boldly) was a darke figure of a figure: but er it be lóg, we fhal enioye it more perfitely and more purely when as the word (that is the fonne of God) fhall drynke the fame newe with vs in the kingdom of his father, opening and teaching the thinges, that now he fheweth not in moft clear wife. For that euer is newe, which of late is knowen. Where as this learned father called our paffeouer that we eate a figure, where of the lawe paffeouer was a figure, terming it the figure of a figure, he afketh leaue, as it were, fo to faye, and confeffeth him felfe to fpeake boldely, alluding as it femeth to S. Paul, or at leaft hauing faft printed in his mynde his doctrine to the Hebrewes: where he calleth the thinges of the lvfe to come, *res ipfas*, the very thinges them felues, the thinges of the newe teftamét *ipfam imaginé rerŭ*, the very image of thinges: and the Olde teftamét, *imaginis vmbrá* the fhadowe of the image. Which doctrine Naziá zene applyeth to the Sacrament of the aulter. And his meaning is this, that although we be goten

Heb.10.

goté out of thofe darknes of the lawe, yet we are not come to the ful lyght, which we looke for in the world to come, where we fhall fee and beholde the very thinges them felues clearely, and we fhall knowe as we are knowen. To be fhorte, by his reporte the faciamentes of the olde teftamét be but figures and fhadowes of thinges to come, the Sacraimétes of the newe teftamét, not fhadowes of thinges to come, but figures of thinges prefent which are cóteined and delyuered vnder them in myfterie, but yet fubftantially: at the ende all figures in heauen fhall ceafe and be abolifhed, and there fhall we fee al thofe thinges that here be hydden, clearely face to face. And where Chrift fayeth, that he will drinke his paffeouer newe with vs in the kingdom of his father, Nazianzen fo expowndeth that word (*Newe*) as it may be referred to the maner of the exhibiting, not to the thing exhibited: not that in the world to come we fhall haue an other body of our lord, which now we haue not, but that we fhall haue the felfe fame body, that now we haue in the Sacrament of the aulter in a myfterie, but yet verely and fubftantially, after an other forte and maner, and in that refpecte newe. for fo had without myfterie or couerture in cleare fight and moft ioyfull fruition, it is newe in comparifon of this prefent knowledge.

Th' the word figure reporteth not alwaies

Y 4   the

the absence of the truth of a thing, as we see,
but the maner of the thing either promyled,
or exhibited : that for as much as it is not
clearly and fully sene, it be called a figure. So
of Origen it is called *imago rerū*, an image of
the thinges, as in this place. *Si quis verò tran-*
fire potuerit ab hac vmbra, veniat ad imaginem
rerum, & videat aduētum Christi in carne faĉtū,
videat eum pontificem offerentē quidem & nunc
patri hostias, & postmodum oblaturum, & intel-
ligat hæc omnia imagines esse spiritualium rerum,
& corporalibus officys cœlestia designari. Imago
ergo dicitur hoc quod recipitur ad præsens, & in-
tueri potest humana natura. And if any man
(sayeth he)can passe and departe frō this sha-
dow, let him come to the image of thinges,
and see the cōming of Christ made in fleshe,
let him see him a bishop that bothe now offereth facrifice vnto his father, and also hereafter shal offer. And let him vnderstand, that all
these thinges be images of spirituall thinges,
and that by bodily seruices heauenly thinges
be resembled and set forth. So this which is at
this present receiued, and may of mannes nature be sene, is called an image. In this saying
of Origen this word image doth not in signification diminish the truth of thinges, so as
they be not the very thinges in dede, for the
thinges that Christ dyd in fleshe, were true
thinges: but when they are termed the image
of thinges, thereby is signified, so farre, as the
condition

In Psal.38.
homil.2.

condition and nature of man can beholde
and see them.

This is most plainely vttered by *Oecumenius* a Greke writer vppon these wordes of saint Paul to the Hebrewes. *Non ipsam imaginem rerum.* Not the image it selfe of thinges, Hebr.10. *id est, veritate rerum,* that is the truth of thinges, sayeth he. and addeth further. *Res appellat futurā vitam, imaginem autē rerum, Euāgelicam politiam, vmbram verò imaginis rerum, vetus Testamentum, imago enim manifestiora ostendit exemplaria: adumbratio autē imaginis obscurius hæc manifestat, nam hæc veteris testamenti exprimit imbecillitatem.* The sense of which wordes may thus be vttered in English. S. Paul calleth the lyfe to come, the thinges, and the ordināce or dispositiō of the thinges in the gospell, he calleth the image of thinges, and the olde testamēt, he nameth the shadowe of the image of thinges. For an image sheweth samplers more manifest: but the adumbratiō or shadowing of the image sheweth these thinges but darkely, for this doth expresse the weakenes of the olde testament. By this place of *Oecumenius* we see, that although it be proper to an image to exhibite the truth of thinges, and therefore by interpretatiō he sayeth, *Imaginem, id est, veritatem,* the image, that is, the truth: yet the proper and right taking of the word, signifieth the waye or maner of a thing to be exhibited, not the thing it selfe: that

what

what the image hath lesse then the thing it self, it is to be vnderstanded in the maner of exhibiting, not in the thing it selfe exhibited.

Hitherto we haue brought examples too declare that the wordes, figure and image, signifie the truth of thinges exhibited in dede, though in secrete and priuie maner. Certaine fathers vse the wordes *signum & sacramentum*, that is, signe and Sacrament, in the same significatiõ. Saint Augustine *in libro Sententiarum Prosperi*, sayeth thus. *Caro eius est, quam forma panis opertam in sacramento accipimus, & sanguis eius, quem sub vini specie & sapore potamus, caro videlicet carnis, et sanguis est sacramentum sanguinis, carne & sanguine, vtroque inuisibili, spirituali, intelligibili, signatur visibile domini nostri Iesu Christi corpus, & palpabile, plenum gratia omnium virtutũ & diuina maiestate.* It is his flesh that we receiue couered with the forme of bread in the Sacramét, and his bloud, that vnder the shape and fauour of wine we drinke, soothly flesh is a Sacrament of flesh, and bloud is a Sacrament of bloud: by the flesh and the bloud bothe inuisible, spirituall, intelligible, our Lorde Iesus Christ his visible and palpable body full of the grace of all vertues ad diuine Maiestie, is signified, or as it were with a signe noted.

In these wordes of S. Augustine we see the flesh of Christ called a sacrament of his flesh, and the bloud a Sacrament of his bloud, in as
much

De consecrat. dist. 2. can. Vtrum sub figura.

much as they be coouered with the forme of
bread and wyne, yet verely and in substance
present, and likewise he letteth not to call
this veritie or truth of the thinges them selues thus couertly exhibited, a signe of Christes visible and palpable body: so that the
naming of a signe doth not importe a separa-
tion from the truth, but sheweth a distincte
maner of the truth exhibited: And therefore
according to the truth of the maner of exhibiting, it is not the flesh of Christ, but the
sacrament of the flesh of Christ, for that the
flesh doth not exhibite it selfe in his owne sha
pe, but in a Sacrament. And therefore in an
other place he writeth thus. *Sicut ergo cœlestis*   De cōsecra:
panis, qui caro Christi est, suo modo vocatur cor-   dist. 2. can.
pus Christi, cum re vera sit sacramentum corpo-   Hoc est
ris Christi, illius videlicet quod visibile, quod pal-   quod dici-
pabile, mortale in cruce positū est, vocaturque ipsa   mus.
immolatio carnis, quæ sacerdotis manib' fit, Chri-
sti passio, mors, crucifixio, non rei veritate, sed si-
gnificante mysterio: Sic Sacramentum fidei, quod
Baptismus intelligitur, Fides est. As the heauēly
bread (sayeth S. Augustin) which is the flesh
of Christ, in his maner is called the body of
Christ, when as in very dede it is the sacramēt
of Christes body, euē of that which is visible,
which is palpable, and being mortall was put
on the crosse, and the sacrificing it selfe of his
flesh which is done by the pristes handes, is
called the passion, the death, the crucifying
                       of Christ,

of Chrijt not in truth of the thing, but in my sterie signifying: So the Sacrament of faith, which is vndestãded to be baptisme, is faith. By heauẽly bread he vnderstdãded not wheaten bread, but that heauẽly meate, which he sayeth to be the flesh of Chrijt, and this farre he affirmeth the truth of his flesh it selfe, which he sayeth to be called *suo modo* in his maner the body of Chrijt: as who should saie, whose truth notwithstanding if ye behold on the behalfe of the maner of exhibiting, in very dede it is a Sacrament of Chrijtes body, which is in visible shape, so as he speaketh of Chrijtes body, that hath suffred.

In Psal.98. Agayne S. Augustine sayeth in an other place. *Non hoc corpus quod videtis comesturi estis*. Not this body which ye see, shall ye eate. And In 1.cap. Ephes: Saint Hierom sayeth, *diuinam & spiritualem carnẽ manducandam dari, aliam quidem ab ea quæ crucifixa est*. that diuine and spiritual flesh is geuen to be eaten, other beside that, which was crucified. Wherefore in respecte of the exhibiting, the flesh is diuided, that in it selfe is but one: and the flesh exhibited in mysterie, is in very dede a Sacramẽt of Chrijtes body visible and palpable, which suffred on the crosse. And thus it foloweth of conuenience, whereas the flesh is not the same according to the qualities of the exhibiting, which was crucifyed, and which now is sacrificed by the handes of a priest: againe where as the passiõ, death

death and resurrection are sayde to be done not in truth of the thing, but in mysterie signifying: it foloweth (I saye) that the flesh is not the same in qualities, so as it was on the crosse, though it be the same in substance.

Many mo auctorities might be alleaged for the opening of this matter, but these for this present are ynough, if they be not too many, as I feare me they will so appeare to the vnlearned reader, and to such as be not geué to earnest studie and diligent serche of the truth. By these places it is made cleare and euident, that these names *figure*, *image*, *signe* *token*, *sacrament*, and such other the like, of force of their signification, doo not allwaies exclude the truth of thinges: but doo onely shewe and note the maner of presence. Wherefore to conclude this matter, that is somewhat obscure to senses litle exercised, the figure of the body, or the signe of the body, the Image of the body, doth note the coouertnesse and secretnes in the maner of the exhibiting, and doth not diminsh any whitte the truth of presence. So we doo accorde with M. Iuel in this article touching the forme of wordes, but withall we haue thought it necessary, to declare the true meaning of the same, which is contrary to the doctrine of the Sacramentaries.

Or

Or that it was lawfull then to haue xxx. xx.
xv.x. or v.Masses said in one church in one daie.

Of pluralitie of Masses in one church in one daie.

ARTICLE XIII.

S M . Iuell here descendeth by diuerse proportions and degrees, frō
xxx. to v . first by taking awaie . x .
the thirde parte of the whole, and
then v. from rhe rest three times: So it might
haue pleased him also to haue také awaie three
frō fiue the last remanét, and so to haue lefte
bút two in al. Which if he had done, thē shul-
de we so haue made vp that núber , as in this
audite he might not otherwise doo, in regarde of his owne free promisse , but allowe our
accompte for good and sufficiét. For that nūber we are wel able to make good. And what
reason hath moued the auncient fathers gouernours of the church , to thinke it a godly
and a necessarie thing , to haue two Masses in
one churche in one daie , the same reason in
cases either hath, or might haue moued them
and their successours after them likewise , to
allowe three or four Masses , and in some cases fyue or mo.

Now if that reckening could duely be made of our parte , M . Iuell perhappes woulde
then saie , as commonly they saye that cōfesse
their errour in núbring, that he had mistolde
him

him felue . Albeit here it is to be marueiled, that he appointeth vs to proue a number of Maſſes in one churche in one daie , that vtterly denyeth the Maſſe , and would haue no Maſſe in any church any daie at all . And ſtanding in the denyall of the whole ſo peremptorely as he doth, it may ſeme ſtraunge, that he ſhuld thus frame this Article . For what reaſon is it to chalenge vs for proufe of ſo great a number, ſith he taketh awaie all together?

It appeareth that being not vnwitting how good proufes we haue for the Maſſe it ſelfe, he thinketh to blanke vs by putting vs to the proufe of his number of xxx. xx. xv. x. or v. Verely this kynde of men fareth with the church much like vnto ſtrong theeues , who hauing robbed an honeſt welthy man of all his monney , ſaie afterwardes vnto him vncourteouſly, ah carle how cameſt thou by ſo much olde golde? Or if it like not them to be compared with theeues, in regard of the Rome they haue ſhuffled them ſelues into , they may not vnfittely be likened to a Iudge of the Stemerie at Lidford in Deuonſhire , who (as I haue heard it commonly reported) hanged a felone among the Tynners in the fore- noone, and ſate vppon him in iudgemét at afternoone. And thereof to this day ſuch wrongfull dealing in a common prouerbe is in that countrie called Lidford lawe . Sith that you

Lydford lawe vſed by the goſpellers.

M.Iuell

M. Iuell and your felowes that now sitte on
the benche, require of vs the proufe of mo
Masses in one church in one daie, as it were a
verdite of twelue men : of equitie and right
ye shuld haue heard our verdite, er ye had geuen sentence and condemned the Masse.

Pluralitie
of Masses
in one
church in
one daye.

Now concerning the number and iterati-
on of the Masse, first we haue good and auncient auctoritie for two Masses in one church
in one daie.

That eloquēt and holy father *Leo* the first,
writeth thus to *Deoscorus* bishop of *Alexan-*
dria. Volumus illud quoque custodiri, vt cum sō-
lenniōr festiuitas conuentum populi numerosioris
indixerit, & ad eam tanta multitudo conuenit,
quæ recepi basilica simul vna non possit, Sacrificij
oblatio indubitanter iteretur, ne ijs tātum admis-
sis ad hanc deuotionem, qui primi aduenerint, vi-
deantur ij qui postmodum confluxerint, non re-
cepti. Cum plenum pietatis atque rationis sit vt
quoties basilicam, in qua agitur, præsentia nouæ
plebis impleuerit, toties sacrificiū subsequens offe-
ratur. This order we will to be kepte, also
that when a number of people cometh to
church together at a solemne feaste, if the
multitude be so great as maye not well be receiued in one churche at once, that the oblation of the Sacrifice hardely be done againe:
least if they onely shuld be admittted to this
deuotion who came firſt, they that come afterward maye seme not to be recceiued. for as
much

much as it is a thing full of godlynesse and reason, that how oftetimes the church where the seruice is done, is filled with a newe companie of people, so oftentymes the Sacrifice there eftesones be offered,

By this father, whom the great Generall Councell of Chalcedon agnised for supreme gouernour of the churche of Christ, and honoured with the singular title of the Vniuersall Bishop, it is ordeined, that if any where one churche could not conueniently holde all the people together at one time: they that came after the first copanie, shuld haue their deuotion serued by hauing an other Masse celebrated againe. And least perhappes some might doubte wether that were laufull so to be done or no, or because then some doubted thereof, as now likewise some seme to doubte of it : to put the matter out of doubte, he sayeth assuredly, *Sacrificÿ oblatio indubitanter iteretur* . Let them not sticke to iterate or doo againe the oblation of the Sacrifice, that is to saie, let the Masse be celebrated againe, *indubitäter*, without casting peril, without sticking, staggaring, or doubting. In that epistle he sheweth two great causes, why mo Masses then one maye be done in one churche in one daie. The one is, least the aftercomers shuld seme reiected, *non recepti*, not receiued, the other is, that the one parte of the people be not defrauded of the benefite of
Z   theír

their deuotion: As him selfe sayeth, *Necesse est autem vt quædam pars populi sua deuotione priuetur, si vnius tantum Missa more seruato sacrificium offerre non possint, nisi qui prima diei parte conuenerint.* It must nedes be that a parte of the people be berefte of their deuotiõ, if the custom of hauing one Masse onely kepte, none maye offer the sacrifice, but such as came to church together in the morning or first parte of the daye. Now the people may neither be reiected, whõ God hath chosen, nor sparkled abroade, whõ our lord hath gathered together, neither ought they to be defrauded of their deuotiõ by withdrawing the Masse frõ thẽ, but rather to be styrred therevnto by their deuout presence at the celebratiõ of the same, where the death and passion of our lord is liuely represented before their eyes, the very same body that suffered on the crosse of them by the ministerie of the priest offered to the father, in a mysterie, but truly, not to be a newe Redẽption, but in commemoration of the redemption allready performed, the vertue of thesame euerlastingly remayning and continewing.

By this testimonie we fynde, that it was laufull within syx hundred yeres after Christ, (for *Leo* lyued about the yere of our lord 450.) to haue two Masses in one churche in one daie, for so much the word *iteretur* doth importe at least, and if there were mo, the

case

case so requyring, the word will beare it well L. veluti §.
ynough, as by good auctoritie of the ciuil la- hæc vox, ff.
we we learne. de edendo.

Now by this holy bishoppes godly will, the
custome of hauing one Masse onely in one
daie was abrogated, and this decreed, that in
tyme of two sundry resortes of people to
church, two sundry Masses shuld be celebrated, for the auoiding of these two incouenié-
ces, least the aftercommers shuld seme not
receiued, but reiected like excomunicate persones, and that a parte of the faithfull people
shuld not be put besyde their deuotiō. Whe-
reuppon I make this reason. The causes standing, the effectes folowe: But the danger of
the peoples seeming to be reiected, and the
defrauding of their deuotiō, which are causes
of iterating the Masse in one daie, did in that
age in some holy daies of likelyhod thrise, yea
iiij. or v. tymes happen, and in our tyme most
certainely doth comonly so often, or oftener
happen: wherefore the Masse may so many
tymes be sayd in a daye in one churche.

Where great multitude of Christen people is, as in townes, we see some resorte to
churche early in the morning, making their
spirituall oblations to th'intent to serue God
er they serue man in their worldly affaires.
All can not come so early: others come at
their conuenient oportunitie, some at syx,
some at seuen, some at eight, some at nyné

or ten of the clocke. If they which through
laufull lettes can not come at the firſt houres, comming afterward be rowndly tolde
by the prieſt, come ye at ſuch or ſuch houres,
or elles ye gette no Maſſe here: ſhall not they
according to *Leo* his ſaying ſeme to be reiected, and defrauded of their deuotiō? All wel
diſpoſed people about Powles can not come
to the Apoſtelles Maſſe at four or fyue of the
clocke in the morning, neither at high Maſſe
there. Shall all ſuch in a Terme or Parlament
tyme when great reſorte is, be denyed that
ſpirituall conforte? And if they bee, ſhall not
they ſeme reiected and put from their deuotion? Which inconuenience that it might not
happé, *Leo* willeth not onely twoo, but three,
four, or mo Maſſes to be done on a daye,
for his wordes reporte no leſſe . *Cum ple-*
num pietas atque rationis ſit, vt quoties baſilicam
in qua agitur, præſentia nouæ plebis impleuerit,
toties ſacrificium ſubſequens offeratur, Let there
be no ſticking at the iterating of the Maſſe.
For as much as (ſayeth he) it is a thing
full of godlyneſſe and reaſon , that how often
the churche where the ſeruice is done, is
fylled with a newe companie of people , ſo
ofte the Sacrifice there efteſones be offered.
Here he willeth plainely that Maſſe be done,
toties quoties , at euery newe reſorte of the
well diſpoſed people ; and that for theſe weighty cauſes, leaſt parte of the people ſhuld
seme

seme not receiued, and that they be not defrauded of their deuotion. Wherefore, they that reproue the pluralitie of Masses in one church in one daie, after the iudgement of this worthy father be reiectours of the faithfull people and robbers of their deuotion. But they that haue vtterly abrogated the Masse, which is the outward and the euerenduring Sacrifice of the newe Testament, by verdite of Scripture, be no lesse then the forerunners of Antichrist.

Here that I maye adde somewhat more for proufe of this article, If the pluralitie of Masses in one churche in one daye had bē vtterly vulawfull, the fathers of the councell of *Antisiodorum* would not haue decreed, that it shuld not be lawfull to celebrate two Masses vpon one aulter in one daye: neither where the Byshop had sayde Masse, that a priest might not saye the same daye at the same aulter. For besyde that the prohibition presupposeth the thing prohibited to haue ben before vsed, (elles prohibitiō had ben superfluouse, and so farre forth it appeareth that before the making of that decree mo Masses were sayde at one aulter in one daye) the argument of this decree serueth very well for proufe, that by force of this councell, it was then lawfvll to saye mo Masses in one churche in one daye. For this prohibition of the councell is not generall but speciall, re

Non licet super vno altario in vna die duas Missas celebrare, nec in altario, vbi Episcopus Missas dixerit presbiter illa die Missas dicat. Concil Antisiodoren.can.10. an.domini 613.

Z 3   stricted

strict to a particular place of the churche,
in vno altario, at one aulter, which includeth
not of any reason a more generall and larger
matter then it selfe, as neither at any other
aulter in the same church the same daye it
shal be lawfull to saye Masse: But of côsequét
this being but one speciall case forbydden
inferreth a permission and good leaue in the
reste *eiusdem generis & subiecti*, that be of the
same kynde, and about the same matter, and
not included by wordes of reason in that prohibition. So that we may not argue by reason in this sorte, it is forbidden to saye mo
Masses at one aulter in one daye, *ergo* it is
forbidden to saye many Masses at all in one
churche in one daye vppon diuerse aulters:
but the contrary reason foloweth, *ergo* ye
may saye many Masses vppon diuerse aulters
in one daye. And likewise ye may not saye
Masse that day on th'aulter where the bishop
hath sayde, *ergo* ye may lawfully saye that daye at an other aulter. For other wise the lawe
would haue forbydden generally, ye shall not
saye Masse in the church where the bishop
hath sayde that daye: and then ye had bé for-
byddé that aulter and all aulters there at one
worde. But in forbidding the one aulter, the
lawe grawnteth you the vse of the reste there.

And this kynde of reasoning and arguing
of the lawe, that forbyddeth one case specially, to affirme the reste that is not métioned

in

in the prohibitiō, the lawiers will defende by
their principles againſt M. Iuell, who I thinke will not wade farre to ſtande againſt them
in this macche. For they ſaye, an edicte prohi- In genere
bitorie in ſuch thinges which are not wholy permiſſo-
in their kynde vnlawfull, forbydding ſpeciall nia intelli-
caſes, graunteth the reſte, and doth permitte gitur per-
all that, which is not ſpecially forbydden. miſſa, quæ
And by that, all may be witneſſes which are ſpecialiter
not ſpecially forbydden, all may make their riuntur
proctoures to anſwere for them in iudgemēt prohibita.
which are not forbydden in the ſpeciall prohibition, for that the edictes of proctoures
and witneſſes are prohibitorie. And becauſe L.Iulia.ff.
Lex Iulia dyd forbydde a woman condem- de teſti-
ned for adulterie to beare witneſſe in iudge- bus.
ment, thereof the texte of the Ciuill lawe cō-
cluded, that women maye beare witneſſe in
iudgement.

And they ſaye further that exception in Exceptio
one caſe, confirmeth the generall rule, and confirmat
maketh the reſte that is not excepted, more regulam,
ſure and ſtable, and to be in force in contrary ceptis.
ſenſe to the exception.

But I wil not bring M. Iuell out of his pro-
feſſed ſtudie to farre to ſeeke lawes. For in dede we nede not go to lawe for theſe matters,
wherein the church hath geuen ſentence
for vs, but that our aduerſaries refuſe the
iudge after ſentēce. Which if they had done,
when order permitteth it at the begynning,

Z 4   and

and had plainely (as I feare me some of them thinke) denyed them selues to be Christians, or at least of Christes courte in his catholike churche : we shuld not haue stryued so long about these matters. We would haue imbraced the truth of God in his church quietly, whiles they sought an other iudge according to their appetites and phantasies, as Turkes and infidelles doo.

Now if M.Iuell be not so precise in his iudgement of allowing the first six hūdred yeres after Christ, as to cōdemne the churche that folowed in the nexte generation : then we may alleage vnto him the twelfth councell of Toledo in Spaine , holdēn in the yere of our lorde 680. for proufe that many Masses were celebrated in one churche in one daye. For the same appeareth plainely by this decree of the fathers there.

Can.5.

Relatum nobis est quosdam de sacerdotibus non tot vicibus communionis sanctæ gratiam sumere, quot sacrificia in vna die videntur offerre: sed in vno die, si plurima per se Deo offerāt sacrificia , in omnibus se oblationibus à communione suspendunt , & in sola tātum extrema sacrificij oblatione communionis sanctæ gratiam sumunt. quasi non sit toties illis vero & singulari sacrificio participandum, quoties corporis & sanguinis Domini nostri Iesu Christi immolatio facta constiterit. Nam ecce Apostolus dicit : Nōnne qui edunt hostias , participes sunt altaris? Certum est quod

quàd hi qui sacrificantes non edunt, rei sunt do- 1.Cor.10.
minici sacramenti. Quicunque ergo sacerdo-
tum deinceps diuino altario sacrificium oblatu-
rus accesserit, & se a communione suspenderit,
ab ipsa qua se indecenter priuauit,gratia commu-
nionis anno vno repulsum se nouerit. Nam quale
erit illud sacrificiũ,cui nec ipse sacrificãs particeps
esse cognoscitur? Ergo modis omnibus est tenendũ,
vt quotiescunq, sacrificans corpus & sanguinem
Iesu Christi Domini nostri in altario immolat,to-
ties perceptionis corporis & sanguinis Christi se
participem præbeat.

It is shewed vnto vs, that there be certaine
priestes, who doo not receiue the grace of
the holy communion so many tymes, how
many sacrifices they seme to offer in one
daye. But if they offer vp to God many sacrifices by thē selues in one daye, in all those
oblations they suspend them selues from the
communion, and receiue the grace of the
holy communion onely at the last oblation
of the sacrifice, as though they ought not so
oftentymes to be partakers of that true and
singular sacrifice, as the sacrifice of the body
and bloude of our lorde Iesus Christ hath
ben done. For beholde the Apostle sayeth: *Be* 1.Cor.10.
not they which eate sacrifices partakers of the aul-
ter? It is certaine, that they, who dooing sacrifice doo not eate, be gylty of our lordes sacrament. Wherefore what priest so euer hereafter shall come vnto the holy aulter to offer
sacrifice,

sacrifice, and suspend him selfe from the
communion, be it knowen vnto him, that
he is reppelled and thrust awaye from the
grace of the communion, whereof he hath
vnsemely bereued him selfe, (whereby is
meant that he standeth excommunicate)for
the space of one yere. For what a sacrifice shal
that bee, whereof neither he him selfe that
sacrificeth, is knowen to be partaker? wherefore by all meanes this is to be kepte, that
how oftentymes so euer the priest doth sacrifice the body and bloude of Iesus Christ
our lorde on the aulter, so oftentymes he receiue and make him selfe partaker of the body and bloude of Christ.

Sacrifice
taken for
the Masse.

Here by the word Sacrifice and offering of
the sacrifice, the fathers vnderstande the
dayly sacrifice of the church, which we call
the Masse. For though the word *Missa* be
of great antiquitie and many tymes fownde
in the fathers, yet they vse more commonly
the word Sacrifice. Neither can the enemies
of this sacrifice expounde this canon of the
inward sacrifice of a mannes harte, but of
that sacrifice, which the priest cometh to the
holy aulter to offer, of the sacrifice of the
body and bloude of Christ our lorde offered
on the aulter, (for so be their wordes) where
he receiueth the grace of the holy communion, which is the participation of the body
and bloude of our lorde.

This

This much graunted, as by any reasonable
vnderstanding it can not be drawen , nor by
racking cā be stretched to any other sense:we
haue here good auctoritie for the hauing of
many Masses in one churche in one daye.
And where as the fathers of that councell allowed many Masses in one daye sayde by one
priest,there is no reason , why they shuld not
allowe the same sayd by sundry priestes in
one daye. If our aduersaries saye , this might
haue ben done in sundry places , whereby
they may seme to frustrate our purpose touching this article : we answere , that besyde
th'approuing of the Masse by them so confessed, it were vaine and fryuolouse to imagi-
ne such gadding of the priestes from churche to churche for saying many Masses in one
daye.Doubtelesse the fathers of that Toleta-
ne Coūcel meant of many Masses sayd in one
place in a daye , as *Leo* dyd , for seruing the
faithfull peoples deuotion , that resorted to
churche at sundry houres , as we see the people doo now, that so all might be satisfied.
Which shuld not haue ben , if one Masse
onely had ben sayde.

If M.Iuell agnise and accepte for good the
auctoritie of this Councell , as the churche
doth , then must he allowe these many thinges, which the Sacramentaries to the vtter-
most of their power and cunning labour
to disproue and deface . First , the blessed
sacrifice

1 sacrifice of the Masse, which the fathers of
this councel call the true and singular sacrifice, the sacrifice of the body and bloud of our
lord IESVS CHRIST, the sacrifice of the
body and bloud of Iesus Christ our lorde,

2 which the priest offereth on the aulter, Nexte, the truth and reall presence of the body
and bloud of our lorde in the sacrifice offe-

3 red. Then aulters, which this councell calleth
diuine or holy, for the diuine and holy thinges on them offered, the body and bloud of

4 Christ. Furthermore, the multitude of Masses in one daye, for they speake of many sacrifices, that is, many Masses, *plurima sacrificia*.

5 Lastly, priuate Masses. For the wordes *nec ipse
sacrificans* rightly constrewed and weighed,
importe no lesse. For where as no worde in
this decree is vttered, whereby it maye appeare the people to be of necessitie requyred
to receiue, if the priestes had receiued them
selues at euery Masse, no faulte had bē fownde. And if the people had receiued without
the priestes, in this case it had bē reason, this
decree shuld other wise haue ben expressed.
And so it is cleare, that at that tyme priuate
Masses were sayde and done.

Now if M. Iuell refuse and reiecte the auctoritie of the churche represented in that
councell, then he geueth vs a manifest noti-
ce, what marke we ought to take him to be
of. Then may we saye vnto him the wordes
of

ofS.Paul· *Nos talem consuetudinem non habe-* I.Cor.II.
mus,nec eccesia Dei . We haue no such custome, neither the churche of God hath not, to
condemne the churche: And in this case he
must pardon vs, if according to the precepte
of Christ,for that he will not heare the chur- Matth.18.
che,we take him for no better, then a hethen
and a publican.

Or that Images were then set vp in the Chur- Iuell.
ches , to the intet the people might worship them.

Of Images.
ARTICLE XIIII.

That Images were set vp in churches within syx hundred yeres: after Christ , it is certaine, but not
specially either then,or sithens to
the intent the people might worship them.
The intet and purpose hath ben farre other,
but right godly, as shall be declared. Wher e-
fore the imputing of this entent to the catholike church, is both false, and also sclaun-
derouse. And because for the vse of images,
these newe maisters charge the church with
reproche of a newe deuise, breache of Gods
commaundement , and idolatrie : I will here
shewe,first, the Antiquitie of Images, and by 1
whom they haue ben allowed . Secondly, to 2
what entent and purpose they serue,Thirdly, 3
how they maye be worshiped without offence.

Concerning

Antiquitie of Images.

Concerning the Antiquitie and originall of images, they were not first inuented by man, but commaunded by God, brought in to vse by traditiō of the Apostles, allowed by auctoritie of the holy fathers and all councelles, and by custome of all ages sith Christes being in the earth. When God would the Tabernacle with al forniture thereto belonging to be made, to serue for his honour and glorie, he commaunded Moses among other thinges to make two Cherubins of beaten golde, so as they might couer bothe sydes of the propitiatorie, spreading abroade their whinges and beholding them selues one an other, their faces tourned toward the propitiatorie, that the Arke was to be couered with all. Of thole Cherubins S. Paul speaketh in his epistle to the Hebrewes. Which images *Beseleel* that excellent workeman made at the commaundement of Moses, according to the instruction by God geuen. Againe Moses by the commaundement of God made the brasen Serpent, and set it vp on high for the people that were hurt of serpentes in wildernes to behold, and so to be healed. In the temple also that *Salomon* buylded were images of Cherubins, as the scripture sheweth. Of Cherubins mention is made in sundry places of the scriptures, specially in *Ezechiel* the prophet. *cap. 41. Iosephus* writeth of the same in his third and eight booke *antiquitatū Iudaicarum.*

Exod. 25.

Cap. 9.

Exod. 37.

Num. 21.

3. Reg. 6.
2. Paral. 3.

Iudaicarum. The image of Chrerubins repre-
fenteth angels, and the word is a word of an-
gelicall dignitie, as it appeareth by the third
chapter of *Genefis,* where we read that God
placed Cherubins before paradife, after that
Adam was caft forth for his difobedience.

It were not much befyde our purpofe here
to rehearfe the place of *Ezechiel* the prophet, Ezech. 9.
where God commaunded one that was clo-
thed in lynnen, and had an ynkhorne by his
fyde, to go through the myddes of Hieru-
rufalem, and to prynt the figne of *Tau,* that is In cōmen-
the figne of the Croffe(for that letter had the tar.in Eze-
fimilitude of the Croffe amōg the old Hebre chuelem.
we letters as S.Hierom witneffeth) in the fo-
reheddes of the mē, that moorned and made
mone ouer all the abhominatiōs of that citie.

Touching the figne, Image, or figure of the
Croffe in the tyme of the new teftament, God The figne
femeth by his prouidence and by fpeciall of the Crof
warninges, in fundry reuelations and fecrete fe cōmen-
declarations of his will, to haue commended ded to men
the fame to men, that they fhuld haue it in prouidēce.
good regard and remembraunce. When
Conftantine the Emperour had prepared
him felfe to warre againft *Maxentius* the ty- Eufeb. ec-
raunt, cafting in his mynde the great daūgers clef.hift. li.
that might thereof enfue, and calling to God 1.cap.9.
for helpe, as he lookte vp, beheld (as it were
in a vifion) the figne of the croffe appearing
vnto him in heauē as brigḥt as fyer, and as he

was

was aftonied with that ftraunge fight, he
heard a voice fpeaking thus vnto him. Conftantine *in this ouercomme.*

ἐν τούτῳ νί-
κα.
Sozomen.
triparr.
hift.lib.5.
cap.50.

After that Iulian the Emperour had forfa-
ken the profeſsion of Chriften Religion, and
had done facrifice at the temples of painyms,
mouing his fubieɛtes too doo the like : as he
marched forward with his armie on a daye,
the droppes of rayne that fell downe out of
the ayer in a fhewer, formed and made tokens
and fignes of the croſſe, both in his, and alfo
in the fouldiers garmentes.

Ecclef. hi-
ftor.lib.10.
in fine.

Rufinus hauing declared the ftraunge and
horrible plages of God, whereby the Iewes
were frayed and letted frō their vaine attēpte
of buylding vp againe the temple at Hierufa-
lem, leaue thereto of the Emperour Iulian in
defpite of the Chriftians obteyned: in the ende fayeth, that leaft thofes earthquakes and
terrible fyers which he fpeaketh of rayfed by
God, whereby as well the work houfes and
preparations toward the buylding, as alfo
great multitudes of the Iewes were throwen
downe, caft abroade, and deftroyed, fhuld be
thought to happen by chaunce: the night folowing thefe plages, the figne of the croſſe ap
peared in euery one of their garmétes fo euidently, as none to cloke their infidelitie, was
able by any kynde of thing to fcowre it out
and put it awaye.

When the temples of the painims were
deftroyed

destroyed by the Christians in *Alexandria,* about the yere of our lord 390. in the chiefe temple of all, which was of the Idol *Serapis,* the holy and mysticall letters called ἱεϱογλυ- φικά, by Gods prouidence, were fownde grauen in stones representing the figure of the crosse, the significatiō whereof after their interpretation was, life to come. Which thing espyed by the Christians and by the painimes present at the spoile, serued maruelously to furtheraunce of the Christen faith, no lesse then the inscription of the aulter at Athens, *Ignoto Deo, vno the vnknowē God,* serued to the same purpose through S. Paules preaching. Which all together was before wrought by Gods holy prouidence, as *Socrates,* one of the writers of the ecclesiasticall stories, reporteth.

Thus it appeareth plainely, how Gods prouidence hath cōmended vnto true beleuers, the signe of the crosse. For which cause and for remembraunce of our Redemption, it hath ben in olde tyme and allwayes sithens much frequented and honoured. For besyde that we reade hereof in Tertullian, who was neare the Apostles tyme, *in Apologetico,* we finde in the writers of the ecclesiasticall stories, *that the Christen people of Alexandria,* after they had pulled downe and taken awaye the armes and monumēts of *Serapis* the Idol, euery man caused the signe of our lordes crosse in place of them to be painted and

A a   set vp

Histo. tripart. lib. 9. Cap. 29. γϱάμμιπά ἱεϱογλυφι- κά.

Actor. 17.

Cap. 16.

Eccl. hist. lib. 11. cap. 29. auctore Rufino.

set vp in their postes, entreis, windowes, walles and pillours, that where so euer the eye was tourned, it shuld light on the holy signe of the crosse.

Histor. tripart. lib. 1. cap. 9.

Constantine the Emperour loued and honoured this signe so much, that he caused the same to be paineted in al his flagges and banners of warre, to be stroken in his coines and monneys, to be purtraited in his armes, scutchins and targets. Of this *Aurelius Prudētius* maketh mention.

Lib. 1. cōtrà Symmachūm.

Christus purpureum gemmanti textus in auro,
Signabat labarum, clypeorum insignia Christus
Scripserat, ardebat summis crux addita cristis.

The sense whereof is this much in English. The chiefe banner which was of purple, had the image of Christ in it wrought in golde and stones. The targets were paineted al ouer with Christ. The Crosse shyned fyerbright in the crestes of theire helmettes. That the *ban-*

Vide histo. tripart. lib. 1. cap. 5.

ner cōmonly borne before the Emperour in warre, in Latine called *Labarum,* was of this sorte, it appeareth by an epistle, that S. Ambrose wro-

Lib. 5. epistol. 29.

te to *Theodosius* the Emperour. Neither was the figure of the crosse then onely in flagges and banners, paineted, wouen, embrodered, or otherwise wrought, in golde or pretiouse stones: but also made in whole golde and set vpon a long staffe or pole, and borne before men, (as the maner is now in processiōs) as it semeth plainely by these verses of *Prudentius.*

Agnoscat

Agnoscas Regina lubens mea signa necesse est,
In quibus effigies crucis aut gemmata refulget,
Aut longis solido ex auro præfertur in hastis.

It houeth you Madame, that gladly you
acknowledge myne enseignes, in which the
figure of the Crosse is either glittering in stones, or of whole golde is borne on lōg staues
before vs. This much haue I gathered out of
the auncient fathers writinges cōcerning the
signe of our lordes crosse, the sight whereof
the professours of this newe gospell can not
abyde; to the entent the diuersitie of our tyme and of olde tyme maye appeare, to the
maners of which for a perfite reformation,
these preachers would seme to bring the
world againe.

Concerning the images of Christ and of
his sainctes, that they haue ben greatly estemed and vsed in houses, churches, and places
of prayer from the Apostles tyme foreward, it
is so euident, that it can not be denyed. *Atha-*
nasius writeth that Nicodeme, who came to
I ɛ s v s by night, made an image of Christ
with his owne handes, and that when he laye
in his death bedde, he delyuered it to *Gama-*
liel, who was S. Paules scoolemaister. *Gamaliel*
when he sawe he shuld dye, lefte it to Iames,
Iames lefte it to Simon and *Zachæus*. This
image came from hand to hand by successiō,
and continewed a long tyme in Hierusalem.
From Hierusalē it was caried in to *Syria*, and

Images frō the Apostles tyme.

A a 2   at length

at length it was brought to the citie *Berytus*, not farre from Tyre and Sydon. Where how despitefully it was vsed of the Iewes, and what wonders ensued thereupon, who list to knowe, may he reade it largely declared in a litle booke written by *Athanasius* of that matter. *Eusebius Casariensis* in the seuenth booke of his ecclesiasticall storie, writeth of the auncient image of Christ made in brasse, and of the woman, that was healed by our Sauiour of her bloudy flixe in the citie of *Phænicia* called *Casarea Philippi*, whereof that woman was a citizen. Which image he sayeth he sawe, as likewise the images of Peter and Paul kepte by some of olde tyme. And there he consesseth, that the images of Peter and Paul and of our Sauiour were in his tyme made, and painted in tables and set forth. After *Eusebius* death Iuliã the renegate tooke downe this image of Christ, and set vp his owne in the same place. Which with violent fyer that fell from heauen, was clefte asunder in the brest, the hedde broken of with a peece of the necke, and stickt in the grownde. The rest of it so remayned long after, as a token of lightning and Gods displeasure might be reserued. That image of Christ after that the painimes had haled, pulled, broken, and mangled it villainously, by the christians was taken vp, set together, and placed in the churche, where it is yet reserued, sayeth

Socrates

Cap. 14.

Lib. 6. Tri-
part. ca. 41.

Socrates of his tyme. Of the miraculouse herbe that grewe at the foote of this image, which after that it had growen so high, at it touched the images skirtes, taken and miniſtred was a medicine and preſent remedie for all diſeaſes, as *Euſebius* writeth: becauſe it perteineth not ſpecially to the matter of images, I rehearſe nothing.

It is euident by Chryſoſtomes Maſſe, that there was ſome vſe of images in the church of Conſtãtinople in his tyme, for he ſpeaketh of the image of the crucifixe. Who ſo euer is deſyrous to ſee teſtimonies of the fathers for prouf of images, let him read the ſeuenth generall councell holde in Nicea the citie of *Bithynia* againſt Imagebreakers, and there he ſhall fynde no ſmall number.

I will not let here to recite ſome, which, ſo farre as I remẽber, be not fownde there, one onely excepted which is of S.Baſile, euery one of right good and auncient auctoritie.

Simeon Metaphraſtes a greke writer de ſcribing the lyſe of S. Luke th'euangeliſt ſayeth that he made the images of Chriſt and of his mother Mary. Saint Ambroſe witneſſeth, that in his tyme the Images of the Apoſtles were vſed in pictures, for where he declareth the maruelous appearing of the holy martyrs *Geruaſius* and *Protaſius* vnto him in a viſiõ, be ſayeth, that a third perſon appeared with them that tolde him where their bodyes

In vita Geruaſij & Protaſij.

Aa 3   laye.

laye, which semed like to S. Paul the Apostle, as he vnderstoode his face by viewe of his picture.

Gregorie Nyssene S. Basiles brother writing the lyfe of *Theodorus* the martyr, bestoweth much eloquence in the praise of the church, where his holy relikes were kepte, commending the shape of lyuing thinges wrought by the keruer, the smoothenes of marble poolished like syluer by the mason, the liuely resemblaunce of the martyr him selfe and of al his worthy actes, expressed and excellently set forth to the eye in imagerie with the image of Christ by the paynter. In which images he acknowlegeth the sightes of the martyr to be declared no lesse, then if they were described and written in a booke.

Paulinus the bishop of *Nola* in his booke that he made in verses of the lyfe of *Felix* the In decimo martyr, prayseth the church which the martyrs bodye was layed in, for the garnishing of it with painted images in bothe sydes, of bothe kindes men and women, the one kinde on the one syde, and the other kinde on the other syde. Where he speaketh expressely by name of the Images of scabbed Iob, and blynde Tobye, of fayer *Iudith*, and great quene *Hester*, for so he nameth them.

Athanasius hath one notable place for hauing the Image of our Sauiour Christ, which is not common, where he maketh Christ and the

the church to talke together as it were in a dialogue, *in sermone de sanctis patribus & prophetis*. The greke may thus be tranflated. *Age (inquit) dic mihi, cur oppugnaris? Oppugnor, (inquit Ecclesia) propter doctrinam Euangelij, quam diligenter & acuratè teneo, & propter verum & firmum Pascha quod agito, et propter religiosam & puram imaginem tuam, quam mihi Apostoli reliquerunt, vt haberem depictam arram humanitatis tuæ, in qua mysterium redemptionis operatus es, Hic Christus, Si propter hoc (inquit) te oppugnant, ne grauiter feras, néve animum despondeas, cum sciaς, si quis Pascha neget, aut imaginem, me eum negaturum coram patre meo, & electis angelis. Rursus verò qui compatitur mecum propter Pascha, côglorificaturum. An non audisti quid Moysi præceperim? Facies, inquam, mihi duos Cherubinos in tabernaculo testimonij, scilicet ad præfigurandã meã imaginẽ, &c.*

The Englifh of this Latine or rather of the Greke is this. Come on (quoth Chrift to the church) tell me, wherefore art thou thus inuaded and vexed? declare me the matter. Forfooth lord (quoth the church) I am inuaded and vexed for th'exacte obferuing of the gofpel, and for the keping of the feaft of the true and firme Eafter, and for thy reuerent and pure image, which thy holy Apoftles haue lefte to me by tradition, to haue and kepe for a reprefentation of thine incarnation. Then (quoth our lord) if this be the matter for

which

which thou art inuaded and set against, be not dismayed, be of good cōfort in hart and mynde, being assured hereof, that who so de- * ἄχειπ]ον. nyeth Easter, or my * cleane image, I shall de- nye him before my heauenly father and his chosen Angels. And he that suffereth perse- cution with me for keping of Easter, the sa- me shall also be glorified with me. Hast not thou heard, what I commaunded Moyses the lawegeuer to doo? Make me (sayd I) two Che- rubins in the tabernacle of the testimony, to be a prefiguratiō or foretokening of my ima- ge, &c.

Of all the fathers none hath a playner te- stimonie bothe for the vse and also for the worshipping of Images, then S, Basile, whose auctoritie for learning, wisedom, and holy- nes of lyfe, besyde antiquitie, is so weighty in the iudgement of all men, that all our newe maisters layed in balance against him, shall Citatut ab be fownde lighter then any fether. Touching Adriano this matter, making a confession of his faith Papa in in an epistle inueghing against Iulian the epistola renegate, he sayeth thus. Euen as we haue re- Sinodica ceyued our Christian and pure faith of God, ad Constā- as it were by right of heretage : right so I ma- tinū & Ire- ke my confession thereof to hym, and therein nem. I abyde. I beleeue in one God father almigh- ty, God the father, God the sonne, God the holy ghoste. One God (in substance) and the- se three (in persones) I adore and glorifie. I

confesse

confesse also the sonnes incarnation. Then afterward sainct Mary, who according to the fleshe brought hym foorth, callyng her *Deiparam*. I reuerence also the holy Apostles, Prophetes, and Martyrs, which make supplication to God for me : that by their mediation our most benigne god be mercifull vnto me, and graunt me freely remissiō of my synnes. Then this foloweth. *Quam ob causam & historias imaginum illorum honoro, & palàm adoro : hoc enim nobis traditum à sanctis Apostolis, non est prohibendum, sed in omnibus ecclesijs nostris eorum historias erigimus.* For the which cause I doo both honour the stories of their images, and openly adore them. For this being delyuered vnto vs of the holy Apostles by tradition, is not to be forbidden. And therefore we set vp in all our churches their stories. Lo M. Iuell here you see a sufficient testimonie, that Images were set vp in the churches long before the ende of your syx hūdred yeres, and that they were honoured and worshipped not onely of the simple christen people, but of bishop Basile, who for his excellent learning and wisedom, was renoumed with the name of Great.

Now that there hath ben ynough alleaged for the Antiquitie, originall and approbatiō of Images, it remayneth, it be declared, for what causes they haue bē vsed in the church. We fynde that the vse of images hath ben *Three causes vvhy images haue ben vsed in the church.*

Aa 5   brought

brough into the church for three caufes. The
firft, is the benefite of knowledge. For the
fimple and vnlearned people, which be vtterly ignorant of letters, in pictures doo as it
were reade and fee noleffe then others doo
in bookes, the myfteries of chriften Religion,
the actes and worthy dedes of Chrift and of
his fainctes. What writing performeth to
them that reade, the fame doth a picture to
the fimple beholding it, fayeth S. Gregory.
For in the fame the ignorant fee, what they
ought to folowe, in the fame they reade,
which can no letters; therefor Imagerie fer-
ueth fpecially the rude natiõs in ftede of wri-
ttng, fayeth he.

To this S. Bafile agreeth in his homilie
vpon the forty martyrs. Bothe the writers of
ftories (fayeth he) and alfo paineters do fhewe and fet forth noble dedes of armes and
victories, the one garnifhing the matter with
eloquence, the other drawing it lyuely in tables, and bothe haue ftyrred many to valiant
courage. For what thynges the vtterance of
the ftorie expreffeth through hearing, the fame doth the ftille picture fet forth through
imitatiõ. In the like refpecte in olde tyme the
worke of excellent poetes was called a fpeaking picture, and the worke of payneters, a
ftille poetrie. And thus the vfe and profite of
writing and of pictures, is one. For thinges
that be read, when as they come to our eares,
then

Ad Serenũ
epifcopum
Maſsilien.
lib.9.epi-
ſtol.9.

Pictura lo-
ques,poe-
ma tacens.

then we conueigh them ouer to the mynde, and the thinges that we beholde in pictures with our eyes, the same also doo we imbrace in our mynde. And so by these two, reading and painting, we acheue one like benefite of knowledge.

The second cause of the vse of Images, is the styrring of our myndes to all godlynes. For whereas the affecte and desyre of man is heauy and dull in diuine and spirituall thinges, because the body that is corruptible wei-gheth downe the mynde: when it is set forth before our eyes by images, what Christ hath done for vs, and what the Sainctes haue done for Christ: then it is quickned and moued to the like will of doing and suffering, and to all endeuour of holy and vertuouse life. As when we heare apte and fitte wordes vt-tered in a sermon or an oration: so when we beholde lookes and gestures liuely expres-sed in images, we are moued to pitie, to wee-ping, to ioye, and to other affectes. Wherein verely, it hath alwayes ben though, that pai-neters haue had no lesse grace, then eitheir oratours or poetes.

Sapient. 9.

Who listeth to see exaples hereof, he may peruse the second Nicene councell, where he shall fynde among other most notable thin-ges concerning this point, one of sainct *Eu-phemia* the martyr, an other of *Abraham* sacrificing his sonne *Isaac* worthy of euer-lasting

Action. 4.

lasting memorie, that of *Asterius* the holy bishop, this of Gregory Nyssene, very elegātly described. Virgil maketh *Æneas* to weepe, to hope for better fortune, to gather courage of mynde, to take good aduise and order for redresse and helpe of his great calamities, by occasion of beholding a painters worke at *Carthago*, wherein the bataile of Troye was expressed. Which that wise poete would not haue done, were not that pictures haue great force to moue mennes hartes.

Ouide likewise in the epistle of *Laodamia* to *Protesilaus* her husbād being forth at warres, maketh her so to write of his image, which she had caused to be made of waxe for her conforte in his absence, as it may well appeare, that images haue a meruelouse power to stirre vehement affectes, and to represent thinges absent, as though in maner they were present, in the myndes of the beholders.

Among all other examples for this purpose, that semeth to me most notable, which *Appianus* writeth of *C. Iulius Cæsar. lib. 2. de bellis ciuilib.* After that *Cæsar* had ben murdered of the Senatours in the counsaile house, one of his frendes to shewe te crueltie of the facte to the people, layed Cæsars bedde in the open market place, and tooke forth of it his image made of waxe, which represented three and twenty woōdes after a beastly sorte stabde in to his face and all the reste of his body, yet dy, yet gaping and as it were freſhe bleeding. With which ſhewe he ſtyrred the people to more wrath and rage, then he could haue done with any oration or geſture. Which was declared forth with. For as ſone as the people ſawe it, not able to beare their griefe nor ſtaye their furie any lenger, wrought great and ſtraunge cruelties againſt them, that were fownde to haue committed that murder.

The third cauſe why images haue ben ſet vp in Churches, is the keping of thinges in memorie neceſſary to our ſaluatiõ. For when we caſt our eyes on thẽ, our memorie whjch otherwiſe is fraile and weake, gathereth together and embraceth the benefites and merites of our Sauiour Chriſt, and the vertuouſe examples of Sainctes, which we ought to folowe: that if we bee ſuch as they were, we may by Gods grace through Chriſt atteine the blyſſe they be in, and with them enioye lyfe euerlaſting. And verely they that haue images in regard and reuerence, muſt be ſo mynded, as they beholde not onely the thinges by them repreſented, but alſo performe the ſame in dede with moſt diligent imitation.

And now we are come to declare, how Images maye he worſhipped and honoured without any offence. That godly worſhip which conſiſteth in ſpirite and truth inwardly, and is declared by ſignes outwardly in recong

Hovvimages may be vvorſhipped vvithout offéce.

in recognizing the supreme dominiō, which
properly of the diuines is called *Latria* is deferred onely to the bleſſed Trinitie. As for
the holy images, to thē we doo not attribute
that worſhip at all, but an inferiout reuerēce
or adoration, for ſo it is named. Which
is nothing elles, but a recognizing of ſome
vertue or excellencie proteſted by outward
ſigne, as reuerent kiſſing, bowing downe,
kneeling, and ſuch the like honour. Which
kynde of adoration or worſhip, we fynde in
the ſcriptures oftentymes geuē to creatures.
The whole acte where of is notwitſtanding
referred not to the images principally, but
to the thinges by them repreſented, as
being the true and proper obiectes of ſuch
worſhip. For although the honour of an
image paſſeth ouer to the originall or firſt
ſampler, which the learned call *archetypum*
as S. Baſile teacheth : yet that high worſhip
called *Latria*, belongeth onely to thē bleſſed
Trinitie, and not to the reuerēt images, leaſt
we ſhuld ſeme to be worſhippers of creatures
and of matters, as of golde, ſyluer, ſtones,
woodde, and of ſuch other the like thinges.
For we adore not images as God, ſayeth *At-*
hanaſius, neither in them doo we put hope of
our ſaluation, ne to them doo we geue godly ſeruice or worſhip, for ſo dyd the gentiles,
but by ſuch adoratiō or reuerēce, we declare
onely a certaine affection and loue, which we
beare

Li. ad Am
philoch.
cap. 18.

In queſtio-
nib. ad An-
tiochum
Principem.

beare toward the originales . And therfore
if it happen their figure and shape to be defaced and vndone , we let not to burne the
stoekes, as very woodde , and being of other
stuffe,to conuert the same to any vse, it maye
serue best for.

S.Gregory praysing much one *Secundinus*, Lib.7.
for that he desyred the Image of our Sauiour Epist.53.
to be sent vnto him, to th'entent by hauyng
his image before his eyes,he might the more
be stirred to loue him in his hart:after a fewe
wordes vttered in this sense,he saieth further.
We knowe thou demaundest not the image
of our Saiour to th'entent to worship it,as
God: but for the remembrance of the sonne
of God,that thou mightest be enkédled with
the loue of him, whose image thou desyrest
to beholde . And verely we fall not downe
before it , as before God . But we adore and
worship him , whom through occasion of the
image , we remember either borne , or done
to death for vs , or sitting in his throne.
And whiles we reduce the sonne of God to
our memorie by the picture no lesse then by
writing , it bryngeth either gladnes to our
mynde by reason of his Resurrection , or
consort by reason of his Passion. Thus farre
S. Gregorie.

And if men praye kneelyng before any
image or triumphant signe of the holy Crosse , they worship not the woodde or stone
figured,

figured, but they honour the highest God. And whom they can not beholde with senses, they reuerence and worship his image representing him according to auncient Institution, not resting or staying them selues in the image, but transferring the adoration and worship to him that is represented.

Much might be alleaged out of the fathers concerning the worshipping of Images, but this may suffise. And of all this one sense redowndeth, that what reuerence, honour, or worship so euer is applyed to Images, it is but for remembrance, loue and honour of the primitiues or originalles. As when we kysse the gospell booke, by that token we honour not the parchemét, paper and incke, wherein it is written, but the gospell it selfe. And as Iacob, when he kyssed his sonne Iosephes cote embrewed with kyddes bloud, holding and embracing it in his armes, and making heauy mone ouer it, the affection of his loue and sorowe rested not in the cote, but was directed to Ioseph him selfe, whose infortunat death (as he thought) that blouddy cote represented: So Christen men shewing tokés of reuerence, loue and honour before the Image of Christ, of an Apostle, or Martyr with their inward recognition and deuotion of their hartes, they staye not their thoughtes in the very Images, but deferre the whole to Christ, to the Apostle, and to the Martyr, geuing

Gen.37.

geuing to eche one in dewe proportion, that which is to be geuen, putting difference betwen the almighty Creatour and the creatures, finally rendring all honour and glory to God alone, who is maruelous in his sainctes. Such worshipping of Images is neither to be accompted for wicked, nor to be dispysed, for the which we haue the testimonies of the auncient fathers, bothe Grekes and Latines: vnto which further auctoritie is addded by certaine generall Councelles, that haue condened the brekers ad impugners of the same.

Or that the laye people was then forbydden to **Iuell.** *reade the word of God in their owne tonge.*

Of the peoples reading the Bible in theire owne tonga.

ARTICLE. XV.

Hat the laye people was then forbidden to reade the word of God in their owne tōge, I fynde it not. Neither doo I fynde, that the laye people was thē, or at any other tyme commaunded to reade the word of God in their owne tonge being vulgare and barbarous. By vulgare and barbarous tōges, I vnderstād, as before, all other, besyde the three learned and principall tonges, Hebrew, Greke and Latine. Which as they were once natiue and

B b   vulgare

vulgare to those thre peoples, so now to none
be they natiue and vulgare, but common to
be obteined by learning for meditatiõ of the
scriptures, and other knowledge.

Three sundry opiniõs concerning the scriptures to be had in a vulgare tonge.

They that treate of this Article, cõcerning
the hauing of the scriptures in a vulgar tonge
for the laytie to reade, bee of three sundry
opinions.

1   Some iudge it to be vtterly vnlaufull, that
the Bible be translated into any tonge of the
2   common people. Some thinke it good it be
translated, so that respecte be had of tyme,
3   and of place, and of persones. Some be of the
opinion, that the holy scriptures ought to
be had in the mother and natiue tõge of euery nation, without any regard of tyme, place,
or persones. The first opiniõ is holde of fewe,
and commonly mysliked. The third is maineteined by al the sectes of our tyme, the Swenk-
feldians excepted, who would the scriptures
to be in no regard. The second is allowed
best of those that seme to be of most wisedõ
and godlynes, and to haue most care for the
helth of the churche, who haue not seuered
them selues from the faith which hath continewed from the begynning. Here that I saye
nothing of the first opinion; as they of the
third reproue the moderation of the secõd,
so they of the second, can not allowe the generalitie of the third.

That the scriptures be not to be set forth
in the

in the vulgare tonge to be reade of all sortes **Fiue consi-**
of people, euery parte of them, without any **derations**
limitation of tyme, place, and persones, they **vvhy the**
seme to be moued with these cósyderations. **are not to**
First, that it is not necessary: nexte, that it is **be set forth**
not conuenient. thirdly, that it is not profi- **for al sortes**
table. Fourthly, that it is dangerous and hur- **of people**
tefull. And lastly, although it were accorded **to read the**
the commó people to haue libertie to reade **vvithout li-**
the Bible in their owne tonge, yet that the **mitation.**
translations of late yeres made by those that
haue diuided them selues from the catholike
churche, be not to be allowed as worthely
suspected, not to be sównde and assured.

First, that the common people of all sortes **1**
and degrees ought of necessitie to reade all
the holy scriptures in their owne tonge, they
saie, they could neuer fynde it hytherto in
the same scriptures. *Ireneus* writeth, that the **Li. 3 aduer-**
Apostles preached to the aliantes and barba- **sus hereses.**
rous people the faith of Christ, euen to tho- **cap. 4.**
se, that were aliátes and barbarous in language, and sayeth that hauing heard the gospell
preached, they beleued in Christ, and keping
the order of tradition which the Apostles dé-
lyuered vnto thé, had their saluatió and faith
writté in their hart without prynte, penne, or
ynke, and vtterly without letters. And further he sheweth, that if the Apostles had lefte
to vs no scriptures at al, yet we shuld be saued
by the tradition, which they lefte to thé, whó

they

they committed their churches vnto, as many nations of aliantes be saued by the same.

Prologo in explanatione Psal. *Hilarius* likewise declaring that the mysterie of Gods will, and th'expectation of the blessed kingdom, is most and chiefly preached in the three tóges, in which Pilate wrote on the Crosse, our lord Iesus Christ to be king of the Iewes : confesseth notwithstanding that many barbarous nations haue atteined and goté the true knowledge of God, by the preachíg of the Apostles and the faith of the churches remayning amongest them to that daie. Whereby he doth vs to vnderstand, that the vnlearned barbarous peoples had their faith without letters or writíg whereof they had no skill, by tradition and preaching, as well as the other nations, who were holpen by the benefite of the learned tonges, Hebrewe, Greke and Latine.

That it is not conuenient nor semely, all sortes of persons without exceptió to be admitted to the reading of the holy scriptures, I nede to saye nothing, euery reasonable man may easely vnderstand the causes by him selfe. This is certaine, diuerse chapters and stories of the olde testament, cóteine such matter, as occasió of euill thoughtes is like to be geuen, if women, maydens, and young mé be permitted to reade rhem. Gregorie Nazian- Li.1. Theologiæ. zene, whom the grekes called the diuine, sayeth, moued with great considerations, that

it is

it is not the parte of all perſons to reaſon of
God and of godly thinges, neither behoofull
the ſame be done in all tymes and places, nor
that all thinges touching God be medled
withal. Which aduertiſemēt taketh no place,
where all be admitted to the curiouſe reading
of the ſcriptures in their owne vulgare tōge.

And the ſcripture it ſelfe (ſaye they) ſheweth plainely, that of couenience the ſcriptures ought not be made common to all perſons. For Chriſt affirmeth the ſame with his
owne wordes, where he ſayeth to his Apoſtles. *Vnto you it is geuen to knowe the ſecretes*
of the kingdom of God : but to other in parables,
that whē they ſee, they ſhuld not ſee, and whē they
heare, they ſhuld not vnderſtande. They to whō
it is geuen to knowe theſe ſecretes, be none
other then the Apoſtles and their ſucceſſours
or diſciples. They to whom this is not geuen, but muſt learne parables, be they, for
whom it were better to be ignorant of the
myſteries, then to knowe them, leaſt they
abuſe them and be the more grieuouſly condemned, if they ſette litle by them, which we
ſee cōmonly done among the cōmon people.

It is reported by ſundry auncient writers
of great auctoritie, that among the people of
Iſael, the ſeuenty Elders onely could reade
and vnderſtande the myſteries of the holy
bookes, that we call the Bible. For whereas
the letters of the Hebrewe tonge haue no

Lu.x.8.

Vide Hila-
rium in
Pſal.2.

Bb 3   vocalles

vocalles, they onely had the skill to reade the
scripture by the consonantes: and therby the
vulgare people were kepte from reading of it
by special prouidéce of God, as it is thonght,
that pretiouse stones shuld not be caste before swyne, that is to saye, such as be not called
thereto, as being for their vnreuerent curiositie and impure life, vnworthy.

3   Here I nede not to spende tyme in reher-
sing the manifolde difficulties of these holy
letters, through which the reading of them
to the simple and vnlearned people, hauing
their wittes exercised in no kynde of learning, their myndes occupied in worldly ca-
res, their hartes caryed awaye with the loue of
thinges they luste after, is not very profita-

Bernard. Su   ble. As the light shyneth in vaine vpő blinde
per cantica.   eyes (sayeth a holy father) so to no purpose
or profite is the labour of a worldly and naturall man taken for the atteining of thinges
that be of the spirite. Verely emonges other,
this incommoditie is sene by dayly experience hereof to procede, that of the people, such
as ought of right to take lest vpon them, be
now becomme censours and iudges of all,
despysers of the more parte, and which is
cőmon to all heretikes, mockers of the whole
simplicitie of the churche, and of all those
thinges, which the churche vseth as pappe or
mylke to nourrish her tender babes withall,
that it were better for them not to reade, thé

by

by reading so to be pufte vp and made info-
lēt. Which euill cometh not of the scripture,
but of their owne malice and euil dispositiō.

The dangers and hurtes which the com- 4
mō peoples reading of the scriptures in their
one language bryngeth, after the opinion of
those that reproue the same, be great, sundry
and many. I will here, as it were but touche
a fewe of them, leauing the whole matter it
selfe to the iudgement of the churche. First,
seing the poyson of heretikes doth most in-
fecte the common people, and all heretikes
drawe their venyme, out of the Bible vnder
pretence of Gods worde: it is not thought
good by these men, to lette euery curiouse
and busie body of the vulgar sorte, to reade
and examine the Bible in their common language. Yet they wouldnot the learned discrete and sober laye men to be imbarred of that
libertie.

Againe if heresie spring of wrong vnder- De Trini-
standing, not of the scriptures, (as *Hilarius* tate lib. 2.
sayeth, heresie is of vnderstanding, not of scri
pture, and the sense not the worde is a crime)
who shall sooner fall to heresie, then the
common people, who can not vnderstande
that they reade? verely it semeth a thing hard
to beleue, that the vnlearned people shuld
vnderstāde that, which the best learned men
with long studie and great trauaill can scarcely at length atteine.

Bb 4   Whereas

Whereas Luther would the scriptures to be tranflated into euery vulgare tonge, for that they be lyght and eafie to vnderftande, he is confuted by the scripture it felfe. For both S. Peter, and alfo S. Paul, acknowlegeth in them to be great difficulties, by occafion whereof fome mifconftrue them to their owne damnation, fome vnderftande not what thinges they fpeake, nor of what thinges they affirme, and to fome the gofpell that S. Paul preached is hydden, euen to them which perifhe. If the fcriptures were playne, how erred *Arius*? how *Macedonius*? how *Eunomius*? how *Neftorius*? how many mo, men of great learning? fpecially feing they all tooke occafion of their errours of the fcripture not rightly vnderftanded?

a.Pet.3.
1.Tim.1.
a.Cor.4.

Luther fayeth, that S.Hieröe was ouerfeen in the vnderftanding of the fcripture, that S. Auguftine erred in thefame, that S.Ambrofe, Cyprian, Hilary, Bafile, and Chryfoftome, the beft leraned doctours of Chriftes churche, were oftentymes deceiued. And yet in the preface of his booke *de captiuitate Babilonica* he fpeaketh of them very honorably, and graunteth, that they haue laboured in the lordes vineyarde worthely, and that they haue employed great diligéce in opening the fcriptures. If thefe being of fo excellent learning after long exercife in the holy letters, after long ftudie and watche, after long
and

and feruent prayer, after mortification of
them felues, and purgation of carnall affections were deceiued, as he witneffeth: how can
he faye they are cleare, plaine and eafye to be
vnderftanded? And if thefe worthy fathers
were deceiued in one pointe or two, is it not
likely the common people may be deceiued
in many, fpecialy their diligence and ftudy
not being comparable to theirs, and their
lyues not being fuch, as the cleanneffe of their inward affectes might lighten their vnderftanding, and the annointing of god might
teach them?

And leaft all the vnlearned laye people
fhulde feme hereby vtterly reiected from
hope of vnderftanding gods worde without
teaching of others, it may be graunted, that it
is not impofsible a man (be he neuer fo vnlearned) exercifed in long prayer, accuftomed
to feruent contemplation, benig brought Pfal.72.
by God into his inward cellares, may from
thence obteine the true vnderftanding and
interpretation of the holy fcriptures, no
leffe then any other alwaies brought vp in
learning. Of what forte S. Antony that holy
and perfecte man the Eremite of Egypt, was.
Who, as faint Auguftine writeth, without Prologo in
any knowledge of letters, both canned the libros de
fcriptures by hart with hearing, and vnder- doctrina
ftode them wifely with thinking. And that Chriftiana.
holy man, whom S. Gregorie fpeaketh of,

who lying bedred many yeres for fiknes of body, through earneſt prayer and deuout meditation, obteined helth of mynde, and vnderſtanding of the ſcriptures neuer hauing learned letters, ſo as he was able to expounde them to thoſe that came to viſite him, who comming vnto him with pretence to bring conforte, through his heauenly knowledge, receiued conforte. But amõg the people how great number is there of lewed locelles, gluttons and dronckeerds, whoſe bealy is theire god, who folowe their vnruly luſtes? is it to be thought this ſorte of perſones may without meditation and exerciſe of prayer pearſe the vnderſtanding of the ſcriptures, and of thoſe holy myſteries, which god hath hidden (as Chriſt confeſſeth) from the learned and wiſe men?

Matth.11.
The goſpellers diui
ded in to
contrarie
ſectes.

And whereas learned men of our tyme be diuided intocontrarie ſectes, and write bitterly one againſt an other, eche one imputing to other miſtaking of the ſcriptures, if amongeſt them who would ſeme to be the leaders of the people, be controuerſies and debates about the vnderſtanding of the ſcriptures: how may the common people be thought to be in ſafe caſe out of all danger of errours, if by reading the Bible in their owne tonge, they take the matter in hande?

If any man thinke, I ſclaunder thẽ, for that I ſaye they be diuided into cõtrary ſectes, let
him

him vnderstand, their owne countrie men, I
meane them of Germanie, and speciall setters
forth of this newe doctrine, report it in their
bookes, and complaine lamentably of it. Namely *Nicolaus Amsdorffius* in his booke intituled, *Publica confessio pura doctrinæ euangelij*
&c. Also *Nicolaus Gallus*, in his kooke of *The-*
ses and *Hypotyposes* : who acknowlegeth the
strifes and debates that be amongest them, to
be not of light matters, but of the high articles of christian doctrine. For euen so be his
wordes in Latine. *Nõ sunt leues inter nos concer-*
tationes de rebu leuibus , sed de sublimibus doctri-
næ Christianæ articulis, de lege & euangelio &c.
The same man in the last leafe of his forsayde
booke, with great vehemencie reporteth , *hæ-*
reses permultas esse præ manibus, plerasque etiam-
nùm hærere in calamo , that very many heresies
be allready in hande, and many as yet sticke in
the penne, as though he meant, they were ready to be set forth.

Of late there haue ben put out in printe
two great bookes, one by the Prīces of Saxo-
nie, the other by the Erles of Mansfeld, chiefe maineteiners of the Lutheranes : in which
be recited eleuen sectes, and the same as detestable heresies cõdemned, they are conteined
in this cataloge or rolle. *Anabaptistæ, Seruetia-*
ni, Stancariani, Antinomi , Iesuitæ, Osiandrini,
Melanchthonici, Maioristæ, Adiaphoristæ, Suëc-
feldiani, Sacramentarij. Albeit the Iesuites haue
wronge

wrong to be numbred amõg thé. This much is confessed of the sectes and controuersies of our newe gospellers by their owne princes, that stande in defence of the confession of Auspurg, and by two of the Lutherane superintendentes.

Fridericus Staphylus. No man hath so exactly declared to the world the number and diuersitie of the sectes of our tyme, which hath sprong out of Martin Luther, as *Fridericus Staphylus* a man of excellent learning, one of the Emperours counsaile that now is, who might wel haue knowledge herein, for as much as he was a diligent student ten yeres at Wittenberg amõg the chiefe doctours of them, and for that tyme was of their opinion, and afterward by consyderation of their manifold disagreeinges and contentions within them selues induced to discredite them, and through the grace of God reduced to a whole mynde and to the catholike faith, and now remayneth a perfecte member of the churche. This learned man in his Apologie sheweth, that out of Luther haue sprong three diuerse heresies or sectes: the Anabaptistes, the Sacramentaries, *Protestantes.* and the Confessionistes, who made confession of their faith in open diete before the Emperour Charles, the princes and states of Germanie at Auspurg, *anno domini* 1530. and for potestation of the same there, are called Protestantes. Now he proueth further by testimonie

teſtimonie of their owne writinges, that the
Anabaptiſtes be diuided into ſyx ſectes, the
Sacramentaries into eight ſectes, the Con-
feſſioniſtes and they which properly are called proteſtátes, into twenty ſectes, euery one Proteſtátes
hauing his proper and particular name to be diuided in-
called and knowen by. This lamentable diui- to twventy
ſió of learned men into ſo many ſectes in the Sectes.
countries where the goſpell (as they call it)
hath theſe forty yeres and is yet moſt buſely
handled, may be a warning to the gouernours
of Chriſtendome, that they take good aduiſe-
ment, how they ſuffer the rude and raſhe
people to haue the ſcriptures common in
their owne tonge.

The perill of it is knowen by ſundry examples bothe of tymes paſt, and alſo of this preſent age. For out of this roote hath ſprong
the ſecte of the *Valdenſes*, otherwiſe called Valdenſes.
Pauperes de Lugduno. For Valdo a merchant
of Lyós their firſt author, of whom they were
named *Valdenſes*, being an vnlearned laye má,
procured certaine bookes of the ſcripture to
be tranſlated into his owne language, which
when he vſed to reade and vnderſtoode not,
he fell into many errours. Of the ſame well-
ſpring yſſued the fylthie puddels of the ſectes called *Adamitæ* or *Picardi*, *Bogardi*, and
Turelupini, and of late yeres beſyde the ſame
ſecte of Adamites newly reuiued, alſo the A-
nabaptiſtes, and Suenkfelldians. Wherefor
that

that edicte or proclamation of the worthy
Princes *Ferdinando* and *Elizabeth* kyng and
Quene of Spayne, is of many much commēded, by which they gaue streight commaundement, that vnder great penalties no man
shuld trāslate the Bible into the vulgare Spa-
nish tōge, and that no man shuld be fownde
to haue the same translated in any wise. These and the like be the reasons and consyde-
rations, which haue moued many men to
thinke, the setting forth of the whole Bible,
and of euery parte of the scripture in the vulgare tonge, for all sortes of persons to reade without exception or limitation, to be a
thing not necessary to saluation, nor otherwise conuenient nor profitable, but contra-
rywise dangerous and hurtefull.

Yet it is not meant by them, that the people be kepte wholly from the scripture, so as
they reade no parte of it at all. As the whole
in their opinion is too strong a meate for
their weake stomakes, so much of it they
may right holesomely receiue and brooke,
as that which perteineth to pietie and necessary knowledge of a christen man. Wherein
they would the examples of the olde holy fathers to be folowed. S. Augustine hath gathered together into one booke, all that maketh for good lyfe out of the scriptures which
booke he intituled *Speculum*. that is to saye,
a myrrour or a looking glasse, as *Possidonius*
wit-

VVhat par-
tes of the
scriptures
apperteine
to the peo-
ple to kno-
vve.

witnesseth in his lyfe. S. Basile hath set forth
the like argument almost in his fourescore
morral rules perteining all together to good
manners. S. Cyprian also hath done the like
in his three bookes *ad Quirinum*. Such godly bookes they thinke to be very profitable
for the simple people to reade . But how
much and what partes of the scripture the
common people may reade for their conforte and necessary instruction , and by whom
the same may be translated; it belongeth to
the iudgemēt of the churche. Which church
hath already condemned all the vulgare trās-
lations of the Bible of late yeres , for that
they be founde in sundry places erroneous
and parciall in fauour of the heresies , which
the translatours mainteine. And it hath not
onely in our tyme condemned these late trā-
slations , but also hytherto neuer allowed
those fewe of olde tyme. I meane S. Hieromes translation into the Dalmaticall tonge,
if euer any such was by him made , as to some it semeth a thing not sufficiently proued:
And that , which before S. Hierome *Ulphi-
las* an Arian bishop made and commended
to the nation of the Gothes , who first inuented letters for them , and proponed the
scriptures to them trāslated into their owne
tonge , and the better to bring his Ambassa-
de to the Emperour *Valens* to good effecte,
was persuaded by the heretikes of Constantinople

tinople and of the courte there, to forſake the catholike faith, and to communicate with the Arians, making promiſe alſo to trauaile in bringing the people of his countrie to the ſame ſecte, which at legth he performed moſt wickedly.

As for the church of this land of Britaine, the faith hath continewed in it thirten hundred yeres vntill now of late, without hauing the Bible tranſlated into the vulgare tonge, to be vſed of all in common. Our lord graunt, we yelde no worſe ſoules to God now hauing the ſcriptures in our owne tonge, and talking ſo much of the goſpell, then our aunceſters haue done before vs. This Iland saieth Beda (ſpeaking of the eſtate the church was in at his dayes) at this preſent, according to the number of bookes that Gods lawe was written in, doth ſerche and confeſſe one and the ſelfe ſame knowlege of the high truth and of the true highte, with the tonges of fiue nations, of the Engliſhe, the Britons, the Scottes, the Pightes, and the Latines, *Quæ meditatione ſcripturarum cæteris omnibus eſt facta communis*. Which tonge of the Latines (ſayeth he) is for the ſtudie and meditation of the ſcriptures made comõ to all the other. Verely as the Latine tonge was then common to all the natiõs of this lande being of diſtincte languages, for the ſtudie of the ſcriptures, as Beda reporteth: ſo the ſame onely hath

Hiſt. eccleſiaſt. lib. 1.

hath alwayes vntill our tyme, ben common
to all the cowntries and nations of the Occidentall or West churche for the same purpose, and thereof it hath ben called the Latine
churche.

Wherefore to conclude, they that shewe
them selues so earnest and zelous for the trá-
slation of the scriptures into all vulgare and
barbarous tonges, it behoueth thé after the
opinion of wise men to see, first, that no faultes be fownde in their translatiós, as hytherto
many haue ben fownde. And a small faulte
committed in the handling of Gods worde,
is to be taken for a great crime. Nexte, that
for as much as such translations perteine to
all christé people, they be referred to the iudgement of the whole churche of euery language, and commended to the layetie by the
wisedó and auctoritie of the clergie hauing
charge of their soules. Furthermore that there be some choïse, exception, and limitation
of tyme, place, and persons, and also of partes
of the scriptures, after the discrete ordinaunce of the Iewes. Amongest whom it was not
laufull, that any má shuld reade certaine partes of the Bible, before he had fullfilled the
tyme of the priestly ministerie, which was the
age of thirty yéres, as S. Hierome witnesseth. Præfatione
Lastly, that the setting forth of the scriptures in Ezechie-
in the commó language be not commended lem.
to the people as a thing vtterly necessary to
C c saluation,

ſaluation, leaſt thereby they condemne ſo many churches, that hytherto haue lackt the ſame, and ſo many learned and godly fathers, that haue not procured it for their flocke, finally, all that haue gonne before vs, to whom in all vertue, innocencie, and holynes of lyfe, we are not to be compared. As for me, in as much as this matter is not yet determined by the church, whether the common people ought to haue the ſcriptures in their owne tonge to reade and to heare, or no, I define nothing. As I eſteme greatly all godly and holeſome knowledge, and wiſhe the people had more of it then they haue, with charitie and meekeneſſe: ſo I would, that theſe hote talkers of gods worde had leſſe of that knowledge, which maketh a man to ſwell, and to be proude in his owne conceite: and that they would depely weigh with them ſelues, whether they be not conteyned within the lyſtes of the ſaying of S. Paul to the Corinthians, *If any man thinke that he knoweth any thing, he knoweth nothing yet as he ought to knowe.* God graunt all our knowledge be ſo ioyned with meekeneſſe, humilitie and charitie, as that be not iuſtly ſayd of vs, which S. Auguſtine in the like caſe ſayde very dredfully to his dere frende *Alipius. Surgunt indocti, & cœlum rapiunt, & nos cum doctrinis noſtris ſine corde, ecce vbi volutamur in carne & ſanguine?* The vnlearned and ſimple aryſe vp, and catche

1. Cor. 3.

Cōfeſſ. lib. 3. cap. 8.

eatche heauen awaie from vs, and we with all
our great learning voyed of heart, lo where
are we wallowing in fleshe and bloude?

Or that it was the lawfull for the priest, to pro- Iuell.
nounce the wordes of Consecrati on closely and
in silence to him selfe.

Of secrete pronouncing the Canon of the Masse.

ARTICLE XVI.

He matter of this article is neither
one of the highest mysteries, nor
one of the greatest keyes of our
religion, how so euer Maister Iuell
pleaseth him selfe with that reporte, thinking thereby to impaire the estimation of the
catholike churche. The diuersitie of obseruation in this behalfe sheweth the indifferencie
of the thing. For elles if one maner of pronouncing the wordes of consecration had
ben thought a necessarie point of religion, it
had ben euery where vniforme and inuaria-
ble. That the breade and wyne be cōsecrated
by the wordes of our lord, pronounced by
the priest, as in the person of Christ, by vertue of which through the grace of the holy
ghoste the breade and wyne are chaunged into our lordes body and bloude: this thing
hath in all tymes, and in all places, and
with consent of all inuariably ben done,

and

and so beleued. But the manner of pronouncing the wordes concerning silence or open
vtteraunce, according to diuersitie of places,
hath ben diuerse.

The maner of pronouncing the consecration in the Greke and Latine churches diuerse.

In libello de Sacramento Eucharistiæ.

The grekes in the East church haue thought
it good to pronounce the wordes of consecration, *clara voce,* as we finde in Chrysostomes Masse, and as *Bessarion* writeth, *alta voce,*
that is, plainely, out alowde, or with a lowde voice. *Sacerdos alta voce iuxta Orientalis
Ecclesiæ ritum verba illa pronunciat, hoc est
corpus meum, &c.* The priest (sayeth *Bessarion*) after the rite or maner of the east churche pronounceth with a lowde voice those
wordes, *this is my body, &c.* Which manner
of lowde pronouncing was thought good to
be vsed in the Greke churche, as it may be
gathered by that *Bessarion* writeth (who being
a Greke borne and brought vp in learning
amongest the Grekes knewe rightwell the order of that churche) to the intent the people might therby for the better mainetenau-
ce of their faith be styrred and warned to
geue token of consent and of beleefe thereto. When the priest (sayeth he) pronunceth
those wordes with a lowde voice, the people
standyng by, *in vtraque parte,* that is, first, at
the consecration of the body, and agayne at
the consecration of the bloude, answereth
Amen: as though they sayde thus, truly so it
is, as thou sayest. For where as *Amen* is

an

an aduerbe of afûrimyng in Hebrue, in Gre-
be it signifieth so much as truly. And there
fore the people answering *Amen* to those
wordes, verely saie they, these giftes sette
forth are the body and bloude of Christ. So
we beleue, so we côfesse. This farre *Bessarion,*
It is declared by Clement, *lib. 8. constitut.
Apostol carum,* that the people sayde *Amen,*
when the wordes of consecration had ben
pronunced. Whereby we vnderstande, that
order to haue ben taken by the Apostles.
The same custome also maye be gathered
out of S. Ambrose, who sayeth thus. *Dicit tibi
sacerdos, corpus Christi, & tu dicis, Amen, hoc
est verum: quod confitetur lingua teneat affectus.
de sacramentis lib. 4. cap. 5.* The priest sayeth,
the body of Christ, and thou sayest, *Amē,* that
is to saye, true. Holde with thy harte that
which thou confessest with thy tonge. He
sayeth hereof likewise, *de ijs qui initiantur
mysterijs. cap. 9. Frustrà ab illis respondetur
Amen, &c. Amen* is answered in vaine by
them, who dispute against that, which is
receiued, sayeth Leo.

Serm. 9. de ieiunio. 7. mensis.

And that the people shuld geue their consent and applie their faith to this truth without errour and deceite, and that by saying
Amen, they shuld then beleue and confesse
the breade and wine to be made the body
and bloude of Christ, when it was made in
deede, and not elles, for so were it a great

Cc 3   errour

De eccle-
siasticis di-
uersis ca-
pitulis con-
stitut. 123.
errour: for this cause Iustinian the Emperour
made an ordinaunce, that the bishoppes and
priestes shuld to this intent pronounce their
seruice plainely, distinctly, and so, as it might
he vnderstanded, that the people might answere *Amen*, (which is to be referred to eche
parte of the seruice, but specially to the consecration) that they might beleue and confesse
it was the body and bloude of Christ, when it
was in deede, and not so confesse, when it was
not, which might happen, if they hearde not
the wordes of consecration plainely pronounced. And hereunto specially that Constitution of Iustinian is to be restrayned, as
perteining onely to the Greke churche, wherein he lyued, and not to be stretched further to serue for proufe of all the seruice to
be had and sayde in the vulgare tonge in the
West churche, as to that purpose of our newe
teachers it is vntruly alleaged.

Now in this West churche, which is the
latine churche, the people hauing ben sufficiently instructed touching the beleefe of the
body and bloude of our lord in the Sacramét:
it hath ben thought by the fathers coueniént,
the wordes of consecration to be pronounced by the priest closely and in silence, rather
then with open voice. Where in they had
speciall regarde to the dignitie of that high
mysterie. And doubteles for this point they
vnderstoode, as Saint Basile writeth, that the
Apostles

Apostles and the fathers which at the begyn- Lib. de spi-
ning made lawes for the order of Ecclesia- ritu sancto.
sticall thinges, mainetened the mysteries in cap. 27.
their due auctoritie by keping them secrete
and in silence . For it is not (sayeth he) any
mysterie at all , which is brought forth to the
popular and vulgar eares , whereof he wrote
very truly before . *Ei quod publicatum est,*
& per se apprehendi potest , imminere contem-
ptum . Ei verò quod remotum est ac rarum,
etiam naturaliter quodammodo esse coniunctam
admirationem . That , what is done openly
and made common , and of it selfe maye be
atteined , it is like to come in contempte and
be dispysed . But what is kepte farre of , and
is sildom goten , that euen naturally in maner is neuer without wondering at it . And
in such respecte Christ gaue warning , that
pretiouse stones be not strewed before hog-
ges .

If in the olde lawe priestes were chosen
(as Saint Ambrose writeth) to coouer the
arke of the Testament , because it is not lawfull for all persones to see the deapth of my- Num. 4.
steries : If the sonnes of *Caath* by Gods ap- Vide Ori-
pointment dyd onely beare the arke and genem ho-
those other holy thinges of the Taberna- mil. 5. in
cle on their shulders , when so euer the chil- Nu. cap. 4.
dre of Israel remoued and marched foreward
in wildernes , being closely folded and lapte
within vailes , courteines and palles , by the

Cc 4 priestes,

priestes : and might not at no tyme touche
nor see the same vpon payne of death, which
were but figures of this : how much more is
this high and worthy mysterie to be honoured with secretnes, closenes, and silence?

In fragmē-
to Caroli
Mag. de ri-
tibus vete-
ris ecclesie.

For this cause as they reporte, sayeth *Ca-*
rolus Magnus that noble, vertuouse and learned Emperour, wryting to his Schoolemai-
ster *Alcuinus* our cowntrie man, and first teacher of Philosophie in Paris, it is become a
custome in the church, that the Canon and
consecration be sayde by the priest secretly,
that those wordes so holy and perteining to
so great a mysterie, shuld not growe in contempte, whiles all in maner through common vse bearing them awaye, would syng
them in the high wayes, in the stretes, and in
other places, where it were not conuenient.
Whereof it is tolde, that before this custome was receiued, shepherdes, when they
sang them in the fielde, were by Gods hande
strooken. Luther him selfe *in praeceptorio*, is
much against them, that would haue the Canon of the Masse to be pronounced with a
lowde voice for the better vnderstanding.

VVhat per-
sons the
primitiue
church ex-
cluded frō
presence of
the sacra-
ment.

The fathers of the primitiue churche had
this Sacramēt in such reuerence and honour,
that they excluded some sortes of faithfull
people from being present at the celebratiō
of it, thinking them vnworthy not onely
to heare the mystical wordes of consecration
pronounced,

pronounced, but also to see the formes of
the outward elemẽtes, and to be in the churche, whiles that most holy Sacrifice was
offered. They were these, *Cathechumeni*,
Energumeni, and *pœnitentes*, The first were
learners of our beleese, who as they were daily instructed, beleued in Christ, and as Saint
Augustine writeth, bare Christes crosse in Tractatu in
their forehead and marked them selues with Ioan. 11.
the same. The second were such, as notwithstanding they had ben christened, yet for
the inconstancie of their mynde, were vexed
with vncleane spirites. The third sorte were
they, who for their synnes committed, had
not yet made an ende of doing their open
penaunce. Al these were iudged by the gouer
nours of the churche at the begynning vnworthy to be present at these holy misteries.

Now if this great reuerence towardes the
holy thinges in them was iustly praised, the
admitting of all sortes of people not onely
to be present and to beholde the same, but
also to heare and vnderstande the wordes
of consecration, (that had thus allwaies
ben honoured with silence and secretnes) can
not seme to wise zelouse and godly men
a thing commendable: specially in these
tymes, in which the holy Christen discipline of the churche is loosed and vtterly
shaken of, and no difference nor accompte
of any diuersitie made betwen the perfite and

godly

godly people, and them, that ought to doe open penaunce, that be possessed with deuilles, and be infamouse for heynouse and notoriouse crimes committed. Where as in olde tymes, when by holesom discipline the faithfull people were kepte in godly awe and obedience, that prayer also which was sayde ouer the oblation before consecration, was pronounced closely and in silence, and therefore it was called of the latines, *secreta*, of the Grekes *mystica oratio*, meaning thereby, that it ought not to be vttered openly and made common.

Or that

Or that the priest had then auctoritie, to offer Iuell.
vp Christ vnto his father.

Of the priestes auctoritie to offer vp Christ to his father.

ARTICLE XVII.

 H R I S T is offered vp to his father Threefold
after three manners. figuratiuely, oblatiō of
truly with bloud shedding, and sa- of Christ.
cramentally or mystically. In figu-
re or signification, he was offered in the sacrifices made to God bothe in the tyme of the
lawe of nature, and also in the tyme of the
lawe written. And therefore Saint Iohn cal- Agnus oc-
leth Christ the lambe, which was killed from cisus est ab
the begynning of the world, meaning in fi- origine
gure. The sacrifices of *Abel*, *Noe*, and *Abra-* mundi.
ham, and al those of the people of *Israel* com- Apoc.13.
maunded by the lawe of *Moses*, figured and
signified Christ. For which respecte chie
fly, the law is reported of Saint Paul, to Heb.10.
haue the shadowe of the good thinges to
come. Saint Augustine writing against *Fau-* Lib.6.ca.5.
stus the heretike, sayeth: *Testamenti veteris*
sacrificia omnia multis & varijs modis vnum sa-
crificium, cuius nunc memóriam celebramus, si-
gnificauerūt. All the sacrifices of th'olde testamēt, signified by many and sundry waies this
one sacrifice, whose memorie we doo now
celebrate. And in an other place he sayeth; De fide ad
that in those fleshely sacrifices, there was a Petrū diaco
signi- nū. cap.16.

significatiõ of Christes flesne, which he shuld offer for synnes, and of his bloude, which he shuld shedde for the remission of our synnes.

Truly and with bloude shedding, Christ was offered on the Crosse in his owne persone, where of S. Paul sayeth: *Christ gaue him selfe for vs, that he myght redeme vs from all iniquitie:* And againe: *Christ hath loued vs, and hath delyuered him selfe for vs an oblation and sacrifice to God into a swete sauour.*

Tit. 2.
Ephes. 5.

Sacramentally or in mysterie, Christ is offered vp to his father in the dayly sacrifice of the churche vndei the forme of breade and wine, truly and in dede, not in respecte of the manner of offering, but in respecte of his very body and bloude really (that is in dede) present, as it hath ben sufficiently proued here before.

The two first manners of the offering of Christ, our aduersaries acknowlegde and confesse. The third they denye vtterly. And so they robbe the churche of the greatest treasure it hath or may haue, the body and bloude of our Sauiour Christ once offered vpon the crosse with painefull suffering for our redemption, and now daily offered in the blessed Sacrament in remembraunce. For vvhich we haue so many proufes, as for no one point of our Christen religion moe. And herein I am more encombred with store, then straighted vvith lacke, and doubte more vvhat I

may

may leaue, then what I may take. Wherefor thinking it shall appeare to the wise more skylle to shewe discretion in the choise
of places, rather then learning in recitall of
number,though we are ouer peartely thereto
prouoked by M. Iuelles vaunting and inso-
lent chalenge : I intend herein to be shotte,
verely shorter, then so large a matter requireth : and to bring for proufe a fewe such auctorities, I meane a fewe in respecte of the
multitude that might be brought) as ought
in euery mannes iudgement to be of great
weight and estimation.

The scripture it selfe ministring euident
proufe for the oblation of Christ to his father by the priestes of the newe testament, in
the Institution of this holy Sacrament, in
the figure of *Melchisedech*, and in the prophecie of Malachie the prophete: the auctorities of the fathers neded not to be alleged,
were not the same scripture by the ouerth-
warte and false interpretations of our aduersaries wrested and tourned to a contrary sense,to the horrible seducing of the vnlearned.
For where as the holy Euangelistes reporte,
that *Christ at his last supper tooke breade ,gaue
thākes,brake it,and sayde,this is my body, which
is geuen for you.* Againe, *this is my bloude which* Luc.22.
is shedde for you in remission of synnes : By these
wordes, being wordes of sacrificing and offering, they shewe and set forth an oblation
in acte

in acte and dede, though the terme it selfe of oblation or sacrifice be not expressed. Albe it to some of excellent knowledge, *datur* here sowndeth no lesse, then *offertur* or *immolatur*, that is to saye, is offered or sacrificed, specially the addition *pro vobis*, withall consydered. For if Christ sayde truly, (as he is *truth it selfe, and guile was neuer fownde in his mowth*) then was his body presently geuen and for vs geuen, at the tyme he spake the wordes, that is, at his supper. For he saide *datur*, is geuen, not *dabitur*, shal be geuen: And likewise was his bloude shedde in remission of synnes, at the tyme of that supper: for the texte hath *funditur*, is shedde. But the geuing of his body for vs, and the shedding of his bloud in remission of synnes, is an oblatiō of the same. *Ergo* Christ offered his body and bloude at the supper. And thus *datur*, signifieth here as much as *offertur*.

1.Pet.2.

Now this being true, that our lord offered him selfe vnto his father at his last supper, hauing geuen cōmaundemēt to his Apostles to doo the same that he there dyd, whō then he ordeined priestes of the newe testamēt, sayig *doo this in my remembraunce*, as Clement doth plainely shewe, *lib.8. Apostolicarum cōstitut. cap.vltimo:* the same charge perteining no lesse to the priestes that be now the successours of the Apostles in this behalfe, then to the Apostles thē selues: it doth right well appeare,

how

how so euer M. Iuell assureth him selfe of the contrary, and what so euer the deuill hath wrought and by his ministers taught against the sacrifice of the Masse, that priestes haue auctoritie to offer vp Christ vnto his father.

That Christ offered him selfe to his father in his last supper, and that priestes by those wordes, *Doo this in my remembraunce*, haue not onely auctoritie, but also a speciall commaundement to doo the same, and that the figure of *Melchisedech*, and the prophecie of Malachie perteineth to this sacrifice, and maketh proufe of the same: let vs see by the testimonies of the fathers, what doctrine the Apostles haue lefte to the churche.

Eusebius Cæsariēsis hath these wordes. *Horrorem afferentia mensa Christi sacrificia supremo Deo offerre, per eminentissimum omnium ipsius Pontificem edocti sumus*. We are taught (sayeth he) to offer vnto our supreme God the sacrifices of Christes table, which cause vs to tremble and quake for feare, by his bishop highest of all. Here he calleth Christ in respecte of his sacrifice, Gods bishop highest of all bishops, the sacrifices of Christes table he calleth, the body and bloud of Christ, because at the table in his last supper he sacrificed and offered the same, and for that it is his very body and very bloud, imagination onely, phantasie, and figure set apparte, he termeth these sacrifices, as cōmonly the
auncient

De demō-strat. Euā-geli. lib. 1. cap. 10.

auncient fathers doo, dredfull, causing trembling and feare. And where as he sayeth we haue ben taught to offer these sacrifices to God, doubteles he meaneth by these wordes of Christ: *Doo this in my remembraunce, this is my body, which is geuen for you: this is my bloud which is shedde for you.* Clement in his eight booke often cited, speaking of the sacrifice offered by the Apostles, commonly addeth these wordes, *secundum ipsius ordinatione,* or, *ipso ordinante:* Whereby he confesseth it to be Christes owne ordinance.

That Christ sacrificed him selfe at his supper, *Hesychius* afirmeth with these wordes. *Quod Dominus iussit (Leuit. 4.) vt sacerdos vitulum pro peccato oblaturus, ponat manũ super caput eius, & iugulet eum coram Domino, Christum significat, quem nemo obtulit, sed nec immolare poterat, nisi semetipsum ipse ad patiẽdum tradidisset. Proper quod non solum dicebat, potestatem habeo ponendi animam meam, & potestatem habeo iterum sumendi eam: sed & praeueniens semetipsum in cœna Apostolorum immolauit, quod sciunt, qui mysteriorum percipiunt virtutem.* That our Lord commaunded (sayeth he the priest which shuld offer a calfe for synne, to put his hand vpon his hedde, and to sticke him before our lord, it signifieth Christ, whõ no man hath offered, neither could any man sacrifice him, excepte he had delyuered him selfe to suffer. For the which he sayde not onely,

Ioan. 10.

onely, *I haue power to laye downe my soule, and I* Ioan.10. *haue power to take it agayne.*: But also preuenting it, he offered vp him selfe in sacrifice in the supper of the Apostles, which they knowe, that receiue the vertue of the mysteries. By these wordes of *Hesychius* we learne, that Christ offered and sacrificed his body and bloud twise. First in that holy supper vnbloudely, when he tooke bread in his handes and brake it, &c. Without diuision of the sacrifice, for it is but one and the same sacrifice. And afterward on the crosse, with shedding of his bloude, and that is it he meaneth by the word preuenting.

And at the same very instãt of tyme, (which is here further to be added as a necessary poĩt of Christen doctrine) we must vnderstand, that Christe offered hym selfe in heauen inuisibly (as dõcerning man) in the sight of his hauenly father, and that from that tyme foreward that oblation of Christ in heauen was neuer intermitted, but contineweth allwaies for our attonement with God, and shal without ceasing endure vntill the ende of the worlde. For as S. Paul sayeth, *Iesus hath not en-* Heb.9. *tred into temples made with handes, the samplers of the true temples, but into heauen it selfe, to appeare now to the countenaunce of God for vs.* Now as this oblation and sacrifice of Christ endureth in heauen cõtinually, for as much as he is rysen frõ the dead and ascẽded

D d　　　　into

in to heauen with that body which he gaue
to *Thomas* to feele, bringing in thither his
bloud, as *Hesychius* sayeth, and bearing the
markes of his woondes, and there appeareth before the face of God with that thorne
prikte, naileboared, spearepearsed, and other
wise woonded, rent, and torne body for vs:
(whereby we vnderstand the vertue of his
oblation on the crosse euer enduring, not
the oblation it selfe with renewig of payne
and sufferaunce continewed) so we doo per-
petually celebrate this oblation and sacrificing of Christes very body and bloud in the
Masse, in remembraunce of him, commaunded so to doo vntill his comming.

Wherein our aduersaries so foolishly as
wickedly scoffe at vs, as though we sacrificed
Christ agayne so as he was sacrificed on the
crosse that is, in bloudy maner. But we doo
not so offer or sacrifice Christ agayne, but
that oblation of him in the supper, and oures
in the Masse, is but one oblation, the same sacrifice, for this cause by his diuine ordinaûce
left vnto vs, that as the oblation once made
ont he crosse continually endureth and appeareth before the face of God in heauen for
our behalfe, continewed not by newe suffering, but by perpetuall interceßion for
vs: So the memorie of it may euer vntill
his second comming be kepte amongest vs
also in earth, and that thereby we may apply

and

and bring vnto vs through faith the great benefites, which by that one oblation of him
felfe on the croſſe he hath for vs procured,
and daily doth procure.

Now for further proufe of the offering
and ſacrificing of Chriſt of thoſe wordes of
our lord, *Doo this in my remembraunce*, to
recite ſome teſtimonies of the fathers: Firſt,
Dionyſius Saint Paules ſcoler, and biſhop
of Athenes, writeth thus. *Quocirca reue-* Ecclefiaſ.
renter ſimul & ex Pontificali officio, poſt ſa- Hierarch.
cras diuinorum operum laudes, quòd hoſtiam cap.3.
ſalutarem, quæ ſuper ipſum eſt litet, ſe excuſat,
ad ipſum primò decentèr exclamans, Tu dixi-
ſti: Hoc facite in meam commemorationem.
Wherefore the biſhop (ſayeth he) reuerently, and according to his biſhoply office,
after the holy prayſes of Gods workes, he
excuſeth him ſelfe, that he taketh vpon him
to offer that helthfull ſacrifice, which is
aboue his degree and worthynes, crying
out firſt vnto him in ſeemely wiſe, lord
thou haſt commaunded thus, ſaying, *Doo*
this in my remembraunce. By theſe wordes
he confeſſeth, that he could not be ſo har-
dy, as to offer vp Chriſt vnto his father,
had not Chriſt him ſelfe ſo commaunded,
when he ſayde, *Doo this in my remembraunce.*
This is the doctrine touching this article
that Saint Paul taught his ſcolers, which
M. Iuell denyeth.

Irenæus

Irenæus receiued the same from Saint Iohn the Euangelist by *Polycarpus* Saint Iohns scoler. He declareth it with these wordes. *Eū. qui ex creatura panis est, accepit, & gratias egit, dicens, Hoc est corpus meum. Et calicem simili-ter ; qui est ex creatura quæ est secundum nos, suum sanguinem confessus est, & noui testamen-ti nouā docuit oblationem, quam Ecclesia ab A-postolis accipiens, in vniuerso mundo offert Deo. De quo in duodecim prophetis Malachi-as sic præsignificauit, Non est mihi voluntas in vobis dicit Dominus excituum : & munus non suscipiam de manu vestra.* He tooke that which by creation is bread, and gaue than-kes, saying, this is my body. And likewise the cuppe full of that creature which is he-re with vs, and confessed it to be his bloud, and thus taught the newe oblation of the ne-we testament, which the churche receiuing of the Apostles, doth offer to God through the whole worlde, whereof Malachie one of the twelue prophetes dy prophecie thus *I haue no lyking in you, sayeth our lord almigh-ty, neither will I take sacrifice of your handes: because from the rysing of the sunne to the going downe of the same, my name is glorified among the nations, and incense is offered to my name in euery place, and pure sacrifice, for that my name is great among the nations.* What can be vnderstanded by this newe oblation of the newe testament other, then the oblation

tion of that, which he sayde to be his body,
and confessed to be his bloude. And if he
had offered bread and wine onely, or the figure of his body and bloud in bread and
wine, it had ben no newe oblation, for such
had ben made by *Melchisedech* long befor-
re. Neither can the prophecie of Malachie
be vnderstanded of the oblation of Christ
vpon the crosse, for as much as that was done but at one tyme onely, and in one certaine place of the world, in Golgoltha a place without the gates of Ierusalem neare to
the walles of that citie. Concerning the sacrifice of a contrite and an humbled heart,
and all other Sacrifices of our deuotion that
be mere spirituall, they can not be called
the newe oblation of the Newe testament,
for as much as they were done as well in the
olde testamēt as in the newe, neither be they
all together pure. Wherefore this place of
Ireneus, and also the prophecie of Malachie,
wherewith it is confirmed, must nedes be
referred to the sacrifice and oblation of the
body and bloud of Christ dayly throughout
the whole world offered to God in the Masse, which is the externall Sacrifice of the
churche and proper to the newe testament:
which, as *Irenæus* sayeth, the church receiued
of the Apostles, and the Apostles of Christ.

Now let vs heare what S. Cyprian hath
written to this purpose. Because his workes

be common, to be shorter, I will rehearse his
wordes in Englilh . If in the Sacrifice, which
is Chrilt , none but Chrilt is to be folowed ,
soothly it behoueth vs to obey and doo that,
which Chrilt dyd , and commaunded to be
donne. For if *Iesus* Chrilt our lord and God,
very he him selfe be the high priest of God
the father , and him selfe first offered sacrifice to God the father , and commaunded
the same to be done in his remenbraunce:
verely that priest doth occupie the office of
Chrilt truly, who doth by imitation the same thing that Chrilt dyd. And then he offereth to God the father in the church a true
and a perfite sacrifice , if he begynne to offer
right so as he seeth Chrilt him selfe ro haue
offered. This farre S : Cyprian. How can this
Article be auouched in more plaine wordes?
he sayeth that Chrilt offered him selfe to his
father in his supper , and likewise commaunded vs to doo the same.

Here we haue proued, that it is lawfull, and
hath alwaies frō the begynning of the newe
testament ben lawfull for the priestes to offer
vp Chrilt vnto his father, by the testimonies
of three holy martyrs, two Grekes, and one
Latine, most notable in sundry respectes , of
antiquitie, of the rome they bare in Chrilles
churche, of learning, of cōstācie, of faith stedfastly kepte to death, suffred in places of fame
and knowledge, at Paris, at Liōs, at Carthage.

Our

Our aduersaries crake much of the sealing
vp of their newe doctrine with the bloud of
such and such, who be written in the booke
of lyes, not in the booke of lyfe, whom they
will nedes to be called martyrs. Verely if
those Moonkes and freres, Apostates and
renegates, wedded to wiues, or rather (to vse
their owne terme) yoked to sisters, be true
martyrs: then must our newe Gospellers pull
these holy fathers and many thousandes mo
out of heauen. For certainely the faith, in
defence of which either sorte dyed, is vtterly contrary. The worst that I wishe to them
is, that God geue them eyes to see, and eares
to heare, and that he shut not vp their hartes,
so as they see not the light here, vntil they
be throwen awaye in to the owtward dar-
kenes, where shall be weeping and grynting Matt. 25.
of teeth.

Leauing no small number of places, that
might be recited out of diuerse other doctours, I will bring two of two worthy bishopes, one of Chrysostome, the other of S.
Ambrose, confirming this truth. Chrysostomes wordes be these. *Pontifex noster ille est,
qui hostiam mundantem nos obtulit: ipsam offerimus & nunc, quæ tunc oblata quidem consumi
non potest. Hoc autem quod nos facimus, in com-* Chrysost.
memorationem fit eius, quod factum est. Hoc in epist. ad
enim facite, inquit, in mei commemorationē. He Heb. Ho-
is our bishop, that hath offered vp the hoste mil. 17.

which

which cleanseth vs. The same doo we offer also now, which though it were them offered yet can not be consumed. But this that we doo, is done in remembraunce of that which is done. For doo ye this sayeth he, in my re-

In Psal. 38. membraunce. S. Ambrose sayeth, thus. *Vidimus principem Sacerdotum ad nos venientem, vidimus & audiuimus offerentem pro nobis sanguinem suum: sequamur vt possumus Sacerdotes, vt offeramus pro populo sacrificium, etsi infirmi merito, tamen honorabiles sacrificio: Quia etsi Christus non videtur offerre, tamen ipse offertur in terris, quando Christi corpus offertur.* We haue sene the prince of priestes come to vs, we haue sene and heard him offer for vs his bloud: Let vs that be priestes folowe him as we maye, that we may offer sacrifice for the people, being though weake in merite, yet honorable for the sacrifice. Because albeit Christ be not sene to offer, yet he is offered in earth, when the body of Christ is offered. Of these our lordes wordes, *which is geuen for you*, and, *which is sheddde for you and for many*, Here S. Amhrose exhorteth the priestes to offer the body and bloud of Christ for the people. And willeth the to be more regarded, then commoly they be now a dayes, for this sacrifices sake, though otherwise they be of lesse deserte.

Now for proufe of the sacrifice and oblation of Christ by the doctoures mynde vpon

the

the figure of *Melchisedech* : firſt S. Ciprian Lib.2.
ſayeth thus . *Qui magis ſacerdos Dei ſummi,* epiſt.3.
quàm Dominus noster Ieſus Christus, qui ſacri-
ficium Deo patri obtulit, & obtulit hoc idem, quod
Melchiſedech, id eſt, panem & vinum, ſuum ſci-
licet corpus & ſanguinem , Who is more the
prieſt of the higheſt God, then our lord *Ieſus*
Chriſt , who offered a ſacrifice to God the
father, and offered the ſelfe ſame, that *Mel-*
chiſedech dyd, that is, bread and wine, that is
to ſaye, his owne body and bloud. S. Hierome
in an epiſtle that he wrote for the vertuouſe
womé *Paula* and *Eustochium* to *Marcella*, hath
theſe wordes, *Recurre ad Geneſim & Melchi-*
ſedech regem Salem. Huius principem inuenies
ciuitatis , qui iam in typo Chriſti panem &
vinum obtulit, & mysterium christianum in Sal-
uatoris ſanguine & corpore dedicauit . Retourne
to the booke of *Geneſis,* and to *Melchiſedech*
the king of *Salem* . And thou ſhalt fynde the
prince of that Citie, who euen at that tyme in
the figure of Chriſt offered bread and wine,
and dedicated the myſterie of Chriſtians in
the body and bloud of our Sauiour . Here
this learned father maketh a plaine diſtincti-
on betwen th'oblation of the figure, which
was bread and wine , and the oblation of the
truth, which is the myſterie of Criſté people,
the bloude and the body of Chriſt our Sauiour. Of this S. Auguſtine ſpeaketh largely
in his firſt ſermon vpon the 33. Pſalme.

and in the 17. booke *de ciuitate Dei, cap. 20.*

Of all other *Oecumenius* ſpeaketh moſt plainely to this purpoſe vpon this place of S. Paul alleaged out of the Pſalme, *Tu es Sacerdos in æternum ſecundum ordinem Melchiſedech.* Thou art a prieſt for euer after the order of *Melchiſedech.* his wordes be theſe, *Significat ſermo, quòd non ſolum Chriſtus obtulit incruentam hoſtiam (ſiquidem ſuum ipſius corpus obtulit) verum etiam qui ab ipſo fungentur ſacerdotio, quorum Deus Pontifex eſſe dignatus eſt, ſine ſanguinis effuſione offerent. Nam hoc ſignificat (in æternum,) Neque enim de ea quæ ſemel à Deo facta eſt oblatio & hoſtia, dixiſſet in æternum, ſed reſpiciens ad præſentes ſacrificos per quos medios Chriſtus ſacrificat, & ſacrificatur, qui etiam in myſtica cœna modū illis tradidit huiuſmodi ſacrificy.* The meaning of this place is (ſayeth he) that not onely Chriſt offered an vnbloudy ſacrifice, for he offered his owne body, but alſo that they which after him ſhall doo the office of a prieſt (whoſe biſhop he voucheſaueth to be) ſhall offer without ſhedding of bloud. For that ſignifieth the word *(for euer.)* For concerning that oblation and ſacrifice which was once made by God, he would neuer ſaye, *(in æternum)* for euer. But (he ſayd ſo) hauing an eye to thoſe priſtes that be now, by the mediation of whom Chriſt ſacrificeth and is ſacrificed, who in his myſticall ſupper taught them by

tradition

tradition the maner of such à sacrifice.

Concerning the prophecie of Malachie for proufe of this oblation, though the place of *Irenæus* aboue recited may stand in stede of many auctorities, yet I will not lette to rehaerse the sayinges of a father or two, for confirmation of this Article. Chrysostom sayeth very plainely, *In omni loco sacrificium offertur* In Psal. 95. *nomini meo, & sacrificium purum.Vide quàm luculenter quánque dilucide mysticam interpretatus est mensam, quæ est incruenta hostia. In euery place a sacrifice shall be offered to my name, and that a pure sacrifice.*See how plainely and clearely he interpreted the mysticall table, which is the vnbloudy sacrifice.

Saint Augustine hath many euident sayinges touchig this matter in his workes. One shal suffise for all which is in a litle treatise he made *contra Iudæos*, vttered in these wordes. *Aperite oculos tandem aliquando, & videte ab* Cap.9. *Oriente sole vsque ad Occidentem, non in vno loco, vt vobis fuit constitutum, sed in omni loco offerri sacrificium Christianorum, non cuilsbet Deo, sed ei, qui ista prædixit sDeo Israel.* Open your eyes at last you Iewes, and see that from the rysing of the sunne to the setting, not in one place, as it was appointed to you, but in euery place the sacrifice of the Christen people is offered, not to euery God, but to him that prophecied of these thinges before, the God of Israel. And euen so with that protestation

teſtation which ſaint Auguſtine made to the Iewes, I ende this red
iouſe matter conſiſting in maner altogether in allegatiõs to M.Iuell.
Open open your eyes at laſt M.Iuell, and ſee how all the holy and learned fathers, that haue preached the faith of Chriſt from the ryſing of the ſonne to the ſetting, haue taught this doctrine, by word and writing lefte to the poſteritie, that they which vnder Chriſt doo vſe the office of a prieſt after the order of *Melchiſedech*, haue not onely auctoritie, but alſo expreſſe commaundement to offer vp Chriſt vnto his father. The proufe of which doctrine, although it depend of the weight of one place, yet I haue thought good to fortifie it with ſome good number, that it may the better appeare to be a moſt vndoubted truth, not moued greatly with the blame of tediouſnes, where no thankes are ſought, but onely defence of the catholike Religion is intended.

Or that.

Or that the priest had then auctoritie to com-   **Iuel.**
municate and receiue the Sacramét for an other,
as they doo.

Of the priestes saying Masse for an other.

ARTICLE XVIII.

Vhat you would saye M. Iuell, I   The priest
wote not, what you saye, well I wo- receiueth
te. Verely we do not communicate not the Sa
ne receiue the Sacrament for an cramét for
an other.
other. Neither hath it euer ben taught in the
catholike churche, that the priest receiue
the Sacrament for an other. We receiue not
the Sacrament for an other, no more then
we receiue the Sacrament of Baptisme, or the
Sacrament of penaunce, or the Sacrament of
Matrimonie, one for an other. In dede the
priest sayeth Masse for others, where he receiueth that he hath offered, and that is it
you meane I gesse: In which Masse being the
externall sacrifice of the Newe testament according vnto Christes institution, the thing
that is offered, is such, as maketh our petitions and requestes acceptable to God, as S.
Cypriã sayeth, *In huius (corporis) præsentia non* In serme-
superuacuè mendicant lachrymæ veniam. In the ne de cœ-
presence of this body teares craue not forge- na domini.
uents in vaine.

That the oblation of the Masse is done
for others then for the priest alone which celebrateth, it may sufficiently be proued by an
hundred

hundred places of the fathers, the matter
being vndoubted, two or three may suffise.
First Chrysostom writeth thus in an homelie
vpon the Actes. *Quid dicis? in manibus eft ho-*
ftia, & omnia propofita funt bene ordinata: ad-
funt angeli, adfunt archangeli, adeft filius Dei, cū
tanto horrore adftant omnes, adftant illi clamātes
omnibus filentibus, et putas fimpliciter hæc fieri?
Igitur & alia fimpliciter, & quæ pro ecclefia, &
quæ pro facerdotibus offerūtur, & quæ pro pleni-
tudine ac vbertate? abfit. Sed omnia cū fide fiunt.

In Acta.
homil. 21.

What fayeft thou hereto? the hofte is in
the prieftes handes, and all thinges fet forth
are in due order. The Angels be prefent, the
Archāgels be prefēt, the fonne of God is prefent. Whereas all ftād there with fo great feare, whereas all they ftand there crying out tō
god, and all other holde their peace, thinkeft
thou thefe thinges be done fimply anp without great caufe? Why then be thofe other
thinges done alfo fimply, bothe the thinges
which are offered for the church for the prieftes, for plentie and abūdaunce? God forbydde, but all thinges are done with faith. Saint
Ambrofe in his funerall oration made of the
death of Valētiniā the Emperour, calling the
Sacramēt of the aulter the holy and heauenly
myfteries, and the oblatiō of our mother(by
which terme he vnderftādeth the church) fayeth, that he will profecute the holy foule
of that Emperour with the fame. This father
writing

writing vpon the 38. Pſalme, exhorteth prieſtes to folowe Chriſt, that as he offered for vs
his bloud, ſo prieſtes offer ſacrifice for the
people, his wordes be theſe, *Vidimus principem ſacerdotum, &c.* We haue ſene the princo
of prieſtes cōming vnto vs, we haue ſene and
hearde him offering for vs his bloud. Let vs
that be prieſtes folowe as we can, ſo as we offer ſacrifice for the people, though weake in
merite, yet honorable for the ſacrifice, &c.

That the oblation of the Maſſe is profitably made for others, S. Gregorie witneſſeth
very plainely, *homilia.* 37. expoūding the place of S. Luke. *cap.* 14. *alioqui legationem mit-*
tens, ea quæ pacis ſunt poſtulat. Elles he ſendeth
forth an ambaſſade, and ſueth for peace, He-
renpon he ſayeth thus. *Mittamus ad Dominū*
legationem noſtram, flendo, ſacras hoſtias offe-
rendo. Singulariter namque ad abſolutionem no-
ſtam, oblata cum lachrimis & benignitate men-
tis, ſacri altaris hoſtia ſuffragatur. Let vs ſend
to our lord our Ambaſſade, with weeping,
geuing almoſe, and offering of holy hoſtes.
For the hoſte of the holy aulter (that is the
bleſſed Sacrament) offered with teares and
with the mercifull bountie of our mynde,
helpeth vs ſingularely to be aſſoyled. In that
homilie he ſheweth, that the oblation
of Chriſtes body in this Sacrament preſent,
which is done in the Maſſe, is helpe and con-
fort not onely to them that be preſent, but
also

also to them that be absent, bothe quycke and dead, which he proueth by examples of his owne knowledge. Who so listeth to see antiquitie for proufe hereof, and that in the Apostles tyme bishops and priestes in the dredfull sacrifice offered and prayed for others, as for euery state and order of mē, and also for holesomnesse of the ayer, and for fertilitie of the fruites of the earth, etc. Let him reade the eight booke of the constitutions of the Apostles set forth by Clement.

Juell.

Or that the priest had then auctoritie to applye the vertue of Christes death and Passion to any man by the meane of the Masse.

Of the application of the benefites of Christes death to others by meane of prayer in the Masse.

ARTICLE XIX.

He vertue of Christes death and passion is grace and remission of synnes, the appeacing of Gods wrath, the reconciliation of vs to God, delyueraunce from the deuill, hell and euerlasting damnation. Our aduersaries imputing to vs, as though we sayde and taught, that the priest applyeth this vertue, effecte and merite of Christes death to any man by the meane of the Masse, either belye vs of igno raūce, or sclaunder vs of malice. Verely wq

saye

faye not fo. Neither doth the prieſt applye
the vertue of Chriſtes paſſion to any man by
the meane of the Maſſe. He doth but applie
his prayer and his intent of oblation, befe-
chig almighty God to applye the merite and
vertue of his ſunnes death, (the memorie
whereof he celebrateth at the Maſſe) to
them, for whom he prayeth.

VVhat ap-
plyeth the
prieſt vnto
vs in the
Maſſe.

It is God and none other, that applyeth to
to vs remiſſion of ſynne, the prieſt doth but
praye for it, and by the commemoration of
his ſonnes death, moueth him to applye. So
as all that the prieſt doth, is but by waye of
petition and prayer, leauing all power and
auctoritie of applying to God, which prayer
is to be beleued to be of moſt force and efficacie, when it is worthely and deuoutly made in the Maſſe: in the which the prieſt bea-
reh the perſon of the whole churche, and offereth his prayer in the ſacrifice, wherein the
churche offereth Chriſt, and it ſelfe through
Chriſt to God. Which his prayer and deuout
ſeruice he beſecheth to be offered vp by the
handes of Angelles vnto the high aulter of
God, in the ſight of the diuine maieſtie. Of
what ſtrength prayer made at the Maſſe is,
the holy biſhop and martyr. S. Cyprian witneſſeth, where he he ſayeth. In the preſence
of this Sacrament teares craue not in vayne,
and the ſacrifice of a contrite harte is neuer
denyed his requeſt.

Sermone
de cœna
Domini.

E o   Or

Iuel. *Or that it was then thought a sounde doctrine, to teache the people, that the Masse ex opere operato, That is, euen for that it is sayde and donne, is able to remoue any parte of our sinne.*

Of opus operatum, vvhat it is, and vvhether it remoue synne.

ARTICLE XX.

N dede the doctrine vttered in this Article is false, and derogatorie to the glorie of our Sauiour Christ. For thereby the honour of Christes sacrifice, whereby he hath once satisfied for the synnes of all, shuld be transferred to the worke of the priest, which were great wickednes and detestable blasphemie. And therefore we will not requyre M. Iuell to yelde and subscribe vnto this Article. For we graunt, this was neuer thought a sounde doctrine within syx hudred yeres of Christes Ascension, nor shall be so thought within syx thousand yeres after the same of any man of sounde beleefe. Neither hath it ben at any tyme taught in the catholike churche, how so euer it liketh our aduersaries to charge the scolasticall doctours with the sclaunderous reporte of the contrary. For it is Christ onely and none other thing, that is able to remoue our synnes, and that hath he done by the sacrifice of his body once done vpon the crosse. Of which sacrifice once performed vpon

vpon the croſſe with ſhedding of his bloud,
this vnbloudy ſacrifice of the aulter, which is
the daily ſacrifice of the churche, commonly
called the Maſſe, is a ſampler, and a commemoration, in the which we haue the ſame body that hanged on the croſſe. Neyther is it a
ſampler or commemoration only, but the
ſelfe ſame ſacrifice which was offered on the
Croſſe: a ſampler or commemoration, in reſpect of the manner, for that it is done without bloud ſhedding, the ſelue ſame for that
the thing which is offered, is the ſame that
was offered on the Croſſe. And whereas we
haue nothing of our ſelues, that we maye
offer vp acceptable to God: we offer this his
ſonnes body as a moſt acceptable ſacrifice,
beſeching him to looke not vppon our worthynes; our acte or worke: but vpon the face Pſal. 83.
of Chriſt his moſt dere ſonne, and for his ſa-
ke to haue mercie vpon vs.

And in this reſpecte we doubte not this Hovv the
bleſſed ſacrifice of the Maſſe to be vaileable Maſſe is
and effectuall, *ex opere operato*, that is, not as vaileable
M. Iuell interpreteth, for that the Maſſe is *ex opere*
ſayde and done, referring *opus operatum* to the *perato.*
acte of the prieſt, not ſo: but for the worke
wrought it ſelfe, which god him ſelfe worketh
by the miniſterie of the prieſt, without reſpecte had to his merite, or acte, which is the body and bloud of Chriſt; whoſe breking and
ſhedding is in this myſtical Sacrifice, ſo farre

Ee 2   as the

as the holy ghost hath thought expedient for mans behoofe, reprefented, fhewed, and recommended to memorie. Which body and bloud when it is according to his commaundement offered vp to God, is not in regarde of our worke, but of it felfe, and of the holy Inftitutiõ of his onely begoten fonne, a moft acceptable facrifice to him, both for quicke and dead, where there is no ftoppe nor lette to the cõtrarie on the behalfe of the receiuer.

De octo quæft, Dulcitij quæf. 2

The dead, I meane fuch onely, as through faith haue recommended them felues to the redemption wrought dy Chrift, and by this faith haue deferued of God, that after their departure hence, as S. Auguftine fayeth, this facrifice might profite them.

Maffe takẽ tvvo vvaies.

But to fpeake, of this matter more particularly and more diftinctly, the terme Maffe maye be takẽ two wayes. Either for the thing it felfe which is offered, or for the acte of the prieft in offering of it. If it be taken for the thing it felfe that is offered, which is the body of Chrift, and is in this refpecte of the fcolafticall doctours called *opus operatum:* no man can iuftly denye, but that it remoueth and taketh awaie fynne. For Chrift in his flefh crucified is our onely facrifice, our onely price, our onely redemption, whereby he hath merited to vs vpon the croffe, and with the price of his bloud hath bought the remiffion of our fynnes: and S. Iohn fayeth, he is the propitiation

1.Cor.6. &
7.
Tit.2.
Apoc.14.
1.Ioan.2.

propiriatiō for our synnes. So *Ocumeni*⁹ saieth *Caro Christi est propitiatorium nostrarū iniqui-* In.3.cap. *tatum.* The fleshe of Christ is the propitia- adRōanos. tion for our iniquities. And this not for that it is offered of the priest in the Masse specially, but for that he offered it once him selfe with shedding of his bloude vpon the crosse for the redemption of all. Which oblation done vpon the Crosse, is become a perpetuall and continuall oblation not in the same maner of offering, but in the same vertue and power of the thing offered. For since that tyme the same *body of Christ appearing* alwaies Heb. 9. before the face of god in heauen, presenteth and exhibiteth it selfe for our reconciliation. And likewise it is exhibiteth and offered by his owne commaundement here in earth in the Masse, where he is both priest and sacrifice, offerer ad oblation, verely and in deede though in mysterie and by waie of commemoratiō, that thereby we may *be made* parterakers of the reconciliation performed, applying the same vnto vs (so farre as in this behalfe man may applye) through faith and deuotion no lesse then if we sawe with our eyes presently his body hanging on the crosse before vs, and streames of bloud issuyng foorth. And so it is a sacrifice in very dede propitiatorie, not for our acte or worke, but for his owne worke already done and accepted. To this onely we must ascribe remiſſion and remouing of our ſynnes.

If the terme Maſſe be taken for the acte of the prieſt, in reſpecte of any his onely doing, it is not able to remoue ſynne. For ſo we ſhuld make the prieſt Gods peere, and his acte equall with the paſſion of Chriſt, as our aduerſaries doo vniuſtly ſclaunder vs. Yet hath the Maſſe vertue and effecte in ſome degree, and is acceptable to God by reaſon of the oblation of the ſacrifice which in the Maſſe is done by the offerer, without reſpect had to Chriſtes inſtitution, euen for the faithfull prayer and deuotion of the partie that offereth, which the ſcoole doctours terme *ex opere operantis*. For then the oblation ſemeth to be moſt acceptable to God, when it is offered by ſome that is acceptable. Now the partie that offereth is of two ſortes. The one offereth immediatly and perſonally: the other offereth mediatly, or by meane of an other, and principally. The firſt is the prieſt that conſecrateth, offereth and receiueth the Sacrament, who ſo doth theſe thinges in his owne perſon, yet by Gods auctoritie, as none other in ſo offering is concurrent with him. The partie that offereth mediately or by meane of an other and principally, is the churche militat, in whoſe perſon the prieſt offereth, and whoſe miniſter he is in offering. For this is the Sacrifice of the whole churche. The firſt partie that offereth, is not it not alwayes acceptable to God, neither alwaies pleaseth him, because oftentymes he is a synner. The second partie that offereth, is euermore acceptable to God, because the churche is alwayes holy, beloued, and the onely spouse of Christ. And in this respecte the Masse is an acceptable seruice to God, *ex opere operantis*, and is not without cause and reason called a sacrifice propitiatorie, not for that it deserueth mercie at Gods hand of it selfe, as Christ doth, who onely is in that principall and speciall sorte a sacrifice propitiatorie: but for that it moueth God to geue mercie and remissiō of synne already deserued by Christ. In this degree of a sacrifice propitiatorie, we may put prayer, a contrite harte, almose, forgeuing of our neighbour, &c. This may easely be proued by the holy fathers.

Origens wordes be very plaine. *Si respicias ad illam commemorationem, de qua dicit Dominus, Hoc facite in meam commemorationem, inuenies, quòd ista est commemoratio sola, quæ propitium faciat Deum.* If thou looke to that commemoration, whereof our lord sayeth, *Doo this in my remembraunce, or in commemoration of me*: thou shalt fynde, that this is the onely commemoration, that maketh God mercifull. Saint Augustine sayeth thus. *Nemo melius præter martyres meruit ibi requiescere, vbi & hostia Christus est, & sacerdos, scilicet, vt propitiationem de oblatione hostiæ consequantur.*

In Leuit. Hom. 13.

E e 4 *quantur.*

quantur. No man hath deserued better then the martyrs to reste there, where Christ is bothe the hoste and the priest, (he meaneth to be buried vnder the aulter)to the intent they might atteine propitiation by the oblation of the hoste. But here to auoyd prolixitie in a matter not doubtefull, I leaue a number of places whereby it may be euidently proued, that the Masse is a sacrifice propitiatorie in this degree of propitiation, bothe for the quicke and the dead, the same not being specially denyed by purporte of this Article. Thus we haue declared, as we might superficially treating of this Article, that the Masse is a sacrifice ppitiatorie both *ex opere operato*, that is through the merite of Christes body that suffered on the crosse, which is here *opus operatum*, and is by Christ through the ministerie of the priest in the Masse offered, truly, but in mysterie, and also *ex opere operante*, that is through the doing of the priest, if he haue the grace of God and so be acceptable, but in a farre lower degree of propitiation, which is called *opus operans* or *opus operantis*. And this is the doctrine of the churche, touching the valour of the Masse *ex opere operato*, whereby no parte of Christes glorie is impayred.

Or that.

Or that then any Christian man called the Iuell.
Sacrament his lord and God.

Of calling the Sacrament lord and God.

ARTICLE XXI.

 His word Sacramēt(as is declared Sacrament
before)is of the fathers taken two tvvo vva-
wayes. Either for the onely out- yes taken.
ward formes of bread and wine,
which are the holy signe of the very body and
bloud of Christ present and vnder them con
teined: Or for the whole substance of the Sacrament, as it consisteth of the outward formes, and also of the very body and bloud of
Christ verely present, which S. Augustine In sent.
calleth the inuisible grace and the thing of Properi. de
the Sacrament. And *Irenæus*, calleth it *rem* conse. dist.
cælestem, the heauenly thing, as that other, cap.34.
rem terrenam, the earthly thing. Taken the
first waie, no Christen man euer honoured
it with the name of lord and God. For that
were plaine Idolatrie, to attribute the name
of the Creatour, to the creature. But taken in
the second signification, it hath alwayes of
Christen people and of the learned fathers
of the churche, ben called by the name of
lord and God. And of right so ought it to be,
for elles were it impietie and a denyall of
God, not to call Christ the sonne of God, by
the name of lord and God, who is not onely
Ee 5   in truth

in truth of flesh and bloud in the Sacrament,
after which maner he is there *ex vi Sacramen-*
ti, but also the inseparable coniunction of
bothe natures in vnitie of person, *ex necessa-*
ria cōcomitantia, whole Christ, God and man.
That the holy fathers called the Sacrament
taken in this sense lord and God, I might
proue it by many places, the rehearsall of a
fewe may serue for many. Origen in a homilie speaking reuerently of this blessed Sacrament, sayeth, that when a man receiueth it,
our lord entreth vnder his rooffe, and exhorteth him that shall receiue it, to humble him
selfe and to saye vnto it: *Domine non sum dig-*
nus vt intres sub tectum meum. Lord I am not
worthy that thou enter vnder my rooffe.

In diuersos
Euāgelij lo
ees, hom. 5

S.Cyprian *in Sermone de lapsis*, telleth, how
a man, who had denyed God in tyme of persecution, hauing notwithstanding (the sacrifice by the priest done) priuely with o-
thers receiued the Sacrament, not being able
to eate it nor to handle it, opening his handes, sownde that he bare asshes. Where he
addeth these wordes. *Documento vnius osten-*
sum est, dominum recedere cum negatur. By this
example of one man it is shewed, that our
lord departeth awaie, when he is denyed.
The same S. Cyprian in th'exposition of the
Pater noster, declaring the fourth petition
of it, *Geue vs thys daye our daily bread* vnderstandeth it to conteine a desyre of the
holy

holy communion in this blessed Sacrament,
and sayeth. *Ideo panem nostrum, id est, Christū
dari nobis quotidie petimus, vt qui in Christo
manemus & viuimus, à sanctificatione & corpore eius non recedamus.* Therefore we aske
our daily bread, that is so saye, Christ, to
be geuen vnto vs, vhat we which abyde and
lyue in Christ, depart not from the state of
holynes, and communion of his bodye. Here
S. Cyprian calleth the Sacrament Christ, as
he is in dede there present really, so as in the
place alleaged before he calleth it lord. And
I wene our aduersaries will imbarre the Sacrament of the name of Christ, no lesse then
of the name of lord or God, Onlesse they
make lesse of Christ, then of lord and God.
Verely this holy martyr acknowlegeth this
sacrament not for lord and Christ onely, but,
also for God, by these wordes in his sermon
*de cana Domini.Sicut in persona Christi huma-
nitas videbatur, & latebat diuinitas, ita sacramento visibili ineffabiliter diuina se infudit essen-
tia.* As in the person of Christ, the manhode
was sene, and the godhed was hydden, so the
diuine essence (or substaunce of God) hath
infused it into the visible sacrament vnspeakeably.

Chrysostom doubteth not to call the Sacrament God in this plaine saiyng. *Nolimus
obsecro, nolimus impudentes nos ipsos interimere,
sed cum honore & mūditia ad Deum accedamus
& quando*

In priorem
ad Cor.
Homil. 24 *quando id propositum videris, dic tecum: propter hoc corpus non amplius terra & cinis ego sum, non amplius captiuus, sed liber.* Let vs not, let vs not for gods sake be so shamelesse, as to kill our selues (by vnworthy receiuing of the sacrament) but with reuerence and cleannesse let vs come to God. And when thou seest the sacrament set forth, saye thus with thy selfe: by reason of this body, I am no more earth and ashes, no more captiue, but free.

And least this sense taken of Chrysostom shuld seme ouer straunge, this place of Saint Ambrose, who lyued in the same tyme, and agreeth with him thoroughly in doctrine, may seme to leade vs to the same. *Quid edamus,* De ijs qui
mysterijs
initiantus
cap. 9.
Psal. 33. *quid bibamus, alibi tibi per prophetam Spiritus sanctus expressit, dicens: gustate & videte, quonia suauis est Dominus, beatus vir qui sperat in eo, in illo Sacrameto Christus est, quia corpus est Christi.* What we ought to eate, and what we ought to drinke, the holy ghost hath expressed by the prophete in an other place, saying: Taste and see, how that our lord is sweete, blessed is the ma that trusteth in him. In that Sacrament is Christ, because there is the body of Christ. Here S. Ambrose re- In collectaneis in
10. cap.
prioris ad
Corinth. ferring those wordes of the psalme to the sacrament, calleth it lord, and that lord, in who the man that trusteth, is blessed, who is God.

Agreeably to this sayeth S. Augustine, in a sermon *de verbis Euangelij*. as Beda reciteth.

Qualem

Qualem vocem Domini audiſtis inuitantis nos?
Quis vos inuitauit? Quos inuitauit? Et quis præ-
parauit? Inuitauit Dominus ſeruos, & præpara-
uit eis cibum ſeipſum . Quis audeat manducare
Dominum ſuum? Et tament ait , qui manducat
me , viuet propter me . What maner a voice is
that ye haue heard of our lord inuiting and
bydding vs to the feaſt? who hath inuited?
whom hath he inuited? And who hath made
preparation ? The lord hath inuited the ſer-
uantes , and hath prepared him ſelfe to be
meate for them. Who dareth be ſo bolde as
to eate his lord? And yet he ſayeth, he that eateth me, ſhall lyue for cauſe of me.

    Cyrillus accōpteth the ſacramēt for Chriſt, In Ioan.
and God the word , and for God , in this lib.4.cap.
ſaying. *Qui carnem Chriſti manducat , vitam* 15.
habet æternam. Habet enim hæc caro Dei verbū,
quod naturaliter vita eſt. Proptereà dicit: Quia
ego reſuſcitabo eum in nouiſſimo die . Ego enim Ioan.6.
dixit, id eſt, corpus meum quod comedetur reſuſ-
citabo eum. Non enim alius ipſe eſt, quàm caro
ſua, &c. He that eateth the fleſhe of Chriſt,
hath lyfe euerlaſting . For this fleſhe hath the
word of God, which naturally is lyfe. Therefore ſayeth he , that I will raiſe him in the laſt
daie. For I, quoth he, that is to ſaye , my body
which ſhall be eaten , ſhall raiſe him vp agayne, for he is no other, then his fleſhe, &c.

    No man more expreſſely calleth the Sacra-
ment by the name of God, then S. Bernard in
                   his

his godly sermon *de cœna Domini ad Petrum presbyterum.* where he sayeth thus. *Comedunt angeli Verbum de Deo natum, Comedunt homines Verbum fœnum factum.* The angels eate the Word borne of God, men eate the Word made haye, meaning hereby the sacrament, which he calleth the Word made haye, that is to witte, the Word incarnate. And in an other place there, he saieth. *Hæc est verè indulgētia cœlestis, hæc est verè cumulata a gratia hæc est verè superexcellens gloria, sacerdotē Deū suū tenere, & alijs dando porrigere.* This is verely an heauenly gyfte, this is verely a bountifull grace, this is verely a passing excellent glorie, the priest to holde his God, and in geuing to reache him forth to others. In the same sermon speaking of the meruelouse sweetnes that good bishopes and holy religiouse men haue experience of, by receiuing this blessed Sacrament, he sayeth thus. *Ideo ad mensam altaris frequentius accedunt, omni tempore candida facientes vestimenta sua, id est, corpora, prout possunt, melius, vtpote Deum suum manu & ore coutrectaturi.* For this cause they come the oftener vnto the bourd of the aulter, at all tymes making their garmentes that is to saye, their bodyes, so white, as they can possibly, as they, who shall handle their God with hand and mowth. An other place of the same sermon, for that it conteineth a holesom instruction besyde the affirming

ming of our purpose, I can not omitte. I remitte the learned to the Latine, the Englilh of it is this.

They are meruelous thinges brethré, that be fpoken of this Sacrament, faith is neceffarie, knowledge of reafon is (here) fuperfluous. This, let faith beleue, let not vnftderftanding require, leaft that either not being fownde, it thinke it incredible, or being fownde out, it beleue it not to be finguler and alone. And therfor it behoueh it to be beleued fymply, that can not be fearched out profitably. Wherefor ferche not ferch not, how it may bee, doubt not whether it bee. Come not vnto it vnreuerently, leaft it bee to you to death, *Deus enim eſt, & quanquám panis myſteria habeat, mutætur tamē in carnē.* For it is God, and though it haue myſteries of bread, yet is it chaunged into fleſhe. God and man it is that witneſſeth bread truly to be made his fleſhe. The veſſell of election it is, that threatneth iudgement to him that putteth no difference in indging of that fo holy fleſhe. The felfe fame thing thinke thou o Chriſten man of the wyne, geue that honour to the wine. The creatour of wine it is, that promoteth the wine to be the bloud of Chriſt. This farre holy Bernard.

Here let our aduerfaries touching this Article, confyder and weigh with them felues, whether they be Lutherans, Zuinglians, or Geneuians,

1.Cor.11.

Geneuians, what englifh they can make of thefe wordes vfed by the fathers, and applyed to the Sacrament in the places before alleaged. *Dominus, Chriftus, Diuina effentia, Deus, Seipfum, Verbū Dei, Ego, Verbum fœnum factū, Deum fuum.* The number of the like places that might be alleaged to his purpofe, be in maner infinite. Yet M. Iuel promyfeth to geue ouer ād fubfcribe, if any one may be fownde: Now we fhal fee, what truth is in his word.

In the weighing of this doctrine of the churche, litle occafion of wicked fcoffes and blafphemies againft this bleffed facramēt fhal ramaine to them, that be not blinded with that groffe and fond errour, that denyeth the infeparabilitie of Chrift, but affirmeth in this myfterieto be prefent his flefhe onely, without bloud, foule, and godhed. Which is confuted by plaine fcriptures. Chrift rayfed from the dead, now dyeth no more. *Rom.6.* He fuffereth him felfe no more to be diuided *1. Cor. 1.* Euery fprite that lofeth Iefus, this is Antichrift, *1. Ioan. 4.* Hereof it foloweth that if Chrift be verely vnder the forme of bread in the Sacrament, as it is other wheres fufficiently proued: then is he there entier and whole: flefhe, bloud, and foule, whole Chrift, God and man, for the infeparable vnion of bothe natures in one perfon. Which matter is more amply declared in the Article of the adoration of the Sacrament.

Or that

Or that the people was then taught to beleue, Iuell. *that the body of Christ remayneth in the Sacrament , as long as the Accidentes of the bread remayne there without corruption.*

Of the remayning of Christes bodye in the Sacrament so long as the accidentes be entier and whole.

ARTICLE XXII.

Hese fiue articles here folowing are Scoole pointes, the discussion whereof is more curiouse, then necessary . Whether the faithfull people were then, that is to saye, for the space of six hundred yeres after Christ, taught to beleue concerning this blessed Sacrament precisely according to the purporte of all these articles or no, I knowe not. Verely I thinke , they were taught the truth of this matter simply and plainely , yet so as nothing was hydden from them , that in those quiet tymes , (quiet I meane touching this point of faith) was thought necessary for them to knowe. If sithe there hath ben more taught , or rather if the truth hath in some other forme of wordes ben declared for a more euidence and clearnesse in this behalfe to be had , truth it selfe alwaies remayning one: this hath proceded of the diligence and earnest care of the churche, to represse the pertinacie of heretikes , who haue within these last syx hundred yeres impugned

Ff the

the truth herein, and to meete with their peruerse and froward obiections : as hath ben
thought necessary to finde out such wedges, as
might best serue to ryue such knotty blockes.
Yet this matter hath not so much ben taught
in open audience of the people, as debated
priuatly betwen learned men in scooles, and
so of them set forth in their priuate writinges. Wherein if some perhappes through con-
tentiō of wittes haue ben either ouer curious
or ouer bolde, and haue ouershotte the marke, or not sufficiētly confirmed the point they
haue taken in hande to treate of, or through
ignoraunce, or fauour of a parte, haue in some
thing swarued from reason, or that maening
which holy church holdeth: it is great vncour-
rosie to laye that to our charge, to abuse their
ouersightes to our discredite, and to reproue
the whole churche for the insufficiencie of a
fewe.

Now concerning this Article, whether we
are able to auouche it by such authorities as
M. Iuell requireth, or no, it shall not greatly
force. The credite of the catholike faith dependeth not of olde proufes of a fewe newe
controuersed pointes, that ben of lesse importaunce. As for the people, they were taught
the truth plainely, when no heretike had af-
saulted their faith craftely. The doctrine of
the churche is this. The body of Christ after
due consecration remayneth so long in the Sacrament,

The do-
ctrine of
the chur-
che.

crament, as the Sacrament endureth. The Sacrament endureth so long as the formes of breade and wine continewe. Those formes continewe in their integritie, vntill the other accidentes be corrupted and perishe. As if the colour, weight, sauour, taste, smell, and other qualities of bread and wine be corrupted and quite altered, then is the forme also of the same annichilated and vndone. And to speake of this more particularly, sith that the substāce of bread and wine is tourned into the substāce of the body and bloud of Christ, as the scriptures, auncient doctours, the necessary cōsequent of truth, and detetmination of holy churche leadeth vs to beleue: if such chaunge of the accidentes be made, which shuld not haue suffised to the corruption of bread and wine, in case of their remaindre: for such a chaunge the body and bloud of Christ ceaseth not to be in this Sacrament, whether the chaunge be in qualitie, as if the colour, sauour, and smell of bread and wine be a litle altered, or in quantitie, as if thereof diuision be made in to such portions, in which the nature of bread and wine might be reserued. But if there be made so great a chaunge, as the nature of bread and wine should be corrupted, if they were present: then the body and bloud of Christ doo not remaine in this Sactament, as whē the colour and sauour and other qualities of bread and wine are so farre chaunged, as

the nature of bread and wine might not bear
it : or on the quantities syde, as if the bread be
so small crōmed into dust, and the wine dispersed into so small portions, as their formes remaine no lenger: then remaineth no more the
body and bloud in this Sacrament. Thus the
body and bloud of Christ remayneth in this Sa
crament, so long as the formes of bread and
wine remaine. And when they faile and cease
to be any more, then also ceaseth the body and
bloud of Christ to be in the Sacrament. For
there must be a conueniēce and resemblaunce
betwen the Sacraments and the thinges whereof they be sacraments, which done awaie and
loste at the corruption of the formes and acci-
dents, the Sacraments also be vndone and perishe, and consequently the inward thing and
the heauenly thing in them conteined, leaueth
to be in them

Here because many of thē, which haue cutte
them selues from the churche, condemne the
reseruation of the Sacrament, and affirme that
the body of Christ remayneth not in the same,
no longer then during the tyme whiles it is receiued, alleaging against reseruation the exam
ple of the Paschall lambe in the olde lawe,
wherein nothing ought to haue remained vntill the morning, and likewise of manna: I will
rehearse that notable and knowē place of *Cyrillus Alexandrinus*, his wordes be these. *Audi
quòd dicant mysticam benedictionem, si ex ea re-
manserint*

Margin notes:
August. ad
Bonifaciū
epist. 23.

Of reserua
tion of the
Sacrament.

Exod. 11.
Ad Colosy
rium Arse-
noitēn. Epi
scopū. citat
Thomas
parte 3: q.
76.

*manſerint in ſequentem diem reliquiæ, ad ſanctifi-
cationem inutilem eſſe.Sed inſaniunt hæc dicentes.
Non enim alius fit Chriſtus,neque ſanctū eius corpus immutabitur, Sed virtus benedictionis & vi-
uifica gratia manet in illo.* It is tolde me , they
ſaye,that the myſticall bleſſing (ſoo he calleth
the bleſſed Sacrament) in caſe portions of it
be kepte vntil the nexte daie,is of no vertue to
ſanctification. But they be madde , that thus
ſaye.For Chriſt becommeth not an other, neitheir his holy body is chaūged: but the vertue
of the conſecration and the quickening or lyfe
geuing grace,abydeth ſtill in it. By this ſaying
of *Cyrillus* we ſee that he accōpteth the errour
of our aduerſaries in this Article , no other
then a mere madnes.The body of Chriſt(ſaieth
he)which he termeth the myſticall bleſſing,be
cauſe it is a moſt holy myſterie done by conſecration,once cōſecrated is not chaunged , but
the vertue of the conſecration and the grace
that geueth lyfe,wherby he meaneth that fleſh
aſſumpted of the Word, remayneth in this Sacramēt,alſo whē it is kepte: verely euen ſo lōg,
as the outward formes cōtinewe not corrupte.

*Or that a Mouſe or any otther worme or beaſte   Iuell.
maye eate the body of Chriſt , for ſo ſome of our aduerſaries haue ſayd and taught.*

VVhat is that the Mouſe or vvorme eateth.

ARTICLE XXIII.

VVhereas M. Iuell imputeth this vile aſſe-
ueration but to ſome of the aduerſaries of

Ff 3   his

his syde, he semeth to acknowledge, that it is not a doctrine vniuersally taught and receiued. The like may be sayde for his nexte Article. And if it hath ben sayd of some onely, and not taught vniuersally of all, as a true doctrine for Christen people to beleue: how agreeth he with him selfe, saying after the rehearsall of his number of Articles, the same, none excepted, to be the highest mysteries and greatest keyes of our religion. For if that were true, as it is not true for the greatest parte, then shuld this Article haue ben affirmed and taught of all. For the highest and greatest pointes of the catholike Religion be not of particular, but of vniuersall teaching.

Concerning the matter of this Article, what so euer a mouse, worme, or beaste eateth, the body of Christ now being impassible and immortall, susteineth no violence, iniurie, ne villanie. As for that which is gnawen, bytten, or eaten of worme or beaste, whether it be the substaunce of bread, as appeareth to sense, which is denyed, because it ceaseth through vertue of consecration: or the outward forme onely of the Sacrament, as many holde opinion, which also onely is broken and chawed of the receiuer, the accidentes by miracle remayning without substance: In such cases happening contrary to the intent and ende the sacrament is ordeined and kepte for, it ought not to seme vnto vs incredible, the power of
God

God confydered, that God taketh awaye his body from thofes outward formes, and permitteth either the nature of breade to retourne, as before confecration, or the accidentes to fupplye the effectes of the fubftãce of breade. As he commaunded the nature of the rodde which became a ferpent, to retourne to that it was before, when God would haue it ferue no more to the vfes it was by him appointed vnto.

The graue auctoritie of S. Cyprian addeth great weight to the balance for this iudgement in weighing this matter, who in his fermon *de lapfis*, by the reporte of certaine miracles fheweth, that our Lordes body made it felfe awaie frõ fome, that being defyled with the facrifices of idols, prefumed to come to the cõmunion, er they had done their due penaunce. One (as he telleth there) thinking to haue that bleffed body, which he had receiued with others in his hande, when he opened the fame to put it into his mowth, fownde that he helde afhes. And thereof S. Cyprian fayeth, *Documento vnius oftenfum eft, dominum recedere, cum negatur*. By the example of one man it was fhewed, that our lord departeth awaye, when he is denyed. It is neither wicked, nor a thing vnworthy the maieftie of that holy myfterie, to thinke our lordes body likewife done awaye, in cafes of negligence, villanie, and prophanation.

Or that.

Or that when Christ sayde, Hoc est corpus me-um: this word, Hoc pointeth not the bread, but Indiuiduum vagum, as some of them saye.

VVhat this pronoune Hoc pointeth in the vvordes of consecration.   ARTICLE XXIIII.

VVhat so euer *hoc* pointeth in this saying of Christ after your iudgement, M.Iuel, right meaning and plaine Christen people, (who through Gods grace haue receiued the loue of truth, and not the efficacie of illusion to bele-ue lying) beleue verely, that in this sacrament fter cōsecratiō, is the very body of Christ, and hat vpon credite of his owne wordes, *Hoc est orpus meum.* They that appoint them selues to folowe your Geneuiā doctrine in this point, deceiued by that ye teache them (*hoc*) to point the breade, ād by sundry other vntruthes, in ste de of the very body of Christ in the Sacrament rightly ministred verely present, shall receiue nothing at your communion, but a bare piece of bread not worth a point. As for your some saye, who will haue *Hoc* to point *indiuiduū va-gū*, first learne you wel, what they meane, and if their meaning be naught, who so euer they be, handle thē as you lyste, there with shall we be offended neuer a deale. How this word *Hoc* in that saying of Christ is to be taken, and what it pointeth, we knowe who haue more learnedly more certainely, and more truly treated there of, then Luther, Zuinglius, Caluin, Cranmer, Peter Martyr, or any their offspring.

Or

Or that the accidētes, or formes, or shewes of bread   Iuell.
and wine, be the Sacramentes of Christes body and
bloud, and not rather the breade ad wyne it selfe.

VVho are the Sacramētes of Christes bodye and bloud,
the accidentes, or the bread and vvyne.

ARTICLE XXV.

FOr as much as by the almighty power of
gods word pronounced by the priest in
the consecration of this Sacrament, the body
and bloud of Christ are made really present,
the substance of breade tourned into the substance of the body, and the substance of wine
into the substance of the bloud : the breade
(which is consumed awaie by the fier of the diuine substance, as Chrysostom sayeth, and now   In homil.
is becomme the breade which was formed by   Paschali.
the hand of the holy ghost in the wombe of
the virgine, and decocted with the fyer of the
passion in the aulter of the crosse, as S. Ambrose sayeth:) can not be the Sacrament of the   De consc.
body, nor the wine of the bloud. Neither can   dist. 1. cap.
it be sayde that the breade and the wine which   omnia.
were before, are the sacramentes, for that the
breade is becomme the body, and the wine the
bloud, and so now they are not, and if they be
not, then neither be they sacramentes. Therefore that the outward formes of breade and
wyne which remaine, be the sacramentes of
Christes body and bloud, and not the very
bread and wine it selfe : it foloweth by sequell

Ff 5   of reason

of reason or consequent of vnderstanding deduced out of the first truth, which of S. Basile in an epistle *ad Sozopolitanos*, speaking agaynst certaine that went about to raise vp againe the olde heresie of *Valentinus*, is called, τὸ ἐν διανοίαις ἀκόλουθον. Of which sequell of reason in the matter of the Sacrament many cōclusions may be deduced in case of wante of expresse scriptures. Which waye of reasoning Basile vsed against heretikes, as also sundry other fathers where manifest scripture might not be alleaged.

Epist.65.
In latino
codice.

And whereas there must be a lykenesse betwen the Sacrament and the thing of the Sacrament, (for if the Sacramentes had not a likenesse of thinges whereof they are Sacramētes, properly and rightely they shuld not be called Sacramentes : as the Sacrament of baptisme, which is the outward washing of the fleshe, hath a likenesse of the inward washing of the soule) and no likenesse here appeareth to be betwen the formes that remaine, and the thing of the Sacramēt, for they consist not, the one of many cornes, the other of grapes, for thereof cometh not accidēt, but substāce: hereto may be sayde, it is ynough, that these Sacramētes beare the likenesse of the body ād bloud of Christ, for as much as the one representeth the likenesse of breade, the other the likenesse of wyne, which S. Augustine calleth *visibilē speciem elemētorū*, the visible forme of the elemētes.

Aug.epist.
22.ad Bo-
nifacium
Episcopū.

De conse.
dist.2. cap.
Hoc est
quod di-
cimus.

Thus

Thus the formes of breade and wine are the
sacramentes of the body and bloud of Christ,
not onely in respecte of the thing signified,
which is the vnitie of the churche, but also of
the thing conteined, which is the very fleshe
and bloud of Christ, whereof the truth it selfe
sayde: *The breade that I shall geue, is my fleshe for* Ioan. 6.
the lyfe of the worlde.

Or that the Sacrament is a signe or token of the Iuell.
bodye of Christ, that lyeth hydden vnderneathe it.

Of the vnspeakeable maner of the being of Christes bodye and bloud vnder the formes of breade and vvine.

ARTICLE XXVI.

THat the outward forme of bread, which is
properly the sacrament, is the signe of the
body of Christ, we confesse, yea of that body,
which is couertly in, or vnder the same, which
S. Augustine calleth, *carnem domini forma panis* Id libro
opertam: the fleshe of our lord couered with Sen'ent.
the forme of bread. But what is meant by this Prosperi-
terme (*Lyeth*) we knowe not. As through faith
grounded vpon gods worde, we knowe that
Christes body is in the Sacrament, so that it
lyeth there, or vnderneathe it, by which terme
it may seme a scoffe to be vttered, to bring the
catholike teaching in contempte, or that it sitteth or standeth, we denye it. For lying, sitting,
and standing, noteth situation of a body in a
place, according to distinctio of membres and
circunscription of place, so as it haue his partes
in a

in a certaine order correspondent to the partes of the place. But after such maner the body of Chriſt is not in the Sacrament, but without cir cumſcriptiō, order, and habitude of his partes to the partes of the body or place enuirōning. Which maner of being in, is aboue all reache of humaine vnderſtãding wonderouſe, ſtraunge and ſingular, not defined and limited by the lawes or bōdes of nature, but by the almighty power of God. To conclude, the being of Chriſtes body in the Sacrament is to vs certaine, the maner of his being there to vs vncertaine, and to God onely certaine.

<table>
<tr><td>

Juell.

</td><td>

Or that Ignoraunce is the mother and cauſe of true deuotion and obedience.

</td></tr>
</table>

Aiſter Iuell had great nede of Articles, for ſome ſhewe to be made againſt the Catholike church, when he aduiſed him ſelfe to put this in for an Article. Verely this is none of the higeſt myſteries, nor none of the greateſt keyes of our Religion, as he ſayeth it is, but vntruly, and knoweth that for an vntruth. For him ſelfe imputeth it to D. Cole, in his replyes to him as a ſtraũge ſaying by him vttered in the diſputatiō at Weſtminſter, to the wondering of the moſt parte of the honorable and worſhipfull of this realme. If it were one of the higheſt myſteries and greateſt keyes of the Catholike Religion, I truſt the moſt parte of the honorable and worſhipfull

ſhipfull of the realme, would not wonder at it. Concerning the matter it ſelfe, I leaue it to D. Cole. He is of age to anſwere for him ſelfe. Whether he ſayde it or no, I knowe not. As he is learned, wiſe, and godly, ſo I doubte not, but, if he ſayde it, therein he had a good meaning, and can ſhewe good reaſon for the ſame, if he may be admitted to declare his ſaying, as wiſe men would the lawes to be declared, ſo as the mynde be taken, and the word ſpoken not alwayes rigorouſly exacted. Ioan.9.

κατὰ τὴν διάνοιαν, καὶ μὴ κατὰ τὸ ῥητόν.

Auguſt. de Trinit. lib.1.cap.4.
Hæc mea fides eſt: quoniam hæc eſt catholica fides.
This is my faith, for as much as this is the catholike faith.

THE CONCLVSION EXHOR-
ting M. Iuell to ſtande to his promiſe.

Hus your Chalenge M. Iuell is anſwered. Thus your negatiues be auouched. Thus the pointes you went about to improue, by good auctoririe be proued, and many others by you ouer raſhely affirmed, clearly improued. Thus the catholike Religion with all your forces layd at and impugned, is ſufficiently defended. The places of proufes, which we haue here vſed, are ſuch, as your ſelfe allowe for good and lawfull. The ſcriptures, examples of the Primitiue church, auncient Councelles, and the

the fathers of syx hundred yeres after Chrift.
You might and ought likewise to haue allowed
Reason, Tradition, Cuftome, and auctoritie of
the Church, without limitation of tyme. The
maner of this dealing with you, is gétle, sober,
and charitable. Put awaye all myftes of blynde
felfe loue, you shall perceiue the fame to be so.
The purpose and intent towardes you, right,
good, and louing, in regard of the truth, no leffe then due, for behoofe of Chriftē people, no
leffe then neceffary. That you hereby might be
enduced to bethinke your felfe of that, wherein you haue done vnaduifedly, and ftayde from
hafty running forth, prickte with vaine fauour
and praife of the world, to euerlafting damnation, appointed to be the reward at the ende
of your game: that truth might thus be tryed,
fet forth and defended: and that our brethren
be leadde as it were by the hāde, from perilous
erroures and danger of their foules, to a right
fenfe and to fuertie.

Now it remaineth, that you performe your
promife. Which is, that, if any one cleare fente-
ce or claufe be brought for proufe of any one
of all your negatiue Articles: you would yelde
and fubfcribe. What hath ben brought, euery
one, that wilfully will not blindefold him felfe
may plainely fee. If fome happely, who will
feme to haue both eyes and eares, and to be right learned, will faye hereof, they fee ne heare
nothing·no marueill. The fauour of the parte,
wherete

whereto they cleaue, hauing cutte of them selues from the body, the difpite of the catholike
religiõ, and hatred of the church, hath ſo blinded their hartes, as places alleaged to the diſ-
prouſe of their falſe doctrine being neuer ſo
euident, they ſee not, ne heare not, or rather
they ſeing ſee not, ne hearing heare not. Verely Matt.13.
you muſt either refuſe the balance, which your
ſelue haue offred and required for trial of thes
Articles, which be the ſcriptures, examples,
councelles, and doctours of antiquitie: or, the
better weight of auctoritie ſweaing to our ſyde, that is, the truth founde in the auncient
doctrine of the catholike church, and not in
the mangled diſſenſions of the Goſpellers: ad-
uiſedly retourne, from whence vnaduiſedly
you haue departed, humbly yelde to that you
haue ſtubbernly kickte againſt, and imbrace
holeſomly that, which you hated damnably.

Touching the daily ſacrifice of the Church, **1.**
commaunded by Chriſt to be done in remembrance of his death, that it hath ben, (and may
be well and godly) celebrated without a number of communicantes with the prieſt together in one place, which you cal priuate Maſſe,
within the compaſſe of your ſyx hundred yeres
after Chriſt: That the communion was then **2**
ſometymes, (as now alſo it is and may be) miniſtred vnder one kynde: Of the publike Serui- **3**
ce of the church, or common prayers in a tonge not knowen to all the people: That the
Biſhop

4   Bifhop, of Rome was fometyme called vniuer-
     fall bifhop, and both called and holden for
5   head of the vniuerfall church : That by aun-
     cient doctoures it hath ben taught, Chriftes
     body to be really, fubftantially, corporally, car-
     nally, or naturally in the bleffed Sacrament of
6   the aulter : Of the wonderous, but true being
     of Chriftes body in mo places at one tyme: and
7   of the Adoration of the Sacrament, or rather
     of the body of Chrift in the Sacrament: we ha-
     ue brought good and fufficient proufes, allea-
     ging for the more parte of thefe Articles the
     fcriptures, and for all, right good euidence out
     of auncient examples, councelles, or fathers.
8. 9. 13. Concerning Eleuation, Referuation, Remay-
     ning of the Accidentes without fubftance, Di-
11.   uiding the hofte in three partes, the termes of
12.   figure, figne, token, &c. applyed to the Sacra-
13.   ment, many Maffes in one church in one daye,
14.   the reuerent vfe of Images, the fcriptures to
15.   be had in vulgar tonges for the common peo-
     ple to reade, which are matters not fpecially
     treated of in the fcriptures by expreffe ter-
     mes : all thefe haue ben fufficiently auouched
     and proued, either by proufes by your felfe al-
     lowed, or by the doctrine and common fenfe
     of the churche.
12.   As for your twelue laft Articles, which you
     put in by addition to the former, for fhewe of
     your courage and confidence of the caufe, and
     to feme to the ignorant to haue much matter
                             to

to charge vs withall, as it appeareth: they repor
te matter (certaine excepted) of lesse importance. Some, of them conteine doctrine, true, I
graunt, but ouer curiouse, and not most necessary for the simple people. Some others be
through the maner of your vtterance peruer-
ted, and in termes drawe fro the sense they haue be vttered in by the church. Which by you
beig denyed, might of vs also be denyed in regard of the termes they be expressed in, were
not a sleigh of falsehed, which might redoude
to the preiudice of the truth: therei wortthely
suspected. Verely to them all we haue sayde so
much, as to sober, quiet and godly wittes may
seme sufficient.

Now this being so, what you mynde to doo,
I knowe not, what you ought to doo, I knowe
right well. I wishe you to doo that, which may
be to your owne ad to the peoples soule helth,
that being by you and your felowes deceiued,
depede of you, to the settig forth of the truth,
to the pcuring of a godly cocorde in Christes
church, and finally, to the glory of God. This
may you doo, by forsaking that, which perhappes semeth to you truth, and is not: that, which
semeth to you learning, and is but a floorishe
or vernishe of learning: that which semeth to
you cleare light, and is profounde darknes, and
by retourning to the church, where cocerning
the faith of a christen man, is all truth, and no
deceite, right learning, and the very light, euen
that, which lightneth euery man coming into Ioan. 1.

Gg this

this worlde, which is there to be fownde onely and not elles where, for as much as the head
is, not separated from the body.

O that you would once mynde this serious-
ly M. Iuell. As for me, if either speaking, writing, or expending might further you therto, I
shuld no spare tonge nor penne, nor any portion of my necessary thinges, were it neuer so
dere. I would gladly powre out all together, to
helpe you to atteine that felicitie. But ô lord
what lettes see I, whereby you are kepte from
that good. Shame, welth of your estate, your
worldly acquaintáce, besyde many others. But
Syr, touching shame, which alwayes irketh tho
se, that be of any generositie of nature; if you
call your better philosophie to counsell, you
shall be taught not to accompte it shameful, to
forsake errour for loue of truth, but rather wilfully to dwell in errour, after that it is plainely
detected. Asfor the welth of your estate, which
some assure you of, so long as you maineteine
that parte: I cã not iudge so euil of you but that
you thinke, how fickle and fraile these wordly
thinges bee, and how litle to be estemed in res-
specte of the heauenly estate, which remaineth
to the obediét childré of the church, as the cõtrarie to the rebelles, Apostates, and renegates.
Touching your acquaintáce, what shal the fami
liaritie of a fewe deceiued persõs staye you frõ
that felicitie, which you shal acheue with the lo
ue and frédship of all good mé, of whose good
opinion onely ryseth fame and renome, and
also

also with the reioising of the Angels in heaue? Luc.15.

This your happy chauge, the better and wiser sorte of men will impute to grace mightely by gods power in you wrought, which sundreth light from draknes, and maketh light shyne out Genes.1. of darknes. Neither shall they iudge that incon-1.Cor.4. stancie, where is no chaunge in will, but onely in vnderstanding. Where the will remaining one, alwayes bent to the glorie of God, the deceiued vnderstanding is by better instruction corrected and righted: there is not inconstacie to be noted; but amendment to be praysed. Neither shall you in this godly enterprise be alone. Many both of olde tyme, and of our dayes haue gone this waye, and haue broken the yse before you. *Eusebius of Cæsarea in Palestina, Beryllus of Bostra in Arabia, and Theodoritus of Cyrus in Persie:* who forsooke haynouse heresies against Christ, and by grace retourned to the catholike faith againe. So haue done in *our* tyme *Georgius Wicelius, Fridericus Staphylus, Franciscus Balduinus Nocolaus Villagagno,* ād many mo.

Thus hauing called to my mynde the considerations, that are like to withholde you frō yelding to the catholike faith, from retourning to the church, and from performing your promise: I fynde no bandes so strong, to kepe you fast in the chayer of pestilence, which this long tyme you haue sitten in that through Gods grace working humilitie and denyall of your selfe in your hart, whereof I spake in my preface, you shuld not easely loose and be in liber-

tie,

tie, where you might clearly see the light spred abroad ouer the whole Church, and espie the darknes of the particular sectes of your newe gospell, which you lyued in before.

But al this notwithstanding, peraduenture your hart serueth you to stande stowtly according to the purport of your chalenge, in the defence of the doctrine you haue professed, and for which you haue obteined a bishoprike, thiking great skorne, to be remoued from the same, by any such meanes, as these to you may seme. And now perhappes you enter into meditatió with your selfe and conferéce with your brethté, to frame an answere to this treatise, and by cótrary writing to fortifie your negatiues. Well may you so doo. But to what purpose, I praye you? Well may you make a smoke and a smooder to darken the light for a tyme, as mé of warre are wont to doo to worke a feate secretly against their enemies. But that can not long cótinewe. The smoke will sone vanishe awaye, the light of the truth will eftesones appeare. Well may you shutte the light out of a fewe houses, by closing dores and windowes, but to kepe awaye the bright sunne fró that great Citie which is set on high vpó a hill, doo what ye can, therein all your trauaill, your deuises and endeuours, shall be vaine and frustrate.

Matt. 5.

As iron by scowring is not onely not consumed, but kepte from ruste and canker, and is made brighter: so the church by the armutes and hostilitie of heretikes is not wounded,

but

but through occasion strengthned, ſtyrred to defence, and made inuincible. When it is opreſſed, then it ryſeth, when it is inuaded, then it ouercometh. When by the aduerſaries obiections it is chekte and controlled, then it is acquitted and peruaileth. Wherefore talke, preache, and write againſt the doctrine of the church whiles ye will, ye ſhall but ſpurne againſt the ſtone, where at ye may breake your ſhynnes and be cruſhed to pieces, the ſame not moued. Ye ſhall but kicke againſt the pricke. Ye ſhall but torment youre owne conſcience condemned in your owne iudgement, as witting that ye reſiſt the church, and for the lyfe to come encreace the heape of euerlaſting dānation. All the reward ye ſhall wene hereby, is the vaine fauour of a fewe light and vnſtable perſons by you deceiued. Whom the blaſtes of your mutable doctrine, ſhall moue and blowe awaye from Gods floore the church like chaffe, the good and conſtant people ramaining ſtill like weighty and ſownde wheate.

Te argumentes and reaſons you ſhall make againſt the doctrine of the church, may happely perſuade ſome of the worldly wiſe, who be fooles in Gods iudgement, as the reaſons of them, that haue commēded infamouſe matters, haue perſuaded ſome. Of whom one praiſed the feuer quratane, an other drōkennes, an other baldnes, an other vnrighteouſnes: and in our tyme one, ignorance, and an other fooliſhnes. Which by the auctours had bē done onely

Matt. 21.

Act. 9.

Tit. 3.

Matt. 3.

Phauorinus.
Syneſius.
Glaucus apud Platonē. Cornelius Agrippa.
Eraſmus.

Gg 3   for

for an exercise of wittes, ād rather to the wōde̅-
ring, the̅ corruptīg of the Readers. Would God
of all the writinges of your sect against the catholike faith, which be no lesse besyde reasō and
truth, the intēt were no worse, the dāger ensuīg
no greater. And as for cōme̅datiō of those vnsemely and vnworthy thinges, those Rhetoriciās
haue not brought good ād true reasōs, but onely a probabilitie of talke: right so confirmatiō of
your negatiue diuinitie, ād of many newe strau̅-
ge ād false doctrines, you haue no suer proufes,
but shadowes, colours, ād shewes onely, that p-
happes may dasell bleare eyes, and deceiue the
vnlearned: but the learned wise, ād by any wayes
godly wise, wil sone cōte̅ne the same. For they be
assured, how probably so euer you teach or write, that the church allwayes assisted and prōpted
by the holy Ghoste the spirite of truth, in poītes
of faith erreth not, and that against truth allready by the same spirite in the vniuersall church
taught and receiued, no truth can be alleaged.

As he is very simple, who, being borne in
hānde by a Sophister, and driuen by force of sophisticall argume̅ts to graunt, that he hath hor-
nes, thinketh so in dede, and therfore putteth
his hānde to his forehed: So who so euer through
your teaching fall from the catholike Church
into the errours of our tyme, from the streightnes of Christian lyfe, into the carnall libertie of
this newe gospell, from deuotion into the in-
sensibilitie which we see the people to lyue in,
from the feare of God, to the desperat contempte

tépte of all vertue ãd goodnes:hereby they shewe,thé felues to be fuch,as haue vnftable hartes,
which be geué ouer to the luftes of their flefhe,
which haue no delite ne feeling of God , which
like Turkes ãd Epicures feekig onely for the cõ-
modities and pleafures of this world , haue no
regard of the lyfe to come. But the godly forte,
whofe hartes be eftablifhed with grace, who pãt
and labour to lyue after the fpirite , continually
mortifying their flefhe , whofe delite is to ferue
God,who be kepte ãd holdé within the feare of
God: though they geue you their hearing , and
that of conftraint not of wil,yet wil not they geue you their lyking nor confenting.

Wherefore M,Iuell feing we haue performed
that,which you haue ouer boldly fayde we were
not able to doo:feig for proufe of thefe Articles
we haue brought more, thé you bare your hea-
zers in hãde we had to bring:feing you perceiue
your felfe hereī to haue done more, thé ftãdeth
with learning,modeftie,or good aduife:feing in
cafe of any one claufe or fentéce for our parte
brought,you haue with fo many proteftatiõs p-
myfed to yelde ãd to fubfcribe vnto vs:feing by
performing your promife, you may do fo much
good to the people and to your felfe : feing nothing can be iuftly alleaged for kepíg of you frõ
fatisfyíg your pmife,ãd retourníg to the church
againe:feig fo great refpectes both of téporal ãd
of heauély prefermétes inuite you and call you
frõ partes ãd fectes,wher you remaine withmoft
certaine dãger of your foule,to the fafe porte of
Gg 4   Chriftes

Christes church:seing by so doojng,you shuld not doo that which were singular,but cómó to you with many others,men of right good faıne and estimation:finally seing if you shall, as all-wayes for the most parte heretikes haue done, cótinew in the professió of your vntrue doctrine, and trauaille in setting forth erroneouse treatises for defence of the same,you shal gaingne thankes of no other, but of the lightest and worst sorte of the people , and persuade none but such as be of that marke : we trust you will vpon mature deliberatió, in your sadder yeres chaunge the counsell which you lyked in your youth : we trust you will examine better by learning the newe doctrine , which you with many others were drawé vnto by swea of the tyme , when by course of age you wanted iudgement : we trust you will call backe your selfe from errours and heresies aduisedly, which you haue maineteined rashly, and set forth by word and write busyly, and therein assured your selfe of the truth cófidently.Thus shal your errour seme to procede of ignorance not of malice. Thus shal you make some recópence for hurt done: thus shal you in some deree discharge your selfe before God and men, thus shall you be receiued into the lappe of the church againe , out of which is no saluation: whether being restored , you may from hence forth in certaine expectation of the blessed hope,leade a lyfe more acceptable to God,to whó be all prayse, honour, and glorie, Amen.

Tit.2.

A TABLE

A TABLE OF THE
ARTICLES VTTERED AF-
firmatiuely, against M. Iuelles
Negatiues.

A TABLE OF THE CHIEFE

pointes in these *Articles* vttered.

The number shevveth the leafe, A, the first syde, B, the second
syde of the leafe, &c. noteth the matter further prosecuted
in that as folovveth.

ARTICLE I.

Light

Offyx

Liber

*Liber hic Anglicano idiomate conscriptus ab
eximio Doctore Theologo, Anglo D. Thoma
Hardingo, examinatus est diligenter à viris
doctis & probis Anglicani idiomatis peritis.
Qui mihi attestati sunt, catholicam fidem &
religionem, quæ grauissimè in Anglia oppugna-
tur hac tempestaté, solidè, erudite, & strenuè in
eo propugnari, & magnum fructū popularibus
Angliæ hominibus allaturum.*

Ita attestor Iudocus Tiletanus Doctor
Theologus & Præpositus VValcurien.
hæreticæ prauitatis inquisitor.